Evaluation in Organizations

Also by Darlene Russ-Eft and Hallie Preskill

Human Resource Development Review (co-editors, with Sleezer)

Also by Darlene Russ-Eft

Everyone a Leader: A Grassroots Model for the New Workplace
(with Bergmann and Hurson)

What Works: Assessment, Development, and Measurement
(co-editor, with Bassi)

What Works: Training and Development Practices
(co-editor, with Bassi)

Issues in Adult Basic Education (with Rubin and Holmen)

Also by Hallie Preskill

Evaluative Inquiry for Learning in Organizations (with Torres)

Evaluation Strategies for Communicating and Reporting:
Enhancing Learning in Organizations (with Torres and Piontek)

Evaluation in Organizations

A Systematic Approach to Enhancing Learning, Performance, and Change

Darlene Russ-Eft
Hallie Preskill

PERSEUS PUBLISHING
Cambridge, Massachusetts

Many of the designations used by manufacturers and sellers to distinguish their products are claimed as trademarks. Where those designations appear in this book and Perseus Books was aware of a trademark claim, the designations have been printed in initial capital letters.

A CIP record for this book is available from the Library of Congress.

Copyright © 2001 by Darlene Russ-Eft and Hallie Preskill

Find us on the World Wide Web at http://www.perseuspublishing.com

Perseus Publishing books are available at special discounts for bulk purchases in the U.S. by corporations, institutions, and other organizations. For more information, please contact the Special Markets Department at the Perseus Books Group, 11 Cambridge Center, Cambridge, MA 02142, or call 617-252-5298.

Text design by Heather Hutchison
Set in 11-point Adobe Caslon by Perseus Publishing Services

First printing, June 2001
2 3 4 5 6 7 8 9 10—03 02 01

Contents

Part II: Designing and Implementing the Evaluation

Part III: Maximizing Evaluation Use

Figures and Tables

Tables

Preface

This book has been in the making for several years. During the past two decades, each of us has been involved not only in conducting program, process, and product evaluations in a wide variety of organizations and communities, but we have been teaching and training others about evaluation as well. We have always used a wide variety of resources in helping others learn about evaluation, primarily because no one book addressed the theory of evaluation as well as its practice in sufficient detail. Finally, we decided that it was time to address this issue, and this book is the culmination of years of reading, research, teaching, consulting, and training.

Evaluation means many things to many people, and in this book, we show how evaluation practice can effectively inform decision-making and action within organizations, specifically around issues of learning, performance, and change. However, the content of the book reflects general evaluation practice, and as such, should be helpful within other kinds of organizational contexts as well. The philosophy and ideas that have influenced our writing, thinking, and practice are grounded in certain assumptions and beliefs we have about doing good evaluation work. These suggest that evaluation should be:

Learning oriented
Integrated with daily work practices
Inclusive
Stakeholder focused
Change oriented
Sustainable
Useful
Focused on capacity building
Grounded in organizational reality

Process as well as product oriented
Contextual
Dynamic
Systems oriented
Improvement oriented
Collaborative and participatory
Holistic
Adaptive and flexible
Meaningful
Responsive

Evaluation's potential has barely been tapped in most organizations; its many benefits have been largely ignored over the years. Thus, it is our hope that as you read this book, you will find the knowledge and inspiration to conduct useful, high-quality, and meaningful evaluations within your organization.

This book is intended to help practitioners be more effective evaluators in all aspects of their work. We strongly believe that evaluation is important enough to be integrated into the daily work of organizations, and as such, all employees should understand evaluation's purpose, processes, and uses. Specifically, however, we believe this book will be of particular interest to trainers, managers, organization development specialists, human service professionals, nonprofit agency staff, teachers, management consultant professionals, community organizers, and others interested in understanding the effects of learning, performance, and change interventions or initiatives.

As you read this book, you will likely notice that we often advocate using a participatory and collaborative evaluation approach. Although there will be many situations where such an approach may not be possible or even appropriate, we believe that involving stakeholders in the evaluation's design and implementation significantly affects the extent to which and the ways in which evaluation findings are used. To this end, we strongly believe that evaluations should be conducted with a clear intention to use the findings in some way.

Although individual chapters can be read on an as-needed basis, we recommend reading the book from beginning to end if possible. Since we provide a systematic and comprehensive approach to the theory and practice of evaluation, reading the book from cover to cover will provide a more holistic understanding of the evaluation enterprise. In the first four chapters, we describe what evaluation is, where it came from, how it has evolved over the years, and the politics and ethics of evaluation practice. These four chapters provide the necessary context for understanding not only the theory of evaluation, but why and how it is practiced. Since there is no "one size fits all" for any evaluation, these first chapters set the stage for making critical decisions about an evaluation's design and implementation. The next eight chapters (Chapters 5–12) focus on what needs to be known about designing and implementing an evaluation; from how to focus the evaluation to selecting an evaluation design, data collection methods, validity and sampling issues, and methods of data analysis. The remaining four chapters (Chapters 13–16) address how to communicate and report the evaluation's activities and findings, how to plan, budget, and manage an evaluation, how to evaluate an evaluation, and finally, how to integrate evaluation into the organization. These chapters describe issues that are present throughout an evaluation and should be considered from the beginning of an evaluation effort.

Evaluation can be viewed as a catalyst and opportunity for learning—learning what works and doesn't work, learning about ourselves and the organization, and learning about how to improve what we do in the workplace. As such, it can provide new understandings and insights into our programs, processes, products, and systems. Furthermore, evaluation can provide us with the confidence with which to make decisions and take actions that ultimately help employees and organizations succeed in meeting their goals. We wish you much success as you go forth and evaluate!

Acknowledgments

Preparing for and writing this book has been a learning, performance, and change experience for both of us. We would like to thank the many AchieveGlobal clients who have participated in specific evaluation projects, as well as those who attended various seminars on evaluation. We are also grateful to the scores of students in the Organizational Learning and Instructional Technologies Program at the University of New Mexico who have taken Hallie's evaluation courses over the last several years. Their thoughtful and provocative questions and feedback contributed greatly to her thinking and writing about evaluation. Both of these groups have significantly influenced our evaluation thinking and practice.

We are very grateful for the review and excellent feedback on the manuscript provided by Edward R. Del Gaizo and Rosalie T. Torres. Their insights contributed greatly to the clarity and coverage of the text. In addition, Rosalie served not only as a reviewer, but because of her long-term work and expertise in the area of evaluation communicating and reporting, she graciously agreed to contribute a chapter on this topic.

We also want to thank Roz Madden for helping us with the challenges of various graphics and illustrations, and Jennifer Roberts and Ruth Pangilinan for helping with needed administrative support.

Jerry W. Gilley deserves our thanks for supporting our work and for introducing us to Nicholas Philipson of Perseus Books. We want to acknowledge Nick's promptness in responding to all of our questions and his being as excited about this book as we are.

Darlene wants to give special thanks to her husband, Jack. He endured countless late dinners and working weekends, and his understanding and encouragement has made this work possible. She also wants to acknowledge her daughter, Natalie, who, though at a distance, offered words of support throughout the many months.

Hallie would like to thank her husband, Stephen, and son, Benjamin, for their love and support—their patience, understanding, and belief in this book were unwavering and made the process all the more delightful.

PART ONE

Background and Context of Evaluation

Background and Context of Evaluation

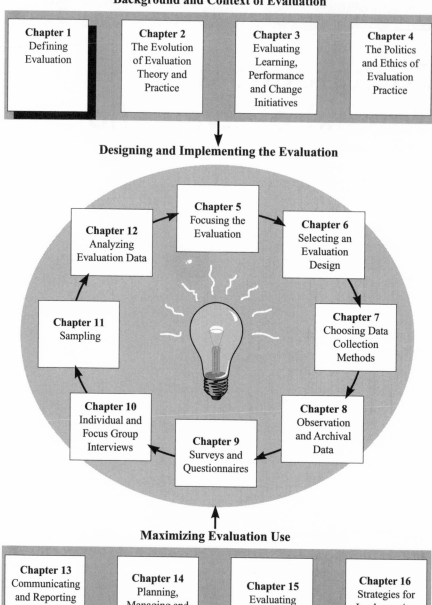

Chapter 1
Defining
Evaluation

Chapter 2
The Evolution
of Evaluation
Theory and
Practice

Chapter 3
Evaluating
Learning,
Performance
and Change
Initiatives

Chapter 4
The Politics
and Ethics of
Evaluation
Practice

Designing and Implementing the Evaluation

Chapter 12
Analyzing
Evaluation Data

Chapter 5
Focusing the
Evaluation

Chapter 6
Selecting an
Evaluation
Design

Chapter 11
Sampling

Chapter 7
Choosing Data
Collection
Methods

Chapter 10
Individual and
Focus Group
Interviews

Chapter 9
Surveys and
Questionnaires

Chapter 8
Observation
and Archival
Data

Maximizing Evaluation Use

Chapter 13
Communicating
and Reporting
Evaluation
Activities
and Findings

Chapter 14
Planning,
Managing and
Budgeting
the Evaluation

Chapter 15
Evaluating
the Evaluation

Chapter 16
Strategies for
Implementing
Evaluation in
Organizations

chapter 1

Defining Evaluation

- What Evaluation Is and Isn't
- The Relationship Between Evaluation and Research
- What Can Be Evaluated?
- Why Evaluate?
- Top Ten Reasons Evaluation Is Neglected
- Kinds of Evaluations
- The Logic of Evaluation
- Evaluation Use
- Internal and External Evaluation

The word *evaluation* means many things to many people. Say the word in your organization and you may receive a wide variety of responses and reactions. For some it means viewing something more clearly to gain a better understanding of the properties of a phenomenon. Images such as a pair of glasses, a microscope, binoculars, a lightbulb, and a magnifying glass come to mind for those who see evaluation with this lens. Still, for others, *evaluation* is thought of in terms of testing and measurement. Images of exams, report cards, checklists, and people standing around with clipboards are often associated with this view. Pictures of a scale, ruler, or thermometer reflect evaluation's relationship to measurement. *Evaluation* also reminds people of auditing procedures or statistics. In many cases, *evaluation* is associated with performance assessment or performance management and, more often than not, perceived to be a dreaded and sometimes threatening activity.

All of these interpretations are viable ways of thinking about evaluation, yet the notion itself remains a mystery to many. What we wish to do in this book is demystify and clarify what evaluation is and isn't, and how evaluation can be conducted in ways that provide useful information within an organizational context. For too long, organizations have neglected integrating evaluation into their work processes and activities. We believe this is due, in part, to a lack of understanding of the full range of possibilities that evaluation can offer an organization and what skills and knowledge are necessary for doing quality evaluation work. When evaluation is viewed as a form of inquiry that seeks to improve organizational decisionmaking, learning, and action, images such as a puzzle with interlocking pieces, employees working together, a spider's web, or a question mark may be evoked.

What Evaluation Is and Isn't

A myriad of evaluation definitions have been offered over the last thirty years. One of the earliest definitions still commonly used was offered by Michael Scriven:

> Evaluation refers to the process of determining the merit, worth, or value of something, or the product of that process. Terms used to refer to this process or part of it include: appraise, analyze, assess, critique, examine, grade, inspect, judge, rate, rank review, study, test. . . . The evaluation process normally involves some identification of relevant standards of merit, worth, or value; some investigation of the performance of evaluands on these standards; and some integration or synthesis of the results to achieve an overall evaluation or set of associated evaluations. (1991, p. 139)

The "something" Scriven refers to is called the *evaluand*; it is the object of the evaluation—that which is being evaluated. In judging "the merit of something, one is judging its inherent value, but when one judges the worth of something, one is judging its value within a particular context, and the two judgments might be quite different" (Mathison, 1994, p. 469). For example, an organization might develop a career development system that is judged to be "cutting edge" and meritorious for its intent, but since the organization is experiencing significant financial challenges, it might be judged not worth the cost to implement such a program.

Another definition, which stems from evaluation's long history with social programs and takes on a social science research perspective, comes from Rossi and Freeman:

> Evaluation research is the systematic application of social research procedures in assessing the conceptualization and design, implementation, and utility of social intervention programs. . . . In other words, evaluation research involves the use of social research methodologies to judge and to improve the planning, monitoring, effectiveness, and efficiency of health, education, welfare, and other human service programs. (1985, p. 19)

A third definition used by many today is from Patton, who emphasizes the use of evaluation findings:

> Program evaluation is the systematic collection of information about the activities, characteristics, and outcomes of programs to make judgments about the program, improve program effectiveness, and/or inform decisions about future programming. (1997, p. 23)

Finally, Preskill and Torres offer a definition that focuses on evaluative activities specifically conducted within organizations for the purpose of organizational learning and change. They write,

> We envision evaluative inquiry as an ongoing process for investigating and understanding critical organization issues. It is an approach to learning that is fully integrated with an organization's work practices, and as such, it engenders (a) organization members' interest and ability in exploring critical issues using evaluation logic, (b) organization members' involvement in evaluative processes, and (c) the personal and professional growth of individuals within the organization. (1999a, pp. 1–2)

Although each definition takes a slightly different view of evaluation, there are important commonalties among them. First, evaluation is viewed as a systematic process. It should not be conducted as an afterthought; rather, it is a planned and purposeful activity. Second, evaluation involves collecting data regarding questions or issues about society in general and organizations and programs in particular. Third, evaluation is seen as a process for enhancing knowledge and decisionmaking, whether the decisions are related to improving or refining a program, process, product, system, or organization, or for determining whether to continue or expand a program. In each of these decisions, there is some aspect of judgment about the evaluand's merit, worth, or value. Finally, the notion of evaluation use is either implicit or explicit in each of the above definitions. The importance of using what was learned from the evaluation is critical. Insofar as evaluation constitutes a significant allocation of time and resources, organizations cannot afford to engage in evaluation activities unless the findings are used in some way. Ultimately, evaluation concerns asking questions about issues that arise out of everyday practice. It is a means for gaining better understanding of what we do and the effects of our actions in the context of society and the work environment. A distinguishing characteristic of evaluation is that unlike traditional forms of academic research, it is grounded in the everyday realities of organizations.

Evaluation's origins, methods, theories, and context are related to many different disciplines and has thus been called a "transdiscipline" (Scriven, 1991). Scriven explains, "Transdisciplines such as statistics, logic, or evaluation, are disciplines whose subject matter is the study and improvement of certain tools for other disciplines. . . . Transdisciplines often have several semiautonomous fields of study connected with them (for example, biostatistics, formal logic)" (p. 364). Scriven uses the analogy of an estate to explain: "Transdisciplines are the utilities—electricity, water, gas, sewers, telephone, data lines or microwave systems, cable or satellite televisions, radio, roads, and public transportation. . . . Transdisciplines thus exist to serve . . ." (pp. 15, 17). Thus, evaluation as a transdiscipline serves many fields and is a tool of learning and decisionmaking for many kinds of organizations.

Because there is often confusion between the terms *data, information,* and *knowledge,* we think it is important to clarify what these terms imply, especially as they relate to evaluation. *Data* can be thought of as facts and figures, or feedback. Data may be in the form of sales figures, ratings on a postcourse training evaluation survey, or the comments made during an interview. *Information* has its root in Latin and means "to give form to, to form an idea" (Allee, 1997, p. 42), or to find patterns in the data (O'Dell and Grayson, 1998). Turning data into information requires a process of interpretation that gives meaning to the data. *Knowledge,* however, occurs when information intersects with a user. As O'Dell and Grayson point out, "we are awash in information, but until people use it, it isn't knowledge" (1998, p. 4). Consequently, information becomes knowledge when it focuses on action or decisions that imply change. Though organizations have reams of information documented on paper or in their information systems, until someone uses that information, it cannot become part of a knowledge base. Knowledge exists within the context of the individual and is the result of cognitive processes that convert that data into information, which, when acted upon, becomes knowledge. Evaluation, therefore, collects data, which is turned into information that, when used, becomes knowledge at the individual level. If shared with others in the organization, that knowledge may then lead to organizational-level learning.

So, what isn't evaluation? Well, evaluation shouldn't be considered simply a survey that's put together the night before a training workshop. Nor should it be catching a few people in the hallway to see what they think about the new process or system. Evaluation shouldn't be considered an activity that's done solely to support a political agenda. Finally, evaluation isn't the same as research.

The Relationship between Evaluation and Research

In many organizations, the terms *evaluation* and *research* are used interchangeably, and one often carries more positive connotations than the other. Although there are some clear similarities between the two forms of inquiry, we believe it's important to distinguish characteristics that make evaluation a unique endeavor. There has been increasing interest in conducting "action research" within organizations in the last several years, which has some similar characteristics to evaluation, but we wish to highlight some differences between traditional forms of research and evaluation.

As can be seen in Figure 1.1, although the two forms of inquiry employ the same data collection and analysis methods, they differ significantly in at least three ways:

FIGURE 1.1 Relationship between Evaluation and Research

	Evaluation	**Research**
Purpose	Provide information for learning and decision making (intention is use) Seeks to describe particular phenomena Undertaken at the behest of a client—is service oriented	Develop new knowledge Seeks conclusions Seeks new laws, new theories Topic and questions are determined by the researcher
Audience	Clients (Internal and External)	Other researchers
Focusing the study	Identifies background of evaluand and purpose of evaluation Identifies evaluation stakeholders and audiences Develops key questions that will guide the evaluation	Develops a problem statement Reviews the literature on the topic Develops theory-based hypotheses or research questions Identifies terms and definitions Identifies variables to be studied
Study design	Naturalistic/qualitative Experimental/quantitative Often bounded by organization's timeframe requirements	Naturalistic/qualitative Experimental/quantitative Is based on researcher's timeline and available funding
Data collection methods	Tests, surveys/questionnaires, observation, interviews, archival analysis, unobtrusive measures	Tests, surveys/questionnaires, observation, interviews archival analysis, unobtrusive measures
Reliability and Validity	Pilot testing, member checks, controlling variables through triangulation, test/retest reliability measures Is rooted in values and politics Generalizability of findings not a major goal or concern	Pilot testing, member checks, controlling variables through designs, triangulation, test/retest reliability measures Attempts to be objective and value free Seeks to establish generalizable findings

FIGURE 1.1 *(continued)*

Data analysis	Inferential and descriptive statistics Content analysis/grounded theory	Inferential and descriptive statistics Content analysis/grounded theory
Results of Study	Reports results to evaluation clients Makes recommendations relevant to evaluation questions Rarely publishes the results	Reports results to other researchers and practitioners Makes suggestions for future research Often publishes study's findings

1. They are often initiated for different purposes.
2. They respond to different kinds of audience or client questions and needs.
3. They communicate and report their findings in different ways and to different groups.

So, even though evaluation and research both provide information about questions of interest, they are typically undertaken for different reasons. As Scriven explains, "what distinguishes evaluation from other applied research is at most that it leads to evaluative conclusions, and to get to them requires identifying standards and performance data, and the integration of the two" (1991, pp. 143–144). Although it is important to understand the difference between these two forms of inquiry, we acknowledge that for some scholars, this difference may be perceived as merely technical and not particularly practical. Therefore, we believe that what is important is the inquiry itself, and not necessarily what it is called. Thus, if organization members refuse to "do" *evaluation*, but are willing to engage in *research*, then we suggest they call it what they will. The bottom line is the collection of quality information that will inform and guide learning, decisionmaking, and practice.

What Can Be Evaluated?

In this book, we will talk about how evaluation can be applied to many aspects of organizational work, with specific emphasis on learning, performance, and change initiatives. *Programs*, for example, can be evaluated. A program can be thought of as a "set of planned activities directed toward bringing about specified change(s) in an identified and identifiable audience" (Smith, 1989). In the learning and performance arena, programs may be thought of as courses, seminars, or modules that make up a content area (for example, a twelve-week customer service training program).

Evaluation can also focus on specific *initiatives, processes,* and *systems* within organizations. For example, organization members may have questions about how an on-line training registration system or the process for hiring outside consultants works. The data that result from the evaluation may provide organization members with information needed to make minor adjustments to these processes and systems or to totally revise them if necessary.

Most of us are very familiar with *product* evaluation. We constantly make evaluative decisions about products in the course of everyday life. When we choose a restaurant, buy a car or computer, or determine which movie to see, we are doing a product evaluation. Scriven suggests that product evaluation is "probably the best-developed and oldest *practice* within evaluation" (1994, p. 46). In this book, we'll also talk about ways to evaluate products that provide information to both internal and external customers and clients.

In a very short period, we have gone from being an industrial economy to a service and knowledge economy. This means that the majority of organizations are providing some kind of *service* to their internal and external customers or clients. Evaluation can be a critical tool for determining how effective these services are—if they are meeting the needs of customers, what additional services are needed, and what changes are required. An example of how customers' interests and habits are being evaluated today is the increasing use of the "mystery shopper" evaluation technique that provides a unique way for companies to see how they are viewed from the customer's perspective. For example, consultant Barbra Zuckerman posed as a mystery shopper for Harley Davidson in Albuquerque, New Mexico, in an effort to evaluate customers' experiences. After pretending to be a shopper, she completed a short checklist and wrote a narrative about her experiences. The checklist included specific close-ended items that the evaluation's client had developed based on their definitions of high-quality customer service (for example, "Were you greeted by a salesperson within three minutes of entering the store?"). The narrative included both the sequence of events (what time she entered the store, at what time the salesperson approached her, what questions the salesperson asked her), as well as her feelings about the visit (frustrated, satisfied, overjoyed). Once the data from the mystery shoppers were collected, they were analyzed and shared with the stakeholders. Mystery shopping as an evaluation technique can focus on customer service and satisfaction, employees' problem-solving strategies, their sense of professionalism and product knowledge, and the effectiveness of training programs.

Finally, *people* can be evaluated. In every organization, the means to evaluate employee performance ranges from simple to complex. These evaluation systems are often called performance management or appraisal systems. In this book we will not focus on this aspect of evaluation—books have been written on how to develop employee performance systems. However, when we evaluate programs, processes, systems, products, or services within organizations, it is impossible and irresponsible to ignore the human element. Therefore, we treat the individual as one component or characteristic of any program's success, but do not focus on how to develop performance appraisal systems per se.

Why Evaluate?

At this point you may be saying to yourself, organizations and people evaluate all the time. This is certainly true. On a daily basis we evaluate what we will wear, what we will eat, which road to take to the office, how people will respond to our ideas, and so on. Evaluation is part of what we do in the normal course of everyday living. However, the systematic and professional conduct of evaluation is undertaken when there is some decision to be made or some form of learning is necessary in order to take action in the short or long term. It is conducted when there is sufficient evidence that the answers to evaluative questions are important enough to warrant expending resources to undertake a more formal or systematic approach, versus an informal/ad hoc kind of judgment. For example, would you agree to a decision to undergo surgery based on a doctor's statement, "I have a hunch that this may help you"? Most likely, you would ask for further information or a second opinion. The important point here is to understand how systematic and professional evaluation adds value to the organization and the work of its members. We believe that evaluation should be integrated into an organization's work practices for the following reasons (see Figure 1.2). Each of the benefits described depends on the evaluation findings being used.

- *Evaluation can contribute to improved quality.*

Evaluation measures quality and then allows people to improve quality. When an evaluation is conducted around concerns of program or product quality, for example, both internal and external customers or clients may be more confident in using, participating in, or purchasing the program or product. The data collected for the evaluation provides evidence of quality according to some predetermined set of standards. For example, a training program vendor might use the evaluation results of specific workshops to advertise the quality of its programs in company brochures.

- *Evaluation can contribute to increased knowledge among organization members.*

Evaluation leads to increased knowledge among organization members in at least two ways. First, those who participate in the evaluation come to know and understand that which is being evaluated (the evaluand) more fully. Second, they learn about good evaluation practice if they are involved in the design and implementation of the evaluation and thus might be more willing and able to facilitate future evaluations. For example, program staff in a nonprofit agency who have had limited involvement in formal evaluation activities learn that the program is having a significant impact on one set of clients, but is missing the boat on another segment. For a long time, they had hunches about this, but now the evaluation confirms what they thought was true. As a result, they are now

FIGURE 1.2   Reasons to Evaluate

Evaluation ensures quality.

Evaluation contributes to increased organization members' knowledge.

Evaluation helps prioritize resources.

Evaluation helps plan and deliver organizational initiatives.

Evaluation helps organization members be accountable.

Evaluation findings can help convince others of the need or effectiveness of various organizational initiatives.

Experience with evaluation is fast becoming a marketable skill.

---

able to discuss the specifics of the program's logic and identify strategies for revising the program. They also learn that evaluation does not have to be a threatening activity, and they should be developing plans for one or more evaluations during the year.

- *Evaluation can help prioritize resources*

Given the multiple demands placed on organization members today, there are usually more needs for services and programs than can possibly be met with available personnel and financial resources. Evaluation can help identify the programs, services, and products that are most critical to the organization's success. It can also help prioritize those things that the organization needs to pay attention to sooner than later. As a decision-making tool, evaluation helps determine what is worth developing or continuing. In short, evaluation makes good economic sense. For example, many organizations have small training and organization development or performance improvement departments, and they can't meet all the organization's needs at once. To help prioritize what to do first, a trainer might conduct a needs assessment to better understand the organization's priorities in terms of improving performance, and as a result, develop a plan for implementing a variety of learning, performance, and change initiatives for the coming year. Without the needs assessment data, the trainer would only be guessing if she were designing and offering appropriate and timely training.

- *Evaluation can help planning and delivery of organizational initiatives.*

Evaluation can be used to plan, organize, and deliver various organizational initiatives. Data collected from an evaluation can identify areas of opportunity as well as strengths and weaknesses of the organization that would inhibit or support new organizational ventures. Thus, evaluation can be used as a diagnostic tool before any organizational change or learning intervention. For example, what if your organization was considering a reorganization of its core functions that would require employees to work in crossfunctional teams? This would represent a significant change in how work had been previously accomplished. You could be asked to evaluate the organization's readiness for team-based work. You might conduct interviews with various levels of employees, observe current work practices, and survey a sample of employees to ascertain their knowledge, attitudes, and skills regarding team-based work. Based on the evaluation's results, you would be able to recommend a series of strategies that will help employees shift to working in teams.

- *Evaluation can help organization members be accountable.*

Evaluation can be used as a means of showing the value certain efforts add to the organization. In days of cost-cutting, layoffs, and outsourcing, organization members must be able to show the impact and consequences of their work if they are to be part of the organization's long-term strategy. Without evaluation data that provides evidence of the usefulness of this work, organization members remain vulnerable to decisions made without data. Evaluation findings can help clarify what and how certain programs, processes, and products promote the organization's mission and goals. It provides the necessary accountability function that is often needed in these turbulent times. For example, consider an organization that is experiencing a significant downturn in its financial profits. Its first instinct is to cut its customized training programs that are offered through the learning and performance department. When confronted with this scenario, the department gathers the evaluation data that have been aggregated and stored in a knowledge management database, and is able to show how the department's efforts have actually improved employees' performance. In addition, they are able to demonstrate that cutting training programs during difficult economic times is contradictory to what the literature suggests about productivity and profitability.

- *Evaluation findings can help convince others of the need or effectiveness of various organizational initiatives.*

Oftentimes we find that we need to lobby for additional time, resources, personnel, or materials to do our jobs better or to provide more effective service. Without data to back up our requests, we have little with which to argue. Evaluation findings can be used to illustrate the effects of a program, process, or initiative on employee morale, learning, motivation, organizational culture and climate, productivity, sales, or efficiency. For example, a human resources department has been piloting a mentoring program with a sample of new employees in the home office as a means to acculturate them to the organization and to help them develop a career path. The evaluation of this pilot program has found it to be highly successful. One of the important indicators is that the turnover rate has been significantly reduced, resulting in great cost savings to the organization. In addition, new employees express satisfaction with their jobs, feel connected to the organization's mission, and say they plan to stay with the organization for at least three years. The manager of the mentoring program uses the evaluation data to lobby for increasing the program's availability to employees in the field offices.

- *Experience with evaluation is fast becoming a marketable skill.*

In spite of many organizations' reluctance to engage in systematic, ongoing evaluation work in the past, there is growing recognition that evaluation skills and knowledge are important to a wide variety of jobs. A review of classified ads for positions in training, organization development, career development, instructional technology, performance technology, management development, and others reveal that evaluation knowledge, skills, and experiences are becoming part of many job requirements.

Top Ten Reasons Evaluation Is Neglected

In spite of the many reasons to evaluate, there are at least ten reasons why evaluation has not been widely implemented in organizations (see Figure 1.3). We've summarized these into the following explanations:

10. Organization members misunderstand evaluation's purpose and role.

Many people within organizations have not had formal training or experience with evaluation and thus lack an understanding of what evaluation is and can do for the organization. Oftentimes their assumptions about evaluation are faulty and lead to negative expectations for evaluation work.

9. Organization members fear the impact of evaluation findings.

Some organization members worry that an evaluation's findings will lead to their being fired or laid off or some other form of punishment. This fear is often well grounded in organizations where there is a culture of distrust. In addition, some members do not wish to be held accountable for their actions.

8. There is a real or perceived lack of evaluation skills.

In some situations organization members would like to conduct evaluations but they and others lack the necessary evaluation knowledge and skills. In many cases, they may not even be aware of what specific skills are needed; they just know that they and their colleagues can't do it in a way that would be considered competent or credible by the intended users of the evaluation results.

7. Evaluation is considered an add-on activity.

In organizations where planned and systematic evaluations designed for use have not been conducted, and there is a lack of evaluation knowledge and

FIGURE 1.3   Top 10 Reasons Evaluation is Neglected

10. Organization members misunderstand evaluation's purpose and role.

 9. Organization members fear the impact of evaluation findings.

 8. There is a real or perceived lack of evaluation skills.

 7. Evaluation is considered an add-on activity.

 6. Organization members don't believe the results will be used; data are collected and not analyzed or used.

 5. Organization members view evaluation as a time-consuming and laborious task.

 4. The perceived costs of evaluation outweigh the perceived benefits of evaluation.

 3. Organizational leaders think they already know what does and does not work.

 2. Previous experiences with evaluation have been either a disaster or disappointing.

 1. No one has asked for it.

skills, employees tend to view evaluation as one more thing to do that is not central to their daily work. When viewed this way, evaluation is often relegated to the "back burner" and rarely done. Historically, evaluation has not been designed into organizational change or learning interventions.

6. Organization members don't believe the results will be used; data are collected and not analyzed or used.

Most people in organizations have been asked at one time or another to complete an organizational culture or climate survey, to respond to an organization development consultant's interview questions, or have been observed performing various work tasks. We have usually been told that managers are very interested in employees' opinions and that the results will be used in some way. However, we rarely hear or learn about the findings or see any tangible changes made as a result of our feedback. Repeated experiences such as these may affect organization members' trust in evaluation efforts. Employees may wonder why they should participate if they don't believe their experiences and opinions will be heard and acted upon.

5. Organization members view evaluation as a time-consuming and laborious task.

There is no question that good evaluation takes time and energy. However, it does not have to consume months and years to complete. Some evaluations that are limited in scope can be conducted in just a few weeks; other evaluations that seek to answer more complex and critical issues may take several weeks to six months or more. Given that evaluation is to inform decisionmaking and learning, evaluation must be conducted in timely and efficient ways.

4. The perceived costs of evaluation outweigh the perceived benefits of evaluation.

Because evaluation is often thought to be a lengthy process involving outside consultants, there is a related belief that the benefits of evaluation cannot possibly outweigh such costs. However, engaging clients in early discussions about how the results will be used can resolve this issue. Costs for a systematic evaluation can be compared with the benefits that are likely to be realized if changes are made based on the evaluation findings. This view is often linked to organization members' previous history with evaluation efforts that did not lead to use of the findings. Another related issue that inhibits organizations from evaluating is the short-term nature of organizational decisionmaking. In many cases, the short-term costs of evaluation need to be balanced with the long-term benefits of whatever changes are made based on the evaluation results. For example, an evaluation might have a high cost, yet the impact of the changes made as a result of the evaluation will not benefit the organization for several months to a year. Given management's impatience for results, this is a significant challenge to evaluation work.

3. Organizational leaders think they already know what does and does not work.

We have often heard managers and other organizational leaders say that they don't need to conduct evaluations because they already know what employees think, or that they have a good handle on how to solve the issues at hand. They believe that the information they've collected informally is sufficient, and thus view more formal, systematic evaluation activity as a waste of time. How accurate their perceptions are may vary considerably.

2. Previous experiences with evaluation have been either disastrous or disappointing.

In these cases there may have been: 1) broken promises that the findings would lead to certain changes and none were made, 2) blatant misuses of the findings or the evaluation process, 3) reports developed but unread and unused, 4) certain issues which were totally ignored, or 5) only "easy" recommendations offered and implemented. It is understandable why organization members would not want to engage in further evaluation efforts if they feel that it is a waste of time. These previous experiences have promoted a culture of "why bother?" when it comes to evaluation.

1. No one has asked for it.

Many people have told us that the number one reason they don't conduct evaluations is because no one has asked for any evidence of the success, impact, or effectiveness of their work. We believe times are changing and it is in the best interests of employees and organizations that evaluation activities be undertaken. During times of continuous change, limited resources, competition, and hard decisions, evaluation is one approach to solving organizational issues that may yield unanticipated, positive benefits.

Ultimately we must ask, "Can an organization afford *not* to evaluate?" How much does it cost to not know how well certain programs, services, or products are doing, or what effect they are having? How much does it cost to make the same mistakes repeatedly? How much does it cost to limit a program's effects to only a few in the organization when many more could benefit? These are not flippant questions, but are questions that must be asked if we are serious about what we do in organizations. In spite of these fundamental questions, we know that organizations have often been reluctant to engage in evaluation activities.

Kinds of Evaluations

As should be clear now, evaluation is conducted to serve several purposes: 1) to gain information before a program's development, 2) to improve a program, and 3) to make final judgments about a program (or other kind of evaluand). The following are some ways to describe these different kinds of evaluation.

Developmental Evaluation

Developmental evaluation is a recent concept that has expanded our understanding about the possible roles for evaluators. Patton introduced the term to "describe certain long-term, partnering relationships with clients who are, themselves, engaged in ongoing program development" (1994, p. 312). In his role as an external evaluator, he has discovered through his years of evaluation service that a developmental role is the most satisfying evaluation role he can play with organizations. Departing significantly from previous roles for evaluators who traditionally were expected to be the value-free, external experts who evaluate a program once it's been implemented, developmental forms of evaluation place the evaluator as:

> Part of a design team helping to monitor what's happening, both processes and outcomes, in an evolving, rapidly changing environment of constant feedback and change. These relationships can go on for years, and in many cases, never involve formal, written reports. (p. 313)

A developmental approach to evaluation positions the evaluator as a guide throughout a program's development. This kind of evaluation is most closely associated with needs assessment forms of evaluation. A needs assessment has been defined as "A systematic set of procedures undertaken for the purpose of setting priorities and making decisions about program or organizational improvement and allocation of resources. The priorities are based on identified needs" (Witkin and Altschuld, 1995, p. 4).

Needs assessments have typically been the role of the program designers and have rarely been thought of as evaluation activity in the learning, performance, and change literature. Yet, in every way, a needs assessment is an evaluation—it is an evaluation of *need*. Patton suggests that the evaluator's role during this phase "is to ask evaluative questions and hold their [clients'] feet to the fire of reality testing" (1997, p. 104). The developmental evaluator sits side by side with the designers, providing feedback that can be used to increase the likelihood that the program will be successful when implemented. Patton emphasizes that developmental evaluation is not a model; rather, it is a "relationship founded on a shared purpose: development" (1994, p. 313). Questions a developmental evaluation might address are:

- What are the right set of activities and strategies for this program?
- What is the best design?
- What are the appropriate goals and objectives?
- What and whose needs is this program addressing?
- What processes should be in place to make implementation effective?
- What criteria or standards are being used to design this product?

Formative Evaluation

Scriven was the first to coin the terms *formative* and *summative* as ways of describing evaluation's main purposes or functions. He explains that formative evaluation "is typically conducted *during* the development or improvement of a program or product (or person, and so on) and it is conducted, often more than once, *for* the in-house staff of the program *with the intent to improve*" (1991, pp. 168–169, italics in the original). Thus, formative evaluation is usually conducted by internal evaluators (though not always), for the purpose of developing or improving the evaluand. The findings from the evaluation are fed into an improvement-focused process that further develops, refines, or revises the object being evaluated. The reports that result from a formative evaluation typically remain internal to the organization. Examples of questions that formative evaluation might address include:

- How well is the program being implemented? What are the barriers to implementation?

- How effective are the program's strategies and activities?
- How might the product be improved to appeal to a larger audience?
- To what extent is the staff prepared to implement the program's objectives?
- How might the process be refined to make it more user-friendly?
- What aspects of the service are working well? Which are not meeting clients' needs?

Summative Evaluation

Summative evaluation is implemented for the purpose of determining the merit, worth, or value of the evaluand in a way that leads to a final evaluative judgment. It "is conducted after completion of the program (for ongoing programs, that means after stabilization) and for the benefit of some external audience or decision maker (for example, funding agency, oversight office, historian, or future possible users)" (Scriven, 1991, p. 340). Examples of summative evaluations include grades in a course, a merit bonus based on performance, a decision of which vendor to use, or the elimination of a program that has outlived its usefulness or is not meeting the current needs of participants. Summative evaluations are often conducted by external evaluators (though not always). Stake (quoted in Scriven, 1991) is credited with helping us understand the difference between formative and summative evaluations with the following analogy: "When the cook tastes the soup, that's formative; when the guests taste the soup, that's summative" (p. 19). Questions a summative evaluation might address include:

- To what extent did the program meet its goals?
- What were the learning outcomes?
- Were the results worth the project's costs?
- What components of the program are reproducible in other locations?
- In what ways did participants benefit from the program?
- To what extent is the product viable?
- To what extent has the process improved employee productivity?

Summative evaluations come in a variety of shapes and sizes. The following are four common kinds of summative evaluation.

1. Monitoring and Auditing

Monitoring is often associated with the need to determine if a program is being administered in ethical or legal ways; it is a means for checking on the program's implementation. A monitoring kind of evaluation would focus on the extent to which program administrators were wasting funds, inappropriately using staff resources, or ineffectively tracking participants' involvement in the program. Monitoring kinds of evaluation are typically undertaken for accountability purposes and serve as a means to prove that the program is being implemented as designed and approved (Rossi and Freeman, 1985). However, internal auditors are increasingly taking on the role of looking at program effectiveness in addition to costs. Auditing kinds of evaluation are more focused on the program's financial accountability and are implemented to investigate the degree to which a program has used its funds appropriately (Scriven, 1991).

2. Outcome Evaluation

Outcome measurement "is the process and set of procedures for assessing, on a regular basis, the result of an agency's programs for its participants" (United Way of America, 1996). An outcome-focused evaluation seeks to understand intended changes in knowledge, attitudes, and practices that result from a program or project's intervention. In so doing it collects information on the inputs, activities, and outputs of the program. In essence, outcomes refer to "benefits or changes in participants' knowledge, attitudes, values, skills, behavior, condition, or status" (Plantz, Greenway, and Hendricks, 1997, p. 17).

3. Impact Evaluation

Impact evaluation focuses on what happens to participants as a result of the intervention or program. Caracelli suggests that impact evaluation is a form of outcome evaluation in that it "assesses the net effect of a program by comparing program outcomes with an estimate of what would have happened in the absence of the program" (personal communication, April 7, 1999). Berard sees impact evaluation related to changes in the status of program participants that result from changes in their knowledge, attitudes, and practices. He explains:

> In a project focusing on improving service delivery through improved local governance, an example of "outcomes" might be the extent to which community members: a) know more about their rights and obligations vis-à-vis locally elected officials, b) modify their attitudes of distrust/detachment, and c) change their behavior in regards to participating in decision making processes. The "impact" might be, a) community needs being better served, and b) improved socio-economic status as measured through educational attainment and/or morbidity factors. (personal communication, April 7, 1999)

4. Performance Measurement

Newcomer explains, "performance measurement is the label typically given the many efforts undertaken within governments and in the nonprofit sector to meet the new demand for documentation of results" (1997, p. 5). It focuses on program activities (process), direct products and services delivered by a program (outputs), and/or the results of those products and services (outcomes) (Caracelli, personal communication, April 7, 1999). Performance measurement has been promoted in the United States for more than twenty years and has received increasing attention as the public's distrust of government has grown. Canada has been implementing performance measurement kinds of evaluation since the mid-seventies, as has Australia since 1984 (Winston, 1999). In the 1990s performance measurement became a rallying cry within the U.S. government arena as a means to hold local, state, and federal agencies accountable. The result was the Government Performance and Results Act of 1993 (GPRA), which

> Requires each federal program to identify indicators of outcome for major programs, to provide targets at the beginning of each fiscal year for each indicator, and to report on the actual values for each outcome indicator within six months after the end of the fiscal year. (Hatry, 1997, p. 32)

GPRA focuses specifically on government performance "in terms of planning, budgeting, measurement, monitoring, and evaluation. The Act's intent is to focus government activity on results, rather than on inputs or process . . . "(Wargo, 1994, p. 65).

Current Thinking about Implementing Developmental, Formative, and Summative Evaluations

Some have suggested that summative evaluation is not as common today as it once was. As Cronbach, Ambron, Dornbusch, Hess, Hornik, Phillips, Walker, and Weiner argued two decades ago, "The hope that an evaluation will provide unequivocal answers, convincing enough to extinguish controversy about the merits of a social program, is inevitably disappointed" (1980, p. 52). A survey of evaluation use topical interest group members of the American Evaluation Association confirmed that formative evaluation is much more prevalent today than summative evaluation (Preskill and Caracelli, 1997). When asked to indicate how important formative and summative approaches to evaluation were ten years ago as compared to today, 81 percent said summative was "greatly or extremely important" ten years ago versus 64 percent who said it was "greatly or extremely important" today. Their responses to the importance of formative evaluation are even more telling; 38 percent said formative evaluation was "greatly or extremely important" ten years ago compared with 78 percent believing it is "greatly or extremely" important today. It appears that employees are now seeking more information for improvement purposes, perhaps in response to a continued call for implementing continuous improvement efforts and program accountability.

It should be noted that developmental, formative, and summative evaluation are not necessarily linear in their implementation. Rather, they should be viewed as circular, interwoven, and fluid. For example, if an evaluator worked with a design team to develop a program and used evaluation to help guide the program's design *(developmental evaluation)*, the team might decide later to conduct a *formative evaluation* of the program to see how it's working. A few months or years later, they might decide to conduct a *summative evaluation* to determine the continued need for the program. These results might lead to a new program design, which then may again call for a developmental evaluation.

The Logic of Evaluation

Evaluation is said to have a particular logic that undergirds all evaluation activity and makes it a somewhat unique enterprise. This logic refers to the specific principles of reasoning that underlie the inference processes in the field of evaluation (Scriven, 1995). Most often, the logic of evaluation relates to understanding how one determines the processes and impact of a program. As Fournier (1995) explains, the logic of evaluation involves the following:

- Establishing criteria
  On what dimensions must the evaluand do well?
- Constructing standards
  How well should the evaluand perform?
- Measuring performance and comparing with standards
  How well did the evaluand perform?
- Synthesizing and integrating evidence into a judgment of worth
  What is the worth of the evaluand?

We believe that evaluation logic also includes the development of recommendations for future action. However, it is important to note that evaluation theorists differ significantly on this point. Some suggest that external evaluators do not have the experience or authority to make such recommendations. Others would argue that it is the evaluator's responsibility to make recommendations. Still others believe that the evaluator and clients together should develop recommendations based on the evaluation's findings (Shadish, Cook, and Leviton, 1995).

An example of applying evaluation logic might go like this if we were to evaluate the ability of an organization's web site to motivate people to register for a particular training workshop:

Establishing Criteria.   Here we would ask, "What are the criteria of a good web site? Is it readability, color, interactivity, navigability?" These criteria might come from subject matter experts or the research literature.

Constructing Standards.   Here we are concerned with how well the web site should perform—what are our expectations for offering this web site? What constitutes a rating of effectiveness? For example, we may set a standard that if 1,000 people per day visited the web site and 25 percent signed up for a training course, it would be deemed successful.

Measuring Performance and Comparing with Standards.   Based on the standards we've outlined, the question here is, "How well is the web site accomplishing its goals of attracting trainees? Does the web site attract 1,000 visitors per day or more and lead to 25 percent of those registering?"

Synthesizing and Integrating Evidence into a Judgment of Worth. Based on what we learn from the evaluation relative to the criteria and standards we've set forth, we learn that the web site attracts on the average 700 visitors per day and, of those, 15 percent register for a training course. The question then becomes, "Is it worth it for the organization to continue offering and supporting this web site?"

Developing Recommendations.   Based on the determination of worth, the evaluator might make a recommendation that the cost of the web site, as currently designed, is not worth the resources to maintain it. Therefore, a recommendation might be to either redesign the site to attract more visitors or to eliminate the site and develop another process for marketing and registering trainees.

Developing the logic of evaluation addresses the steps one undertakes to come to an evaluative judgment about the merit, worth, or value of the evaluand.

Evaluation Use

Implicit in all the reasons for doing evaluation is the underlying belief that evaluation should always be conducted with the intention of using the results. *We will go so far as to say that if there is no clear intention to use the findings, then an evaluation should not be undertaken.* When evaluations are conducted and there is no concerted effort or intention to use the results in any way, then organization members may wonder why they participated in the evaluation. If the results are not used, everyone who participated in the evaluation has been cheated, and the organization has missed a critical opportunity to learn about its practices. Reflecting on the realities of evaluation, Patton asserts that "the central challenge to professional [evaluation] practice remains—*doing evaluations that are useful and actually used!*" (italics in the original, 1997, p. xiv). In fact, Patton has labeled his approach to evaluation *Utilization-Focused Evaluation*. He writes:

> Evaluations should be judged by their utility and actual use; therefore, evaluators should facilitate the evaluation process and design any evaluation with careful consideration of how everything that is done, *from beginning to end*, will affect use . . . the focus in utilization-focused evaluation is on *intended use by intended users*. (p. 20)

Our strong commitment to use has resulted from many years of working in the learning, performance, and change professions and with evaluation clients who, when asked about what kinds of evaluation activities they've been involved with, proudly point to piles of surveys on a desk or floor and filing cabinet drawers packed tight with several years' worth of surveys. Yet when asked what they've learned from the results of these surveys or how they've used the findings (typically postcourse reaction forms), they somewhat guiltily admit, "Not much." However, many are quick to point out that the surveys are reviewed for any problems and these often lead to some kind of follow-up with concerned individuals if names are provided. Although the collection of these surveys is certainly an evaluation act, it is nonetheless incomplete. When the data are not aggregated, analyzed, and reported in any form, the evaluation has failed to achieve its full potential.

Use of Findings

Over the last twenty-five years, many evaluation researchers have studied the topic of evaluation use or utilization (for example, Alkin, Daillak, and White, 1979; Cousins and Leithwood, 1986; Leviton and Hughes, 1981; Patton, 1978). One theme of this research has been to better understand how evaluation findings may be used.

When we think of evaluation use, we most often think of it in terms of actively employing the findings in ways that are tangible and observable. This type of use has been called *instrumental use* and refers to the direct application of what has been learned from the evaluation. The effects of use can be seen, heard, or felt in some way.

For example, in evaluating a knowledge management system, the designer learned that those who were using the system were confused about how to navigate through the site to find the information they needed. As a result of evaluating how organization members used the system (through interviews and observation), she redesigned the cues that guided people to the information they sought in the system. She was able to immediately apply the findings from the evaluation to improve the knowledge management system's design and implementation. Formative evaluation such as this often leads to instrumental uses of evaluation findings.

Evaluation findings can also be used to clarify an individual or group's conceptualization or perception of the evaluand. This type of use is called *conceptual* or *knowledge use,* and usually occurs as a result of hearing a verbal presentation or reading the evaluation report or executive summary. The individual might not be in a position to immediately apply the results *(instrumental use),* but he might come to a better understanding of the issues the evaluation raises. In effect, the person's schema or thinking changes because of learning the findings. Again, although individuals might not use the evaluation information to make instrumental changes or actions, a decision they make later on might be influenced in part by the evaluation's findings.

A third type of use has been referred to as *political, symbolic,* or *persuasive use.* This type of use walks a fine line between legitimate use and misuse (see Chapter 4 for a discussion on how politics influence the misuse of evaluation findings), but it is important to recognize that many evaluations are conducted in response to external requirements to evaluate or to symbolically demonstrate that the program has been evaluated. For example, there are times that an evaluation is conducted to solicit funding or refunding, to meet accreditation requirements, or to show others that the program is doing as was intended. If the evaluation is rigorously designed and implemented, and the findings accurately reported, then this type of use is perfectly justifiable.

It is often the case that an evaluation is interested in all three types of use. Chapter 5 will further explain the importance of talking with the evaluation's clients about what kinds of use they expect to make of the evaluation's results. It is always better to have this conversation earlier in the evaluation process than later. Discussing how the evaluation results might be used when focusing the evaluation ensures that conflicting goals for the evaluation are negotiated and managed.

Process Use

In the last few years, various evaluators have noticed that when using a participatory and collaborative approach to evaluation, another type of use often occurs (Cousins and Earl, 1992; Patton, 1997; Preskill and Torres, 1999a, 1999b). They have discovered that the very process of being involved in the evaluation leads to participants' increased understanding and knowledge, not only about the evaluand and its role within the organization, but about the practice of evaluation. This type of learning is different from what individuals learn from the evaluation findings. Patton coined the term *process use* to explain this phenomenon. He defines process use as:

> Individual changes in thinking and behavior, and program or organizational changes in procedures and culture, that occur among those involved in evaluation as a result of the learning that occurs during the evaluation process. Evidence of process use is represented by the following kind of statement after an evaluation: "The impact on our program came not just from the findings but from going through the thinking process that the evaluation required." (1997, p. 90)

Process use is particularly important if evaluation is to be integrated into daily work practices, if organizational learning is desired, and if a team approach to evaluation is encouraged.

Challenges to Evaluations Being Useful

As you've probably observed so far, evaluation is not a simple endeavor. Consequently, it's helpful to consider some of the challenges evaluators face when conducting an evaluation that may impede the evaluation finding's usefulness.

Changes in Clients During the Evaluation or Limited Involvement of These Clients. As we will discuss in more detail in Chapter 5, it is important to involve those who have a vested interest in the program being evaluated in the design and if possible, the implementation of the evaluation. These individuals help determine the evaluation's questions and they are often those who will make the greatest use of the evaluation's findings. However, there are situations where such individuals leave the organization or are transferred to another part of the organization and lose their connection with the evaluand and the evaluation. When this happens the likelihood of use is diminished since they are not around to use the findings. Use is also limited when we don't include the full range of individuals who could potentially use the findings in some way.

Changes in the Evaluand During the Evaluation. As we know all too well, organizations are not static entities; they are constantly changing. We have observed situations when during a program's evaluation, for example, a new instructor is hired or the population being served changes or the program is summarily discontinued. Each of these situations changes the program in a way that might not have been accounted for in the evaluation's design. As a result, the evaluation may be collecting data on something that no longer exists, or is so changed that the original evaluation questions are no longer adequate. This situation severely limits the usefulness of whatever evaluation results are then generated.

Evaluator's Credibility Is Compromised. The evaluator's credibility is something that is usually earned as a result of a consistent pattern of work. People come to respect evaluators for their expertise, professionalism, and honesty. (Chapter 4 addresses the ethics and standards of evaluation.) In other words, they trust that the evaluator will act in ways that are appropriate and ethical. However, there may be times when organization members question the evaluator's credibility. This may be a result of how an evaluator responded to an ethical dilemma, how much expertise they are perceived to have, or the position of the evaluator within the organization relative to the current political environment. If the evaluator's credibility is questioned, then it is quite possible that the evaluation itself will be distrusted. If this happens, organization members are less likely to have confidence in the evaluation and will be less inclined to use the findings.

Changes in Political Winds. Because evaluation is a political act, it is subject to internal and external political influences. Therefore, how the evaluand is viewed at any given time may change during the evaluation, depending on what political forces are at play. For example, a new mentoring program has been developed and made highly visible by a high-level manager. Sometime during the evaluation's data collection phase, this individual changes his position regarding the program because of some political influence within the organization (such as another new program that is highly regarded by the CEO and diverts his attention and interest from the current program's evaluation). If this were to happen, it is highly likely that the use of the evaluation's findings would be minimal.

Insufficient Communication Channels Within the Organization. For evaluation findings to be used, they must be made available to all clients and relevant audiences in a variety of formats (how to communicate and report evaluation findings is discussed in Chapter 13). This requires that the organization have open channels for communication and systems for disseminating the evaluation findings. When an evaluation report or summary of findings goes no further than the program staff, the organization misses an opportunity for other organization members to learn from the evaluation and its results.

Timeliness of the Evaluation Information. Part of the success of any evaluation effort is the timeliness of the evaluation findings. If evaluations are undertaken to resolve some issue or to understand some problem or concern more completely, then there are usually time requirements for this information. Sometimes these are related to the budgeting cycle, a deadline for a request for funding, a production and delivery launch date, or a "need to know" before taking other actions. When evaluations miss these deadlines, their findings may be of limited use.

In general, whether we're discussing how to identify the questions that will guide the evaluation, how to develop an effective survey, or how to communicate evaluation findings, the issue of use will always be present and part of the conversation.

Internal and External Evaluation

Today's evaluators reflect a wide variety of academic and professional backgrounds. Though management review and internal auditing functions have been present in government agencies for many years, most program evaluators have been external to the programs they've evaluated. That is, they have responded to a request for proposals by one of the federal or state government agencies to evaluate a project or program.

Most external evaluators are university-based professors, independent consultants, or consulting firms that specialize in research and evaluation. More and more, however, individuals within organizations are being asked to conduct evaluations of their own internal programs, processes, systems, products, and projects.

Internal Evaluation

Perhaps one of the most exciting developments over the last several years is the increasing number of organizations that are creating internal evaluation units or teams. To illustrate this growth, Sonnichsen observes the following trends in internal evaluation:

- Lengthy program evaluations will be replaced by shorter, management issue–oriented studies.
- Increased client focus will drive the internal evaluation process.

- Analysis, not compliance or accountability, will become the focus of evaluative efforts.
- Cooperative relationships with program managers will become necessary.
- More marketing efforts by evaluators will be required.
- Additional tasks for evaluation staffs will be necessary for their survival.
- Measuring and evaluating performance will become primary tasks for internal evaluators.
- External evaluation consultants will be used more frequently to train internal evaluators, add expertise to evaluative efforts, bring outside perspectives to the organization, and analyze and critique internal evaluation staff work.
- The notion of advocacy will become more accepted and recognized as an integral feature of internal evaluation.
- A diversity of evaluation approaches will be applied within organizations. (2000, pp. 9–10)

In an informal survey reported by Sonnichsen (2000), internal evaluation was found to be increasing across the world. The survey results estimate that in Korea, for example, nearly 95 percent of all evaluations are internal. In Canada and France, it's close to 75 percent, and in the United Kingdom and United States, it's about 50 percent (p. 40). Although some of these internal evaluators have experience with evaluation, more often than not most have limited education and training in the field. As interest in conducting evaluations grows, evaluation is fast becoming a core competency for many jobs in a variety of organizations. Though the practice of evaluation is essentially the same for internal and external evaluators, each role brings with it certain nuances and challenges. Before beginning any evaluation, it is important to consider whether the evaluation should be conducted by a) an external evaluator, b) an internal evaluator/team, or c) a combination of internal and external evaluators.

These trends symbolize an action-oriented, participatory, pluralistic, and utilization-focused approach to evaluation. There are, however, a number of advantages and challenges in conducting internal evaluations. In terms of advantages:

- There is a greater likelihood that the evaluation will be tailored to the information needs of organization members.
- There will be greater access to data.
- Organization members can develop evaluation expertise.
- There is a greater chance of evaluation becoming a sustained, institutionalized practice that is integrated with other work tasks and strategic planning.
- The evaluation results have a greater probability of being used for decisionmaking and action.
- Knowledge of the organization and its members may provide greater insights into the evaluation's design, implementation, and results.

At the same time, internal evaluators also face very real challenges. In some cases or in some organizations, the internal evaluator might face more resistance to evaluation if the organization has little experience with it. In addition, organizational politics may be more likely to impede the conduct of evaluation and the use of its results. Internal evaluators may not have the credibility or clout to conduct the evaluation and may lack the technical skills to conduct a competent evaluation.

How an internal evaluator defines her role is critical to how evaluation is represented within the organization. For example, Love (1991) points out that if an internal evaluator assumes or projects the role of spy, hatchet person, number cruncher, organizational conscience, or organization memory, she will not be successful. If, however, the internal evaluator assumes the role of management consultant, decision-support specialist, management information specialist, systems generalist, expert troubleshooter, advocate, or systematic planner, then she may be much more successful in implementing useful evaluations.

External Evaluation

As Sonnichsen's trends (2000) suggest, there will always be a place for external evaluators, though their role may shift in the coming years. Instead of being primarily responsible for the majority of evaluation work, their role may take on more of an auditing, summative, or technical assistance/coaching/mentoring function. At the same time, there are situations when an external evaluator may be preferred to using internal evaluators. Advantages to employing an external evaluator may include:

- Increased evaluation expertise
- Greater independence
- Ability to see the whole picture and provide a different perspective
- Less susceptibility to cooptation
- Evaluation may be completed in a more timely way
- Organization members may be more honest with an outsider
- Greater credibility of the findings (Sonnichsen, 2000; Torres, Preskill, and Piontek, 1996; Worthen, Sanders, and Fitzpatrick, 1997)

However, external evaluators are a) limited by their lack of knowledge about the organization's policies, procedures, systems, and culture, b) often dependent on the cooperation of internal organization members to gain access to data and individuals within the organization, and c) external evaluations are typically more expensive. When organization members don't believe in the evaluation, collecting reliable and valid data can be a formidable challenge.

Because both internal and external evaluators bring unique strengths to an evaluation it is often a good idea to seriously consider using a mixed-team approach whenever possible. This might be especially true if the program being evaluated is the subject of much attention and debate, or is one that consumes significant resources.

Keep in Mind . . .

- Evaluation is:
  A systematic process; a planned and purposeful activity;
  A mechanism for collecting data on questions or issues;
  A process for enhancing knowledge and decisionmaking;
  A means of judging the evaluand's merit, worth, or value;

Not the same as research.

- Evaluations should be conducted with the intention of using the results.
- Evaluations may be developmental, formative, summative, or any combination of these.
- Internal or external evaluators can conduct evaluations.

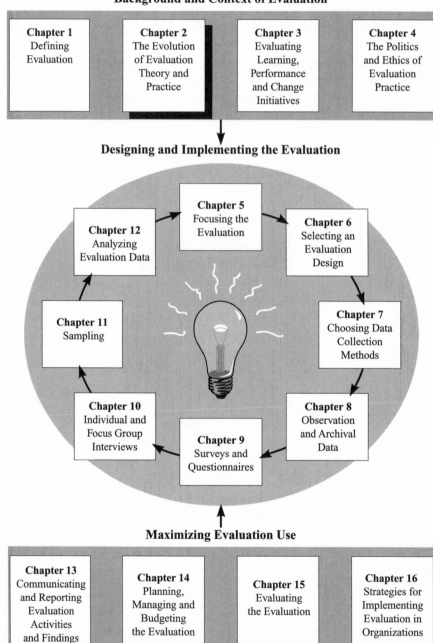

Background and Context of Evaluation

Chapter 1 Defining Evaluation	**Chapter 2** The Evolution of Evaluation Theory and Practice	**Chapter 3** Evaluating Learning, Performance and Change Initiatives	**Chapter 4** The Politics and Ethics of Evaluation Practice

Designing and Implementing the Evaluation

Chapter 5 Focusing the Evaluation

Chapter 12 Analyzing Evaluation Data

Chapter 6 Selecting an Evaluation Design

Chapter 11 Sampling

Chapter 7 Choosing Data Collection Methods

Chapter 10 Individual and Focus Group Interviews

Chapter 9 Surveys and Questionnaires

Chapter 8 Observation and Archival Data

Maximizing Evaluation Use

Chapter 13 Communicating and Reporting Evaluation Activities and Findings	**Chapter 14** Planning, Managing and Budgeting the Evaluation	**Chapter 15** Evaluating the Evaluation	**Chapter 16** Strategies for Implementing Evaluation in Organizations

chapter 2

The Evolution of Evaluation

- The Role of Evaluation in Today's Organizations
- The (Really) Early Days of Evaluation
- The Transformation of Evaluation into a Profession
- Types of Evaluation Models and Approaches

The Role of Evaluation in Today's Organizations

Evaluation has probably been around since the beginning of the human race. As we acknowledge in Chapter 1, we all evaluate things every day, though most often informally. Evaluation as a planned, formal, and professional practice, however, is a recent phenomenon. In this chapter, we present an overview of how evaluation has become a means for providing information for learning, decisionmaking, and action. We believe this context is critical to understanding current evaluation practice and the value of evaluation for learning, performance, and change professionals. As such, evaluation is a dynamic field of practice that continues to evolve.

The (Really) Early Days of Evaluation

The concept and practice of evaluation has been around for a long time, though it has gone through various incarnations over the centuries. Some writers suggest that evaluation goes back to the Chinese dynasties that used examinations to consider individuals for membership in professional and civil service jobs (Guba and Lincoln, 1981; Mathison, 1994; Worthen, Sanders, and Fitzpatrick, 1997). Some even cite Socrates and

39

other Greek teachers in the fifth century as evaluators for introducing questioning practices into the learning process (Stufflebeam and Shinkfield, 1985; Worthen, Sanders, and Fitzpatrick, 1997).

Modern-day conceptions of evaluation are closely linked with efforts to test students in public education owing to the public's dissatisfaction with educational programs. The first cited instance of widescale assessment of student achievement came in the 1840s, when Horace Mann and the Boston Board of Education introduced essay examinations as a replacement for oral examinations and recitation in grammar schools. Later, in 1897, Joseph Rice's study on the effects of spelling drills with 33,000 students was the first to use a comparative research design to assess the quality of educational programs. Rice was concerned that the schools' curriculum was "bogged down, with most of the pupil's time going into drill on a few basic skills" (Cronbach et al., 1980, p. 26), so he studied the extent to which the time spent on spelling drills made a difference in students' spelling performance. His findings indicated that the amount of time spent on spelling drills made no difference on students' spelling performance.

Large scale surveys employed in the early part of the twentieth century grew out of the use of quantitative surveys used during the seventeenth and eighteenth centuries that measured mortality and health (Worthen, Sanders, and Fitzpatrick, 1997). It was also during the early twentieth century that the business community became devoted to making its work more efficient. One example appears in the work of Frederick W. Taylor (1911), an American engineer and efficiency expert. He sought to optimize industrial efficiency by performing time-and-motion analyses in an effort to optimize employees' skills. Management became mechanized as it developed an extensive management structure to organize and supervise employees. As such, management's goal was to minimize individual responsibility to maintain an efficient and uniform manufacturing process.

During World War I, the development of mental tests to screen and classify personnel for military induction received significant attention and resources. The first group intelligence test was developed during this time by the American Psychological Association at the request of military leaders (Guba and Lincoln, 1989). At the same time, a movement toward accrediting U.S. universities and secondary schools was under way. Throughout the 1920s norm-referenced testing in schools became commonplace for measuring students' performance—"by the mid-1930's, more than half of the United States had some form of statewide testing, and standardized, norm-referenced testing, including achievement tests and personality and interest profiles" (Worthen, Sanders, and Fitzpatrick, 1997, p. 28). A study conducted in 1933 by Gertrude Hildreth of the University of Minnesota identified more than 3,500 mental tests and rating scales. By 1945, the number of tests and scales had increased to more than 5,200 (Guba and Lincoln, 1989). With the focus on measurement and assessment during this period, evaluation was more of a technical endeavor where the evaluator's role was that of a *technician* concerned with research design and statistics (Guba and Lincoln, 1987).

It was during these early years that America's interest in and reliance on test score data became synonymous with evaluation. During the 1930s, Ralph Tyler at the University of Chicago conducted an eight-year study on the differential effects of traditional and progressive high schools. In 1949, Tyler wrote, "the process of evaluation is essentially the process of determining to what extent the educational objectives are actually being realized" (p. 69). His study was unusual because instead of making judgments about the impact of different educational experiences based on test scores or accumulated credits (as was the norm of the day), he suggested that students' attainment of educational objectives should be the object of measurement. His work denoted a shift from focusing on individual student outcomes in relation to test norms to making evaluation a "mechanism for continuous curricular and instructional improvement" (Guba and Lincoln, 1981, pp. 5–6). Tyler's work later led to the development of criterion-referenced testing as a replacement for norm-referenced testing (Worthen, Sanders, and Fitzpatrick, 1997). Because of his emphasis on measuring the attainment of objectives and being the first to do so, Tyler is often referred to as the "father of educational objectives."

At the same time, because of the depression and President Roosevelt's New Deal programs, numerous government services and agencies were established. Social science researchers employed by these organizations began to study a wide variety of issues associated with these programs. Although a few used the terminology of "evaluation," most researchers approached their work with a strict social science research orientation.

World War II brought with it an intense need to again evaluate individuals' ability to perform in various wartime tasks and thus precipitated another surge in the use of mental and personality tests. One example appears in the work of U.S. Air Force psychologists who explored and developed new methods for testing aptitude and ability. At the same time, most education assessment efforts were focused on developing standardized tests, using quasi-experimental designs to compare programs, educational surveys, and accreditation. Educators were also being trained on how to develop explicit measurable behavioral objectives that could guide their teaching and assessment activities (Worthen, Sanders, and Fitzpatrick, 1997). After the war, up until 1957, there was a major expansion of education, thanks to postwar optimism and new tax resources. Madaus, Scriven, and Stufflebeam refer to this period as the "Age of Innocence," or alternatively, the "Age of Ignorance," in that there is little evidence to suggest that "data were used to judge and improve the quality of programs or even that they could have been useful for such a purpose" (1983, p 10).

Modern-Day Evaluation

Up until the late 1950s and early 1960s, evaluation was mainly focused on educational assessment and was conducted by social science researchers in a small number of universities and organizations. "Almost all systematic evaluative studies were privately supported and pretty much in the spirit of basic research, or else they were carried out as part of an internal management of a governmental unit, safely insulated from political storms" (Cronbach et al, 1980, p. 30). That changed, however, with the launching of *Sputnik* by the Russians in 1957. For the first time, another country had issued a scientific challenge to the United States, resulting in new and significant efforts to increase the educational requirements of America's public school children, particularly in the areas of math and science. President Lyndon Johnson's War on Poverty and the Great Society in the 1960s spurred a large investment of resources in social and educational programs. Programs to improve education and mental health and to reduce unemployment, crime, urban deterioration, and welfare were developed as innovations and demonstrated throughout the country. In particular, the National Defense Education Act (1958) provided millions of dollars of funding for many different curriculum development projects. In addition, two programs, Project TAL-

ENT and Project PLAN, were implemented as the first large-scale, longitudinal studies that sought to understand what factors led to students' choosing particular occupations. The Elementary and Secondary Education Act (1965) provided compensatory education to disadvantaged children through "tens of thousands of federal grants to local schools, state and regional agencies, and universities" (Worthen, Sanders, and Fitzpatrick, 1997, p. 32). These two bills were major stimuli for large-scale evaluation studies. Senator Robert Kennedy, concerned "that the federal money provided for disadvantaged children would not be used to benefit those children, but would be spent by educators without producing significant improvement . . . delayed the passage of the legislation until an evaluation clause was attached to the bill" (House, 1993, p. 17). Some saw Kennedy's motivation as a way for parents to hold schools accountable for educating disadvantaged children (McLaughlin, 1975). The resulting bill required the local education agency to submit an evaluation plan and the state agency to provide a summary report. This report had to describe not only how the money was spent, but it was required to describe the effectiveness of the program based on objective measures of student achievement that resulted from the money provided (Cronbach et al, 1980). Consequently, evaluation requirements became part and parcel of every federal grant from then on (House, 1993; McLaughlin, 1975; Rossi and Freeman, 1985). It has been said that Senator Kennedy's concerns were responsible for the overnight birth of program evaluation (Worthen, Sanders, and Fitzpatrick, 1997).

Early evaluations "were primarily experimental, quasi-experimental, or survey in methodology, utilizing quantitative outcome measure to meet the demand for surrogate measures of economic growth" (House, 1993, p. 5). The expectation was that these approaches would illuminate the causes of social problems and the clear and specific means with which to fix social problems. Also during this time, various government officials suggested that educational and social programs be evaluated by conducting cost-benefit analyses that would lead to decisions for continuing and eliminating various programs. Without question, the impact of federal social and educational program legislation stimulated an unprecedented interest in evaluation—by 1978, it was estimated that $140 million was spent on evaluating federal social programs (Levitan and Wurzburg, 1979). As House explains,

After 1965, the field resembled the early California gold camps, with large numbers of individuals from many disciplines straggling in to offer their ideas about how evaluation should be done. In addition to measurement specialists, there were psychologists, sociologists, economists, administrators, and even a few philosophers. Although the field was dominated initially by a psychometric view of research, a new brew of people, ideas, and problems simmered. (1993, p. 2)

"By the late 1960's—in the United States and internationally—evaluation research, in the words of Wall Street, had become a 'growth industry'" (Rossi and Freeman, 1985, p. 26). However, it was soon realized that many of these early evaluations were poorly conceived, implemented, and administered. Up until this time, social science researchers who were primarily trained in quantitative social research methods were conducting evaluations. Their efforts were mainly focused on determining what worked and didn't work. Donald Campbell is considered by many to be the most influential individual in helping found modern-day program evaluation. He suggested that the impact of social programs should be studied using experimental designs, that the effectiveness and impact of these programs be continually tested to determine their impact on social change (Campbell, 1969). Yet as increasing number of evaluations were conducted, evaluators and program staff realized that evaluation could do more than make judgments of worth or value; they could lead to program improvement (Patton, 1978).

Other evaluation researchers suggested that evaluations could also provide more than just judgments regarding a program's impact, and began to question the "leap of faith" needed when undertaking an impact evaluation. Specifically, Wholey (1975, 1976, 1979) recommended that evaluators undertake some initial steps prior to conducting an impact or summative evaluation. He urged evaluators to begin the evaluation process by identifying the program's logic, using "If—then" statements. For example, if a federal program receives funding, then that funding is distributed to the states. If the states receive funding, then the money is distributed to local agencies. If the local agency receives money, then it serves clients. By identifying and mapping the program's logic, the evaluator could begin the evaluation by determining whether the outcomes could possibly be achieved. Thus, a federal program that receives no funding cannot be expected to obtain its stated objectives. Such a process could also identify ways in which a program could be evaluated if the initial work determined that an impact evaluation was feasible.

As a result of evaluation's growth and some dissatisfaction with the constraints imposed by a strictly social science view of evaluation, new evaluation theories, models, and strategies began to emerge. Some of these efforts led to establishing evaluation approaches that were not reliant on social science experimental designs and instead focused on more naturalistic, qualitative case study designs. An outgrowth of the burgeoning need for evaluation was the establishment of evaluation centers at various universities (for example, the University of Illinois at Urbana-Champaign, Northwestern University, and Western Michigan University) where several evaluation researchers and theorists were located. These centers not only carried out many federally funded evaluations with faculty and graduate assistants, but they also developed a curriculum that educated and trained future evaluators.

The Transformation of Evaluation into a Profession

As the number of people who conducted evaluations grew, two U.S.-based professional evaluation associations that drew evaluators from all over the world emerged in 1976. One, called the Evaluation Network, consisted mostly of university professors and school-based evaluators, and the other, the Evaluation Research Society, attracted mostly government-based evaluators and some university evaluators. In 1985, these two organizations merged to form the American Evaluation Association (AEA), whose membership of approximately 2,700 individuals includes people from across the globe. In addition, journals devoted to evaluation that provided outlets for sharing evaluators' knowledge and experience began to emerge.

The 1980s saw huge cuts in social programs resulting from President Ronald Reagan's emphasis on less government. He saw to it that the requirement to evaluate was removed from or lessened in federal grants (House, 1993; Weiss, 1998). However, evaluators and evaluation researchers continued to hone their craft. In terms of evaluation's history, House refers to the 1980s as "the quiet decade" (1993, p. 3). However, it was during this time that organizations such as school districts, universities, private companies, state departments of education, the FBI, the Food and Drug Administration, and the General Accounting Office (GAO), developed internal evaluation units (House, 1993). Until this time, external evaluators generally conducted evaluation. However, with the emergence of internal evaluation units, the role of internal evaluators was created.

The 1990s saw the evaluation profession evolve even further. Increased emphasis on government program accountability and organizations' efforts to be lean, efficient, global, and more competitive have led to more urgent calls for evaluation. Although the majority of evaluations are still conducted by government-funded programs, evaluation in the 1990s moved into every type of organization. Today evaluation is conducted to meet not only government mandates today, but to improve programs' effectiveness, to enhance organizational learning, and to make resource allocation decisions in a wide variety of both public and private organizations.

Over the last thirty-five years, evaluation has grown from being monolithic in its definition and methods to being highly pluralistic. It now embraces multiple methods, measures, criteria, perspectives, audiences, and interests. It has shifted to emphasizing mixed method approaches in lieu of only randomized control group designs, and has embraced the notion that few evaluations are value-free and, by their very nature, are politically charged.

The maturing of the profession can also be seen by the myriad of professional journals that are currently available. This maturation is illustrated by the expanding number of national evaluation associations that are developing all over the world. These include the Australasian Evaluation Association, the African Evaluation Association, the Canadian Evaluation Society, the European Evaluation Society, the U.K. Evaluation Society, the Malaysian Evaluation Society, the Central American Evaluation Association, and La Société Français de l'Évaluation. Evaluation has, without a doubt, become a global enterprise.

An additional indicator of a maturing profession is the number of evaluators who claim evaluation as their primary or secondary discipline. For example, in 1989, only 6 percent of American Evaluation Association (AEA) members declared evaluation as their primary discipline (Morell,

1990). Yet eleven years later, 32 percent of AEA members identify evaluation as their primary discipline (American Evaluation Association, 2000). These findings lead us to conclude that people are taking on more and more evaluation responsibilities within organizations or consulting practices and identify themselves as "evaluators" regardless of their professional/organizational title.

Types of Evaluation Models and Approaches

The evaluation models and approaches that underlie much of today's evaluation practice were developed in the late 1960s and 1970s in response to several issues that concerned evaluation researchers and theorists about the definition, design, and implementation of evaluations. These issues included a reliance on quantitative/quasi-experimental or experimental designs and methodologies, the evaluator's role, an overreliance on objectives to guide the evaluation, the perceived lack of use of evaluation results, and the role of program decision-makers in the evaluation process (Guba and Lincoln, 1981). In this section we will briefly describe what we believe are the eleven most influential evaluation models and approaches that have developed during the last four decades in the field of evaluation. We discuss these according to the following characteristics: 1) the authors most often associated with the model/approach, 2) the intended users of the evaluation findings, 3) the degree of client or stakeholder involvement, 4) its underlying assumptions, 5) its primary methodology, and 6) the model or approach's major focusing questions (see Figure 2.1).

Behavioral Objectives Approach

This approach goes back to the 1930s with the work of Tyler (1935) and later by Bloom, Engelhart, Furst, Hill, and Krathwohl (1956), Mager (1962), and Popham, Eisner, Sullivan, and Tyler (1969). An evaluation using a behavioral objectives approach concerns itself with specifying the degree to which a program's goals and objectives have been attained. The major question guiding this kind of evaluation is, "Is the program achieving the objectives? Is the program producing?" Evaluations that follow this approach assume that the program's goals and objectives can be iden-

FIGURE 2.1 Evaluation Models and Approaches

Model or Approach/ Year Developed	Authors most often associated with model or approach	Intended Users	Degree of Stakeholder involvement	Assumptions	Primary Methodology	Major Focusing Questions
Behavioral Objectives (1930's-1960's)	Tyler Bloom Mager Popham	Managers	Limited	All objectives can be prespecified; quantifiable outcomes	Achievement tests Performance data	Is the program achieving its objectives? Is the program producing outcomes?
Responsive (1967)	Stake	Organization members Community members	Moderate	Stakeholders know what they need to know	Mixed methods, though primarily case study using qualitative methods	What does the program look like to different people?
Expertise (1970's) and Accreditation (1800's)	Accreditation groups Eisner	Government agencies Professional Boards Organization members	None	Experts know what is good	Document review Interviews, Observation	How would professionals rate this program?
Goal Free (1973)	Scriven	Consumers	Limited	Criteria can be specified; goals and objectives are unknown to evaluator	Observation Document review Interviews	What are the anticipated and unanticipated effects?

Approach	Author(s)	Stakeholders	Involvement	Assumption	Methods	Key question
Adversary/Judicial (1973)	Owens Wolf & Rosenberg Levine	Government agencies	Limited	Balanced presentation of facts can be provided	Public hearings Mock trial	What are the arguments for and against the program?
Consumer-oriented (1974)	Scriven	Consumers	None	Standards of quality performance can be prespecified	Checklists Usability labs	Would an educated consumer approve of this program or product?
Utilization-focused (1976)	Patton	Organization members Community members	High	Stakeholders know what they need to know—emphasis is on use of findings	Mixed methods, though often qualitative	What are the information needs of stakeholders and what plans are there for using the findings?
Participatory/Collaborative (1987)	Cousins & Earl King Greene	Organization members Community members	High	Grounded in democratic decision-making processes with no political agenda	Mixed methods, though primarily qualitative	What are the information needs of those closest to the program?
Empowerment (1993)	Fetterman Mertens	Community members	High	There is a political agenda underlying the evaluation to empower stakeholders	Mixed methods though primarily qualitative	What are the information needs to foster improvement and self-determination?

(continues)

FIGURE 2.1 *(continued)*

Organizational learning (1990's)	Preskill & Torres Cousins & Earl Owens & Lambert	Organization members	High	The organization is interested in learning from the evaluation and using the findings	Mixed methods	What are the information and learning needs of individuals, teams and the organization in general?
Theory-driven (1987)	Bickman Chen Smith	Government agencies	Moderate	The evaluator can help identify the underlying theory of programs	Mixed methods, though primarily quantitative	How is the program supposed to work? What are the assumptions underlying the program's development and implementation?

tified using behavioral terms, where the evaluator then searches for examples of how and where these objectives have been achieved. Typical methods used to collect these data are achievement tests and other performance measures. The resulting test or performance data are compared with the behaviorally stated objectives to determine if they have been met.

The behavioral objectives approach to evaluation is intended to serve managers' summative decision-making processes. In addition, the objectives approach has been influential in K–12 schools as a means for assessing student achievement. As originally designed, clients or stakeholders are not significantly involved in decisions regarding the evaluation's design or implementation.

Responsive Evaluation

In 1967, Robert Stake first wrote about the need to emphasize the importance of portraying participants' experiences with the program, and to present these observations through qualitative data collection methods in the form of vignettes and case studies. Stake developed the "responsive evaluation" approach in the early 1970s and explained,

> The essential feature of the approach is a responsiveness to key issues, especially those held by people at the site . . . issues are suggested as conceptual organizers for the evaluation study, rather than hypotheses, objectives or regression equations, because the term "issues" draws thinking toward the complexity, particularity, and subjective valuing already felt by persons associated with the program. (1983)

In particular, this approach calls for evaluators to be responsive to the information needs of various audiences—whom Stake calls *stakeholders*, as they are the intended users of the evaluation findings. It assumes that stakeholders know what they need to know. The process of conducting a responsive evaluation includes: a) talking with clients, program staff, and other audiences; b) identifying the program's scope and activities; c) discovering individuals' concerns; d) conceptualizing the issues or problems; e) identifying data needs and instruments; f) collecting data; g) developing case studies; h) validating the data; i) writing reports for different audiences; and j) assembling any required formal reports. The primary question addressed through a responsive evaluation is, "What does the program look like to different people?" To answer this question, responsive evaluations typically use a case study approach that employs both qualitative and quantitative data collection methods.

Goal-Free Evaluation

The goal-free evaluation approach advocated by Scriven takes an opposite stance on the role of objectives, as compared to the behavioral objectives approach described earlier. In goal-free evaluation, it is assumed that the program's objectives and goals are unknown to the evaluator so that the program's managers and staff do not influence the evaluator's observations. Using this approach, the evaluator looks at program materials, observes the program's activities and procedures, and tries to ascertain what the program's goals and objectives might be. Data collection methods typically used are observation, interviews, and document reviews. The fundamental purpose is to infer the program's effects from the activities of the program. As Scriven explained, "You can't do an evaluation without knowing what it is you're supposed to evaluate—the treatment—but you do not need or want to know what it's supposed to do" (1973, p. 322). Thus, goal-free evaluation focuses on actual outcomes rather than intended program outcomes. The hope is that unanticipated side effects will more likely be noticed when the evaluator has minimal contact with the program's managers and staff, who are not aware of the program's stated goals and objectives. The major question addressed in this kind of evaluation is, "What are all the effects?" This evaluation approach assumes that consumers are the intended users of the evaluation results and does not include stakeholders in decisions about the evaluation.

Adversary/Judicial Approaches

The adversary or judicial model of evaluation attempted to adapt the legal paradigm to program evaluation in cases surrounding educational and social program issues (Levine and Rosenberg, 1979; Wolf, 1975, 1979). As Owens wrote, "The adversary proceeding has been established as an administrative hearing process or judging the merits of a case involving opposing parties" (1973, p. 296). In this approach, two teams of evaluators representing two views of the program's effects argue their case based on the evidence (data) collected. Worthen, Sanders, and Fitzpatrick explain: "If trials and hearings were useful in judging truth of claims concerning patents and products, and if human testimony were judged acceptable for determining life or death, as in the judicial system, then might not legal proceedings be a useful metaphor for program evaluation?" (1997, p. 139).

In most cases, a judge (or several judges) decides which side has made a better case and hands down a decision. The purpose of this approach is to provide a balanced examination of all sides of controversial issues or to highlight both strengths and weaknesses of a program. The question this type of evaluation addresses is, "What are the arguments for and against the program?" The primary assumption underlying this approach is that there can be a balanced presentation of facts so that both sides are adequately represented.

This approach was used mostly in the 1970s with an emphasis on government agencies as the intended users of the evaluation findings. However, it was also used in a higher education setting to determine the effectiveness of Indiana University's undergraduate teacher education program (Wolf, 1975). The evaluation involved two evaluation teams, thirty-two witnesses, and a jury of thirteen education experts and occurred over a two-day period.

Consumer-Oriented Approaches

Michael Scriven has probably been the foremost advocate of using a consumer-oriented evaluation approach. As explained earlier, Scriven coined the terms *formative* and *summative* evaluation in an effort to distinguish between different kinds of decisions necessary for evaluating school programs and products. At a time when a large number of educational products were being developed as a result of increased federal funding, he published a checklist that focused on evaluating educational products developed by federally sponsored research and development centers (1974). Over the years, he has vigorously advocated a consumer approach to evaluation that is based on standards set forth and guided by consumers' needs. The original emphasis was to help consumers choose among competing programs or products by providing information that would help consumers in the purchase or adoption process. Data collection methods used in this kind of evaluation include checklists to analyze products, product testing, and usability labs. A question addressed by this evaluation approach might be, "Would an educated consumer approve of this program or product?" It assumes no role for stakeholders and presumes that general standards of quality performance can be prespecified and agreed to. Scriven often cites *Consumer Reports* as a good model for types of product evaluation.

Expertise/Accreditation Approaches

Involving experts in the evaluation of a program is considered one of the oldest approaches to program evaluation (Worthen, Sanders, and Fitzpatrick, 1997). One example is the accreditation model that relies on expert opinion to determine the quality of programs. This kind of evaluation has been implemented for decades in the medical profession, K–12 and higher education institutions, and the legal profession. In this model, the program staff is usually responsible for conducting a self-evaluation before a team of evaluators arrives onsite for one to three days of data collection. During these site visits, evaluators review the self-evaluation reports and conduct numerous interviews and observations of program staff and activities. The purpose of this model is to provide professional judgments of quality, which are typically based on individual knowledge and experience and use consensus and preestablished standards to make their decisions. It assumes that experts know what is good. Other more informal professional reviews are also used under this rubric. For example, blue-ribbon panels that involve prestigious individuals or ad hoc panels that are convened when necessary provide expert testimony regarding a program's quality. The question addressed in this kind of evaluation is, "How would professionals rate this program?" Stakeholders typically are not involved in the evaluation's design or decisions about its implementation.

Utilization-Focused Evaluation

Patton's (1978, 1986, 1997) *utilization-focused evaluation* (UFE) has received a great deal of attention over the years. Patton defines UFE as a "process for making decisions about and focusing an evaluation on intended use by intended users" (1994, p. 317). This approach positions the evaluator as "a facilitator of evaluative decisionmaking by intended users" rather than viewing evaluators as independent judges (1994, p. 317). It also assumes that stakeholders will have a high degree of involvement in the evaluation's design, implementation, and use of the findings. The major question UFE addresses is "What are the information needs of stakeholders and how will they use the findings?" Patton views *UFE* as a user-oriented approach because it focuses on people and "involves incremental improvement processes, conceptual insights, and reality-testing their assumptions or beliefs" (1994, p. 318). He emphasizes that a utilization-focused approach to evaluation does not automatically imply the use of certain data collection methods. Rather, the evaluator and stakeholders choose an evaluation design and data collection methods based on the evaluation questions. Though Patton admits that many UFE questions imply the use of qualitative methods, a UFE approach may collect both quantitative and qualitative data.

Participatory/Collaborative Evaluation

Participatory and *collaborative* approaches grew out of a concern with the mechanistic and insensitive approaches to evaluation that were being used in the late 1960s (Worthen, Sanders, and Fitzpatrick, 1997). Several evaluators began to stress the importance of involving participants or stakeholders in the evaluation process who have firsthand experience with the program being evaluated (Cousins and Earl, 1992, 1995; Greene, 1987, 1988; King, 1995). The emphasis in participatory/collaborative forms of evaluation is to understand and portray the complexities of a program or set of activities so that organization and community members can use the findings in their decisionmaking processes. As Cousins and Earl explain, "Participatory evaluation is best suited for formative evaluation projects that seek to understand innovations (programs) with the expressed intention of informing and improving their implementation" (1995, p. 8). Thus, the major focusing question for a participatory/collaborative approach is "What are the information needs of those closest to the program?" The approach assumes that stakeholders can engage in a democratic decisionmaking process to reach understandings about their programs' effects and effectiveness. It should be noted that there is no ideological or political agenda underlying this approach. The approach relies on a high degree of stakeholder involvement in the evaluation's design and implementation. Evaluations that are participatory and collaborative tend to use a mixed methods approach, but rely heavily on qualitative data that reflects the multiple realities of program participants.

Over the years, a continuum of participatory approaches has been recommended. The increasing number of participatory approaches led Cousins and Whitmore to develop a classification scheme that categorizes participatory evaluations as either pragmatic or emancipatory in their purpose. Evaluations that support program or organizational decisionmaking and problem solving are called *practical participatory evaluation*. Those that are founded on principles of emancipation and social justice, that seek to empower community members or groups who are less powerful, are called *transformative participatory evaluation* (1998, p. 6). Although there are many similarities between the two strands, Cousins and Whitmore write that there are three distinguishing characteristics that influence all forms of participatory evaluation. These are: control of the evaluation process, stakeholder selection, and depth of participation.

Empowerment Evaluation

Several evaluators have been particularly concerned about issues of social justice and fairness in program evaluation (Fetterman, 1994, 1996; House, 1993; Mertens, 1998; Sirotnik, 1990). The approach known as empowerment evaluation is most closely associated with David Fetterman, though its roots lie in community psychology and action anthropology. Fetterman explains that he developed the concept of empowerment evaluation as he explored the ways that "evaluators and social scientists could give voice to the people they work with and bring their concerns to policymakers" (1996, p. 4). He defines empowerment evaluation as:

> The use of evaluation concepts, techniques, and findings to foster improvement and self-determination. It employs both qualitative and quantitative methodologies. Although it can be applied to individuals, organizations, communities, and societies or cultures, the focus is on programs. It is attentive to empowering processes and outcomes. (1996, p. 4)

Evaluations that are conducted with this purpose help program participants improve their own programs through self-evaluation and reflection. In most cases, program participants conduct the evaluations and only use evaluators as technical experts or guides. Fetterman explains that empowerment evaluation is naturally a collaborative activity and that the evaluator is not in a position to empower others; rather, "people empower themselves" (1996, p. 5). Two characteristics that make empowerment evaluation different from other participatory evaluation approaches are: 1) the approach "is political in that it has an agenda—empowerment," and 2) "it has a bias for the disenfranchised, including minorities, disabled individuals, and women" (1996, pp. 26–27). This type of evaluation would be considered an example of emancipatory participatory evaluation according to Cousins and Whitmore's (1998) typology.

Evaluation and Organizational Learning

Another recent development in the theory and practice of evaluation has to do with linking evaluation to the concept of organizational learning. In response to the need for organizations to adapt to (a) a global economy, (b) technological advances, (c) an ever more diverse workforce, (d) increased customer expectations, (e) heightened competition, and (f) various legal requirements, organizations have looked for ways to maximize the value of their employees' work. Many management theorists and organizational leaders have determined that the way to succeed in these turbulent times is to ensure that employees continually learn and share their learning with others in the organization. Argyris and Schon, who have studied organizational learning for the last twenty years, believe that organizational learning occurs when individuals inquire into a problematic situation on the organization's behalf (1996, p. 16). Fiol and Lyles add that organizational learning is the "development of insights, knowledge, associations between past actions, the effectiveness of those actions, and future action" (1985, p. 811). Most theorists agree that organizational learning primarily occurs when individuals and teams engage in dialogue, reflection, asking questions, and identifying and challenging values, beliefs, and assumptions (Preskill and Torres, 1999a; Senge, 1990; Watkins and Marsick, 1996).

The collaborative nature of organizational learning and its reliance on information and inquiry has attracted the interest of several evaluation researchers. These evaluators are particularly interested in how the process of evaluation and the use of evaluation findings foster continuous improvement and change in organizations as we go forward into the next century. In advocating for participatory forms of evaluation, Cousins and Earl "argue for a pragmatic form of participatory evaluation using principles of organizational learning as a theoretical rationale" (cited in Shulha and Cousins, 1997, p. 199). Preskill and Torres (1999a, 1999b) propose that evaluative inquiry for learning in organizations can guide individual, team, and organizational growth and success as organizations adapt to new economic and societal requirements. They suggest that organizational learning is achieved through the social construction of knowledge and can be transformative when stakeholders are able to alter their perceptions and understandings based on evaluation processes and findings. Furthermore, learning from evaluation occurs within the context of the organization and is therefore mediated by the organization's internal systems and structures. Thus, the role of the evaluator is somewhat different from the role advocated by earlier evaluators that often required the evaluator to be external, value-free, and independent. Within an organizational learning context, the evaluator's role is more akin to that of a facilitator, educator, coach, mentor, trainer, and guide (Torres, Preskill, and Piontek, 1996).

Agreeing with those who have written about participatory and empowerment forms of evaluation, Preskill and Torres (1999a) believe that evaluation must be increasingly responsive to the evolving information and decisionmaking needs of organizations. However, they specifically recommend that evaluative inquiry be ongoing and integrated into all work practices rather than be enacted as an add-on activity or only as a product-oriented effort at the end of a program.

Several evaluators continue to theorize and research the role of evaluation in facilitating organizational learning (Cousins and Earl, 1995; Forss, Cracknell, and Samset, 1994; Owen, 1999; Owen and Lambert, 1995; Patton, 1997; Preskill and Torres, 1999a, 2000; Torres, Preskill, and Piontek, 1996). These evaluation professionals envision evaluation as a catalyst for learning in the workplace and believe that evaluation can be a social and communal activity in which evaluation issues considered most critical are constructed by and acted upon by a varied and diverse group of participants.

Theory-Driven Evaluation

Chen wrote that method-driven evaluation has, over the years, dominated program evaluation practice and theory. By focusing our thinking on methods, he believes that we have conceived of evaluation too narrowly, and that this approach has resulted in evaluations reflecting an evaluator's methodological bias resulting in the exclusion of data on critical issues. Since the late 1980s, there has been increasing interest in how theory-driven evaluations can contribute to our thinking about the role of evaluation (Bickman, 1987; Chen, 1990, 1994; Smith, 1994; Weiss, 1997). As Chen explains, evaluation should be designed by looking at:

> Pertinent assumptions and mechanisms underlying a program, such as what must be done in terms of treatment and implementation, what kind of causal processes are involved, and/or what intended and unintended consequences are likely to be generated. The exact features in a program theory to be included in the evaluation model are dependent upon key stakeholders' needs, resources available for research, and evaluators' judgments. (1994, p. 230)

The basic idea is to use the "program's rationale or theory as the basis of an evaluation to understand the program's development and impact" (Smith, 1994, p. 83). By developing a plausible model of how a program is supposed to work, the evaluator is able to consider not only social science theories that relate to the program and its implementation but the program's resources, activities, processes, policy statements, outcomes, and the assumptions that operationalize these (Bickman, 1987).

One way to develop and illustrate a program's theory is to construct a logic model that describes the program's design and implementation in one or two pages (Russ-Eft, 1986; Schmidt, Scanlon, and Bell, 1979; Wholey, 1975, 1976, 1979). In developing the logic model, stakeholders identify the program's underlying assumptions, resources, and other inputs, its activities, goals, and anticipated short- and long-term impacts. As a result of this process, stakeholders understand the program's goals, why the program exists, and where it is likely to be going. Examples of logic models can be seen in Chapter 3 (Figure 3.1) and Chapter 5 (Figure 5.1).

The Role of Evaluation in Today's Organizations

As we've explained in this chapter, evaluation has grown out of a need to hold government-sponsored programs accountable and to find ways to maximize programs' effectiveness. Since the 1960s, evaluations have often been of multisite programs in different states, across widely varying contexts. Although evaluation still plays an important role in social and educational programs at the local, state, and federal levels, there is an increasing need for evaluations at an organizational level.

Many writers on management today believe that the future success of organizations will be dependent on their ability to build core competencies within a context of collaboration. Technology and quick and easy access to information will help create weblike structures of work relationships that will facilitate their working on complex organizational issues (Hargrove, 1998; Helgeson, 1995; Limerick and Cunnington, 1993; Stewart, 1997). We believe evaluation can be a means for collectively identifying information needs, gathering data on critical questions, and providing information that when used, becomes part of the organization's knowledge base for decisionmaking, learning, and action. As organizations have been forced to respond to an increasingly competitive environment that is volatile and unpredictable, and as they are likely to continue being pressured to do things better, faster, and cheaper, they are looking at evaluation as a means to help them determine how best to proceed. In the knowledge era, where we now find ourselves, it is critical that organizations learn from their mistakes, that they see themselves as part of a larger system, and that they use quality information for making timely decisions.

Keep in Mind . . .

- Evaluation has been around for millennia.
- Evaluation as a profession is fairly new.

- Evaluation models and approaches provide options for determining the focus of the evaluation, the level of client or stakeholder involvement, the evaluation design and methods, and the emphasis on using the findings.
- More organizations are recognizing the value of evaluation and are requesting staff to conduct evaluations as part of their jobs.

Background and Context of Evaluation

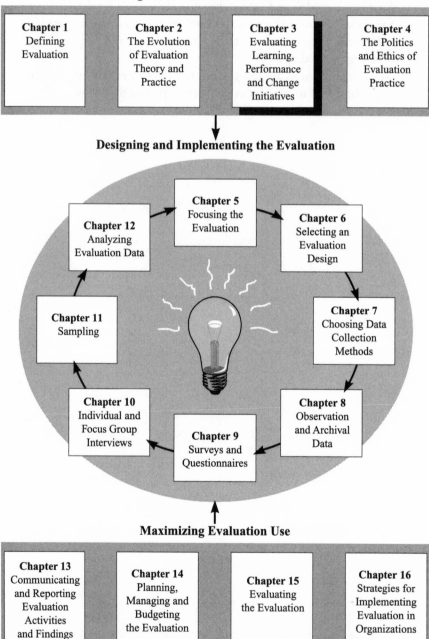

Chapter 1
Defining Evaluation

Chapter 2
The Evolution of Evaluation Theory and Practice

Chapter 3
Evaluating Learning, Performance and Change Initiatives

Chapter 4
The Politics and Ethics of Evaluation Practice

Designing and Implementing the Evaluation

Chapter 12
Analyzing Evaluation Data

Chapter 5
Focusing the Evaluation

Chapter 6
Selecting an Evaluation Design

Chapter 11
Sampling

Chapter 7
Choosing Data Collection Methods

Chapter 10
Individual and Focus Group Interviews

Chapter 9
Surveys and Questionnaires

Chapter 8
Observation and Archival Data

Maximizing Evaluation Use

Chapter 13
Communicating and Reporting Evaluation Activities and Findings

Chapter 14
Planning, Managing and Budgeting the Evaluation

Chapter 15
Evaluating the Evaluation

Chapter 16
Strategies for Implementing Evaluation in Organizations

chapter 3

Evaluating Learning, Performance, and Change Initiatives*

- The Role of the Learning, Performance, and Change Professional
- General Models, Approaches, and Taxonomies for Evaluation Training and Performance Initiatives
- Research on Training Program Evaluation Models

Future Directions for Evaluating Learning, Performance, and Change

As we've discussed in Chapters 1 and 2, today's organizations are experiencing unprecedented changes in how they define themselves and accomplish their work. Some of these changes involve greater shareholder concern for constantly improving returns, increased competition both domestically and globally, increased customer demands for newer, better, and less expensive products, and demands for improved services. Lest we forget the employees, it must be recognized that, in the United States at least, the current high level of employment means that recruiting and retaining skilled and motivated employees is a major imperative for most

*This is an adaptation of the chapter "Evaluating Training" by Joan Hilbert, Hallie Preskill, and Darlene Russ-Eft from the book *What Works: Assessment, Measurement, and Development* published in 1997 by the American Society for Training and Development (ASTD). We would like to thank ASTD for their permission to adapt this material and for their support of our work.

organizations. Underlying and supporting these changes are changes in the work itself. Not only are we seeing the use of computerized tools to accomplish work (whether on an assembly line or in an office), but an increasing number of jobs are requiring employees to be "knowledge workers"—those who produce with their heads, not with their hands. Recognizing the importance of knowledge workers, the new field of managing this "intellectual capital" as well as "knowledge management" has arisen.

The Role of the Learning, Performance, and Change Professional

Nowhere are these changes more evident than within the learning, performance, and change professions (Bassi, Benson, and Cheney, 1996; Dobbs, 1999; McLagan, 1999; Zielinski, 2000). Professionals within this arena are being asked to:

- Shift their emphasis from training to enhancing learning and performance improvement
- Keep up with the pace of reengineering and restructuring
- Manage, develop, retrain, and retain current and new employees
- Maximize learning technologies
- Facilitate learning to achieve the organization's goals
- Know their organization's business inside and out

The above areas of professional practice occur in many places within organizations, though they are often located within human resource development (HRD), training, or organization development departments. Increasingly, however, these departments or organizational units are being called Human Improvement Performance, Organizational Learning, Learning and Performance, Organization and Leadership Change, Organizational Effectiveness, Training and Culture, and Learning and Development (Lackey, 2000). In many small organizations, the learning, performance, and change function exists within the human resources (HR) department, though HR is typically concerned with recruiting, hiring, compensation, and other aspects of the personnel system.

Given today's organizational environment, Gilley and Maycunich suggest that learning, performance, and change professionals, regardless of which department they are in, are vitally important to an organization's success. They describe strategic HRD:

> The process of facilitating organizational learning, performance, and change through organized interventions and initiatives and management actions for the purpose of enhancing an organization's performance capacity, capability, competitive readiness, and renewal. (2000, p. 6)

Accepting this responsibility means that learning, performance, and change professionals must understand:

1. How adults learn
2. How to design and implement learning, performance, and change interventions
3. How individuals, teams, and organizations change
4. How to mediate and manage conflict within teams or groups
5. The nature of group dynamics
6. How to interact and communicate with individuals from diverse backgrounds
7. How to operate within a systems environment
8. The business of the organization
9. The external demands on the organization
10. The effectiveness and impact of their work

Given the scope and importance of these various responsibilities, it is clear that the job of a learning, performance, and change professional is multidimensional, complex, political, and challenging. Whether designing a training program for 100 employees, creating a system for improving a department's performance, or facilitating a large-scale organization change intervention, the importance of evaluation cannot be underestimated. In addition to understanding the value certain programs, processes, or products add to the organization, evaluation can also help decision makers and stakeholders make informed decisions. For example, evaluation can help answer questions about appropriate instruction and program design to achieve maximum benefits or to identify tradeoffs given alternative designs. With the increased demand and use of technology-enhanced learning, evaluation can address what processes must be in place when using certain technologies and what kinds of results might be expected. As organizations continue to be concerned about individual learning and performance in addition to team and organizational learning and performance, evaluation can focus on what implementation strategies seem to contribute to these goals. Finally, with learning and performance strategies needing to lead organizational change, evaluation can inform organization members about what strategies seem to work best and under what conditions. These concerns and others are the focus for today and tomorrow's learning, performance, and change program evaluations.

In the next section, we review the various training and performance evaluation approaches that have been developed over the last forty years, and discuss them relative to the models and approaches that grew out of the evaluation field during the same period. Given that training provided in the public and private sectors equals $54 billion (Industry Report, *Training,* 2000), learning and performance professionals have an ethical obligation, if not a pragmatic one, to invest in developing effective evaluation systems.

General Models, Approaches, and Taxonomies for Evaluating Training and Performance

During the last four decades, numerous models for evaluating training and performance have been proposed. Most of these models follow in the tradition of the behavioral objectives approach described in Chapter 2. Thus, their questions focus on whether programs are achieving their objectives; the data tend to be performance measures.

In 1959, Donald Kirkpatrick created one of the most familiar evaluation taxonomies. He originally called his conceptualization a "four-step approach" to evaluation. Since then, it has been variously called a model, a system, a framework, taxonomy, a methodology, typography, and a vocabulary. The four steps themselves have also been called stages, criteria, types, categories of measures, and most commonly, *levels of evaluation.* Kirkpatrick himself now calls it the four-level model of evaluation (Kirkpatrick, 1994).

As the first attempt to formalize the notion of training and performance evaluation, Kirkpatrick's model offered a solid starting point. Interestingly, the majority of models found in the literature either directly or indirectly build on Kirkpatrick's model. The following section presents the most common and relevant models of evaluation found in the human resource development (HRD) literature over the last forty years, starting with Kirkpatrick's four-level model.

Kirkpatrick's Four-Level Evaluation Model

Kirkpatrick (1959a, 1959b; 1960a, 1960b) noticed that evaluation of training could be conducted with four possible outcomes in mind: *reactions, learning, behavior,* and *results*. A Level 1 evaluation involves gathering reactions to determine if participants enjoyed the training, if the training environment was suitable and comfortable, and if the trainers were capable and credible. At this level, the evaluation question focuses on: What do participants think and feel about the training?

A Level 2 evaluation measures trainees' learning. Such measures determine the extent to which participants have improved or increased their knowledge or skills as a result of the training. The evaluation question at this level is: What do participants know now that they didn't know before?

A Level 3 evaluation focuses on behavior. Here, the evaluation seeks to determine the extent to which trainees are using or transferring their newly learned knowledge and behaviors back on the job. The evaluation question at this level is: In what ways has performance on the job improved?

A Level 4 evaluation focuses on results for the organization. The evaluation focuses on the extent to which the training has affected business results or has contributed to the achievement of organizational goals. Questions asked at this level might be: How has the organization benefited? Has productivity increased? Have customer complaints been reduced? Have scrap and rework decreased? How much has the organization saved?

Kirkpatrick did not explicitly state that his model was hierarchical in nature such that one level would affect the next level. However, the training evaluation literature has tended to accept this model as a hierarchy. That is, trainers have assumed that if trainees like the training (Level 1), they will have learned more (Level 2); if they learn more, they will use what they learn on the job (Level 3); and if they use their new knowledge and skills on the job, then the organization will realize specific benefits (Level 4).

Another implicit assumption in Kirkpatrick's four-level model is that each succeeding step or level is somehow "better" than the previous one. "Better" might be in terms of information gleaned or value to the organization. As we will discuss later in this chapter, there is little research to support these assumptions.

The ubiquity of Kirkpatrick's model stems from its simplicity and understandability. To explore just how pervasive this model is in the field, Hilbert, Preskill, and Russ-Eft (1997) reviewed fifty-seven journal articles in the training, performance, and psychology literature that discussed or mentioned training evaluation models. Of those, forty-four (or 77 percent) included Kirkpatrick's model (either alone or in comparison with another model). A mere thirteen articles discussed a model other than Kirkpatrick's. The fifty-seven articles describe twenty-one different models published between 1959 and 1996. As the numbers below indicate, it's only in recent years that alternative models have been developed:

1959	1960s	1970s	1980s	1990s
1	0	2	3	15

Although it is not exhaustive, this list illustrates the tenacity of Kirkpatrick's model and the lack of challenge until recent years. Even as late as 1993, some asserted, "Kirkpatrick's recommendations continue to represent the state-of-the-art training evaluation" (Kraiger, Ford, and Salas, 1993).

Kirkpatrick's taxonomy, for all the attention it has received over the years, has only been subject to a modest level of scrutiny and has not been widely implemented in its entirety. Most commonly, training interventions are evaluated at the reaction and learning levels. The reliance on reaction and learning measures may be owing to the perceived difficulty and cost in measuring performance or behavior and organizational benefits. Yet with the increased emphasis on the bottom line in many organizations comes concomitant pressure on trainers to "prove" the value of training. In the eyes of management, this often means providing enough evidence to show an acceptable return on investment or other concrete benefits.

Kirkpatrick's taxonomy has provided a foundation for the development of other models as evidenced by a host of evaluation models with a similar "look and feel." The remainder of this section describes the salient features of some of these models, approaches, and taxonomies.

Hamblin's Five-Level Model

Hamblin (1974), also widely referenced, devised a five-level model similar to Kirkpatrick's. In addition to measuring reactions, learning, job behavior, and organizational impact (noneconomic outcomes of training), he adds a Level 5 that measures "ultimate value variables" or "human good" (economic outcomes). As such, it can be viewed as falling into the tradition of the behavioral objectives approach.

Hamblin was more explicit than Kirkpatrick about his model being hierarchical, asserting that reactions lead to learning, learning leads to behavior changes, and so on. Accordingly, evaluation at a given level is not meaningful unless the evaluation at the previous level has been performed.

Training Effectiveness Evaluation (TEE) System

The Training Effectiveness Evaluation System (Swanson and Sleezer, 1987) highlights three evaluation processes. First, they advocate developing an effectiveness evaluation plan, then developing tools for measuring training effectiveness, and finally compiling an evaluation report. Like Kirkpatrick's model, the TEE system focuses on measuring participants' and supervisors' satisfaction, trainees' knowledge and skills, and organizational, process, job, and financial performance. Thus, this can be seen as similar to the behavioral objectives approach as described in Chapter 2.

The model specifies that a minimum of four tools are required to evaluate training: two satisfaction measures, at least one learning measure, and at least one performance measure. Scores from each tool are calculated and used to compile the Effectiveness Evaluation Report that compares before-and-after snapshots of a specific performance goal.

Brinkerhoff's Six-Stage Model

Brinkerhoff's evaluation model provides a cyclical approach, subjecting every phase of the human resource development (HRD) process to evaluation (Brinkerhoff, 1988, 1989). His six-stage model, although similar to Kirkpatrick's, adds a Stage I called goal setting or needs analysis. In Stage I, the training need is clarified and verified before any efforts begin to design a program. Brinkerhoff also adds a Stage II that focuses on evaluating the training program's design. His model then picks up with evaluating the training program's operation or implementation (similar to Kirkpatrick's reactions (Level 1). The six-stage model is to aid in the decisionmaking process throughout the design and implementation of HRD interventions. As formative evaluation, it can be used to improve programs by recycling evaluative information from one stage to the next.

Brinkerhoff's model reflects elements of the behavioral objectives approach, described in Chapter 2. Stages I and II may use a logic model, as described in Chapter 2 (and later in this chapter), to guide the evaluation.

Input, Process, Output Model

Combining and enhancing features of both Kirkpatrick's four-level model and Brinkerhoff's six-stage model, IBM developed its own model for evaluating training. Called Input, Process, Output (IPO), Bushnell (1990) described this model as IBM's corporate education strategy for the year 2000. This approach appears to be most similar to that of program logic models, as described in Chapter 2.

In the early stages of evaluation, it takes into account some of the factors (inputs) that may affect training's effectiveness. Among these factors are trainee qualifications, trainer qualifications, program design, materials, facilities, and equipment. The inputs, themselves subject to evaluation, feed into the process stage where the mechanics of planning, designing, developing, and delivering the training are accomplished. After the delivery of the training, the results are evaluated. These results are subdivided into outputs and outcomes. Outputs, which are defined as short-term benefits, consist of trainee reactions, knowledge and skill gains, and job performance improvement. Outcomes, or long-term results, are associated with the bottom line. Outcome measures include profits, customer satisfaction, and productivity, and they are derived from short-term outputs. Evaluative information from outputs and outcomes are recycled into both the process and input stages, thereby improving the training program cyclically.

Since the goal of training is to affect an organizational level change, the payoff comes when trainees use their new skills, knowledge, and attitudes on the job in a fashion consistent with organizational goals. Ultimately, then, the training impact should be expressible in terms of dollars and cents, rather than in training seats filled or number of favorable reactions generated.

Systemic Model of Factors Predicting Employee Training Outcomes

Richey (1992) provides a systemic model of factors predicting employee training outcomes. This model includes factors affecting training outcomes: knowledge, attitudes, and behavior. It acknowledges that instructional design and delivery do affect training outcomes, but deemphasizes this process in favor of trainee characteristics and perceptions of the organization. Thus, it can be viewed as falling into the tradition of the theory-driven approach as described in Chapter 2.

This model assumes that trainee's attitudes are affected by their background (age, education, training experience, work environment, motivation, and ability to learn) and their perceptions of the organizational climate (working conditions, management style). In turn, trainees' attitudes directly influence knowledge, attitudes, and behavior.

Kaufman, Keller, and Watkins Five-Level Model

In recent years, there has been a new twist to Kirkpatrick's four-level model. Kaufman and Keller (1994) and Kaufman, Keller, and Watkins (1995) expanded Kirkpatrick's model by increasing the scope of the first four levels (enabling and reaction, acquisition, application, and organizational outputs). By adding a fifth level (societal outcomes), they take into account the societal impact of training or of any HRD intervention. The "good neighbor" aspect of the model draws attention to an area in which businesses have not always realized or admitted their impact—the environment outside of their organizations. The effects of their programs on their clients and on society should be a major concern of any organization, according to this model.

Specifically, evaluation at the societal outcomes level seeks to answer whether the clients of the organization have been satisfied and whether the contributions to society have been worthwhile. These "megalevel" results are seen to be vital in determining how an organization benefits the society to which it is inextricably linked (Kaufman, Keller, and Watkins, 1995, p. 375). As an example of a societal outcome, manufacturing organizations would be held accountable for side effects of production such as pollution. This model strives to present a holistic view of the nature and purposes of evaluation and follows in the tradition of the behavioral objectives approach.

Training Efficiency and Effectiveness Model (TEEM)

This model (Lincoln and Dunet, 1995), which labels the evaluation stages as analysis, development, delivery, and results, bears some similarity to Brinkerhoff's six-stage evaluation model. TEEM emphasizes that evaluation should occur throughout the training and development process by using evaluative information to shape the decisions made at each stage. The model also strongly advocates the role of stakeholders in the evaluation process and recommends that trainers identify all those with a "stake" in the program so that all points of view and information needs can be considered in the evaluation's design and implementation.

Because of the focus on the training process, this approach reflects some aspects of the evaluability assessment and program logic approach. In addition, however, this approach acknowledges the importance of stakeholders, which few of the other models do. Therefore, it includes some aspects of the responsive approach as well as the utilization-focused and participatory/collaborative approaches.

Holton's HRD Evaluation Research and Measurement Model

Holton's model (1996) identifies three outcomes of training (learning, individual performance, and organizational results) that are affected by primary and secondary influences. For example, learning is affected by trainees' reactions, their cognitive ability, and their motivation to learn. The outcome of individual performance is influenced by motivation to transfer their learning, the training program's design, and the condition for training transfer. Organizational results are affected by the expectations for return on investment, the organization's goals, and external events and factors. The similarity to Kirkpatrick's Level 2 (learning), Level 3 (behavior), and Level 4 (organizational results) is readily apparent.

This model is unique in that it is the only one to identify specific variables that can affect training's impact. By identifying various objects, relationships, influencing factors, hypotheses, predictions, and limits of generalization, it provides a model that is testable. This can be viewed as related to the theory-driven approach, as described in Chapter 2. Thus, it is an intriguing addition to the roster of models for evaluating training and performance.

Evaluation Models Focused on Training Transfer

Each of the general models for evaluating training described above includes a stage, level, or process that focuses on transfer (Kirkpatrick's Level 3)—to what extent and in what ways are trainees applying their learning? In recent years, transfer has rightly grown to be an important issue in evaluations of training and performance. The extent to which trainees' skills, knowledge, and attitudes are transferred to the workplace highlights the effectiveness of the intervention. Because of its importance, we describe four models of transfer to help conceptualize the components that may affect successful transfer.

A Model of the Transfer Process

Baldwin and Ford's (1988) model conceptualizes the transfer process in three parts: training input, training output, and conditions of transfer. Each of these categories is further reduced to essential components. Similar to Holton's model, this can be considered a theory-driven approach.

Training input includes (1) trainee characteristics such as ability, personality factors, and motivation; (2) training design, which includes principles of learning, sequencing, and delivery of training; and (3) the work environment, consisting of managerial support and opportunity to use new behaviors. Training output includes the actual learning that occurred during training and the retention of that learning at the end of the training intervention. Conditions of transfer include the ability to generalize learned behaviors to the job and to maintain them over time.

Navy Civilian Personnel Command (NCPC) Model

Trainers at NCPC are similarly concerned about the knowledge and competencies gained during training, but go about testing for them in a different fashion (Erickson, 1990). Instead of completing detailed questionnaires, trainees in staffing and placement undergo intensive interviews three to six months after training. The interviews are designed to test their knowledge by presenting real-life situations with which trainees will be or have been confronted. By explaining how to handle the situation to a subject matter expert (SME), trainees divulge their grasp of the course material and the degree to which they have been able to apply the material on the job. The SME uses a checksheet to note which actions the trainee would take to resolve the problem under question. Analyzing the results of many trainees, trainers are able to determine what portions of the training are not working or appear irrelevant. This approach falls within the tradition of the behavioral objectives approach.

Stages of Transfer Model

Foxon's (1994) Stages of Transfer Model illustrates transfer not as an outcome, as it is often described, but rather as a process. From intention to transfer to unconscious maintenance, each of the model's five stages is affected by supporting or inhibiting factors.

Stage 1: Intention to transfer begins when a trainee decides to apply newly acquired knowledge and skills. Motivation to transfer is affected by the training environment, work environment, and organizational environment.

Stage 2: Initiation occurs when the trainee makes a first attempt to apply new knowledge and skills at the job. Factors that affect transfer at this stage include the organizational climate, trainee characteristics, training design, and training delivery.

Stage 3: Partial transfer is when the trainee applies only some of the knowledge and skills learned or applies them inconsistently. Factors affecting training transfer are the opportunity and motivation to apply the learning, skill mastery, and confidence to apply skills and knowledge.

Stage 4: Conscious maintenance occurs when the trainee chooses to apply what was learned in training. Motivation and skills influence transfer.

Stage 5: Unconscious maintenance occurs when trainees apply their new knowledge and skills unconsciously and integrate them completely into their work routines.

Similar to Holton, Baldwin, and Ford, this model can be seen as a theory-driven model.

Transfer Design Model

Garavaglia (1996) combines various aspects of each of the preceding three models to create his Transfer Design Model. As with Foxon's (1994), this model is organized into stages.

Stage 1 establishes a baseline performance measure from which the trainee is expected to improve. Stage 2, systemic design factors, and Stage 3, instructional design factors, operate simultaneously and feed back into each other. Stage 4, the training event, "is where the rubber meets the road, and we begin to get a sense of the effect the training will have on the original performance problem" (Garavaglia, 1996, p. 8). At Stage 5, the maintenance system, concerned with management support, comes into effect as the trainee returns to the work environment. Finally, Stage 6 is implemented to determine the transfer performance measure. This measure, when compared with the initial performance measure (Stage 1), indicates the extent to which the original performance problem has been corrected. If there has been insufficient transfer, the model suggests that the problem may lie in the training program's design or in the maintenance system. Again, as with Foxon's model above, this is a theory-driven model.

Research on Training Program Evaluation Models

Our next discussion focuses on research that has been conducted using various models to evaluate the outcomes of training. Many of the researchers measuring the effects of training have looked at one or more of the outcomes identified by Kirkpatrick (1959a, 1959b; 1960a, 1960b; 1994): reactions, learning, behavior, and results. These possible training outcomes provide a straightforward structure for organizing and reporting the results. Because of its usefulness, we have adopted a similar organization for the following discussion on measuring training's effectiveness.

Evaluating Trainee Reactions

The first level, according to several evaluation models, is to assess trainees' reactions to the training experience. Kirkpatrick pointed out in 1959 that positive reactions to training did not imply that any learning had occurred. Since then, perhaps because of the minimal cost and ease of conducting reaction evaluations, many trainers have apparently forgotten Kirkpatrick's caveat. They routinely use positive reactions as evidence of training's "success."

It may seem reasonable to assume that enjoyment is a precursor to learning, and that if trainees enjoy training, they are likely to learn. Recently, however, cognitive, industrial, and organizational psychologists have argued that adding difficulty or uncertainty to the training (thereby making it less enjoyable) will yield improved results (Hesketh, 1997). At the very least, the issue as to whether reactions are related to any other training outcomes has come under increased scrutiny and has shown mixed results. Some studies have shown that positive reactions to training are related to increased learning or greater use on the job, whereas others have shown no such relationship (see Figure 3.1).

A recent metanalytic study, which combined results from several other studies, showed that ratings of the usefulness of the training were related to later learning and use, whereas ratings of interest and enjoyment were unrelated to any other outcomes (Alliger, Tannenbaum, Bennett, Traver, and Shotland, 1997).

Although the results of these studies are mixed, it seems certain that using only trainee reactions to assess learning or behavior change is risky indeed. Many researchers suggest evaluating other training outcomes, in addition to reactions, to obtain for a more holistic view of training's impact.

Evaluating Trainees' Learning

After reactions, learning measurements are most often used to assess the impact of training. As with studies attempting to relate reactions to

FIGURE 3.1 Evaluating Trainee Reactions

Author(s)/Date	Focus of Research	Design and Methods	Findings
Dixon (1990)	Relationship between trainee reactions and post-training learning scores	1,200 employees of large manufacturing company; pretest/posttest of content and performance demonstration in three courses by employee type	Participants' reactions were not related to how much they learned. Ratings of instructors were related to the participants' level of enjoyment.
Clement (1982)	Relationship between trainee reactions and knowledge test scores	Pretest/posttest control group; fifty new supervisors; knowledge test	Positive relationship between reactions and learning; the more favorable the reactions, the greater the learning
Faerman & Ban (1993)	Relationship between trainee reactions and changes in work behaviors	Three-day managerial leadership training program for first-level supervisors; pretest/posttest at three months; supervisor behavior and reactions	Moderate relationship between participants' reactions and subsequent job behavior
Noe & Schmitt (1986)	Degree of influence of trainee attitudes on training effectiveness	Sixty educators (randomly selected); pretest/posttest of learning, behavior, and performance	No link between trainee reactions and learning
Warr & Bunce (1995)	Relationship between trainee characteristics and reactions to training	Open learning environment with 106 junior managers in a four-month training program; pretest/posttest on performance; reactions and learning assessed during training and reported later	Neither enjoyment nor usefulness is related to learning. Pretraining motivation was related to both enjoyment and usefulness, but not to perceived difficulty.

learning, the studies investigating the relationship between learning and work behaviors have shown mixed results (see Figure 3.2).

For example, some research has shown that trainees' perceptions of how much they have learned are not related to their actual learning scores. This result contradicts the intuitive notion that individuals know whether they've learned. Also, testing or measuring immediately after training may or may not be related to retention at some later time. In addition, although some studies have shown relationships between learning and behavior change, others have failed to demonstrate such relationships. Still other studies have examined trainee characteristics related to learning. In general, trainees' general attitude about training, their motivation for the specific course of training, learning self-efficacy, management experience, and analytic learning strategies are positively associated with learning outcomes. Characteristics shown to be negatively associated with learning outcomes are learning-task anxiety, stress, and (greater) age. Finally, a study that explored how management development interventions have been evaluated between 1986 and 2000 showed that there was no research to justify the relationship between learning and organizational performance (Collins, in press).

Obviously, many questions remain about how to truly evaluate learning from training. Much of the research reported here may be limited in its generalizability, given the lack of the subjects' diversity with regard to gender and race/ethnicity, the small populations studied, the different variables studied, and the variety of environments in which the research took place.

Evaluating Training Transfer

Training transfer is defined as applying the knowledge, skills, and attitudes acquired during training to the work setting. Training for training's sake is not a viable business practice, and today's economic realities mandate highly focused training to remedy organizational deficiencies or to gain business advantage. The paucity of research dedicated to transfer of training belies the importance of transfer issues.

Some of the research on training transfer has focused on comparing alternative conditions leading to training transfer (see Figure 3.3). A typical design might involve one group that receives one training condition

FIGURE 3.2   Evaluating Trainees' Learning

Author(s)/Date	Focus of Research	Design and Methods	Findings
Clement (1982)	Relationship between learning and behavior improvement	50 new supervisors; pretest/posttest control group; measured knowledge, behavior, and performance	No relationship between increase in learning and work behavior
Noe and Schmitt (1986)	Relationship between learning and motivation to learn	60 educators in a two-day administrative and interpersonal skills training program; pretest/posttest of learning, behavior, and performance	Pretraining motivation was weakly related to learning; job involvement and psychological attachment to the job were stronger predictors of learning than attitude.
Baldwin, Magjuka, and Loher (1991)	Relationship between choice of training to trainee motivation and learning	242 divided into three groups that were trained on skill-based performance appraisal and feedback; groups were divided into choice-not-received group, choice-received group, and no-choice group; pretest/ posttest control group design	The choice-received group had higher levels of motivation to learn, but there were not significant differences in terms of learning outcomes between trainees who received their training choice and those who were not given a choice.
Gist, Stevens, and Bavetta (1991)	To determine the impact of self-efficacy on the acquisition and retention of negotiation skills	79 self-selected predominantly white male M.B.A. students; four-hour salary negotiation training program; self-efficacy report, checklist of goal-setting activities, questionnaire	Self-efficacy is positively related to the acquisition and retention of salary negotiation skills; trainees with high self-efficacy negotiated the largest salaries.

(continues)

FIGURE 3.2 (*continued*)

Author(s)/Date	Focus of Research	Design and Methods	Findings
		on self-set goals; trainees randomly assigned to a two-hour workshop; pretest/posttest control group design	
Warr & Bunch (1995)	Relationship between trainee characteristics and training outcomes	106 mostly male junior managers; four-month open learning program for first-line managers	The following characteristics are positively related to learning outcomes: Attitude about training Motivation to learn about the topic Learning self-efficacy Management experience Analytic learning strategy The following characteristics are negatively related to learning: Learning task anxiety (Greater) age

Ree & Earles (1991)	The extent to which specific abilities combined with general cognitive ability predict learning outcomes	78,041 air force enlistees, mostly white, 17–23 years old, high school graduates; battery of tests for cognitive ability; training on one of 82 military job training topics; learning measured by technical knowledge and procedure tests	Test battery predicted general cognitive ability; measures of specific ability were not needed to predict training success
Dixon (1990)	Relationship between trainees' perceptions of how much they have learned and actual learning scores	1,200 employees of large manufacturing company; pretest-posttest of content and performance demonstration in three courses by employee type	No relationship between perception of how much learned and learning scores

FIGURE 3.3   Evaluating Training Transfer

Author(s)/Date	Focus of Research	Design and Methods	Findings
Wexley and Baldwin (1986)	Which of three posttraining strategies best enhanced retention and application of time-management skills	256 university students who attended a three-hour time-management workshop; subjects were randomly assigned to one of four groups: (1) assigned goal setting, (2) participative goal setting, (3) behavior self-management, (4) control; measures included learning and behavioral self-reports	Assigned and participative goal-setting conditions were positively related to behavior performance; learning was not related to experimental conditions.
Gist, Bavetta, and Stevens (1990)	Whether goal-setting or self-management training would better facilitate transfer of learning	Sixty-eight MBA students with a mean age of 29; all participants completed a seven-hour negotiation skills course; independently reported behavior measure of performance; learning was measured by written responses to nine scenarios; subjects were randomly placed into one of the two groups	Trainees in the self-management group negotiated greater compensation on the transfer task than did trainees in the goal-setting group; some form of post training transfer strategy may facilitate training transfer.
Tziner, Haccoun, and Kadish (1991)	To determine whether personal and situational factors affect training transfer	Eighty-one Israeli military instructors; divided about equally by gender, with a mean age of 20; subjects randomly assigned to a relapse prevention module after the training program; other subjects assigned to a control group; nine instruments administered to	Trainees who attended the relapse prevention module learned more, attempted to use transfer skills more often, and used their new skills on the job more often than members of the control group.

Study	Purpose	Method	Findings
(continued)		measure locus-of-control, work environment support, reactions to training, motivation to transfer, content mastery, trainee self-report of skills used, trainee self-report of transfer strategies used	
Rouiller and Goldstein (1993)	Relationship between organizational climate and training transfer	102 assistant managers at a large fast-food franchise; nine-week training program on administration, customer service, and food handling; surveys administered to assess organizational climate; measures of trainees' learning, transfer behavior, and job performance taken; trainers assessed learning during and after training	Learning and transfer were positively related; trainees who learned more also performed well on behavior measures; transfer behavior was found to be positively related to job performance; learning was not related to job performance; the amount of learning combined with transfer climate affects the degree to which training is transferred.
Brinkerhoff and Montesino (1995)	Relationship of management support to training transfer	91 randomly selected employees from a Fortune 500 company; subjects participated in one of five different skill development courses; course members assigned to either the experimental or comparison group; survey questionnaire administered to assess amount of transfer, factors affecting transfer, and meetings held with supervisors	Management support and training transfer are related; trainees who reported more skills transfer also perceived greater supervisor support and reported fewer transfer-inhibiting factors.

and another group that receives a different training condition or no training at all. Unfortunately, these studies have not always used the same research design and have not shown consistent results. For example, comparisons of goal setting versus self-management as a posttraining strategy have shown mixed results. Nevertheless, from this research we know that some form of posttraining transfer strategy facilitates training transfer.

Other researchers have investigated whether personal and situational factors affect training transfer. Several studies have shown the effect of management support and of organizational transfer climate on learning and training transfer.

Evaluating Training Results

One of the hottest training evaluation topics is that of evaluating business results, financial results, and return on investment (ROI). The popular and research literature from 1990 through 1999 is laden with such articles. Most offer anecdotal evidence or conjecture about the necessity of evaluating training's return on investment or financial results and methods trainers might use to implement such an evaluation. Research on this topic, however, is not so voluminous (see Figure 3.4).

Since training and development is a costly endeavor, "it should be evaluated in the same way as other large investments, in terms of costs and benefits" (Mosier, 1990, p. 45). To assist managers in selecting appropriate evaluation approaches, Mosier reviewed numerous common capital budgeting techniques. Among these are payback time, average rate of return, present value or worth, internal rate of return, and cost-benefit ratio. She notes that many managers and trainers still evaluate by the "gut feel" method and insist that a rational financial model is essential for evaluating training's effectiveness. She concludes by speculating that there are four reasons why financial analyses are rarely conducted or reported:

- It is difficult to quantify or establish a monetary value for many aspects of training.
- No usable cost-benefit tool is readily available.
- The time lag between training and results is problematic.
- Training managers and trainers are not familiar with financial analysis models.

FIGURE 3.4 Evaluating Training Results (Organizational Impact)

Author(s)/Date	Focus of Research	Design and Methods	Findings
Russ-Eft, Krishnamurthi, and Ravishankar (1990)	To determine ROI of interpersonal skills training	Pretest/posttest control program group design; fixed and variable costs computed; skill changes from training were converted to monetary benefits using the fixed and variable costs	Training improved interpersonal skills and the program showed a favorable ROI.
Jacobs, Jones and Neil (1992)	To determine whether unstructured or structured on-the-job training produced greater financial benefits	Case study at midwestern assembly plant; studied three critical tasks; performance value and costs calculated for each task	Structured OJT resulted in significantly lower mastery times for all three tasks; structured OJT found to provide almost twice the financial benefits as unstructured OJT for all three tasks.
McLinden, Davis, and Sheriff (1993)	To determine ROI of tax consultant training	Collected reaction, learning, and job performance data; assigned dollar amounts to various training benefits; payback = revenues attributed to training = cost of training	Substantive positive impact on the financial productivity of the tax consultancy; trainees generated more revenue for their organization than did untrained employees.

(continues)

FIGURE 3.4 (continued)

Author(s)/Date	Focus of Research	Design and Methods	Findings
Bernthal and Byham (1994)	To determine the ROI of an interactive skills training program for supervisors	Predominantly white male maintenance supervisors, ages 20–60; pretest/posttest control group design to measure turnover, absenteeism, overtime; five training modules assessed	Training group showed reduced turnover, less absenteeism; results saved organization between $200 and $20,000.

To justify continuation of their training programs, Mosier suggests managers or trainers collect and analyze quantitative data.

In spite of the interest in ROI and cost benefit kinds of outcomes, research on this topic is hard to find and studies that exist do not provide much guidance for trainers in designing and conducting their own ROI evaluations. Generally, the studies reported do not discuss alternative methods for calculating ROI or justify the method ultimately selected.

Bartel identifies some key attributes for determining the ROI of training. Many of these recommendations, such as isolating the effects of training, appear related to the specific research design for the evaluation. However, she recommends that evaluators use the net present value or the internal rate of return method when determining the ROI of training. Both of these methods take into account the time value of money. She further recommends using the net present value, "Because it gives more accurate results when comparing projects of two different sizes or projects that have payout streams of different magnitudes and lengths" (1997, p. 175).

Future research needs to be conducted to identify appropriate financial models for evaluating specific learning, performance, and change initiatives. As Mosier (1990) explains, using the same data and different techniques can result in vastly different ROI results. Learning, performance, and change professionals have a definite interest in determining which models and techniques will best address the questions they seek to answer (Swanson and Gradous, 1988).

Future Directions for Evaluating Learning, Performance, and Change

Although Kirkpatrick's taxonomy has provided many trainers a place to start in evaluating training, criticism about its limited focus is escalating. The taxonomy's lack of diagnostic capability and its inability to account for factors that affect the outcomes at each level are just two of its inherent weaknesses. The same can be true for the vast majority of models, approaches, and taxonomies reviewed in this chapter. Nearly all of these reflect Kirkpatrick's four levels (reactions, learning, behavior, and results) in some way and use similar, if not identical, terminology. Where the labels differ, the underlying ideas embodied share common traits. However, most of these "models" are not true models, but are taxonomies that merely describe anticipated training outcomes. They fail to offer any direction on what critical variables need to be studied or how to conduct a rigorous, credible, useful evaluation in dynamic, evolving, and political environments. Further limiting their usefulness is the fact that very few of these have undergone rigorous forms of research to determine the extent to which they describe training's effects or how training outcomes are affected by various organizational variables. For example, individual trainees have different personalities, skills, motivations, attitudes, and expectations. The organizations in which they work have their own cultures, management structures, organizational goals, and so on. These factors and many more likely affect the conduct and effects of any learning, performance, or change intervention. Yet the models, approaches, and taxonomies that have been proposed provide limited guidance on how these variables interact with and affect individuals, teams, and organizations. To this end, Collins (in press) cautions that "practitioners who use the four-level approach alone are quite likely to arrive at erroneous conclusions about their training programs."

As discussed in this chapter, most of the approaches for evaluating training and performance follow in the tradition of the behavioral objectives approach, with some limited use of theory-driven evaluations. None, however, recommend using a participatory, collaborative, responsive, or use-focused evaluation approach. A future direction for such evaluations would be to apply some of the types of evaluation described in Chapter 2. We provide three examples in the following paragraphs.

1. Using a Goal-Free Approach

The goal-free evaluation (Scriven, 1973), as described in Chapter 2, does not begin by reviewing the objectives and goals of the learning, performance, and change initiative. Rather, the evaluator begins with the program materials and activities and tries to determine the actual outcomes. By doing so, the evaluator cannot "relax" once having found that the intended outcomes are being met. Consequently, this method tends to identify many side effects of the program. Though not often implemented, the goal-free approach may be particularly useful when we want to understand and uncover possible unanticipated outcomes of the learning, performance, and change initiative.

Take, for example, a director of training who decides to hire an external evaluation team to undertake an independent evaluation of a weeklong leadership institute. Over the last three years, the institute had been receiving positive reactions (from a postcourse survey) from attendees. Based on these reactions, various changes had been made to the program. Now, the training director wants to explore the extent to which the institute is achieving its objectives.

The lead evaluator met with the director of training and suggested using the goal-free approach. She recommended this approach because the director of training wanted to know about all of the outcomes of the training, not just those listed in the course curriculum materials. The questions they wanted the evaluation to address included: 1) What is the leadership institute accomplishing? and 2) What appear to be the goals and objectives of the program—what is the institute attempting to do? Based on these questions, an evaluation plan was developed. One of the data collection methods included a comprehensive document review of the materials that were provided to the participants. Two of the evaluation team members participated in the institute as though they were regular attendees (participant observers). Later they interviewed each of the institute's attendees. Based on the materials, their observations, and interviews, they concluded the following:

- Most, but not all, persons attending the institute viewed their participation as a reward.
- Most, but not all, participants read the materials and, therefore, possessed a common understanding and language.
- All participants gained an understanding of the financial operations of the organization.
- All participants developed a network of colleagues, useful in dealing with future crossfunctional issues.

The two participant evaluators presented a draft of the final report to the lead evaluator. After reading it she asked, "But what about the use of leadership skills on the job?" The participant evaluators laughed and stated that they would have to undertake further data collection to confirm whether leadership skills were learned and transferred to the job, since none of their interviewees' responses mentioned their using leadership skills as a result of the institute. The director of training was somewhat surprised by the report, but the results enabled her to make significant changes to the program that would improve future trainees' ability to transfer leadership skills to their work environment.

2. Using a Logic Model

As mentioned in Chapter 2 (and later in Chapter 5), the creation of a "logic map" of the training can help identify objectives, elements, processes, and approaches critical to obtaining specified outcomes. The logic map helps determine the extent to which the program has clearly defined and measurable objectives, a logic or rationale for reaching the program's goals, and a sequence of activities that represent the program's logic or rationale. It shows logical linkages among activities, immediate outputs, and a range of outcomes.

A key distinction in using this approach is that the development of such a logic model is an iterative and collaborative process. Typically, the evaluator involves a stakeholder group in the development of the logic model. The approach can take the form of generating a series of "if—then" statements of the type: If Event X occurs, then Event Y will occur"; or "If trainees participate in training, they will increase their use of the skill being trained." A more structured approach involves the use of specific questions to aid in the model's development. These questions include the following:

- How does this program operate, and what resources are needed?
- Who is reached by these resources in terms of users and clients?
- What results are expected from the program, and why are these results necessary? These results include both direct or immediate outcomes, as well as long-term outcomes.
- What external factors may be influencing each stage of the training and evaluation process?

Data collection to confirm the model can involve surveys, document review, individual and focus group interviews with customers, partners, and stakeholders, and observation. Furthermore, as data are collected, the model may need to be revised to reflect the actual program.

FIGURE 3.5   Logic Model for a Training Process

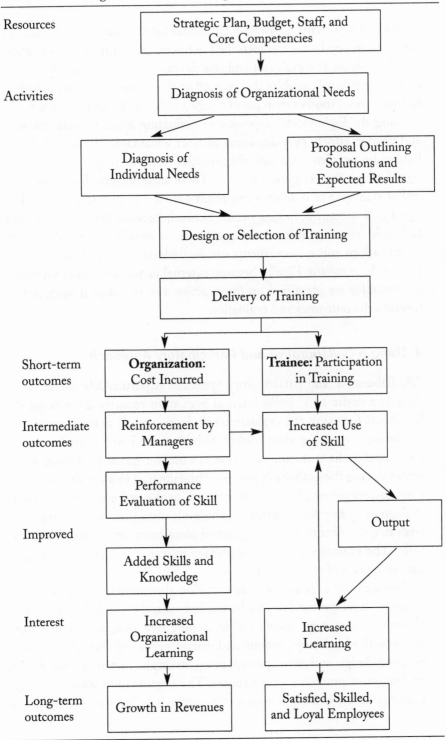

Figure 3.5 presents a simple logic model for this training program. In this case, the evaluator has identified outcomes for both the organization and the trainee. The evaluator and stakeholders can then refine this model to include external variables that may affect the training activities as well as the outcomes. Another example of a logic model can be seen in Chapter 5.

Using the logic model approach to evaluating learning, performance, and change efforts provides some distinct advantages. First, key stakeholders become involved with the initiative from the program's initial design through the evaluation process. These stakeholders should come to realize that specific outcomes can result only if certain resources are allocated and certain activities occur. Second, because the evaluator and stakeholders are examining the process from beginning to end, needed modifications and improvements can be undertaken to enhance the impact of the program. Finally, because external factors and other intervening variables are identified up front, action can be taken if such factors threaten the outcomes and evaluation.

3. Using a Collaborative and Participatory Approach

A collaborative and participatory approach is particularly useful when there is a desire to 1) build internal evaluation capacity, 2) increase the likelihood for using the evaluation's findings, and 3) obtain buy-in and involvement from key stakeholders. Whether one is an internal or external evaluator, the evaluator may serve as a mentor, guide, facilitator, or educator during the evaluation process. Fundamental to a collaborative and participatory approach is that it seeks to involve stakeholders in various evaluation tasks—from designing the evaluation plan to collecting and analyzing the data to developing action plans based on the recommendations. The evaluator might even provide informal or formal training on various aspects of evaluation practice.

Consider, for example, an organization that wants to evaluate their program development process. In the last year, they've designed a comprehensive four-stage system for developing new programs. The system begins with identifying program and market needs and then progresses to program design and development, program implementation, and, finally, evaluation of programs' effectiveness. The organization wants to better understand the extent to which the system is being implemented and how well it is working. Because of the diverse groups of people involved in the system and the organization's interest in having all employees understand the importance of evaluation and how to do it, they've decided to use a collaborative and participatory evaluation approach. To do this, they invite a large number of stakeholders (those who have a vested interest or responsibility for each stage of the program development system) to a meeting whereat they determine the purpose of the evaluation and the questions it will address (see Chapter 5 for how to do this). From this meeting a core group of ten individuals agree to continue with the evaluation. Some of these employees develop and review data collection instruments; collect, analyze, and interpret the data; make recommendations; and develop and implement action plans based on the recommendations. All this time, they work to ensure that the evaluation provides useful and credible information and that others are kept informed about the evaluation's progress and outcomes. In this case, the evaluator's role was negotiated with the group and resulted in her providing evaluation technical assistance and some facilitation of the team's meetings when they got stuck or were unable to resolve an issue. As a result of using the collaborative and participatory approach, employees gained 1) a better understanding about the program development system and its effectiveness, 2) improved evaluation skills, and 3) a greater appreciation for the value of evaluation and its role within the organization.

Developing More Comprehensive Evaluation Models

What we have learned from reviewing the history of training evaluation research is that there are many variables that ultimately affect how trainees learn and transfer their learning in the workplace. Unless we carefully consider and study these variables, we will be unable to describe and explain any effects training may have on individual, team, and organizational performance. Therefore, a comprehensive evaluation of learning, performance, and change would include some representation of the variables shown in Figure 3.6.

In addition, the training evaluation models, approaches, and taxonomies have not been grounded in a philosophy or theory of evaluation. The literature tends to position evaluation as a periodic event that is the sum of a set of technical skills and activities focused on a narrow set of

FIGURE 3.6   Variables that Affect the Effectiveness and Impact of Learning, Performance, and Change Interventions

---

Organization
    risk-taking capacity
    orientation to change
    commitment to training and learning
    resources for training and learning
    extent to which it has systems and structures that support transfer of
       training and learning
    degree of alignment between goals and actions
    experiences with previous change efforts
    financial situation
    orientation towards evaluation
    organization culture
    organization climate

Trainees
    motivation to learn
    work history
    ability to learn
    readiness for training
    motivation to transfer learning
    attitude about and commitment to the job
    expected utility of training content
    personality factors
    enjoyment of the training experience
    opportunity to apply learning
    choice to be in training
    self-efficacy
    learning task anxiety
    (greater) age
    goal setting before training
    locus of control
    involvement in the program's design
    prior experience with training
    perceptions of the organization

FIGURE 3.6 *(continued)*

Trainers
    facilitation skills
    content knowledge
    training delivery skills
    level of interest/enthusiasm
    written and verbal communication skills
    credibility
    demographics
    understanding of adult learning theories and principles
    level of organization and preparedness
    listening skills

Managers
    ability and willingness to coach on new skills
    ability and willingness to model new skills
    expectations of improved job performance
    pre-training meeting with trainees
    provision of time for trainees to use new knowledge and skills
    provision of resources to use new knowledge and skills
    provision of incentives to use new knowledge and skills
    communication of the value of training and learning

Training Program Design
    training program is based on a needs assessment
    training population is clearly identified and have training needs
    goal and objectives are related to the needs identified (focused on
        organizational, team or individual performance improvement)
    a variety of learning/teaching strategies are used to appeal to all learning
        styles and abilities
    design is based on adult learning theories and principles

Training Program Implementation
    materials facilitate learning
    facilities are adequate for delivering the program effectively
    necessary equipment is available for delivery
    trainer's training skills and level of expertise with content matter
    trainees' group dynamics

expected outcomes. Of particular concern is how little learning, perfor-mance, and change professionals and researchers have tapped other disci-plines in their development of evaluation theories, models, and methods. As discussed in Chapter 2, the field of evaluation has matured over the last forty years. This research on evaluation models, methods, philoso-phies, standards, ethics, utilization, and cultural issues has, unfortunately, developed outside of the learning, performance, and change fields and has had limited effect on the evaluation of such initiatives.

As a result, evaluation of training over the last forty years has focused on a limited number of questions using only a few tools and methods. This pattern has led to a constricted view of what evaluation can offer or-ganizations. Training evaluation has been parochial in its approach and, as a result, has failed to show its contribution or value to organizations. We have failed to understand the learning potential from evaluation en-deavors and the concept of intended use (of evaluation findings) by in-tended users (stakeholders). As the role of learning, performance, and change professionals expands and as organizations seek to do things faster and better, these professionals should consider additional and alter-native ways of integrating evaluation into their work. This shift requires establishing a culture focused on gathering and using information in the organization. We should also look to other disciplines to expand our no-tion of evaluation theory and practice. As Scriven reminds us,

> Evaluation is not only a discipline on which all others depend, it is one on which all deliberate activity depends. It follows that significant improve-ments in the core concept and techniques of evaluation, of which we have seen many in recent years, and of which many more could be made within the next few years, have the potential for huge improvement in the quality of life and work, as well as in the level of achievement in all disciplines. (1996, p. 404)

We wish to leave this chapter with a sense of untapped opportunities that exist in establishing effective evaluation processes and systems in their organizations. Our experiences have shown us that when learning, performance, and change professionals become evaluators of their pro-grams, using insightful and well-informed practices, their efforts do not go unnoticed. Organization members become aware of the commitment to continuous improvement and the relationship between learning and performance and the organization's goals. Without ongoing evaluation systems, learning, performance, and change professionals have no basis on which to judge the merits and contributions of what they do in organizations. When well conceived and implemented, evaluation should be considered a key strategic initiative that highlights the critical information needs of designers, trainers, and managers and provides the means to ensuring high-quality learning, performance, and change interventions.

. . . .

Keep in Mind . . .

- The role of learning, performance, and change professionals will increasingly require them to evaluate their own efforts.
- Most training evaluation models, approaches, and taxonomies are derived from Kirkpatrick's (1959) taxonomy.
- The training evaluation models, approaches, and taxonomies do not reflect what has been learned in the evaluation profession. This has significantly limited the value and usefulness of current training evaluation approaches.
- Future learning, performance, and change evaluation models must include not only outcome variables but also the wide variety of variables affecting those outcomes.

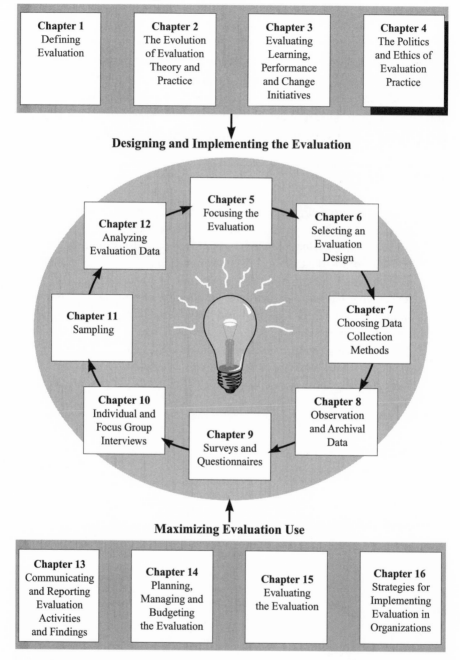

Background and Context of Evaluation

Chapter 1	Chapter 2	Chapter 3	Chapter 4
Defining Evaluation	The Evolution of Evaluation Theory and Practice	Evaluating Learning, Performance and Change Initiatives	The Politics and Ethics of Evaluation Practice

Designing and Implementing the Evaluation

Chapter 12 Analyzing Evaluation Data

Chapter 5 Focusing the Evaluation

Chapter 6 Selecting an Evaluation Design

Chapter 11 Sampling

Chapter 7 Choosing Data Collection Methods

Chapter 10 Individual and Focus Group Interviews

Chapter 9 Surveys and Questionnaires

Chapter 8 Observation and Archival Data

Maximizing Evaluation Use

Chapter 13	Chapter 14	Chapter 15	Chapter 16
Communicating and Reporting Evaluation Activities and Findings	Planning, Managing and Budgeting the Evaluation	Evaluating the Evaluation	Strategies for Implementing Evaluation in Organizations

The Politics and Ethics of Evaluation Practice

- Ways in Which Evaluation Becomes Political
- Political Influences During the Evaluation
- Examples of Evaluation Politics
- Strategies for Managing the Politics of Evaluation
- The Ethics of Evaluation Practice

•••

Vignette #1: Evaluation as a Political Act in MyEightball, Inc.

MyEightball, Inc. prides itself on providing excellent, just-in-time training and development for its members worldwide. Its training is based on the latest adult learning and instructional design principles and is beginning to use technology to deliver a significant portion of its training. In fact, the new CEO of the organization is so committed to integrating learning technologies throughout the organization that this goal is stated in the organization's mission statement. The Learning and Performance Department (LPD) receives a request from the vice president of operations to evaluate its leadership development training programs to determine which ones can be put online. She explains that the CEO wants to eliminate classroom training for its upper-level managers and vice presidents and thus wants to know how soon the LPD can convert the majority of these courses for web-based delivery. The LPD manager calls a meeting of the leadership course designers and trainers and explains the situation. The staff of six expresses great concern over this request, believing that the kinds of training and development experiences they provide these leaders can only be delivered in a face-to-face format, and that the impersonal nature of on-line training will reduce the course's effectiveness. The manager reminds them, however, that they are obligated to act on this request for evaluation and asks them to begin designing the evaluation.

••

In the above scenario, the team is dealing with the politics of evaluation. The way in which they choose to carry out the evaluation has political implications. Let's consider why this is so.

By looking closely at the word "evaluation," you will see the word *value* embedded in it. "Because of its intimate involvement with value issues, evaluation inevitably serves a political agenda and becomes a tool of political advocacy" (Guba and Lincoln, 1987, p. 216). Therefore, in the above vignette, the training team is dealing with their values regarding the content and delivery of the leadership development courses and technology in general, versus the CEO's interests concerning technology's role in the organization's future. These potentially conflicting values ultimately affect how the evaluation will be designed and implemented and how the results will be used.

According to Palumbo, politics refers to "the interactions of various actors within and among bureaucracies, clients, interest groups, private organizations and legislatures as they relate to each other from different positions of power, influence, and authority" (1987, pp. 18–19). Walumbwa describes organizational politics "as those activities taken from within organizations to acquire, develop and use power and other resources to obtain one's preferred outcomes in a situation in which there is uncertainty" (1999, p. 206). We'll come back to the principle of uncertainty a bit later. Politics thus involves the use of power and influence to obtain a certain outcome. It is probably wise to remember that "A theory of evaluation must be as much a theory of political interaction as it is a theory of how to determine facts" (Cronbach et al., 1980, p. 13).

In this chapter, we discuss the *ways in which evaluation becomes political, strategies for managing the politics of evaluation,* and the *standards and ethics of evaluation practice* within a political context.

Ways in Which Evaluation Becomes Political

Carol Weiss was one of the first evaluation researchers to publicly recognize the importance of politics and values within the evaluation and policymaking process. In a paper she presented at the annual meeting of the American Psychological Association in 1973, she identified three ways in which evaluation and politics are related (1987, pp. 47–48):

- The policies and programs with which evaluation deals are creatures of political decisions. They were proposed, defined, debated, enacted, and funded through political processes, and in implementation they remain subject to pressures—both supportive and hostile—that arise out of the play of politics.
- Because evaluation is undertaken in order to feed into decision-making, its reports enter the political arena. There, evaluative evidence of program outcomes has to compete for attention with other factors that carry weight in the political process.
- Evaluation itself has a political stance. By its very nature it makes implicit political statements about such issues as the problematic nature of some programs and the unchallengeability of others, the legitimacy of program goals and program strategies, the utility of strategies of incremental reform, and even the appropriate role of the social scientist in policy and program formation.

As Guba and Lincoln state, "evaluation is always disruptive of the prevailing political balance" (1981, p. 299). This reminds us that even in programs that seem "nonpolitical," there are political implications that result from the mere act of evaluation, not to mention the findings. All this is to suggest that programs themselves are not neutral—not even those that seem small and insignificant. Furthermore, Weiss tells us, programs are not "antiseptic, laboratory-type entities. They emerge from the rough and tumble of political support, opposition, and bargaining" (1987, p. 49). Palumbo even suggests, "the very taking of a position about how well a program is doing [is] inherently and unavoidably political" (1987, p. 12). When we consider that evaluation often surfaces conflicts in values and interests, and that evaluation often leads to changes that some may or may not welcome, we can appreciate why some may be leery of formal evaluation processes.

Think to yourself about the programs with which you work and ask yourself the following questions:

- How did they come into being?
- Who supported their development and implementation?
- In response to whose needs were they developed?
- What and whose values are reflected in the program?
- Who has a vested interest in the continuation of the program—for what purpose?
- What resources are being allocated to your programs? Which programs are not receiving adequate funding?
- Who would stand to gain or lose from the evaluation if the findings were used to make decisions or changes?
- Which individuals or groups have power in this setting or program?
- What level of support is the evaluation being given?

The answers to these questions have political implications for how the evaluation is designed and implemented as well as how the findings are used. After all, the programs themselves are the result of a political decisionmaking process.

With regard to the issue of politics and uncertainty referred to earlier, Patton explains, "the power of evaluation varies directly with the degree to which the findings reduce the uncertainty of action for specific stakeholders" (1997, p. 348). In other words, the greater the amount of uncertainty about an organization's future, relationships, or effectiveness, the more political an evaluation may become. Perhaps this is because there seems to be more at stake with the evaluation's findings. The next section provides examples of how evaluation is political.

Political Influences During the Evaluation

Politics may be present during any phase of the evaluation process. For example, politics may influence the reasons for conducting evaluation and the way in which the evaluation is commissioned (such as in the vignette at the beginning of this chapter). The commissioning stakeholder may wish to prove a program is working to convince funders of the need to continue the program or to secure additional personnel or financial resources for the program. In other cases, the stakeholder may wish to show

how the program is failing to live up to its expectations, and may use the evaluation results to support a decision to channel program funds to some other program or initiative. Therefore, the very act of undertaking an evaluation is often the result of a political decision. The following examples describe how an evaluation may become political during the commissioning and early design phases of the evaluation:

- Choosing which stakeholders should be involved in the evaluation
- Choosing the evaluator
- Determining what role the stakeholder group will play in the evaluation
- Evaluating as a means to placate external requirements for evaluation with no intention to use the results
- Using evaluation to legitimize the evaluand without intent to use the results

How an evaluation is conducted is also political. The following evaluation task can present political challenges:

- Choosing the evaluation design and data collection methods
- Determining which goals and objectives are to be evaluated
- Determining the scope of the evaluation (what is and is not considered)
- The evaluator's values about the program and the population served by the program
- The evaluator's relationship to the primary stakeholders or funding client

Let's consider, for example, an evaluation that seeks to determine the transfer of learning from a weeklong training program. The evaluator decides to observe a sample of the participants back on the job to see the extent to which they've been able to apply their learning. The evaluator's decision regarding which employees to observe, and from which departments, may be influenced by the current politics of the situation or organization. If particular managers are unsupportive of the evaluation, they may deny access to such observations. This would lead to including only a sample of the trainees, which might influence the findings of the evaluation and thus compromise the ability to make decisions based on the evaluation's results. Given that research has shown that managers positively influence trainees' ability and willingness to transfer their learning, we must consider if it's possible that the managers who deny access are also the ones who provide less transfer support. If this were the case, we would need to be extremely cautious in interpreting the results and making decisions based on the evaluation's findings.

In another situation, we might find that in talking with key stakeholders, we learn that they want the evaluation to focus on specific goals they think are important and ignore goals that might be of interest to others in the organization. The choices one makes about whose questions to focus on may indeed be a political act in that the results of the evaluation would serve some individuals' questions, but not necessarily others'. Additional examples of political pressures that affect the implementation of the evaluation and the quality of its findings include:

- Involving in the data collection process only participants who have an opinion that would support a particular political position
- Manipulating the data collection methods to systematically bias the resulting data in a way that will yield the desired results
- Inappropriately manipulating statistical data during the analysis process
- Using less than rigorous qualitative analysis procedures
- Being pressured to complete the evaluation more quickly, thus compromising the quality of the data

The politics of evaluation most often become apparent during the communicating and reporting phase of the evaluation process. Torres, Preskill, and Piontek (1996) found that a significant barrier to reporting evaluation findings was the politics of the organization. This includes changes in the political winds—what was important to one leader is now unimportant to the new leader, the difficulty in balancing positive and negative findings, and a general unresponsiveness to using the findings (which is often the result of a politically motivated decision).

Preskill and Caracelli's (1997) study also found that the greatest misuse of evaluation findings was during the communicating and reporting stage. Examples of how politics influence this phase include the following:

- Reporting the evaluation findings in a way that supports a particular political agenda
- Distorting the data to support a particular political opinion
- Selectively using or withholding evaluation findings to support a political agenda (for example, ignoring negative findings)
- Using the evaluation findings to fire employees or initiate layoffs and to reward or punish staff (when the evaluation's stated purpose was for program improvement)
- Drawing unjustified conclusions—going beyond the data

These findings seem to confirm what Mark Twain once said, "Get the facts first, and then distort them as you please."

To summarize thus far, it is important to remember that because evaluation involves individuals' values and addresses issues of power, resources, and position, evaluation is a political act. Therefore, although the political nature of any evaluation may vary considerably, it is never absent. Before we discuss strategies for managing the politics of evaluation, let's consider more specifically how evaluation politics might affect the evaluation of learning, performance, and change initiatives.

Examples of Evaluation Politics

Learning, performance, and change professionals often find themselves caught between doing what they are asked and doing the right thing. In these times of quick fixes, downsizing, competition for resources and clients, and a general unwillingness to provide enough time for change to occur, learning, performance, and change professionals may find that their evaluation takes a political turn. Examples of such situations include:

- An evaluation of a new hire orientation-training program in which the manager of the department took over conducting the data analysis and reporting tasks himself to be sure that the program was portrayed most positively.

- An evaluation in which a technology training program was transferred from the training department to the management information systems (MIS) department. The MIS department was intent on showing that the technology training program was ineffective so it could be eliminated from their department. This would free up resources that had been diverted when the technology training program was organized under MIS.
- An evaluation where the vice president of human resources rewrote sections of the final report to eliminate negative findings about employees' perspectives on the organization's rewards and compensation systems.
- An evaluation of a web-based training program that decided to limit stakeholders to those who supported the implementation of web-based training. The questions they chose to answer were of a narrow focus almost ensuring a positive outcome.
- An evaluation of the organization's climate where confidentiality of responses is promised and when reading the preliminary analysis, the organization's executives requested to see the individual surveys that could provide information about specific individuals.
- An evaluation of an at-risk youth training program that was supposed to provide formative feedback for improving the program, but funders used the negative findings as reasons to eliminate the program.

You might be asking yourself at this point, could any evaluation not be political? Consider the thoughts of an individual who responded to Patton's question, "What is and is not politics in evaluation, and by what criteria does one judge the difference?" in preparation for his 1988 AEA presidential address (1997, p. 352). His favorite was this anonymous entry:

Evaluation is NOT political under the following conditions:
- No one cares about the program.
- No ones knows about the program.
- No money is at stake.

- No power or authority is at stake.
- And, no one in the program, making decisions about the program, or otherwise involved in, knowledgeable about, or attached to the program, is sexually active.

We rest our case.

Strategies for Managing the Politics of Evaluation

Though we can't escape the political nature of evaluation, there are some things we can do to minimize the negative effects of politics on the evaluation process.

At the Beginning of the Evaluation

The following strategies can be employed at the beginning of an evaluation when the evaluation is just being commissioned and initiated:

- Discuss with stakeholders what they believe are the intended goals of the program and the potential political consequences of answering the evaluation questions.
- Develop a logic model of the program.
- Involve as many stakeholders as possible in planning and implementing the evaluation. If possible, develop an evaluation advisory task force or team.
- Recognize the different kinds of information needs various stakeholders have at different points in the evaluand's life cycle.
- Negotiate a contract or evaluation plan that outlines the evaluation's activities, due dates, and people responsible for various evaluation tasks.
- Ask the stakeholders to consider how they will react if the findings suggest X or Y.
- Determine your role, as well as the stakeholders' roles, in analyzing and writing the final report.

- Discuss with stakeholders possible implications if the findings are misused or used in ways that are clearly political.
- Ask the stakeholders/decision makers how they will judge the success of the program and the evaluation.
- Understand the political conditions under which the evaluation will take place and plan and implement the evaluation accordingly.
- Assess the organization's readiness for evaluation work and for using the findings. (See Appendix A for a sample diagnostic instrument.)

It is also a good time for evaluators to consider their own values and ethical orientations. Patton (1997, p. 364) suggests that evaluators do the following: 1) consider your own intentions and moral groundings, 2) exercise ethical care in selecting projects to work on and stakeholders to work with, and 3) be clear about whose interests are being represented or not represented in the evaluation.

During the Evaluation's Implementation

The following strategies may help to minimize the political situation during an evaluation's implementation phase:

- Explain and communicate the purpose of the evaluation and its design to those involved in the evaluation. Make clear what the evaluation is intended to do, who are the intended users, and how the results are to be used.
- Obtain information from as many sources as possible throughout the evaluation—seek a diversity of voices and perspectives.
- Conduct the evaluation in a professional manner and use the *Program Evaluation Standards* (Joint Committee on Standards for Educational Evaluation, 1994) and the *Guiding Principles* (American Evaluation Association, 1995) to guide your practice (see Figures 4.1 and 4.2).
- Train stakeholders in appropriate methods of data collection, analysis, and how and when to communicate findings.

During the Communicating and Reporting Phase

As explained earlier, the communicating and reporting phase of the evaluation is particularly prone to becoming political. The following are some methods for managing the politics at this point:

- Write the report in a way that clearly and directly communicates the findings. Use language that will not inflame the situation.
- Communicate and report evaluation findings in a variety of formats to a wide variety of audiences and stakeholders.
- Make all efforts to produce a credible study based on sound methods, thus limiting attacks on the methodological quality of the study or partisanship.
- Make all attempts to produce the evaluation report(s) in a timely way.
- Prioritize evaluation findings and recommendations.
- When discussing findings and their implications, translate these into long-term benefits.

We want to emphasize here the value of collaborative evaluation approaches as a means for mediating the political nature of evaluation. By developing a team or group to design and conduct an evaluation, several things can happen that impact the degree to which politics affects the evaluation process. First, collaboration allows various voices to be heard concerning what issues the evaluation should address, what the goals of the program are perceived to be, and the ways in which the evaluation findings might be used. Second, collaboration communicates to others that a diversity of viewpoints is welcomed and will influence the evaluation's design and implementation. Third, collaboration increases the buy-in from those participating in the evaluation and those who are intended users. The evaluation effort may be perceived to be more credible and rigorous, given the diversity of representation on the evaluation team. Fourth, collaboration ensures that one evaluator's experiences and biases do not overly influence the design or implementation of the evaluation process. A team approach creates a form of checks and balances that again increases the likelihood of buy-in and the quality of the evaluation.

Fifth, by having several people on the team, a more diverse group of evaluation skills and knowledge may be present. This would lessen the dependence on an outside evaluator always being called in to do evaluation work. Such an external evaluator might be used for technical assistance and training, but would not need to be the one who "conducted" the evaluation. Finally, as a team engages in evaluation, they learn more about what it means to evaluate and the benefits of evaluation. When they share this learning with others in the organization, a culture of evaluation and learning from evaluation may begin to affect the organization's overall culture regarding evaluation work. This might circumvent future political consequences of evaluation activity. Supporting the use of a collaborate approach, Honea's (1991) research confirmed that the use of evaluation teams prevented unethical dilemmas from occurring, because of the team's ongoing process of deliberation.

We recognize that even if you do all of the things listed here, you may still not be able to avoid the political nature of evaluation. In some cases, you may find yourself faced with an ethical dilemma whereby you have to choose between equally unsatisfactory alternatives involving questions of right and wrong. Fortunately, the evaluation profession has provided evaluators with a set of standards and principles that can help guide evaluation practice in such situations.

The Ethics of Evaluation Practice

One characteristic of a profession is that it has developed a set of ethical standards or principles by which it expects its members to abide. Newman and Brown (1996) define ethics as: "Principles of morality, particularly those dealing with the right or wrong of an action; as the rules of conduct for members of a particular profession; and as the science of the study of ideal human behavior, the concepts of good behavior" (p. 20).

More specifically, the term *ethics* refers "to the science of rules and standards of conduct and practice" (p. 20). The goal of having a code of ethics or set of ethical principles is to guide individuals in determining what are right and wrong actions.

The following two scenarios are examples of where learning, performance, and change professionals are faced with such kinds of decisions.

Scenario 4.1

In his role of learning specialist, Josh Palmer has been asked to evaluate the design of a training program for new salespeople. This new program will require significant changes in how sales are made and the ways in which customers are to be served. In addition to asking subject matter experts to review the curriculum, he also decides to interview a sample of current salespeople to get a better picture of what they think about the new training program's content and design. After reviewing the training program with ten salespeople who have been with the organization more than five years, Josh learns that there are a significant number of these employees who are seriously opposed to the training program. Josh feels that he must raise this issue with the HRD and sales department directors. Without divulging the names of the individuals who are opposed to the training program, he explains that several people believe the program is taking the organization in the wrong direction, and wonders if there might be problems in trying to implement the new program and having the newly trained salespeople work with the veteran salespeople. The director of the sales department is very upset with this information and asks for the names of the salespeople who are opposed to the training program, and promises that the employees will never know that their names were given because the director will discuss the issue with all the salespeople. Josh feels pressured to provide the names of the opposing individuals, and does so.

Questions to Consider:

Did Josh make the right decision?
Which is more important—interviewees' confidentiality or the salespeople's right to a good program?
Did the director of sales have a right to ask for the names of those opposing the program?
Was there an alternative solution?

(Adapted from Newman and Brown [1996], p. 9.)

Scenario 4.2

Yolanda Romero is an internal organization development consultant in a large manufacturing organization that has its home office in a large midwestern city with manufacturing sites in seven cities throughout the United States. Yolanda has been asked to evaluate all the employees' experiences with the use of teams and to determine what additional training employees need so that they may more effectively work in a team-based environment. After developing and pilot-testing a survey and making some minor modifications, she sends it to the vice president of operations at each site with a cover letter, explaining the purpose and procedures for administration. Two weeks later, looking through the completed and returned surveys, she sees that one of the sites had rewritten the survey items before administering it to its employees. As a result, the responses from this group are quite different than they are for the other six sites. Yolanda calls the vice president of operations and asks why he rewrote the survey items. He explains that he didn't think the questions were clearly worded and just wanted to improve the survey's quality. He says that he is quite proud of his site's results as they indicate that they are indeed working as a team and everyone appears to be satisfied with the quality of their team-based decisions. Yolanda isn't sure what to do, but decides to write up her evaluation report omitting the results of this site. Upon seeing the final report, the vice president calls Yolanda's boss and argues that she should be fired.

Questions to Consider:
Did Yolanda make the right decision? Why?
What was the ethical dilemma in this scenario?
Could Yolanda have acted any differently?

The Program Evaluation Standards

In 1975, twelve professional organizations whose members conduct research and evaluation studies came together to form the Joint Committee on Standards for Educational Evaluation. The committee, which is accredited by the American National Standards Institute (ANSI), is housed at the Evaluation Center, Western Michigan University. As a result of public hearings and many rounds of reviews and critiques by hundreds of researchers and evaluators, the Joint Committee published a set of standards in 1981 (Joint Committee on Standards for Educational Evaluation, 1981) which identified thirty standards according to four attributes: utility, feasibility, propriety, and accuracy. After another round of review and revisions in 1994, a second edition was published (see Figure 4.1). The Joint Committee also published *The Personnel Evaluation Standards* in 1988.

The Program Evaluation Standards were developed to guide evaluators through the myriad of decisions and choices they must make throughout an evaluation process. Although the standards do not dictate what to do in different situations, they highlight the necessary expectations (standards) and pitfalls of evaluation practice in the real world. At the very least, they encourage evaluators to consider their practice at each step of the evaluation endeavor, and at best, they confirm and validate what constitutes good evaluation practice. If evaluation is a new activity within an organization or has a bad reputation within an organization based on previous experiences, using the *Standards* to guide an evaluation project may add extra legitimacy to, and support of, the evaluation study.

Although ethical standards of practice exist for several professional organizations whose members conduct research and evaluation studies, no other set of standards currently exists that specifically focuses on the practice of evaluation, which brings with it a different set of expectations, relationships, and outcomes. Organizations such as the American Psychological Association (APA), the American Educational Research Association (AERA), the Academy of Human Resource Development (AHRD), and the Organization Development Network (ODN), have guidelines that are useful to evaluators, but they lack the particular context in which evaluators often find themselves (Newman and Brown, 1996).

As stated earlier, the thirty standards are divided into four categories. The utility standards primarily focus on the need for evaluators and evaluations to be responsive to the needs of their clients (stakeholders).

> In general, the utility standards require evaluators to acquaint themselves with various audiences that have a stake in the evaluation results, to ascertain their information needs, and to report the relevant information to these audiences clearly, concisely, and on time. (Madaus, Scriven, and Stufflebeam, 1983, p. 398)

The feasibility standards pay particular attention to the cost effectiveness and real world constraints of conducting evaluation. Thus, they "require evaluations to be realistic, prudent, diplomatic, politically viable, and frugal" (Madaus, Scriven, and Stufflebeam, 1983, p. 398). Protecting the rights of individuals is the primary focus of the propriety standards. These "require that evaluations be conducted legally, ethically, and with

FIGURE 4.1   The Program Evaluation Standards

Utility

The utility standards are intended to ensure that an evaluation will serve the information needs of intended users.

U1   **Stakeholder Identification.** Persons involved in or affected by the evaluation should be identified, so that their needs can be addressed.

U2   **Evaluator Credibility.** The persons conducting the evaluation should be both trustworthy and competent to perform the evaluation, so that the evaluation findings achieve maximum credibility and acceptance.

U3   **Information Scope and Selection.** Information collected should be broadly selected to address pertinent questions about the program and be responsive to the needs and interests of clients and other specified stakeholders.

U4   **Values Identification.** The perspectives, procedures, and rationale used to interpret the findings should be carefully described, so that the bases for value judgments are clear.

U5   **Report Clarity.** Evaluation reports should clearly describe the program being evaluated, including its context, and the purposes, procedures, and findings of the evaluation, so that essential information is provided and easily understood.

U6   **Report Timeliness and Dissemination.** Significant interim findings and evaluation reports should be disseminated to intended users, so that they can be used in a timely fashion.

U7   **Evaluation Impact.** Evaluations should be planned, conducted, and reported in ways that encourage follow-through by stakeholders, so that the likelihood that the evaluation will be used is increased.

Feasibility

The feasibility standards are intended to ensure that an evaluation will be realistic, prudent, diplomatic, and frugal.

F1   **Practical Procedures.** The evaluation procedures should be practical, to keep disruption to a minimum while needed information is obtained.

F2   **Political Viability.** The evaluation should be planned and conducted with anticipation of the different positions of various interest groups, so that their cooperation may be obtained, and so that possible attempts by any of these groups to curtail evaluation operations or to bias or misapply the results can be averted or counteracted.

F3   **Cost Effectiveness.** The evaluation should be efficient and produce information of sufficient value, so that the resources expended can be justified.

FIGURE 4.1   *(continued)*

Propriety
The propriety standards are intended to ensure that an evaluation will be conducted legally, ethically, and with due regard for the welfare of those involved in the evaluation, as well as those affected by its results.

PI   **Service Orientation.** Evaluations should be designed to assist organizations to address and effectively serve the needs of the full range of targeted participants.

P2   **Formal Agreements.** Obligations of the formal parties to an evaluation (what is to be done, how, by whom, when) should be agreed to in writing, so that these parties are obligated to adhere to all conditions of the agreement or formally to renegotiate it.

P3   **Rights of Human Subjects.** Evaluations should be designed and conducted to respect and protect the rights and welfare of human subjects.

P4   **Human Interactions.** Evaluators should respect human dignity and worth in their interactions with other persons associated with an evaluation, so that participants are not threatened or harmed.

P5   **Complete and Fair Assessment.** The evaluation should be complete and fair in its examination and recording of strengths and weaknesses of the program being evaluated, so that strengths can be built upon and problem areas addressed.

P6   **Disclosure of Findings.** The formal parties to an evaluation should ensure that the full set of evaluation findings along with pertinent limitations are made accessible to the persons affected by the evaluation, and any others with expressed legal rights to receive the results.

P7   **Conflict of Interest.** Conflict of interest should be dealt with openly and honestly, so that it does not compromise the evaluation processes and results.

P8   **Fiscal Responsibility.** The evaluator's allocation and expenditure of resources should reflect sound accountability procedures and otherwise be prudent and ethically responsible so that expenditures are accounted for and appropriate.

Accuracy
The accuracy standards are intended to ensure that an evaluation will reveal and convey technically adequate information about the features that determine worth or merit of the program being evaluated.

A   **Program Documentation.** The program being evaluated should be described and documented clearly and accurately, so that the program is clearly identified.

(continues)

FIGURE 4.1 *(continued)*

A2 **Context Analysis.** The context in which the program exists should be examined in enough detail, so that its likely influences on the program can be identified.

A3 **Described Purposes and Procedures.** The purposes and procedures of the evaluation should be monitored and described in enough detail, so that they can be identified and assessed.

A4 **Defensible Information Sources.** The sources of information used in a program evaluation should be described in enough detail, so that the adequacy of the information can be assessed.

A5 **Valid Information.** The information gathering procedures should be chosen or developed and then implemented so that they will assure that the interpretation arrived at is valid for the intended use.

A6 **Reliable Information.** The information gathering procedures should be chosen or developed and then implemented so that they will assure that the information obtained is sufficiently reliable for the intended use.

A7 **Systematic Information.** The information collected, processed, and reported in an evaluation should be systematically reviewed and any errors found should be corrected.

A8 **Analysis of Quantitative Information.** Quantitative information in an evaluation should be appropriately and systematically analyzed so that evaluation questions are effectively answered.

A9 **Analysis of Qualitative Information.** Qualitative information in an evaluation should be appropriately and systematically analyzed so that evaluation questions are effectively answered.

A10 **Justified Conclusions.** The conclusions reached in an evaluation should be explicitly: justified, so that stakeholders can assess them.

A11 **Impartial Reporting.** Reporting procedures should guard against distortion caused by personal feelings and biases of any party to the evaluation, so that evaluation reports fairly reflect the evaluation findings.

A12 **Metaevaluation.** The evaluation itself should be formatively and summatively evaluated against these and other pertinent standards so that its conduct is appropriately guided and, on completion, stakeholders can closely examine its strengths and weaknesses.

---

due regard for the welfare of those involved in the evaluation as well as those affected by the results" (Madaus, Scriven, and Stufflebeam, 1983, p. 399). The fourth category is the accuracy standards, which are concerned with the degree to which the evaluation is providing valid, high quality, information. "These standards require that the information obtained be technically adequate and that conclusions be linked logically to the data" (Madaus, Scriven, and Stufflebeam, 1983, p. 399).

Ethical Challenges and the Standards

In a study conducted by Newman and Brown that sought to "examine the frequency and seriousness of violations of the 30 evaluation standards" (1992, p. 221), the authors found that the most frequent violations occurred with the utility and feasibility standards. The following are the six most frequent violations reported by their sample (n = 145):

- Evaluator selects a test primarily because of his or her familiarity with it. (A5)
- Evaluation responds to the concerns of one interest group more than another. (F2)
- Evaluation is conducted because it is "required" when it obviously cannot yield useful results. (F3)
- Evaluator conducts an evaluation when he or she lacks sufficient skills or experience. (U2)
- Evaluator fails to find out what the values are of right-to-know audiences. (U4)
- Evaluator loses interest in the evaluation when the final report is delivered. (U8)

These findings suggest that evaluators should make special efforts to identify all possible stakeholders and their concerns, to conduct evaluations with the intention and follow-through of use, and for evaluators to manage their own biases and preferences.

Newman and Brown's survey respondents also indicated what they thought were the most important ethical violations. Though these were less frequent than the others previously mentioned, respondents thought the following five were most serious. It should be noted that three of the five represent the propriety standards:

- Evaluator changes the evaluation questions to match the data analysis. (A8)

- Evaluator promises confidentiality when it cannot be guaranteed. (P5)
- Evaluator makes decisions without consulting with the client when consultation has been agreed to. (P1)
- Evaluator conducts an evaluation when he or she lacks sufficient skills or experience. (U2)
- Evaluation report is written so partisan interest groups can delete embarrassing weaknesses. (P7)

A year later, Morris and Cohn (1993) reported on a study that asked a sample of AEA members (N = 459) to indicate whether they had ever experienced an ethical problem in their evaluation practice. Members who answered in the affirmative were asked to describe the ethical problems they frequently faced and the most serious problem they had faced. They found that 65 percent of their respondents "had encountered ethical problems in their evaluation" (pp. 626–627). Those who had experienced an ethical problem generated 555 different problem descriptions. Of the problems identified, the most frequent and most serious ethical problem was associated with the presentation of evaluation findings. These problems included: "1) Evaluator is pressured by stakeholder to alter presentation of findings; 2) Evaluator is reluctant to present findings fully for unspecified reasons; 3) Evaluator has discovered behavior that is illegal, unethical, dangerous, etc.; 4) Evaluator is unsure of his/her ability to be objective or fair in presenting findings" (p. 630). The second most common problem was misinterpretation or misuse of the final reports. In comparing their results to those of the Newman and Brown (1992) study, Morris and Cohn found little overlap in their findings. "None of the violations that were ranked as most frequent by their group of experienced evaluators involved the types of presentation-of-findings issues that characterized the responses of our sample" (1993, p. 637), though it was rated as serious by both sets of respondents. The finding that the communicating and reporting of findings presents the evaluator(s) with several potential ethical challenges provides further motivation and incentive for understanding the politics of the evaluand and the organization prior to beginning the evaluation.

One final thought should be given to the fact that several evaluation researchers have found that many practicing evaluators have not thought about ethical issues in the conduct of their evaluation work (Honea, 1991; Morris and Cohn, 1993; Newman and Brown, 1996). In reflecting on this, Morris asks the following question: "Why do some evaluators view certain types of work-related problems through an ethical lens, whereas others do not?" (1999, p. 16). He recalls that in his study with Cohn in 1993, they discovered that "internal evaluators were less likely than external ones to report that they had ever faced an ethical conflict" (1999, p. 16). Morris (1999a, 1999b) wonders about the extent to which an organization's culture toward questioning and reflecting on work practices influences employees' inclination to think about their work in ethical ways.

To further explore these differences, Morris and Jacobs surveyed a sample of evaluators and asked them to respond to a set of evaluation scenarios that addressed issues of stakeholder involvement, reporting of results, and informed consent (2000). The results of this study showed a surprising lack of consensus regarding whether the evaluator's behavior was ethical. Of particular interest to us, however, is that in analyzing the demographic information, the authors found that respondents in for-profit, private, or consulting organizations were less likely than those in other settings to identify the evaluator's behavior as unethical. Although Morris and Jacobs point out the limitations of using the scenario approach as a research method, their findings nonetheless confirm that evaluators tend to rely on the specifics of the situation rather than a particular standard or guiding principle.

AEA's Guiding Principles for Evaluators

In response to a perceived need that the AEA should consider developing its own professional set of principles for evaluation practice, the organization developed and published *The Guiding Principles for Evaluators* (American Evaluation Association, 1995) (see Figure 4.2). The five major principles are:

1. Systematic inquiry: Evaluators conduct systematic, data-based inquiries about whatever is being evaluated.

2. Competence: Evaluators provide competent performance to stakeholders.
3. Integrity/honesty: Evaluators ensure the honesty and integrity of the entire evaluation process.
4. Respect for people: Evaluators respect the security, dignity, and self-worth of the respondents, program participants, clients, and other stakeholders with whom they interact.
5. Responsibilities for the general and public welfare: Evaluators articulate and take into account the diversity of interests and values that may be related to the general and public welfare.

These five principles are then operationalized into twenty-two normative statements to guide practice.

Guiding Principles for Evaluators was developed based on an understanding that a) evaluation is a profession that is made up of individuals with varying interests and is involved with evaluation of many different kinds of programs, processes, products, systems, and organizations; and b) evaluators come from different backgrounds, training, experience, and work settings and with this comes varying perceptions of what constitutes evaluation.

The principles are intended to guide evaluation practice and foster the continuing development of the profession, in addition to socializing new members. AEA emphasizes that these principles are not intended to replace the *Standards for Program Evaluation* (AEA remains a cosponsor of this document), but are to represent the official position of AEA on the topic of ethical practice. The task force authors of the *Guiding Principles* also point out that these are based on Western practice, particularly that of the United States, and thus may not reflect the values of those in other countries.

One of the most striking features of the *Guiding Principles* is their inclusiveness, according to Covert. Compared to other sets of standards and principles, he writes, "The AEA principles go to great lengths to ensure that both systematic inquiry and competence are not linked to one paradigm or methodology. Instead, they place emphasis on appropriate training and correct applications of the evaluation approach selected for a particular evaluation problem" (1995, p. 40). On the other hand, Mabry criticizes the *Program Evaluation Standards* and *Guiding Principles* for their lack of atten-

FIGURE 4.2   Guiding Principles for Evaluators (American Evaluation
Association, 1995)

A. Systematic Inquiry: Evaluators conduct systematic, data-based inquiries about
   whatever is being evaluated.
   1. Evaluators should adhere to the highest appropriate technical standards in
      conducting their work, whether that work is quantitative or qualitative in
      nature, so as to increase the accuracy and credibility of the evaluative
      information they produce.
   2. Evaluators should explore with the client the shortcomings and strengths both
      of the various evaluation questions it might be productive to ask, and the
      various approaches that might be used for answering those questions.
   3. When presenting their work, evaluators should communicate their methods and
      approaches accurately and in sufficient detail to allow others to understand,
      interpret, and critique their work. They should make clear the limitations of an
      evaluation and its results. Evaluators should discuss in a contextually
      appropriate way those values, assumptions, theories, methods, results, and
      analyses that significantly affect the interpretation of the evaluative findings.
      These statements apply to all aspects of the evaluation, from its initial
      conceptualization to the eventual use of findings.
B.   Competence: Evaluators provide competent performance to stakeholders.
   1. Evaluators should possess (or, here and elsewhere as appropriate, ensure that the
      evaluation team possesses) the education, abilities, skills, and experience
      appropriate to undertake the tasks proposed in the evaluation.
   2. Evaluators should practice within the limits of their professional training and
      competence and should decline to conduct evaluations that fall substantially
      outside those limits. When declining the commission or request is not feasible
      or appropriate, evaluators should make clear any significant limitations on the
      evaluation that might result. Evaluators should make every effort to gain the
      competence directly or through the assistance of others who possess the
      required expertise.
   3. Evaluators should continually seek to maintain and improve their competencies,
      in order to provide the highest level of performance in their evaluations. This
      continuing professional development might include formal coursework and
      workshops, self-study, evaluations of one's own practice, and working with other
      evaluators to learn from their skills and expertise.
C.   Integrity/Honesty: Evaluators ensure the honesty and integrity of the entire
     evaluation process.
   1. Evaluators should negotiate honestly with clients and relevant stakeholders
      concerning the costs, tasks to be undertaken, limitations of methodology, scope
      of results likely to be obtained, and uses of data resulting from a specific
      evaluation. It is primarily the evaluator's responsibility to initiate discussion and
      clarification of these matters, not the client's.
   2. Evaluators should record all changes made in the originally negotiated project
      plans, and the reasons why the changes were made. If those changes would
      significantly affect the scope and likely results of the evaluation, the evaluator
      should inform the client and other important stakeholders in a timely fashion
      (barring good reason to the contrary, before proceeding with further work) of
      the changes and their likely impact.

(continues)

FIGURE 4.2 *(continued)*

---

3. Evaluators should seek to determine, and where appropriate be explicit about, their own, their clients', and other stakeholders' interests concerning the conduct and outcomes of an evaluation (including financial, political, and career interests).

4. Evaluators should disclose any roles or relationships they have concerning whatever is being evaluated that might pose a significant conflict of interest with their role as an evaluator. Any such conflict should be mentioned in reports of the evaluation results.

5. Evaluators should not misrepresent their procedures, data, or findings. Within reasonable limits, they should attempt to prevent or correct any substantial misuses of their work by others.

6. If evaluators determine that certain procedures or activities seem likely to produce misleading evaluative information or conclusions, they have the responsibility to communicate their concerns, and the reasons for them, to the client (the one who funds or requests the evaluation). If discussions with the client do not resolve these concerns, so that a misleading evaluation is then implemented, the evaluator may legitimately then decline to conduct the evaluation if that is feasible and appropriate. If not, the evaluator should consult colleagues or relevant stakeholders about other proper ways to proceed (options might include, but are not limited to, discussions at a higher level, a dissenting cover letter or appendix, or refusal to sign the final document).

7. Barring compelling reason to the contrary, evaluators should disclose all sources of financial support of an evaluation, and the source of the request for the evaluation.

D. Respect for People: Evaluators respect the security, dignity and self-worth of the respondents, program participants, clients, and other stakeholders with whom they interact.

1. Where applicable, evaluators must abide by current professional ethics and standards regarding risks, harms, and burdens that might be engendered to those participating in evaluation; and regarding informing participants about the scope and limits of confidentiality. Examples of such standards include federal regulations about protection of human subjects, or the ethical principles of such associations as the American Anthropological Association, the American Educational Research Association, or the American Psychological Association. Although this principle is not intended to extend the applicability of such ethics and standards beyond their current scope, evaluators should abide by them where it is feasible and desirable to do so.

2. Because justified negative or critical conclusions from an evaluation must be explicitly stated, evaluations sometimes produce results that harm client or stakeholder interests. Under this circumstance, evaluators should seek to maximize the benefits and reduce any unnecessary harms that might occur, provided this will not compromise the integrity of the evaluation findings. Evaluators should carefully judge when the benefits from doing the evaluation or in performing certain evaluation procedures should be foregone because of the risks or harms. Where possible, these issues should be anticipated during the negotiation of the evaluation.

FIGURE 4.2 *(continued)*

---

3. Knowing that evaluations often will negatively affect the interests of some stakeholders, evaluators should conduct the evaluation communicate its results in a way that clearly respects the stakeholders' dignity and self-worth.

4. Where feasible, evaluators should attempt to foster the social equity of the evaluation, so that those who give to the evaluation can received some benefits in return. For example, evaluators should seek to ensure that those who bear the burdens of contributing data and incurring any risks are doing so willingly, and that they have full knowledge of, and maximum feasible opportunity to obtain any benefits that may be produced from the evaluation. When it would not endanger the integrity of the evaluation, respondents or program participants should be informed if and how they can receive services to which they are otherwise entitled without participating in the evaluation.

5. Evaluators have the responsibility to identify and respect differences the among participants, such as differences in their culture, religion, gender, disability, age, sexual orientation, and ethnicity, and to be mindful of potential implications of these differences when planning, conducting, analyzing, and reporting their evaluations.

E. Responsibilities for General and Public Welfare: Evaluators articulate and take into account the diversity of interests and values that may be related to the general and public welfare.

1. When planning and reporting evaluations, evaluators should consider including important perspectives and interests of the full range of stakeholders in the object being evaluated. Evaluators should carefully consider the justification when omitting important value perspectives or the views of important groups.

2. Evaluators should consider not only the immediate operations and outcomes of whatever is being evaluated but also the broad assumptions, implications, and potential side effects of it.

3. Freedom of information is essential in a democracy. Hence, barring compelling reason to the contrary, evaluators should allow all relevant stakeholders to have access to evaluative information and should actively disseminate that information to stakeholders if resources allow. If different evaluation results are communicated in forms that are tailored to the interests of different stakeholders, those communications should ensure that each stakeholder group is aware of the existence of the other communications. Communications that are tailored to a given stakeholder should always include all important results that may bear on interests of that stakeholder. In all cases, evaluators should strive to present results as clearly and simply as accuracy allows so that clients and other stakeholders can easily understand the evaluation process and results.

4. Evaluators should maintain a balance between client needs and other needs. Evaluators necessarily have a special relationship with the client who funds or requests the evaluation. By virtue of that relationship, evaluators must strive to meet legitimate client needs whenever it is feasible and appropriate to do so. However, that relationship can also place evaluators in difficult dilemmas when client interests conflict with other interests, or when client interests conflict with the obligation of evaluators for systematic inquiry, competence, integrity, and respect for people. In these cases, evaluators should explicitly identify and discuss the conflicts with the client and relevant stakeholders, resolve them

FIGURE 4.2 *(continued)*

when possible, determine whether continued work on the evaluation is advisable if the conflicts cannot be resolved, and make clear any significant limitations on the evaluation that might result if the conflict is not resolved.

5. Evaluators have obligations that encompass the public interest and good. These obligations are especially important when evaluators are supported by publicly generated funds; but clear threats to the public good should never be ignored in any evaluation. Because the public interest and good are rarely the same as the interests of any particular group (including those of the client or funding agency), evaluators will usually have to go beyond an analysis of particular stakeholder interests when considering the welfare of society as a whole.

tion to the matter of values resolution, which she argues is "the heart of evaluation" (1999, p. 203). Nevertheless, she concedes that "familiarity with the Standards and Principles helps; understanding a variety of ethical frameworks and engaging in moral discourse helps" (1999, p. 210).

The *Program Evaluation Standards* and the *Guiding Principles for Evaluators* may be effective tools for helping evaluators negotiate the numerous ethical challenges they face in conducting evaluations. However, because of the nuances of every ethical challenge, these tools are limited in describing what specific actions we can or should take in every situation. Ultimately, how individuals act when facing ethical dilemmas rests on the values, ethics, and sense of morality they bring with them to the workplace. It is part of who they are, who they wish to be, and how they wish to be perceived.

Keep in Mind . . .

- Evaluation is a political act.
- Not all political influences on an evaluation are negative.
- Care must be taken that the politics do not lead to unethical evaluation processes and use of findings.
- Learning, performance, and change professionals should use the following guidelines in their evaluation work: the *Program Evaluation Standards*, the *Guiding Principles for Evaluators*, and the Academy of Human Resource Development's *Standards on Ethics and Integrity*.

PART TWO

Designing and Implementing the Evaluation

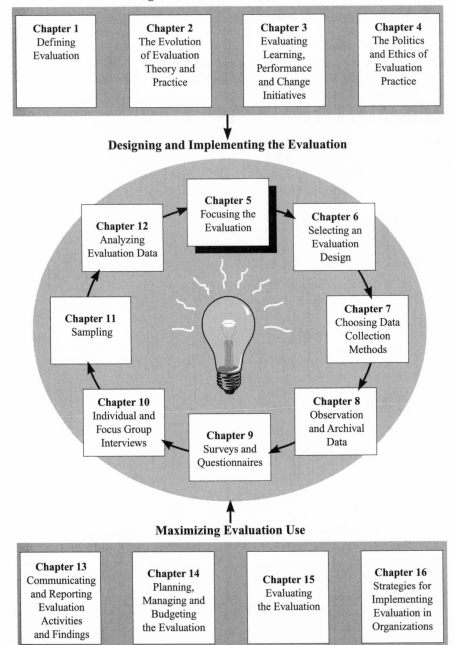

Background and Context of Evaluation

Chapter 1
Defining
Evaluation

Chapter 2
The Evolution
of Evaluation
Theory and
Practice

Chapter 3
Evaluating
Learning,
Performance
and Change
Initiatives

Chapter 4
The Politics
and Ethics of
Evaluation
Practice

Designing and Implementing the Evaluation

Chapter 12
Analyzing
Evaluation Data

Chapter 5
Focusing the
Evaluation

Chapter 6
Selecting an
Evaluation
Design

Chapter 11
Sampling

Chapter 7
Choosing Data
Collection
Methods

Chapter 10
Individual and
Focus Group
Interviews

Chapter 9
Surveys and
Questionnaires

Chapter 8
Observation
and Archival
Data

Maximizing Evaluation Use

Chapter 13
Communicating
and Reporting
Evaluation
Activities
and Findings

Chapter 14
Planning,
Managing and
Budgeting
the Evaluation

Chapter 15
Evaluating
the Evaluation

Chapter 16
Strategies for
Implementing
Evaluation in
Organizations

chapter 5

Focusing the Evaluation

- Developing an Evaluation Plan
- Developing the Evaluation's Rationale and Purpose
- Identifying the Evaluation's Stakeholders
- Developing Key Evaluation Questions

· ·

Vignette #2: Hit-and-Miss Evaluation at MyHome Furnishings.

Judy: You know, we've worked long and hard on designing this new training program. It would probably be a good idea to evaluate its design before we roll it out to the whole organization.

Mark: Yes, you're right. I would hate it not to work in front of 250 employees! How about we invite some subject matter experts and a few future
trainees to a meeting and talk with them about the program's design. Let's
see what they think about it.

Judy: Great idea. I'll jot down a few questions and call a few people to
come to a group interview.

Mark: Okay, let's not keep them longer than thirty minutes; you know how
busy they are.

Judy: Right. I'll be back in touch.

· ·

Although Judy and Mark's idea to evaluate the program's design is a good
one, it is likely that their approach may fall short of providing them accurate and useful information for making decisions about what might work
or need to be changed in the training program's design. What they have
failed to do is reflect on the background and history of the program and
articulate the *rationale and purpose of the evaluation, how the findings will*

127

be used, who the potential stakeholders and audiences might be, and *what key questions the evaluation should answer.* Without addressing these topics, the questions that Judy "jots" down may or may not be helpful or relevant to understanding the program design's effectiveness. Therefore, it is critical that time be taken to discuss the background of what is being evaluated (the evaluand), why it's being evaluated, what questions the evaluation should address, and who the intended users of the evaluation's findings will be. We liken this phase of the evaluation process to developing goals and objectives in the instructional, curriculum, or program design process. As the old proverb goes, "If you don't know where you're headed, you'll likely end up somewhere else." Only after the focus of the evaluation has been developed should we determine which evaluation design and methods could be used to collect the data. When we jump to choosing a design and method before clearly understanding the evaluation's purpose and key questions, we may choose an approach that is less capable of answering the evaluation questions or we may collect data that will not meet our information needs.

In this chapter, we describe the first three steps in designing an evaluation plan. These include:

1. Describing the rationale and purpose of the evaluation
2. Identifying the evaluation's stakeholders
3. Determining the evaluation's key questions

As suggested in the earlier chapters, we strongly recommend that a group or team of people who are interested in the evaluand and the evaluation findings be invited to participate in the evaluation process. We have found that their involvement significantly increases their understanding of evaluation, the program being evaluated, and the use of the evaluation results. These stakeholders tend to feel more connected to the evaluation process that increases their "buy-in" to the evaluation process and its outcomes. Participants' involvement may range from attending one meeting to help focus the evaluation to being responsible for several of the data collection and analysis activities. The number of people may vary throughout the evaluation process, though we have found that a core of three to eight individuals who are committed to the evaluation and are willing to see it through works best. For example, if we were evaluating a customer service–training program, we would likely include a sample of the program's designers, trainers, past participants, future participants, participants' managers, and the organization's customers in designing and implementing the evaluation. We believe that, in most cases, a participatory, collaborative approach that focuses on learning from the evaluation will produce the most usable results from an evaluation study.

Focusing the evaluation may take anywhere from two hours to several hours, depending on the complexity of the evaluation, the political nature of the evaluand, and the number of people attending the meeting. Though we recognize this may sound like a lot of time, it is time extremely well spent. If these issues are not discussed and the goals for the evaluation are unclear, the process and outcomes of the evaluation may be compromised in terms of their quality and usefulness.

Developing an Evaluation Plan

As discussed in Chapter 4, one way to mediate the political forces surrounding the evaluation is to develop an evaluation plan that clearly delineates what is being evaluated, as well as why, how, and when it is being evaluated. An evaluation plan functions as a contract between the evaluator(s) (whether they're internal or external) and the organization, and is the document that guides them through the evaluation process. The evaluation plan further defines the roles and responsibilities of the evaluator(s) so that all organization members and those involved in the evaluation have a clear sense of what the evaluation is intended to accomplish, by whom, and when.

Developing the Evaluation's Rationale and Purpose

Have you ever had the experience of inviting a group of people to a meeting that you thought was going to be straightforward, where you assumed everyone would be on the same page and agreement on the task or goal would be a simple matter, only to discover that your assumption was unfounded? When it comes to discussing the evaluand's background or history, the rationale for the evaluation, and how the evaluation should be conducted, we have learned that the conversation that ensues is strongly influenced by myriad experiences and perceptions of those who have experiences with the evaluand, their stake in the evaluand, and the outcomes of the evaluation. Thus, the task of focusing the evaluation becomes one of clarifying the stakeholders' needs and expectations for the evaluation and negotiating the evaluation's scope and boundaries. The dialogue that takes place during the focusing meeting often surfaces facts, myths, and values people have about the evaluand. Group members may be able to detect differences or errors in their thinking; and it opens them up to new understandings about the evaluand, things they had not thought of before. The discussion of the evaluand's background and history also helps clarify how the evaluation results will be used. If there are competing agendas for the evaluation, these can be negotiated and resolved. The outcome of this dialogue ensures that the most critical issues about the evaluand will be addressed during the evaluation. Examples of two evaluation rationales can be seen in Figures 5.1 and 5.2.

We are totally convinced of the importance and value of collaboratively understanding the evaluand's background and rationale for the evaluation. At the very least, this meeting helps bring clarity about what is being evaluated as well as the evaluation process, reinforces the organization's interest in growing and learning from evaluation, and builds commitment to the evaluation process.

This part of the evaluation plan can be developed in several ways. One process we have used successfully involves asking each group member to first describe his or her experiences with the evaluand (we'll use "program" in this example). This initial conversation often reveals information that others did not know. We might ask each person around the table to discuss the following:

- Their role in the program
- How long they've been involved with the program
- Why they're interested in the evaluation (and level of interest)
- Their concerns about the program; trends they've observed
- What they hope to learn from the evaluation
- What decisions they want to make based on the evaluation results

FIGURE 5.1 Evaluation Plan Example—Focusing the Evaluation*

Background and Rationale

In 1998, the state passed a mandate that required all managers and supervisors employed by public institutions or those that receive public funds to complete a civil rights training program. Early in 1999, an instructional multimedia developer/designer was approached by the local university's human resources department to develop a pilot of an on-line training workshop for their managers and supervisors. The workshop, "Civil Rights at Work," was developed with the input from civil rights subject matter experts and the university's office of equal opportunity.

To help users become familiar with policies and procedures, the workshop was designed as a self-paced program using interactive case-based scenarios. This design was chosen to accommodate employees' busy schedules, the vast amount of written content, and the large numbers of employees who would need to take this course. The resulting on-line training program was an introduction to the civil rights policy and procedures as applied to this particular university setting. To complete the state-mandated civil rights training, the employees would also need to participate in a four-hour classroom-based training course that included in-depth discussions about particular policies and procedures. By developing the on-line workshop, the in-class training time was cut in half.

In the three months the on-line course has been available, 600 employees have completed it and have participated in the follow-up classroom training. Based on anecdotal classroom feedback, the on-line training program appears to have been well received. At the same time there have been an increasing number of requests for other on-line training courses. Before embarking on the development of additional on-line courses, the designers and developers have several questions about the technology and resulting learning that they feel should be answered prior to engaging in any more development work. The Human Resource Department manager agrees with the designers that to strategically plan for future on-line multimedia training projects, an evaluation should first be conducted of the "Civil Rights at Work" web workshop. Thus an evaluation is commissioned.

Purpose of the Evaluation

The purpose of this evaluation is to determine the instructional effectiveness of the "Civil Rights at Work" on-line workshop. The results will be used to make improvements to the workshop as well as to plan for future on-line training courses.

---

*Adapted from an evaluation plan developed by Laura Kratochvil, Alburquerque, NM. Used with permission.

(continues)

FIGURE 5.1 *(continued)*

Stakeholders and Audiences

The following individuals/groups are involved in or will be affected in some way by the results of the on-line training workshop evaluation.

Primary Stakeholders

Human Resources Department Manager. This individual will use the evaluation results to determine the feasibility of future on-line training workshops and make the decision of whether or not to continue developing multimedia on-line training workshops.

Instructional multimedia designers and developers. These individuals are the designers and developers of the on-line workshop and will be responsible for making any revisions in the current on-line program based on the evaluation's findings. They will also be responsible for designing and developing any future on-line courses.

Secondary Stakeholders

University Staff. These stakeholders are directly affected by the decisions of the Human Resource Department with regard to their training. Based on the HRD Manager's decision regarding the future of web-based training, university employees may possibly have new and different opportunities to access training. The staff will be apprised of the evaluation findings and resulting decisions.

Tertiary Stakeholders

Other Multimedia Designers and Developers. The multimedia instructional designers and developers and the HRD manager believe it is important to share the evaluation findings with others who are currently exploring the use of web-based training. They plan to disseminate the evaluations at their yearly professional conference.

Key Questions

1. How well did participants understand the Civil Rights Policies and Procedures presented to them in the on-line training?
2. To what extent did the design, structure, and delivery of the on-line training contribute (or impede) participants' learning?
3. To what extent and in what ways are those who completed the on-line training different from those who did not complete the training?
4. What are the benefits and disadvantages of providing on-line instruction to the university community?
5. What have we learned from evaluating this program that can be applied to future decisions about the feasibility and effectiveness of on-line training?

FIGURE 5.2 Evaluation Plan Example—Focusing the Evaluation

Background and Rationale

The state's Board of Nursing Diversion Program (DP) for chemically dependent nurses is an alternative to formal disciplinary action for nurses who have violated the Nursing Practice Act (NPA). Prior to its inception in 1987, nurses who were reported to the Board of Nursing for violations of the NPA that had to do with drugs or alcohol would face disciplinary action and possible loss of licensure. Given that 78 percent of all violations reported nationwide have to do with drug and alcohol abuse, it was considered more humane as well as cost-effective to develop an alternative program to address this problem.

The state was the third in the nation to develop an alternative program to disciplinary action for chemically dependent nurses. The DP was created by legislative amendment to the Nursing Practice Act in 1987. Since then, nurses who have complaints filed with the Board of Nursing that relate to drug or alcohol issues are automatically offered admission into the DP. If they request admission and agree to be monitored by the DP, they sign a four-year contract, agreeing to abstinence and the submission of regular reports to verify their recovery and abstinence.

The DP functions under the auspices of the Board of Nursing, which directs the program to ensure that nurses remain safe practitioners by maintaining compliance with the DP contract. When nurses does not maintain compliance with their DP contract, they may face disciplinary action. Even with certain disciplinary action, however, nurses can continue to work, and most continue to participate in the DP and regain compliance.

Approximately 95 percent of the nurses who enter the DP successfully complete it, even if they have had issues with non-compliance at some point and received disciplinary action. The 5 percent of nurses who do not comply with the contract or do not regain compliance with the contract are also reported to the Board of Nursing for disciplinary action. If they stop participating in the program, their licenses are revoked, and they are no longer able to practice as nurses. In these cases the Board of Nursing has fulfilled its mandate to protect the public from unsafe practitioners. Since the DP is voluntary, nurses who have lost their license have no obligation to continue the DP program and may drop out if they choose.

The 5 percent dropout rate has been consistent over the last eight years. While this rate may seem low, there are nagging questions about why nurses choose to leave the program, as well as why those who stay choose to stay. Up to this time, no data have been collected from those who leave the program. The DP Coordinator is interested in a more thorough evaluation of the program; both the executive director and the Board of Nursing have expressed support for this effort.

Adapted from an evaluation plan developed by Nancy Darbro Alburquerque, NM. Used with permission.

(continues)

FIGURE 5.2 *(continued)*

Purpose

The purpose of this evaluation is to explore the reasons why nurses either successfully complete or choose to drop out of the DP. The results will be used to improve the quality and effectiveness of the program.

Stakeholders and Audiences

The primary stakeholders for this evaluation include the Board of Nursing executive director, and the seven volunteer members of the Board. These individuals have direct responsibility for monitoring the effectiveness of the DP. The DP's coordinator is also a primary stakeholder due to her responsibility for coordinating and managing the DP as well as implementing any necessary programmatic changes.

The secondary stakeholders include current DP nurse participants and future nurse participants. These individuals will be affected by any modifications to the DP contract or program requirements. They will need to be informed of any recommendations for changing any aspects of the DP. The volunteers of the DP advisory committee who volunteer their time to monitor nurses in the program are also included as secondary stakeholders. These volunteers must be knowledgeable about the requirements for compliance with the DP.

Tertiary stakeholders include all licensed nurses in the state, as they contribute a small percentage of their biannual license renewal fees to fund the DP. The Board of Nursing staff provides clerical and office support to the DP and therefore needs to be aware of the DP's current status. Another tertiary audience is the state legislative body who would be responsible for approving any necessary changes in the Nursing Practice Act.

Key Questions
1. How many and for what reasons do nurses drop out of the DP?
2. What factors contribute to nurses completing the program?
3. What characteristics describe those nurses who relapse after their involvement with the program? To what extent do the same individuals continue to re-enroll in the program?
4. How many dropouts eventually return and complete the program?

- The time frame in which the information is needed to make certain decisions
- Ways they might use the results of the evaluation
- What concerns they have about the evaluation

After each person offers this information, we ask the group members to explain what they believe are the goals of the program. We have often found that people will recite the explicit goals as they are written in the program's documentation, but often add other goals they think are important. This situation creates an opportunity for negotiating which goals should be evaluated, as well as the origin and viability of certain unstated goals.

Patton similarly asks group members to explain what *claims* they wish to make about the program. In other words, if the program were working well, what would you say about it? He also finds that by asking the following questions, the group becomes quite animated and responsive to the task (1997, p. 154):

- What are you trying to achieve with your clients?
- If you are successful, how will your clients be different after the program than they were before?
- What kind of changes do you want to see in your clients?
- When the program works as you want it to, how do clients *behave* differently?
- What do they say differently?
- What would I see in them that would tell me they are different?

The answers to these questions help clarify the explicit, as well as the unstated or tacit, goals and objectives of any program, process, product, or object being evaluated.

By developing a logic model of the program to be evaluated, the evaluator and stakeholders gain an understanding of the evaluand's background and the evaluation's purpose. As discussed in Chapters 2 and 3, a logic model is a visual depiction of how a program is supposed to operate and the theory that drives a program. As McLaughlin and Jordan explain, "the Logic Model is the basis for a convincing story of the program's expected performance" (1999, p. 66). From a discussion about the program's objectives, elements, processes, and approaches, the group can come to understand the history and background of the evaluand. Figure 5.3 provides an example of such a logic model.

The logic model shown in Figure 5.3 was developed for an evaluation of the American Cancer Society's *Look Good . . . Feel Better* (LGFB) program that one of the authors conducted. LGFB is a free, national public service program created to help women look good, have improved self-esteem, and approach cancer and its treatment with greater confidence. A two- to three-hour workshop facilitated by a volunteer cosmetologist shows women how to use makeup, wigs, and scarves to improve their appearance during their cancer treatment.

During the focusing meeting, the group of eight evaluation Advisory Committee members discussed the history of the program, the principles that guide the program, resources the program needs to accomplish its goals, activities that need to take place to ensure the program is delivered successfully, and its short- and long-term goals. Developing the logic model made clear the background of the program, the rationale for the evaluation, and the program's short- and long-term goals.

The overall result of discussing the evaluand's background and developing the evaluation's rationale is a description or summary of what has been agreed upon. Within an evaluation plan, this may be covered in a couple of pages or several, depending on the level of detail necessary to lay the foundation for the evaluation.

Developing the Evaluation's Purpose Statement

Once the rationale for the evaluation has been established and potential uses of the evaluation findings have been discussed, it is helpful to sum up the purpose of the evaluation into a two- or three-sentence purpose statement. It is not unusual for there to be several purposes for conducting an evaluation. For example, the purpose of the evaluation might be to make decisions about the program's improvement, continuance, expansion, or certification, or to monitor a program's implementation for compliance. Other purposes might include obtaining evidence of a program's success to build support for additional resources, or gaining a better understanding of the program's effects on different groups. Whatever the purpose, it should be clearly explained in the purpose statement.

To reinforce the concept of use, we also recommend including a sentence or two that indicates how the evaluation results will be used. Figures 5.1, 5.2, and 5.4 provide examples of purpose statements. As you will notice, they are succinct explanations of what the evaluation will focus on and how the results will be used.

FIGURE 5.3   American Cancer Society's *Look Good ... Feel Better* Program Logic Model (excerpt)*

Assumptions	Resources	Activities	Short-Term Goals	Long-Term Impact
What principles are guiding this program? What claims would we like to make about the program's effect?	*What does the program need to accomplish its goals?*	*What has to happen to make this program successful? What activities will ensure meeting the program's goals?*	*What are the immediate effects of this program? How would we know if the program had a positive impact?*	*What are the longer-term outcomes or effects of the program? What would these look like?*
Nonmedical Product neutral Free of charge Improves patient's outlook about fighting the disease and on life in general Improves how women feel about themselves Enhances patient's feeling of empowerment and control over their lives Improves self-image and self-esteem	**CTFA** Works with cosmetic industry for financial funding and product donations Plans for future needs Provides national promotion **NCA** Marshals volunteer cosmetologists for group sessions **ACS** Recruits and trains volunteer cosmetologists and facility staff	**ACS** Identifies facilities Recruits volunteers from existing volunteer database or through NCA Sends out notices and invitations inviting cosmetologists to participate in the program Plans training for cosmetologists (includes assistance from NCA)	**Patients** Make new friends Continue treatment Are more comfortable buying wigs in stores Feel supported Recognize the joint partnership among the three organizations Are motivated to join support groups Change their image from being a victim to being a survivor	**Patients** Continue using the products beyond their treatment Continue feeling good about how they look Maintain friends made in the session Develop a long-term association and volunteer with ACS Make referrals to LGFB and other ACS programs and services Are better able to deal with recurrences *(continues)*

*Logic Model from the American Cancer Society's evaluation of the Look Good ... Feel Better program, a program co-sponsored by the American Cancer Society, the Cosmetic, Toiletry, and Fragrance Association Foundation, and the National Cosmetology Association. Printed with permission.

FIGURE 5.3 (continued)

Assumptions	Resources	Activities	Short-Term Goals	Long-Term Impact
Gives patients hope for the future	Processes awards (NHO)	Sponsors training	Change their image from being a victim to being a survivor	**Medical professionals** Make more referrals to LGFB
Patients feel renewed	Distributes materials (NHO)	Contacts facilities to see if patients might be interested in the program	Improve their appearance and take control over the treatment's side effects	
Patients feel the positive effects beyond their treatment period	Pays all expenses of design and delivery of the program (NHO)	Patients register	Use the 12-step process	
Doctors become more aware of the importance of looking good		Orders makeup kits from NHO	Use the information learned in the session regarding wigs and scarves	
When a patient looks good on the outside, there is greater healing on the inside		Reminds and confirms patients' participation prior to session	Develop skin care routine	
		Session is conducted by NCA cosmetologist and volunteers (2-3 hour session)	Have a normal appearance	
		Patients receive makeup kit and resource materials	Maintain daily activities	
			Use other ACS resources	

FIGURE 5.4   Sample Purpose Statements

- The purpose of the evaluation is to understand the specific knowledge and attitudes needed by employees in the sales department as they prepare to implement a new sales management software package. The results will be used to develop an on-line training program for teaching salespeople how to use the new software program. *(Needs assessment)*
- The purpose of the evaluation is to identify the strengths and weaknesses of a new six-hour, classroom-based course titled, "Coaching New Employees," prior to rolling it out to all organization members. The results will be used to modify or refine the course's design prior to full-scale implementation. *(Formative evaluation, evaluating a program's design)*
- The purpose of the evaluation is to determine how worthwhile participants found the two-hour classroom-based course on project management. The results will be used to determine whether or not to continue offering this course on a monthly basis. *(Formative and summative evaluation, evaluating participants' reactions to the learning experience)*
- The purpose of the evaluation is to determine what and how much participants learned in the course titled "Preventing Toxic Spills," delivered via distance technologies. The results will be used to determine whether distance technologies will replace classroom-based training on this topic. *(Primarily summative evaluation, evaluating the amount and type of learning)*
- The purpose of the evaluation is to determine the ways in which trainees are transferring their learning back to the workplace. The evaluation will also focus on those things that support or inhibit the transfer of learning to the job. The results will be used to modify the program's content, and/or to determine if additional workplace interventions are necessary to support training transfer. *(Formative evaluation, evaluating the transfer of learning)*
- The purpose of the evaluation is to determine the cost-effectiveness of reorganizing the distribution center that serves the organization's field offices around the world. The results will be used to determine whether this reorganization is cost-effective, as well as whether this serves the organization's needs better than outsourcing the function. *(Summative evaluation, evaluating the cost-effectiveness of a reorganization effort)*

Identifying the Evaluation's Stakeholders

Evaluation is conducted to serve the interests and information needs of several individuals or groups of people. These might be the program's designers, developers, deliverers, customers, future and former participants, community members, members of professional organizations, legislative committees, managers, administrators, and advisory boards. Each of these individuals or groups may have a stake in the outcomes of the evaluation.

The word *stakeholder* dates back to 1708. As William Safire explains:

> When Western land was made available to those who would work and live on it, a stake became a section of land marked off by stakes and claimed by the farmer. By extension, a grubstake was money advanced for food, or grub, as an investment or loan. Stakeholder, in the sense of one who holds the stake of a bet or wager, dates back to 1708; an article in Sporting magazine in 1815 mentions "a Bank of England note, which was lodged in the hands of a stake-holder, as a deposit." (*New York Times*, May 5, 1996, p. 26)

The more recent use of the term *stakeholder* was invented as an analogy for shareholders in 1964 and was later used in the management literature when talking about people who had a direct stake in the organization, such as owners and employees. Interestingly, a survey conducted between 1998 and 1999 by Walker Information Global Network covering twenty-six countries and more than 1,000 large corporations found that many organizations and countries use the term *stakeholder*. Defined as "those groups of individuals who have a stake in or an effect on a business, such as customers, shareholders, employees, and suppliers." South Africa was found to have the most stakeholder-savvy executives (Salopek, 1999, p. 16). The survey found that 99 percent of business leaders in South Africa were aware of the term, and 93 percent of Canadian leaders and 83 percent of U.S. leaders were familiar with the word. However, the overall findings indicated that "one-third of the executives of major corporations world-wide are unfamiliar with the term 'stakeholder' as it relates to business organizations" (1999, p. 16).

In the evaluation field, the word "stakeholder," with regard to a program is,
One who has substantial ego, credibility, power, futures, or other capital in-

vested in the program, and thus can be held to be to some degree of risk with it. This includes program staff and many who are not actively involved in the day-to-day operations—for example, inventors or instigators or supporters of the program. (Scriven, 1991, p. 334)

Evaluation stakeholders are those who have a vested interest in the evaluand, and thus would be in a position to use the evaluation results in some way. As discussed in Chapter 1, some stakeholders who have responsibility for the program might use the findings to make certain decisions (instrumental use), or to better understand the program for future planning (conceptual use). In other cases, stakeholders, because of their relationship to the program, merely have a "right to know" the results and just wish to stay informed about how the program is faring (conceptual use).

We think it's helpful to differentiate various stakeholders by their level of investment and stake in the program and the evaluation findings. For example, primary stakeholders typically are those who allow the evaluand to exist or who make it happen. They are typically responsible for the successful design, development, implementation, and funding of the evaluand. These stakeholders might include the evaluand's:

- Funding agencies, organizations, departments

- Designers
- Developers
- Implementers
- Staff

Secondary stakeholders are often more removed from the daily operations of the program, and may not have financial controls over the evaluation, but have an important stake in the program and the evaluation's outcomes. Examples of secondary stakeholders include:

- Managers
- Administrators
- Students/participants
- Customers
- Clients

- Trainers
- Parents

Tertiary stakeholders are those who have some interest in the evaluation for future planning or decisionmaking, or have some general interest or right to know the evaluation's results. These might include:

- Potential users/adopters
- Professional colleagues
- Professional organizations
- Governing boards
- Community members
- Legislators
- Libraries

Though there is no hard-and-fast rule about what makes an individual or group a primary, secondary, or tertiary stakeholder, it is true that those charged with oversight or implementation of the evaluand tend to make instrumental uses of the findings and thus are often considered to be primary or secondary stakeholders. The more removed individuals or groups are from the evaluand's daily operations and responsibility for funding, the more likely they are to be secondary or tertiary stakeholders. We can also say that primary stakeholders would probably receive the full report of the evaluation's findings, whereas secondary or tertiary stakeholders would normally receive abbreviated versions of the findings (see Chapter 13 for more details on how to communicate and report evaluation findings to various stakeholders).

What is most important in this step is the comprehensive identification of all potential stakeholders. Evaluators should ask themselves the following questions to determine who the stakeholders might be:

- Who has a vested interest in the evaluand and evaluation outcomes?
- Whose position could be affected by the evaluation's findings and actions taken on the findings?
- Who cares about the evaluand?
- How might the evaluation findings be used and by whom?

- What groups will be affected by the evaluation if recommendations are made and acted upon?
- Who are the clients or customers of the evaluand and what stake might they have in the outcomes of the evaluation?
- Who has a "right to know" the evaluation's results?

Answering the above questions helps evaluators make decisions about how inclusive and diverse the stakeholder group should be.

Remember that the identification of stakeholders does not necessarily mean that these are the people from whom you will be collecting data. Although it is entirely possible that you will contact some of these individuals during the data collection phase, it is important not to equate stakeholders with data sources. This step in the evaluation planning ensures that all potential users of the evaluation findings are identified so that maximum use of the evaluation's findings can be made—both from a program improvement standpoint as well as for the purpose of marketing and education. Figures 5.1 and 5.2 provide examples of stakeholders and their potential uses of the evaluation findings.

Developing Key Evaluation Questions

A major outcome of the focusing phase is a list of broad, guiding questions the evaluation will seek to address. They form the boundary and scope of the evaluation and serve to communicate to others what the evaluation will and won't attend to. The questions that are developed are the result of the input and negotiations among the evaluator and stakeholders. When guiding a group through the process of developing these key questions, anywhere from ten to fifty questions may be generated. Given that answering this many questions is often not feasible because of various time and resource constraints, we recommend that the group:

- Examine the questions to make sure that they are truly large, general questions and are not so specific that they might be considered survey or interview questions.
- Group the questions by themes or categories.
- Prioritize the questions in each category according to those that are "need to answer now" versus "would be nice to answer."

- Prioritize the categories of questions to determine if there are some categories that are more important now versus later.
- Determine whether the "would-be-nice-to-answer" questions can be considered as a future evaluation, or can be addressed by another group of individuals.
- Agree on a set of questions that are of the most immediate concern.

It is impossible to say how many questions any one evaluation should seek to answer, but we have found that most program evaluations within an organization include anywhere from three to twelve key questions. It should not be too surprising that the more questions the evaluation addresses, the more complex and comprehensive the evaluation will be. The more comprehensive the evaluation is, the more time and money will be needed for the evaluation. Figures 5.1 and 5.2 provide examples of evaluation questions.

We want to restate here that these key questions focus and guide the entire evaluation process. If we fail to develop these questions and instead jump to writing questions for surveys or interview guides, as Judy and Mark did in the opening vignette of this chapter, we are simply hoping we ask the right questions. We may or may not end up asking questions that will address what we really need to know to make decisions about our programs.

Once you have completed the evaluation's focusing phase, you will: a) understand the background and history of the program being evaluated, b) have developed the rationale for the evaluation as well as its purpose, c) have identified the stakeholder groups, and d) have developed a set of questions that the evaluation will seek to answer. Once this is done, it is time to consider the various evaluation designs and methods to address the key questions. Chapters 6 through 11 will guide you in this process.

··

Keep in Mind . . .

- An evaluation plan should be developed for every evaluation.
- The focusing phase of the evaluation should include the evaluation's:

Rationale and purpose
Stakeholders
Key questions
- It is important that this phase of the evaluation be completed before determining the evaluation's design and data collection methods.

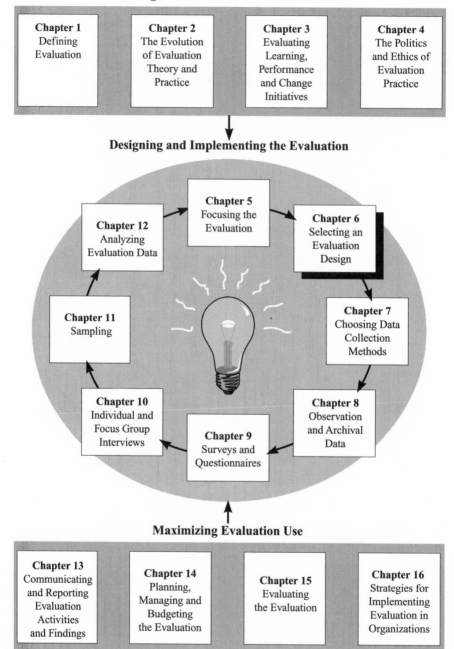

Background and Context of Evaluation

Chapter 1
Defining
Evaluation

Chapter 2
The Evolution
of Evaluation
Theory and
Practice

Chapter 3
Evaluating
Learning,
Performance
and Change
Initiatives

Chapter 4
The Politics
and Ethics of
Evaluation
Practice

Designing and Implementing the Evaluation

Chapter 5
Focusing the
Evaluation

Chapter 6
Selecting an
Evaluation
Design

Chapter 12
Analyzing
Evaluation Data

Chapter 7
Choosing Data
Collection
Methods

Chapter 11
Sampling

Chapter 10
Individual and
Focus Group
Interviews

Chapter 9
Surveys and
Questionnaires

Chapter 8
Observation
and Archival
Data

Maximizing Evaluation Use

Chapter 13
Communicating
and Reporting
Evaluation
Activities
and Findings

Chapter 14
Planning,
Managing and
Budgeting
the Evaluation

Chapter 15
Evaluating
the Evaluation

Chapter 16
Strategies for
Implementing
Evaluation in
Organizations

chapter 6

Selecting an Evaluation Design

- Basic Design Issues
- Commonly Used Evaluation Designs

••

Vignette #3: Testing to No Avail at MyAuto Dealerships

Tim Jenkins, head of the company's human resource development department, wanted to conduct an evaluation of a newly designed sales training
program. Since the program was supposed to increase the participants'
knowledge of specific sales techniques, he decided to administer a test immediately after the last training session to see how much they learned. He
assumed that increased knowledge would result in increased sales revenue.
The test results showed consistently high scores. But when Tim showed the
results to the vice president of sales, the vice president expressed some
skepticism about the usefulness of results and said, "A lot of these folks already knew this stuff."

••

Tim might have avoided this criticism by using a better evaluation design, specifically one that controlled for prior knowledge. Instead of simply using a knowledge test following training, he might have considered
administering a similar test before the training program. This would have
provided valuable information on what the participants actually knew before beginning the sales training program. Alternatively, he might have
randomly selected two groups of salespeople, with one group going
through the training first. Then he could have administered the knowl-

147

edge test to both groups at the same time—which is when the first group had finished training but the second group had not yet started training. This would have provided information on the differences in knowledge between those who had completed the training and those who had not yet started the training.

A variety of evaluation designs currently exist, and one or more of these designs may be appropriate for evaluating a learning, performance, or change initiative. The purpose of this chapter is to provide an overview of some of the most commonly used types of evaluation designs and to highlight their strengths and weaknesses. Before reviewing these designs, however, we discuss some basic issues that need to be considered when designing any evaluation. Note that the issues discussed in this chapter are relevant for both evaluators and researchers, as mentioned in Chapter 1.

Basic Design Issues

Before jumping into a discussion of different designs and related issues, we want to first identify two different views of evaluation and research. One perspective has been called "quantitative," "empirical," and "positivistic." In this view, the evaluator or researcher stands independent and apart from what is being studied. Furthermore, she or he must adopt a neutral stance and control for any biases or preconceived ideas. The purpose or objective of these kinds of studies is to identify cause-and-effect relationships and to discover laws that govern these relationships.

The second view has been called "qualitative," "ethnographic," and "naturalistic." Those who adopt this view believe that evaluators cannot separate themselves from what is being studied—they cannot help but bring their subjectivity and values to the evaluation. The purpose or objective for qualitatively oriented evaluations is to understand, as much as possible, the lived experiences of those being studied.

We have found that most evaluators tend to adopt one view or the other, typically because of their background, education, or training. As a result, these factors often influence the evaluation's key questions, design, and choice of data collection methods. To ensure that both worldviews and preferences are represented, or that one perspective is not embraced to the exclusion of the other, it is a good idea to conduct the evaluation using a team-based approach. Such a team would consist of evaluators possessing quantitative and qualitative expertise. This would then facilitate the collection of both kinds of data (often referred to as "mixed methods").

Validity

The usefulness of evaluation findings is often based on the accuracy and credibility of the results. In this section, we discuss the concepts of internal and external validity for quantitative and qualitative data.

Internal Validity. The internal validity of an evaluation effort refers to the extent to which it correctly answers the questions it claims to answer about what is being evaluated. In other words, are the data an accurate representation of how people think, feel, know, or act about the evaluand? All data collection and analysis efforts are carried out in the context of a set of assumptions (sometimes considered a model) about the program being observed. If those assumptions are wrong, then the findings of the evaluation are meaningless. For example, we might assume that a program that trained people to run a mile faster would improve their performance as a team leader. The evaluation might then focus on whether the training led to faster running times, simply assuming that this would result in improved team leadership. If those assumptions are correct, then the evaluation is internally valid, and the findings from the evaluation are meaningful. Note, however, that the example is one where the assumptions are wrong and therefore the findings are meaningless.

In evaluations, whether using quantitative or qualitative approaches, one major threat to internal validity is that some unmeasured processes (also called confounding factors or variables) might account for the results that were obtained. When evaluating learning, performance, and change initiatives, it is possible that the results are owing to some confounding variables, such as previous knowledge or history with the organization or the job. (This was the criticism leveled by the vice president of sales in our beginning vignette.) The design of the evaluation can help account for such factors or variables. Confounding variables might include the following (words in italics are the technical terms used to describe a particular threat to validity, adapted from Campbell and Stanley [1963]):

- Specific and unexpected events affecting the variables of interest (such as a major downsizing initiative)—*history*.
- Passage of time that leads to changes in attitudes or behavior (such as time on the job resulting in the acquisition of certain skills)—*maturation*.
- Effects of one data collection effort on later data collection (such as the experience of taking a test affecting performance on a later test)—*testing*.
- Changes in the data collection instruments or the observers, which may affect the manner in which measurements are taken (such as multiple untrained observers or changes in item wording on a postsurvey)—*instrumentation*.
- Attrition from the sample (such as job or organizational changes)—*mortality*.

A second type of threat to internal validity, which can affect both quantitative and qualitative data, involves using data collection methods that do not accurately measure the underlying dimensions of concern. For example, one might use an employment test that measures driving ability when the person is being hired to fill a clerical position. In this case, the test scores are irrelevant for making judgments about the quality of the candidates for the job they are seeking. As a second example, in conducting interviews that focus on issues of workplace discrimination, the interview questions might fail to provide needed information, possibly because of respondents' desire to be politically correct, or a fear of repercussions if they were to provide their real opinions. In this situation, more attention to the types of questions being asked may reduce problems with internal validity.

In some evaluations, comparisons are made between a group that receives the learning, performance, or change intervention (sometimes called the experimental or treatment group) and a group that does not receive the intervention. When using comparison designs, another threat to the internal validity is the equivalence between the two groups. In most learning, performance, and change evaluations, treatment and control groups have not been randomly selected and assigned from a predetermined population. Such nonrandom assignment can lead to systematic distortions of the results, particularly if those selected for the intervention are the "best" or the "worst" performers, the "most motivated" or the "least motivated" employees. In addition to problems related to a lack of initial random assignment, the two groups may become nonequivalent over time because more people drop out of one of the two groups. The primary methods for ensuring internal validity are those used to conduct most research studies. These include: a) random assignment to treatment and control conditions, b) identification and measurement of confounding factors, c) control over confounding factors, and d) the use of multiple methods, such as rating forms and interviews, to obtain converging evidence in support of a particular finding (also known as *triangulation*). If an evaluation lacks internal validity, the evaluation will lose credibility in the face of any serious criticism. In such cases, decision makers will turn to other information sources to make important decisions, and the time, effort, and cost of the evaluation will be viewed as a worthless expense.

There are, however, very real costs for increasing an evaluation's internal validity. One example is the increased direct costs for measuring confounding effects. This includes hiring one or more experts to consider all these confounding variables beforehand, the cost of developing and piloting methods for measuring confounding variables, and the costs of collecting and analyzing the additional data.

Therefore, the evaluator must decide whether an evaluation effort needs to incur the costs for increasing internal validity. A high level of internal validity is necessary if the evaluation results are to be used for important decisionmaking purposes. On the other hand, internal validity need not be as great for exploratory evaluations. You may be undertaking an evaluation to pilot some data collection methods or to explore some tentative ideas concerning a particular evaluation issue. In such cases, you may not need high levels of internal validity, because you plan to undertake further evaluation to test conclusions that were tentatively reached from an exploratory study. This does not mean that exploratory evaluations can be conducted in a sloppy way, without pilot tests or concerns for data accuracy. A certain level of internal validity is always needed to justify the collection and analysis of data. At the onset of the evaluation, you should make a rough determination as to the level of validity needed. If that level of validity is unattainable, a decision should be made as to whether to conduct the evaluation. For example, imagine that you have been asked to conduct an evaluation of the organization's performance management system at the same time the organization is being merged with another company. In deciding whether to conduct the evaluation, you consider not only the extent to which employees will agree to be interviewed or surveyed, but you must also judge how honest their responses will be during this unsettling time. You may conclude that given employees' mistrust of management, the resulting data may not be valid, and as a result choose not to pursue the evaluation until things settle down.

External Validity.   This form of validity concerns the extent to which the results can be generalized to other situations. For example, can the results from one site be generalized to the entire organization or to other organizations? Generally, external validity is determined by *sample selection*, whereas internal validity is determined by *sample assignment*. Thus, external validity is increased to the extent that the sample selection reflects the population and the results can be generalized. In contrast, internal validity is increased through random assignment to one or more groups. It must be recognized that such random assignment may not, in fact, be the method by which participants are assigned to learning, performance, and change interventions. For instance, people in the organization may be assigned to particular opportunities because of their location or because they are viewed as "rising stars." So, if in the evaluation you used random assignment, you would increase the internal validity and reduce external validity and generalizability. The results obtained in this case would generalize only to other situations where people were assigned randomly.

Factors that can affect a study's generalizability include:

- Reactions to the pretest that make the results unrepresentative of the general population. In this case, people may be sensitized to certain issues because of the pretest, and such sensitivity would not extend to the larger population.
- Reactions to "experimental" conditions, which again make the results unrepresentative of those outside such conditions. As with the previous factor, such sensitivity or reactions may accompany the specific training setting but would not extend to other learning and performance settings.

- Reactions to multiple treatments, which makes the results unrepresentative of those not receiving the same set of treatments. Many learning, performance, and change initiatives involve more than a single event in isolation. In such cases, the results may not extend to other kinds of interventions.

The value of external validity is the ability to generalize the results to a larger population. Such generalizability, then, depends on drawing a representative sample of the population (see Chapter 11 on sampling). Another approach to maximizing external validity is to repeat the evaluation (replication).

As with internal validity, the expense for achieving external validity comes in the form of direct costs. Obtaining a broad and representative sample involves several technical procedures and may require the cost of involving an expert in sampling procedures. Undertaking replications of an evaluation would require the costs for repeating the data collection and data analyses processes.

Validity and Qualitative Data.   What we have just discussed is the concept of validity primarily in relation to quantitative methods and designs. Again, validity relates to the degree of confidence we have that the data are representing our participants' "truth" or reality. What constitutes "truth," however, is defined in different terms when we use qualitative approaches and methods.

Guba and Lincoln (1981) propose that evaluators and researchers using qualitative designs should still be held accountable for how well they depict the reality of respondents. They recommend that evaluators develop and use "tests of rigor" for establishing such validity. As examples, they provide four criteria of rigor for judging the trustworthiness (validity) of qualitative data.

1. *Truth Value: How can one establish the confidence in the "truth" of the findings of a particular inquiry for the subjects with which—and the context within which—the inquiry was carried out?* Whereas the scientific paradigm asserts that there is one reality and that information is valid when all relevant variables can be controlled and manipulated, a naturalistic or qualitative paradigm assumes that there are multiple realities that exist in the minds of individuals. Thus, when using qualitative methods, the eval-

uator seeks to establish the credibility of individuals' responses. The study must be believable by those who provide the data and by those who will use its findings. Providing a detailed, comprehensive depiction of the multiple perspectives that exist can enhance the data's credibility. For example, trainee satisfaction ratings from a survey, along with interviews of trainees' managers and the training instructors, would provide a more holistic picture of the training experience.

2. *Applicability: How can one determine the degree to which the findings of a particular inquiry may have applicability in other contexts or with other subjects?* How transferable or applicable the findings are to another setting is called generalizability in the scientific paradigm. The goal for qualitative methods is to provide a richly detailed description; such a description can help the reader relate certain findings to his or her own experience. We often think of these as "lessons learned." For example, as a stakeholder reads an evaluation report, he realizes that something very similar has occurred in his own organization, and sees where some of the findings can be used. Although the entire set of findings may not be applicable to his context, some issues identified or lessons learned have applicability in other contexts.

3. *Consistency: How can one determine whether the findings of an inquiry would be consistently repeated if the inquiry were replicated with the same (or similar) subjects in the same (or a similar) context?* In the scientific paradigm, the notion of consistency is called reliability where a study or instrument's consistency, predictability, or stability is measured. Since reliability is necessary for validity, it is critical that data of any kind be reliable. Instead of considering data unreliable if it is inconsistent, evaluators using qualitative methods look for reasons that the data appear unstable (inconsistent). For example, an interviewee might give an opinion one day, and when asked again the following week might say something slightly different. What would be important to understand and capture are the reasons for the change in perception. Such inconsistencies may stem from respondent error, an increase in available information, or changes in the situation. An *audit trail* that includes collecting documents and interview notes and a daily journal of how things are going can help to uncover some of the reasons for such inconsistencies.

4. *Neutrality: How can one establish the degree to which the findings of an inquiry are a function solely of the subjects and conditions of the inquiry and not of*

the biases, motives, interests, and perspectives of the inquirer? Objectivity is often viewed as the goal of most evaluation and research studies. Evaluators and researchers who use qualitative methods don't necessarily believe, however, that true objectivity can ever be fully achieved. They believe that it is impossible to completely separate the evaluator from the method. Instead of trying to ensure that the data are free of the evaluator's biases, the goal is to determine the extent to which the data provide confirming evidence. "This means that data (constructions, assertions, facts, and so on) can be tracked to their sources, and that the logic used to assemble the interpretations into structurally coherent and corroborating wholes is both explicit and implicit" (Guba and Lincoln, 1989, p. 243). Establishing *confirmability*, like consistency, often takes the form of auditing.

To help understand the relationship between these tests of rigor and the scientific terms for validity, Guba and Lincoln (1981, p. 104) provide the following chart:

Aspect	*Scientific Term*	*Naturalistic Term*
Truth value	Internal validity	Credibility
Applicability	External validity	Fittingness generalizability
Consistency	Reliability	Auditability
Neutrality	Objectivity	Confirmability

Techniques for Establishing the Validity of Quantitative or Qualitative Data

To ensure that you do everything possible to enhance the validity of evaluation data, consider implementing the following techniques:

- Carefully check the accuracy in data recording and coding—ensure that all of the data are ready and available for analysis.
- Make repeated and persistent observations—build trust and rapport with participants so they are more likely to provide valid information. The longer one is on-site, the more trust can be built, and the more complete the observations will be.
- Member checking is a means for testing categories, interpretations, or conclusions through continuous checking of data with

stakeholders or other participants after various data collection activities, or when a draft of a final report has been written.

- Triangulation is a means for contrasting and comparing information drawn from different sources, methods, and theories. The term "triangulation" comes from land surveying and navigation where multiple reference points are used to locate an object's exact position. "Knowing a single landmark only locates you somewhere along a line in a direction from the landmark, whereas with two landmarks you can take bearings in two directions and locate yourself at their intersection" (Patton, 1990, p. 187). Therefore, the more information you have from as many sources as possible, which have been subject to various interpretations, the greater the likelihood the data are trustworthy. Denzin describes four kinds of triangulation that are commonly used today.

  1. Data triangulation—collecting data from a variety of sources. For example, in evaluating the transfer of learning from a three-hour workshop, the evaluator collects information from the training participants, their managers, and their peers. In this case, three different sources have been queried.

  2. Methodological triangulation—using more than one method to collect data. For example, we may interview 20 percent of a department's employees and survey the remaining 80 percent. By using two methods, the weaknesses of one may be compensated by the other.

  3. Investigator triangulation—involving two or more evaluators in the inquiry. The maxim "Two heads are better than one" applies to this kind of triangulation. When two or more evaluators can plan, implement, debrief, and interpret the findings, the data will likely be richer and trustworthier.

  4. Theory triangulation—using different theoretical perspectives to interpret the same data. By applying different theories to make sense of the data, it is possible to see how different assumptions and beliefs influence one's interpretations. By making these explicit, stakeholders can see how their assumptions might influence various actions taken because of the findings. (1978)

- Peer debriefing—engaging in formal or informal discussions with a peer about what was seen, heard, experienced, and interpreted. This helps explore alternative explanations and emerging themes and patterns.
- Audit trail—allows an auditor to determine the trustworthiness of the study. The auditor may review interview guides, field notes, documents, peer debriefing notes, journals, and any other documents that have been used or collected.
- Pilot testing—trying out each of the data collection instruments with a sample of the population (or one similar to it). This enables the evaluator to determine if the questions are likely to elicit the kinds and quality of information being sought. Revisions can be made before implementing the instruments to the total sample or population.
- Rival explanations—looking for multiple ways of organizing the data that might lead to different findings.
- Negative cases—considering cases that do not fit a pattern. These cases may lend insights into emerging issues or new perspectives on a recurring problem.

Commonly Used Evaluation Designs

The following section describes various types of evaluation designs. After explaining each design, we provide an example and a list of the design's strengths and weaknesses. Further details on these and other designs can be found in Campbell and Stanley (1963) and Cook and Campbell (1979).

One-Shot Design

The term "one-shot" refers to the fact that the measurement takes place at one time only. This can be depicted as shown in Illustration 6.1.

The one-shot design is commonly used in evaluating learning, performance, and change interventions, whereby after the event, a postcourse or postevent survey is administered to participants. This design assumes that the respondents are providing reactions to the intervention, and only

Sample   Intervention   Posttest

ILLUSTRATION 6.1   One-Shot Design

to the intervention; they are not reacting to the latest announcements about organizational change or other aspects of their environment.

Another example of the one-shot study involves measuring learning and performance outcomes following training on a specific procedure or piece of equipment, such as was described in the vignette at the beginning of the chapter. In that case, Tim decided to measure the effects of sales training by using a test at the end of the workshop. Thus, if the content of the test was not known before the training, it may be reasonable to assume that the correct description of how to implement those steps as recorded on the test resulted from the training. Furthermore, if the trainees do, indeed, remember the relevant course material for the test, it is often assumed that they can successfully apply the material to the job.

A major advantage of this design is that it is simple and cost-effective. A limited amount of data are collected at one time only. In many cases, these data can be gathered as part of the learning, performance, and change initiative.

One-shot designs make several assumptions, however. They assume that the measurement is related in some way to the intervention rather than to some other factor. That assumption may or may not be accurate. For example, negative reactions to a training program may be the result of some recent organizational communication regarding downsizing and may have nothing to do with the training program's quality. As another example, the correct use of some procedure or equipment may be the result of previous knowledge and experience and not the training. However, if the procedure or equipment had not been previously used, it may be assumed that correct usage resulted from the intervention. A final problem with the one-shot design involves the low level of external validity. Since this takes place with only one group, it is not clear whether the results can be generalized to other populations. Such generalization may be addressed if participants were randomly selected for the intervention.

Advantages of the one-shot design:

- Is simple and cost-effective to conduct
- Reduces the costs and time for data collection and analysis
- Produces data that can be analyzed in a timely and cost-effective way
- Gathers data as part of the learning, performance, or change event
- Provides needed information when using an ideal comparison

Disadvantages of the one-shot design:

- Does not control for the effects of other factors, such as organizational issues or prior knowledge
- Assumes that positive reactions and knowledge tests lead to behavior changes
- Findings do not necessarily generalize to other populations

Retrospective Pretest Design

In this variation of the one-shot case study design, data are collected from participants following the learning, performance, or change intervention; however, the participants report retrospectively on their attitudes, knowledge, or skills. As a result, the evaluator can compare these retrospective preassessments with their postassessments.

This design depends on the accuracy of participants' recall, as well as their willingness to provide "truthful" data. For example, in communication skills training, trainees may or may not be aware of their prior skill level until after completing the training. In these cases, the retrospective design may provide a more accurate picture of pretraining skills than data gathering before training.

One example of this design would be the administration of a survey measuring attitudes toward customers following participation in a customer service training program. The survey would ask the respondents about their attitudes before the program as well as their current attitudes. In the case of the sales training vignette at the beginning of this chapter, Tim could ask trainees about the steps they used before training as well as those used after training. Another variation of this design is to ask participants to estimate how much the training has contributed to their skill development.

Like the one-shot design, the appeal of the retrospective design is its simplicity and ease of data collection. In addition, you can obtain a comparison between posttraining data and the retrospective predata. Furthermore, the posttraining data are not contaminated by the experience of pretesting.

One drawback of the retrospective design is that it does not include a control group of people who did not participate in the intervention. As a result, the evaluator cannot rule out the possibility that the results were due to history with the organization or with the job (as is true with the one-shot design). Another problem, particularly with the retrospective reporting, involves possible distortions in the retrospective reports. Such distortions may result from memory problems or from the respondents' current attitudes and beliefs. In some cases, actual preassessments collected from participants, their managers, their peers, and their subordinates often result in inflated scores as compared with retrospective preassessments. Again, the use of or the lack of random assignment to the intervention may increase or decrease the external validity of this design.

Advantages of the retrospective pretest design:

- Is simple and cost-effective
- Reduces the costs and time for data collection and analysis
- Gathers data as part of the learning, performance, or change event
- Compares posttraining data with retrospective predata
- Avoids attrition from the sample being tested or measured
- Decreases the likelihood of testing effects

Disadvantages of the retrospective pretest design:

- Cannot rule out the possibility that results were owing to history with the organization or the job (as is true with the one-shot designs)
- Possible distortions in retrospective reports because of memory or current attitudes and beliefs

One-Group Pretest-Posttest Design

This design involves data collection before the learning, performance, or change intervention as well as following it. This can be depicted as follows:

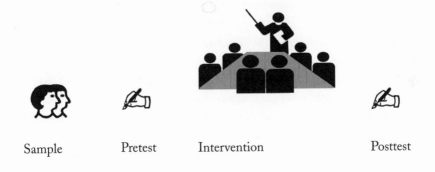

| Sample | Pretest | Intervention | Posttest |

ILLUSTRATION 6.2   One-Group Pretest-Posttest Design

Using the sales training example again, Tim could test trainees on sales protocol procedures before and after the sales training course. This would provide information regarding how much trainees had learned.

A typical scenario for a posttest is to administer it immediately following learning and performance interventions, perhaps even on the last day of the event. Depending on what is being measured, such timing may or may not be appropriate. For example, if you want to measure whether trainees display their newly developed skills on the job, you would want to allow trainees some time to use and become comfortable with these skills. Or you may measure participants' reactions both immediately following the training and some time later to see if their perceptions changed with the passage of time.

If you decide to measure several times, it is important to consider how often data need to be collected (see the Time-Series Design later in this chapter). For example, you might decide to conduct certain observations with greater frequency, such as once a month, rather than less frequently, because you believe that there will likely be significant variation of individual or group performance within the longer period. Annual reports to Congress or to stockholders in a corporation provide examples of a yearly evaluation of certain government programs or of certain aspects of a corporation's operations. On the other hand, economic measures relating to our society, such as cost-of-living indicators, fluctuate seasonally, so these measurements occur several times a year.

Many evaluations of learning, performance, and change initiatives tend to be undertaken on a one-time basis, in which there is no plan for repeated data collection. This may or may not be appropriate. If the initiative is long-term and continues over many years, you may want to consider conducting some evaluation activities on a periodic basis. In such cases, you might consider planning the initial study in such a way that the data provide a baseline for long-term studies.

As with the previous designs, this design is relatively simple and cost-effective. Indeed, the participants could be asked to complete an instrument that focused on attitudes, opinions, knowledge, or skill level at the beginning and at the end of the learning, performance, or change intervention. Since data would be collected as part of the intervention, the evaluator would reduce the costs of data collection and the possibility of attrition from the sample.

However, there are several possible weaknesses with this design. Without a control group of people who have not participated in training, similar problems as those mentioned with the one-shot and retrospective designs can arise. These include the possibility that the results appear because of previous history with the organization and the job (history and maturation). In addition, the pretest itself may cause changes to occur irrespective of the training (testing). For example, a knowledge or skills pretest may actually contribute to the improved knowledge or skills of the people taking the posttest. If so, the posttest measurement not only reflects the effects of the intervention, but it reflects the effects of the pretest *plus* the intervention. Another potential problem involves that of increased effort and resources for follow-up and possible attrition or loss of people from the sample (mortality). With designs that require repeated data collection, you may find respondents disappearing from their positions and from the organization, resulting in a smaller than expected sample (mortality). This becomes particularly problematic when the posttest must take place at some time following the learning and performance intervention. Finally, as with the previous designs, random assignment to the learning, performance, or change intervention can increase or decrease the generalizability of the findings, depending on the organizational circumstances.

Advantages of the one group pretest-posttest design:

- Can be simple to conduct
- Can be cost-effective
- Reduces the costs and time for data collection and analysis
- Gathers data as part of the learning, performance, or change event
- Measures actual attitudes, knowledge, and skills prior to the intervention
- Allows for actual comparison of pretest and posttest data

Disadvantages of the one group pretest-posttest design:

- Cannot rule out the possibility that results were due to history and maturation with the organization or the job (as is true with the one-shot designs)
- Cannot rule out instrumentation effects (because of changes in the instruments or observers)
- Pretest itself may cause changes to occur irrespective of the training
- Is vulnerable to the loss of people from the sample because of job changes
- May require added data collection costs for conducting the posttest

Posttest-Only Control Group Design

Although researchers and evaluators usually emphasize the importance of a pretest, one might want to consider avoiding the use of the pretest to eliminate the effects of the pretest on the posttest results. One can do this by using the posttest-only control group design. This can be depicted as follows:

ILLUSTRATION 6.3   Posttest-Only Control Group Design

In such a design, two groups may be randomly selected, with one group experiencing the learning, performance, or change intervention, and the other receiving no intervention. The two groups are then given a posttest at the same time following the intervention. So, back to our original vignette, Tim could randomly assign salespeople to one of two groups. One group would receive training, and the other group would not receive training (or would receive training at some later time). Following training, the two groups would complete the same posttests.

As previously mentioned, this design avoids the problems associated with using the pretest. Furthermore, random assignment to the two groups provides assurance that no systematic bias exists between the two groups. Concerns over such systematic bias usually lead evaluators to recommend the use of a pretest to determine the similarity of the two groups. Random assignment can, however, overcome this problem, because you can assume that the groups are the same. In addition, data collection is made more simple and easy since it takes place at one time only.

The major limitation, certainly within organizations, is the lack of feasibility of random assignment to various treatment conditions. This problem is exacerbated when you attempt to assign certain people to a "control" condition where they do not receive the intervention. (Or perhaps they receive the intervention later on.) For organizations with the imperative of completing everything *now,* the notion of keeping some people from needed developmental experiences seems inappropriate. In addition, some organizations might consider withholding certain interventions to some people as unethical. Finally, there is a likely possibility that someone within the organization insists that certain people or groups of people must participate in the training at the time of the evaluation. If so, such insistence violates any notion of random assignment.

Advantages of the posttest-only control group design:

- Enables some control of the effects of history and maturation
- Can be accomplished with one data collection time
- May be conducted as part of the intervention
- Rules out possible testing and instrumentation effects
- Allows a comparison of those who have experienced the intervention with those who have not

Disadvantages of the posttest-only control group design:

- Assumes random assignment to treatment and control groups, which may prove impractical in an organizational setting
- Raises potential ethical problems when withholding the intervention from a certain group
- May require added data collection costs for conducting the posttest
- Does not rule out the possibility that everyone knew this information or had these skills prior to the intervention

Time Series Design

So far, we have only looked at two separate data collection times—a pretest and a posttest. Another possible design involves repeated data collection before and following the learning, performance, or change intervention, as shown below.

Sample   Pretest 1   Pretest 2...   Intervention   Posttest 1   Posttest 2...

ILLUSTRATION 6.4   Time Series Design

Using this design, one would graph the results obtained at each time. If charting the results, such as sales revenue, showed some dramatic change only from the time immediately before to immediately after training, one could assume that the training had some impact on the results. Conducting several pretests establishes a stable baseline to use for comparing posttraining results. Let us return to the vignette at the beginning of this chapter. Let's say Tim decides to chart the revenue of salespeople over time. If training took place in early April and the graph of sales revenue looked something like that shown in Illustration 6.5, Tim would have reasonably strong evidence that the sales training program had some effect.

A strength of this design is the fact that you have shown that time in the organization or on the job by itself did not result in changes in attitudes or behavior. For example, let us assume that you measured performance each month for six months showing a gradual improvement over time. Then you show a large and significant improvement in performance following an intervention. Time or history alone would probably not account for such a large improvement unless accompanied by the intervention (or some specific organizational change).

There are, however, several problems with this design. First, as mentioned above, you cannot easily isolate various organizational influences that could affect one's performance separate from the learning, performance, and change intervention. In addition, you would have to undertake repeated data collection with the participants. Such repeated mea-

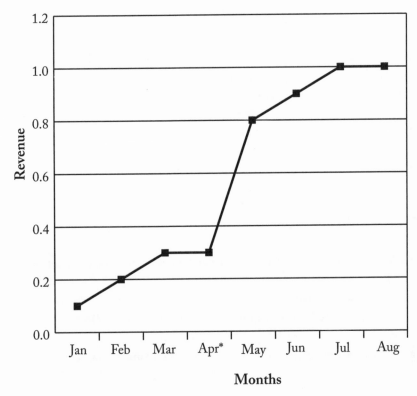

ILLUSTRATION 6.5   Sales Revenue over Time

surements lead to additional costs for the evaluation. Also, the repeated measurement could result in changes in attitudes or behavior simply because of the measurement itself. Since this design takes place over time, there may be attrition from the sample because of people being reassigned or leaving the job and the organization. In addition, whenever someone responds multiple times to the same data collection instrument, the results may not reflect their true knowledge or attitudes; this may be due to familiarity with the content. Finally, some external validity is compromised, since the results are generalizable only to those who undergo such repeated testing.

Another set of issues arises from the use of longitudinal designs. In some cases, different results have been obtained when using a longitudinal design (which tests the same people over time) from those obtained when using a cross-sectional design (which tests different people at different stages at the same time). When considering such designs, you may want to consult some literature on this topic (Russ-Eft, 1999; Schaie, Campbell, Meredith, and Rawlings, 1988).

Advantages of the time-series design:

- Controls for the effects of history
- Provides evidence over time
- Establishes baseline of performance with which to compare postintervention performance

Disadvantages of the time-series design:

- May require more resources because of repeated data collection efforts
- May be expensive because of repeated data collection efforts
- Changes may be the results of the repeated data collection (because of testing or instrumentation effects)
- May experience attrition or loss of people from the sample

Pretest-Posttest Control-Group Design

This design requires two groups, one of which participates in the learning, performance, or change intervention and one that does not. Again, random assignment to the two groups provides greater internal validity to the study but may not be feasible. This design is depicted in Illustration 6.6.

Let us return to Tim's evaluation. To use this design he would first randomly assign salespeople to two groups, one of which would participate in the training first. Each group would complete a pretest at the same time, such as a test on sales procedures. After the first group completed the training, the two groups would receive a posttest at the same time, again on sales procedures.

This design may be considered one of the most rigorous described so far. The random assignment to the two groups eliminates the possibility of any selection bias. The pretest allows the evaluator to determine empirically whether the two groups are similar before training. If random se-

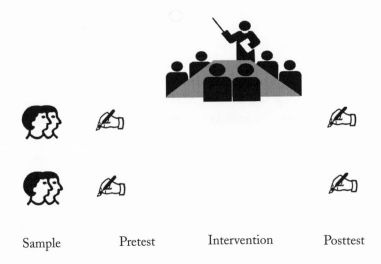

| Sample | Pretest | Intervention | Posttest |

ILLUSTRATION 6.6   Pretest-Posttest Control-Group Design

lection is used, then the groups will likely appear similar before training. In the case described in the paragraph above showing some selection bias, differences will appear in the pretest. For example, if new salespeople were chosen for the group receiving the intervention and the experienced salespeople were chosen for the control group, a knowledge pretest would show that the new salespeople were less knowledgeable than the experienced salespeople. After training, the new salespeople may have gained some knowledge, but they may still receive lower scores than the experienced salespeople. In this case, the decision makers may view the training as unsuccessful, when, in fact, it may have been highly successful. By using comparable groups before training, the posttraining differences between the groups and the gains from pre- to posttraining will be easier to explain.

Since the two groups are tested at the same time after the intervention, differences between the groups cannot be attributed to the following: a) unexpected events or circumstances within the organization, b) the passage of time in the organization or on the job, or c) special attitudes, knowledge, or skills gained as a result of certain organizational changes. The reason is because both groups would have experienced the same events, circumstances, and passage of time.

There are limitations, however, with this design. As mentioned previously, the administration of the pretest may contribute to some of the differences between the groups. For example, the pretest may have the effect of alerting both groups as to what is most important in the intervention. Another problem arises with the use of a control group that does not participate in the intervention. In some organizations, everyone must participate in the intervention at one time, making the use of the control group impossible. Finally, because the design takes place over time, one must expect some attrition from the two groups, given the mobility of today's workforce. If attrition from the two groups were unequal, then this would be a cause for concern.

Advantages of the pretest-posttest control-group design:

- Provides some control for the effects of history and maturation because of the use of a control group
- Provides evidence over time
- Measures actual attitudes, knowledge, and skills prior to the intervention
- Allows for comparison of actual pretest and posttest data

Disadvantages of the pretest-posttest control-group design:

- May require more resources because of repeated data collection efforts
- Changes may be the results of the repeated data collection (because of testing or instrumentation effects)
- May experience attrition or loss of people from the sample
- May have groups that are not similar because of unequal attrition
- May be difficult or impossible to obtain a "control" group

The Solomon Four-Group Design

The Solomon Four-Group Design provides one approach to controlling the effects of pretesting. It is probably the most rigorous design in terms of its ability to control for internal and external threats to validity. In this design, four groups are randomly selected and measured as shown in Illustration 6.7.

| Sample | Pretest | Intervention | Posttest |

ILLUSTRATION 6.7   The Solomon Four-Group Design

In our example with Tim and the sales training program, Tim would have to randomly select four groups; two would receive training and two would not receive training (or would receive the training at a later time). One of the groups going through training would receive a pretest, as would one of the groups not going through training. After training, all four groups would take the posttest.

This design includes all of the benefits listed for the pretest-posttest control-group design. In addition, by including the two groups that do not receive the pretest, it controls for any effects of pretesting. Furthermore, it yields greater generalizability by extending the results to groups who do not take the pretest.

The Solomon Four-Group Design suffers some of the same disadvantages as those of the pretest-posttest control-group design. However, the major disadvantage of this design involves its complexity. Although appropriate for laboratory studies, it may be extremely difficult to obtain four randomly assigned groups and measure them over time within an organization. In particular, it will be difficult to have two groups that are randomly selected not receive the intervention. Also, because the design takes place over time, some unequal attrition from the groups will likely occur and may destroy the assumptions of random selection. Finally, with four groups, it requires a lot of people, a lot of administration, and a lot of data collection.

Advantages of the Solomon Four-Group Design:

- Provides control for the effects of history, maturation, and pretesting
- Provides evidence over time
- Improves generalizability

Disadvantage of the Solomon Four-Group Design:

- May require more resources because of repeated data collection efforts
- May be expensive because of repeated data collection efforts
- Changes may be the results of repeated data collection
- May experience unequal attrition from the sample, resulting in four groups that are not comparable
- May be difficult or impossible to obtain two "control" groups that do not receive the intervention
- Requires a large sample

The Case Study Design

Case studies involve in-depth descriptive data collection and analysis of individuals, groups, systems, processes, or organizations. In particular, the case study design is most useful when you want to answer "how" and "why" questions, and when there is a need to understand the particulars, uniqueness, and diversity of the case (Stake, 1995; Yin, 1994). Case studies typically employ qualitative methods such as individual and focus group interviews, observation, and archival records, though they frequently include quantitative data from surveys or tests. Qualitative methods are emphasized since they are more effective in uncovering individuals' attitudes, beliefs, assumptions, values, practices, and experiences. For example, within the context of learning, performance, and change, we could better understand: a) how employees are using what they learned from a training event, b) why employee performance is at a certain level, c) the ways in which individuals learn from technology-based instruction, d) how the organization supports or inhibits individual, team, and organizational learning and change, or e) what effect reorganization had on a certain group of employees.

A case study design is particularly useful when the evaluator has little or no control over events, and when it is important to study organization members within their "natural setting" (the organization). The evaluator using a case study design does not seek to control or manipulate the environment or any of its variables. Instead, the evaluation focuses on "what is" and tries to explain or make sense of the phenomenon being evaluated according to those who experience it. In evaluating learning, performance, and change initiatives, the goal would be to construct a holistic understanding or gestalt of the organization members' context. To understand the various meanings associated with learning, performance, or change as a result of some intervention or initiative, case studies might use multiple methods and sources of data that are collected over time (this might be one day or several months). Case studies are most effective when the reader of the case vicariously experiences what it might have been like to "be there." Thus, case study designs are particularly appropriate and useful when:

- Context is of critical importance
- Understanding is the primary goal
- Multiple sources of evidence are sought
- The evaluation questions focus on the "how" and "why" of something
- Generalization of findings is not the primary goal

Tim's evaluation of the sales training program could have used the case study method instead of the one-time test. Such a study could have gathered in-depth background information on the trainees, followed by observations and interviews of trainees before, during, and after the training.

Advantages of the case study design:

- Provides descriptive data
- Does not require manipulation or control of individuals or the setting
- Reports include verbatim quotes of those interviewed
- Leads to greater understanding about the context of the evaluand
- May lead to greater understanding about practice
- Tends to gather data using multiple methods (triangulation)
- Provides data that are rich with examples and stories
- Captures what is important to participants
- Portrays the multiplicity of causes associated with various outcomes
- Embraces the diversity of perspectives and experiences of participants
- Allows the evaluator to collect information on outcomes not known or anticipated prior to the learning and performance initiative

Disadvantages of the case study design:

- Results do not lead to scientific generalizability
- Evaluator bias may interfere with validity of findings
- May take too long to conduct
- May produce more data than can be analyzed in a timely or cost-effective way

Once you have decided on the most appropriate evaluation design or designs, you need to describe these in your evaluation plan. Now you can focus on which methods will collect the necessary data.

....

Keep in Mind . . .

- If possible, evaluations should include designs that collect both quantitative and qualitative data.
- Evaluation team members should address issues related to both internal and external validity.
- The choice of one or more evaluation designs should reflect the evaluation's key questions.

Background and Context of Evaluation

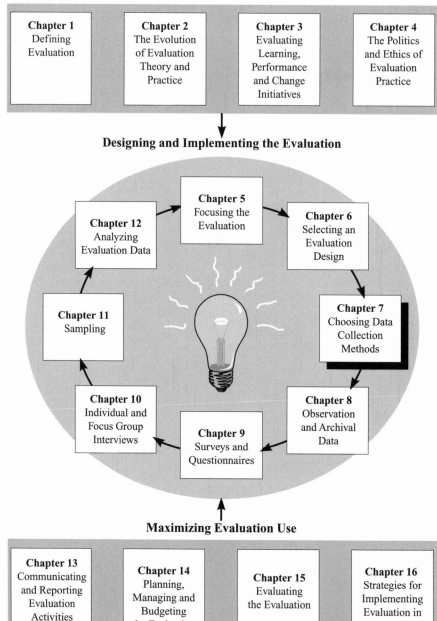

Chapter 1
Defining
Evaluation

Chapter 2
The Evolution
of Evaluation
Theory and
Practice

Chapter 3
Evaluating
Learning,
Performance
and Change
Initiatives

Chapter 4
The Politics
and Ethics of
Evaluation
Practice

Designing and Implementing the Evaluation

Chapter 12
Analyzing
Evaluation Data

Chapter 5
Focusing the
Evaluation

Chapter 6
Selecting an
Evaluation
Design

Chapter 11
Sampling

Chapter 7
Choosing Data
Collection
Methods

Chapter 10
Individual and
Focus Group
Interviews

Chapter 9
Surveys and
Questionnaires

Chapter 8
Observation
and Archival
Data

Maximizing Evaluation Use

Chapter 13
Communicating
and Reporting
Evaluation
Activities
and Findings

Chapter 14
Planning,
Managing and
Budgeting
the Evaluation

Chapter 15
Evaluating
the Evaluation

Chapter 16
Strategies for
Implementing
Evaluation in
Organizations

chapter 7

Choosing Data
Collection Methods

- Menu of Data Collection Methods
- Considerations for Choosing Data Collection Methods
- Using Multiple Data Collection Methods

• •

Vignette #4: Putting the Cart Before the Horse at MyElectronics, Inc.

Tom Winkle, an instructor at MyElectronics Inc., was asked by his manager to evaluate the success of the communications skills training program that had just been rolled out to the organization's service center employees. A couple of days before the workshop, Tom found a survey that had been used in previous training programs, changed a few items, and asked participants to complete the ten-item reaction survey at the end of the workshop.

• •

Tom decided upon a commonly used method for gathering training evaluation data—the ubiquitous postcourse survey. However, he jumped to choosing the data collection method without considering the evaluation's purpose, intended users, uses, and evaluation key questions as described in Chapter 5. In other words, he put the cart before the horse. As a result, it is unlikely that the information Tom collects will be of that much use since the survey questions were not specifically focused on what information was needed for decisionmaking and action. As Mark Twain once stated, "collecting data is like collecting garbage; you must

177

know in advance what you are going to do with the stuff before you collect it."

Unfortunately, selecting the data collection method too often comes as an automatic response to a request for evaluation without any consideration of the strengths, weaknesses, or appropriateness of individual methods. Therefore, in this chapter we describe several commonly used methods for gathering evaluation data and issues for you to consider before choosing any one or more methods. Detailed descriptions of each method can be found in Chapters 8, 9, and 10.

A Menu of Data Collection Methods

One consideration for choosing data collection methods is the degree of intrusiveness the evaluation can tolerate and the extent to which data already exist within the organization. Figure 7.1 classifies various data collection methods by their level of obtrusiveness (from least obtrusive to most intrusive), and describes their characteristics and several examples. This classification suggests, for example, that collecting readily available data from archival records (for example, documents and records) may be the most desirable from the standpoint of unobtrusiveness and immediate availability, particularly if the data are valid, reliable, and relevant. There are often times, however, when sufficiently specific, comprehensive, or valid data cannot be obtained through less obtrusive procedures, in which case surveys, observation, and interviews may be the most appropriate methods for collecting the needed data.

In selecting or developing data collection methods, it is also important to determine how much of the needed information has already been collected or is routinely being collected. In addition, you should decide whether some additional information could be easily gathered in some of the organization's routine data gathering efforts before pursuing other methods of data collection.

Archival Data

Although some evaluators tend to neglect existing data in favor of new data collection, we need to recognize several advantages to using preexisting archival records and documents (see Chapter 8). First, they are easy

FIGURE 7.1   Data Collection Methods Listed in Ascending Order of Obtrusiveness

Data Collection Method	General Characteristics	Examples
Currently available archival data (documents and records)	Nothing new is introduced into the data collection system. The evaluation is based entirely on existing data. These may be selected, combined, and analyzed in new ways.	Employment records Production records Safety records Monthly or quarterly reports
Modified archival data (Documents and records)	The current system must be expanded to provide additional data. The evaluation is based on data available from this expanded system.	Monthly or quarterly reports modified to record specific information, such as number of trainees in each course Technical assistance logs, modified to capture reasons for requesting assistance
Observation in natural settings	The evaluation is based on detailed descriptions of day-to-day behavior that cannot be provided by the existing archival records.	Checklist of meeting-leader behaviors completed by one of the team members Call monitoring form, completed by customer service Qualitative field notes
Observation of artificial or simulated situations	Special stimuli or situations are introduced, and a non-participant observer notes the respondent's reaction or behavior. An evaluation team member gathers the data.	Checklist of meeting leader behaviors performed in a role-play setting completed by the evaluator Checklist of supervisory behaviors performed in a role-play setting completed by the evaluator

(continues)

FIGURE 7.1　*(continued)*

Data Collection Method	General Characteristics	Examples
Surveys and Questionnaires	Special instruments are developed, and respondents complete these. The evaluation is based on data generated from these instruments.	End-of-the-course reaction forms Survey of participants, their managers, and their subordinates
Paper, pencil, or computer-based tests	Commercially produced or specifically developed tests are made to assess knowledge or skills. The evaluation is based on data generated from these exams.	Paper/pencil test at the end of a workshop On-line test thirty days after the end of the workshop Embedded tests in computer-based training modules
Individual and focus group interviews	Interview guides are developed and a skilled interviewer conducts the interview. The evaluation is based on data generated from this interaction.	In-person individual or focus group interviews of participants Telephone interviews of participants

and often cost-effective to use, since they already exist. Second, they can provide quantitative data that may address one or more of the key evaluation questions. Third, they may provide information on the historical context of the program, along with a chronology of events. Fourth, even though archival data may contain errors, they may be less susceptible to distortions and, therefore, be more credible.

To the extent that the needed information has already been collected or can routinely be collected, assembling archival data places fewer demands on evaluation team members. If such data are easily accessible from a central location, a substantial savings in data collection costs can result. On the other hand, attempting to access records held in many different locations may be more costly than using some other data collection procedures. And if the records were not well maintained, comprehensive, or accurate, it would be difficult to trust the accuracy of the data.

Archival data are also useful in longitudinal evaluations. An evaluation question that addresses trends or changes over time may benefit greatly from the collection of archival data. In some cases, the only possible way to address such issues is with existing records from earlier times.

Observation Data

Data collection by observation can range from routine counting of certain occurrences to writing narrative descriptions of what is being observed. More qualitative observations help evaluators understand the program's context and interactions among participants and artifacts of the program, in addition to some of its effects. To ensure that the data are collected consistently and accurately, however, observers must be well trained (see Chapter 8).

Observers can be internal organization members or external consultants. Internal members include program staff, managers, supervisors, and other employees. Since they possess knowledge of the organization and possibly the program, they can be extremely helpful in the data collection process. However, if they are unskilled in observation, can't be trained because of a lack of time or some other reason, or might not appear credible in this role, then external observers should be hired to conduct the observations. Clearly, this could affect the evaluation's overall budget.

Surveys and Questionnaires

There are times when you need to obtain new data from many people who may be in several locations, or you might need to collect quantitative data inexpensively from a large pool of individuals. In these cases, the use of a survey or questionnaire might be called for (see Chapter 9).

An advantage of using surveys and questionnaires is that they allow for easy tabulation of the data, particularly when the questions are closed-ended. However, they are probably the most difficult data collection method to develop well. It takes significant time to construct clearly worded items, and surveys and questionnaires should always be pilot-tested to ensure the resulting data's validity and usefulness. This method is commonly used in organizational research and evaluation. Unfortunately, there is a tremendous amount of unused survey data sitting in files, on desks, or in a corner in most organizations because of the haphazard way postcourse reaction surveys, in particular, have been designed.

Paper, Pencil, and Computer-Based Tests

When the evaluation questions seek information on how much was learned, or what was learned, the use of a test might be appropriate (see Chapter 9). Testing is commonplace in organizations that provide certification or licensure in various technical or safety areas. When testing learning from computer- or web-based training, it is a good idea to embed the necessary tests into the software rather than using a paper-and-pencil form of testing, since it is more consistent with the delivery method.

Although we are all familiar with tests, having experienced many as part of our own education, tests should be used cautiously. First, tests must be developed with strong measures of reliability and validity—that is, they must consistently and accurately measure what was taught. Second, being tested is often perceived as threatening, especially if the results will be used to make performance appraisal decisions. Third, you should check to make sure that your use of the test is legal and will not impinge on the rights of employees.

Individual and Focus Group Interviews

Interviews with individuals or groups, both in person and on the phone, are another means for collecting rich, qualitative information (see Chapter 10). Interviews enable the evaluator (or evaluation team) to interact directly with the respondents and may result in new insights about the program and provide examples, stories, and critical incidents that are helpful in understanding how the program affected individuals, groups, and the organization overall. Furthermore, with some populations, such as those who have difficulty reading, interviews may be the only feasible means of obtaining their opinions or understanding their experiences. At the same time, however, respondents may react to personal characteristics and perceived status of the interviewer, which could affect the data's validity.

Considerations for Choosing Data Collection Methods

Given the variety of data collection methods available, you must decide which ones are most appropriate for a specific evaluation study. In the next several sections, we identify things to consider that may influence your choice of methods.

Evaluation Key Questions

An important factor in selecting data collection methods is the evaluation's key questions. Certain evaluation questions may logically lead to a specific type of data collection method. For example, a key question may ask how much knowledge of a certain process participants retained from a training program. If the evaluation must measure knowledge retention, then an appropriate data collection method would involve some form of written, oral, or observational testing. Or an evaluation question might focus on determining the extent to which employees share their learning with each other. In this case, the most appropriate method might be individual or focus group interviews or qualitative observations. For each evaluation question, you should consider which data collection method or methods could best obtain the needed information. The following are two examples:

Question 1. To what extent do participants find the content from the program useful in performing their job?

- Archival records on program enrollments over time—This provides an unobtrusive but indirect indication of usefulness (with the assumption that people would not enroll if it were not useful). This may not prove useful if the program is mandatory or if external factors might be influencing enrollment (such as layoffs or acquisitions).
- Postprogram survey on usefulness—This provides a more obtrusive but direct indicator of perceived usefulness.
- Postprogram interviews on usefulness—This is also more obtrusive, but it provides direct information on perceived usefulness.

Question 2. To what extent do participants use the skills learned in the program on their jobs?

- Archival records on skill use—Records such as checklists or performance appraisal assessments could provide direct evidence of skill use. (Permission should always be sought in advance before reviewing performance appraisal records.)
- Observations of skills used on the job—Observations may provide direct evidence of skill use, and could be made by colleagues, a supervisor, or by an evaluator.
- Surveys or questionnaires on skill use—These may provide somewhat indirect evidence of skill use and can be administered to the learner, his or her supervisor, and his or her peers.
- Interviews on skill use—Interviews can provide indirect evidence of skill use, but they also allow the evaluator to identify factors affecting the extent to which the skills are being applied, and what obstacles might impede their use.

These examples show that several different data collection methods can potentially be used for each question. You must decide which methods are best suited for a particular evaluation study, given the design, the evaluation team skills, the population, and the organizational context.

Evaluator or Evaluation Team Skills

The skills of the evaluator or the evaluation team can also influence the choice of data collection methods. If the evaluator is skilled in survey design and implementation, this might be a good choice, especially if the evaluation questions can be addressed through this method. Conversely, if the evaluator or evaluation team does not have the skills to effectively use a particular method, such as facilitation skills for conducting focus group interviews, then that method should not be used without the involvement of someone who can provide the appropriate technical assistance. It should be noted that these decisions would likely affect the evaluation's budget.

Resources

The resources needed for a particular data collection method also need to be considered before deciding on a particular method. Resources include not only money but also personnel, equipment, and time. In general, archival methods particularly when the records are located in a central location, tend to require fewer financial resources than observation, surveying, or interviewing. Costs to retrieve and analyze such records do, however, escalate when the materials exist in several locations and in several different formats.

At the same time, archival data may not be available, or you may wish to use other methods to complement the records and documents to create a fuller picture of the program being evaluated. Thus, in choosing another data collection method, it's important to consider how much time, money, and expertise is needed to develop the data collection instruments for observations, interviews, surveys, and tests, and what resources are needed to implement each method. Oftentimes, a predetermined budget and a short time frame will directly influence which methods can be used for a particular evaluation study.

Stakeholders' Preferred Types of Data

The kind of data preferred by the evaluation's stakeholders is another important consideration for choosing data collection methods. For example, in an evaluation undertaken by one of the authors and conducted within an engineering firm, the technical audience demanded a rigorous experimental design and a statistical analysis of observations on employee work behaviors. They wanted to see the "numbers" to determine the success of the program. In another evaluation, the decision makers preferred learning about the program's effectiveness through reading the stories and experiences of program participants. It is often the case that certain stakeholders are looking for either quantitative or qualitative data to inform them of the program's success, effectiveness, value, or impact. Although we usually recommend using a mixed-method approach for most evaluations, one that provides both quantitative and qualitative data, it's important to know what kind of data stakeholders prefer and find credible.

These preferences should be discussed and determined in the focusing phase of the evaluation as described in Chapter 5.

Level of Acceptable Intrusiveness

As discussed earlier, the evaluators and stakeholders should consider how intrusive the data collection activities may be. In other words, methods such as individual and focus group interviews and surveys require that respondents stop what they're doing in the course of their work or lives to participate in the evaluation. In the majority of situations, this is not a problem. However, if you are trying to conduct focus group interviews with plant supervisors during their shift, you must consider what impact taking these employees away from their jobs will have. For example, are there others who can assume the supervisory role? If you wish to conduct a survey with a group of call center employees, might doing so create a shortage of employees available to answer customers' calls? Obviously, most managers would not find this to be acceptable. In circumstances such as these, you might want to consider using unobtrusive methods such as observation and archival data. Unobtrusive methods are those that can be used without disturbing the ongoing program activity or process being evaluated, and as such, produce less interference in the respondents' lives. Unobtrusive data are typically gathered without the person being aware that any information is being collected. For example, if we were studying employees' level of computer use, we could analyze records of use that have been collected and stored in the organization's database. We wouldn't be able to determine the context of their use, as we might through conducting interviews, but we could still gain some understanding on the frequency and duration of such use (see Chapter 8).

Validity

The validity of any measurement is one of the most important aspects of data collection. As described in Chapter 6, validity can apply to the evaluation design as well as the data collection method or instrument. When referring to the data collection method or instrument, validity reflects the extent to which the method or instrument accurately measures the concept or phenomenon being studied. When deciding on which of the various data collection methods to use, you should consider how well the method and instrument chosen will be able to gather both reliable and valid data.

There are three basic approaches to ensuring data collection or instrument validity. Content validity represents the extent to which an instrument represents the full range of concepts that are of interest. For example, in developing the Readiness for Organizational Learning and Evaluation (ROLE) survey (Appendix A), the instruments' authors examined the theoretical literature in evaluation and organizational learning, reviewed existing organizational learning–related instruments, and interviewed organization members who were involved in implementing learning organization efforts. From these sources, the authors developed a set of survey items that exemplified the concepts of organizational learning and evaluation. The authors also wanted to make certain that the instrument had face validity. (This can be considered one aspect of content validity and refers to the extent to which the instrument appears serious and relevant, and that on first impression it looks like it measures what it's intended to measure.)

The second type of validity is called criterion-related validity, which is comprised of two forms. Concurrent validity indicates the degree to which the data correctly measure some condition or criterion, whereas predictive validity indicates the degree to which the data correctly predicts some condition or criterion. In both cases, you are examining the correlation between the measurement and the criterion. One example of concurrent validity might be the administration of a newly developed test of intelligence and some traditional test of intelligence, such as the Stanford-Binet. A high correlation between those two tests would provide some indication that the newly developed test measures intelligence. An example of predictive validity would involve an examination of the correlation of the *Miller Analogies* or *Graduate Record Exam* taken prior to entry into graduate school with some later measure of graduate school success (such as course grades). If individuals who scored high on one of these tests also tended to get high grades in courses that they subsequently took, the test would be said to have high predictive validity for academic success in graduate school.

The third type, called construct validity, is most useful when external criteria are not available. It involves determining whether the instrument or measure behaves as expected according to the model or theory being used. In this case, the variable cannot be viewed as observable or concrete, but it must be viewed as some abstract concept. If we take the example above of an intelligence test, we know that the concept of "intelligence" is simply a concept or a construct. Thus, providing construct validity on a newly developed test of intelligence would require more than simply one correlation with one other test of intelligence. It would involve studies of how the concept of intelligence relates to other concepts, such as motivation and self-esteem.

Reliability

Reliability refers to the consistency of (a) the items within the instrument and (b) data collected using the instrument when those data are collected over time. It is a function of the amount of error in the measurement or an indication that changes in the instrument or data appear unrelated to the phenomenon being measured. Thus, reliability, as with validity, involves correlational analyses, and the correlation ranges from 0.00 (or completely unreliable) to 1.00 (or completely reliable). The instrument or the data can have high reliability but may fail to be valid. Yet to have validity, the instrument or the data must have high reliability.

You need to consider the level of reliability, or alternatively the level of error, in the data collection method being proposed. Errors occur from two primary sources. One source involves an inadequate sampling of the items used to measure a particular concept. If an inadequate sampling occurs, you will find a low level of agreement among different parts of the same instrument. A second source of error can come from situational factors. These situational factors can involve individual variation related to fatigue, mood, or motivation, variations in administrative procedures (such as noise levels), and errors in entering the data. If you want to determine the level of error from both sources of error, you might want to use Cronbach's alpha, which calculates internal-consistency reliability and is available in most statistical software.

Reliability coefficients resulting from a single administration of a test, such as Cronbach's alpha, measure only certain sources of error, however. In cases where respondents are asked to provide data several different times, their responses may vary in ways unrelated to the effects of the intervention. People may be tired, hungry, bored, or pressed for time. In such cases, you may want to calculate the test-retest or repeated measures reliability coefficient (which is simply a correlation between the two measures; see Chapter 12).

Availability of Data

When choosing among data collection methods, it is always a good idea to consider how available certain kinds of data are or will be. For example, if the organization has archival data that pertain to the evaluation's key questions and are accessible to the evaluation team, then you should consider collecting these data. On the other hand, if you want to conduct face-to-face individual interviews with certain people who tend to travel constantly, then this method might not be feasible. In this case, you might need to consider a phone interview or survey instead.

Even when you are able to interview participants or send them a survey, you must also consider how willing they will be to provide honest (valid) information. For example, because of the sensitive nature of certain topics, such as salary, views on the organization's culture or leadership, or issues around sexual harassment, obtaining this information may be difficult. Participants may choose not to respond to certain questions, or may provide false data because they fear the information will be shared with others in the organization. On occasion, if respondents know that organizational decisions may result from their responses, they may be more inclined to suppress their true opinions.

Timeliness

If the evaluation is to serve decisionmaking purposes within an organization, then the data collection process must provide timely information. Thus, it is important to consider the time required to implement certain methods.

One of the reasons for nonuse of evaluation information is that the data were obtained from some earlier data collection efforts by another department. Even though these data can provide useful insights, they may be considered obsolete (or not timely) by some stakeholders. Consequently, even though archival records may exist, decisionmakers might disregard the data because of who collected it and when it was collected.

Objectivity

The degree of objectivity required by stakeholders is another important consideration for choosing among data collection methods. Objectivity relates to the extent to which the data and their interpretation is unbiased or unprejudiced (meaning prejudged). The most objective data are typically tests and structured observations, gathered as part of experimental designs. In most forms of data collection, however, it is extremely difficult to eliminate all sources of bias. In fact, many evaluators (and researchers, for that matter) might argue that we can't divorce ourselves from our experiences, perspectives, or who we are. Therefore, we must understand where our own biases lie and develop ways to minimize the degree of subjectivity in our methods. If you wish to collect attitudinal information, for example, you would likely use a survey. But to ensure greater objectivity of the survey items, you would pilot-test the survey with a sample similar to the respondent population. The same would be true for conducting interviews. In addition, however, you would not only try out the interview guide, but you would pilot-test the interview process to ensure that you were not exhibiting behaviors that might influence the direction or way in which an interviewee responds.

Every form of data collection produces results that approximate the true value of whatever is being measured. At the same time, each data collection method introduces some unintended bias. Figure 7.2 presents various types of measurement bias, along with some examples and procedures to reduce the level of bias.

As shown in Figure 7.2, archival and observational methods can introduce such biases as "changes in record-keeping" or "measurement as change agent." On the other hand, interviews are susceptible to "interviewer effects." Rather than try to classify data collection methods by all

FIGURE 7.2   Types of Measurement Bias

Type of Measurement Bias	Description	Examples	Suggested Procedures
Change in record-keeping procedures	The instrument or record obtains different information at different times.	The definition of a safety violation changes over time, resulting in a higher level of violations.	Calibrate the instrument against a consistent standard.
Measurement itself causes a change	Data collection produces real changes in what is being measured.	Calls are completed more quickly because employees know that their phone time is monitored.	Make the observation unobtrusive or routine.
Guinea pig or Hawthorne effect	Awareness of being tested or observed causes person to act in a different manner than normal.	Person becomes more careful in their work.	Use archival methods or unobtrusive observation.
Response sets	Respondents tend to respond in a certain manner.	Participant marks "strongly agree" on every survey item.	Vary the format of the questionnaire.
Interviewer effects	Respondent reacts to characteristics of the interviewer.	Participants give different responses to male or female interviewers.	Use unobtrusive measures or vary the characteristics of interviewers and test for effects.
Nonresponse bias	Respondents differ from non-respondents in ways related to the variables being measured.	Those who are least satisfied with the organization's work environment are the most likely to respond to an organization culture survey.	Use techniques to increase response rate; interview a sample of nonrespondents and weight data to represent all nonrespondents.

the various kinds of measure biases, it seems best to consider these biases when choosing among different methods in a particular evaluation. At that time, you can determine whether a certain method can be used to overcome the potential bias or whether you need to use multiple methods and examine their convergence, as discussed below.

Degree of Desired Structure

The degree of structure in data collection methods refers to the extent to which the method controls the form of the data to be collected. An example of a highly structured format is a multiple-choice item on a questionnaire where the response option is "choose one." The item would be less structured if it allowed for an "other" response with space to provide a written explanation. Interviews are usually less structured than a survey and allow interviewees to openly discuss their responses—the types of possible responses are not prescribed or limited.

The most unstructured data collection method would involve recording all the available information without predetermining how it is produced. An example would be videotaping ongoing behavior on the job. Following the videotaping, a variety of observational methods could be employed to analyze the observed behaviors. In general, structured data collection requires more time to develop all of the response options, such as the design of a multiple-choice survey or questionnaire, before the data are collected. On the other hand, unstructured data collection requires less up-front time, but more time for the data's analysis.

Structured data collection is more common than unstructured, primarily because the data are more easily analyzed. A more structured approach also ensures that more of the information gathered is relevant to the purpose and the evaluation's key questions. However, there is always the possibility that the results are primarily an artifact of the structure. For example, slight rewordings of an item on a questionnaire and the inclusion or exclusion of certain response categories can produce seemingly contradictory results. Unstructured data collection permits a greater depth of information and is often more palatable to organizational staff, but it also tends to cost more to analyze and requires greater expertise for analysis and interpretation.

FIGURE 7.3   Questions to Consider When Choosing Data Collection Methods

- ☐ Have you considered which methods are best suited for each key question?
- ☐ What skills does the evaluation team have for collecting certain kinds of data?
- ☐ What resources are available to collect the evaluation data (in terms of time, money, and personnel)?
- ☐ What kinds of data or methods do stakeholders prefer—find credible?
- ☐ What level of intrusiveness will the organization tolerate for the evaluation?
- ☐ How will you ensure the content and face validity of the instruments you use?
- ☐ How will you ensure the reliability of the instruments you use?
- ☐ How available and accessible are data sources?
- ☐ What is the time frame for the evaluation and which methods can be implemented successfully within this time frame?
- ☐ What are the requirements for "objectivity"? How can you ensure a certain level of objectivity?
- ☐ How structured should your methods be? Which methods lend themselves to the required level of structure?

Checklist for Choosing Appropriate Methods

To help you choose which methods will be best suited for an evaluation, you might want to use the checklist provided in Figure 7.3. It will raise questions for you to think about as you look at your evaluation key questions, the information needs of your stakeholders, and the kind of data needed to make decisions about the program being evaluated.

Using Multiple Data Collection Methods

The chapter has so far described various data collection methods and some considerations for selecting among those methods. This last section ends with a suggestion that you consider the use of multiple methods when undertaking an evaluation.

As mentioned in the previous section, each data collection method provides certain kinds of information and introduces certain kinds of biases. If the evaluation collects data using only one method, the results will introduce similar kinds of bias (for example, conducting ten individual interviews). In such a case, it will not be possible to determine the extent to which the method is producing biased information. If, however, several different methods are used, the overall results are not likely to be distorted by a single consistent source of bias. For example, individual and focus group interviews introduce similar kinds of bias because they are similar forms of data collection. The results are likely to be influenced by characteristics of the interviewer and by the respondents' desire to accommodate the evaluator and appear cooperative. Archival indicators and observations, on the other hand, have different sources of bias, as do surveys and questionnaires. Using methods that have different inherent sources of bias guards against apparently consistent but actually inaccurate findings. Whenever the results from several different data collection methods agree with each other (a form of triangulation as described in Chapter 6), you can be more certain that the results are not an artifact of the data collection method but rather represent a truer indication of the program being evaluated.

The use of multiple methods and convergent evidence increases the validity, the reliability, and the precision of the information gathered. All of this leads to an increase in the replicability of the evaluation results, even if different data collection methods are employed. On the other hand, the use of multiple methods and convergent evidence increases the resources needed for data collection. Thus, you will need to determine whether the information needs and the resulting decisions require a high level of confidence provided by using multiple methods. (See Greene and Caracelli, 1997, for more information on mixed-method evaluation.)

....

Keep in Mind . . .

- Although it is tempting to automatically assume a survey will do the job, stop and consider whether additional or other data collection methods might best address the evaluation's key questions.

- There are many factors to consider when choosing a data collection method. These factors may affect the usefulness the evaluation's results (see Figure 7.3 for a checklist of questions to consider).

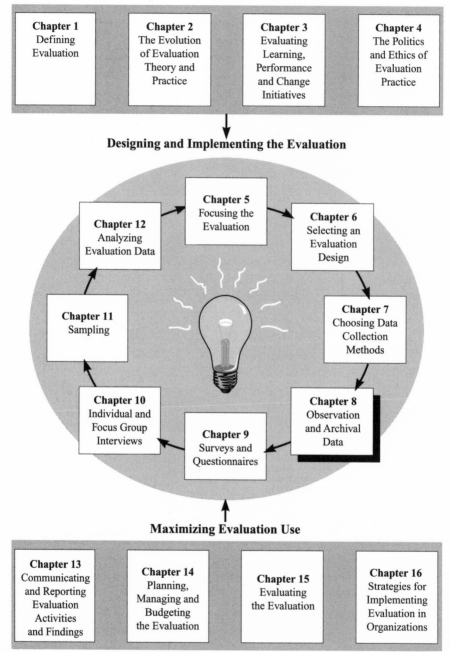

Background and Context of Evaluation

| **Chapter 1**
Defining
Evaluation | **Chapter 2**
The Evolution
of Evaluation
Theory and
Practice | **Chapter 3**
Evaluating
Learning,
Performance
and Change
Initiatives | **Chapter 4**
The Politics
and Ethics of
Evaluation
Practice |

Designing and Implementing the Evaluation

Chapter 5
Focusing the
Evaluation

Chapter 6
Selecting an
Evaluation
Design

Chapter 12
Analyzing
Evaluation Data

Chapter 7
Choosing Data
Collection
Methods

Chapter 11
Sampling

Chapter 10
Individual and
Focus Group
Interviews

Chapter 9
Surveys and
Questionnaires

Chapter 8
Observation
and Archival
Data

Maximizing Evaluation Use

| **Chapter 13**
Communicating
and Reporting
Evaluation
Activities
and Findings | **Chapter 14**
Planning,
Managing and
Budgeting
the Evaluation | **Chapter 15**
Evaluating
the Evaluation | **Chapter 16**
Strategies for
Implementing
Evaluation in
Organizations |

Observation and Archival Data

- Using Methods of Observation
- Observer Roles
- Collecting and Recording Observation Data
- Conducting Observations
- Advantages and Disadvantages of Collecting Observation Data
- Collecting Archival Data—Records and Documents
- Advantages and Disadvantages of Collecting Archival Data

••

Vignette# 5: Evaluating Team Development at MyFountain Hills Healthcare

About six months ago, MyFountain Hills Healthcare reorganized itself into six divisions and nine operating units. Self-directed work teams were implemented throughout the organization to more effectively meet the increasing demands of the vendors, staff, and patients, and to maximize employees' learning from one another. The 200 employees who make up the nine operating units received two weeks of intense team training by an outside consulting organization. The organization's leadership knew that for the new structure to work, everyone had to be able to work in a team-based structure. Since MyFountain Hills was investing a large sum of money in the team-training program, they also knew how important it would be to evaluate the training's impact on employees' ability to work as team members. Given the fact that all employees were involved in this initiative, an outside evaluation consultant was hired. It was agreed that the evaluator would conduct multiple observations of team meetings over a period of two months. During these observations she would focus on 1) the extent to which team members were using the facilitation skills learned in training, 2) the processes used to resolve conflict, 3) the atmosphere and collegiality of the team, 4) how meetings were planned and managed, and 5) the extent to which the team was accomplishing its goals. She would take notes during the meetings and transcribe them shortly thereafter.

....

As the above vignette illustrates, observation can be a useful method for addressing evaluation questions concerning an employee's or group's behavior or actions before, during, or after a training program or other organization initiative. Observing people and environments is particularly helpful in studying processes, relationships among people, and the context of certain events. Although a survey might elicit trainee or employee perceptions of their own or others' behavior, these opinions or perceptions might not always be completely accurate, since it is often difficult to recall past events. And when conducting interviews, participants may not always be comfortable sharing their knowledge or opinions. They might hesitate if they are concerned about the repercussions of their comments, if their responses may not be "politically correct," or if their response might appear insensitive or impolite. Evaluating learning, performance, and change efforts through observation

> Enables one to discover the interrelationships between elements of the whole, such as the interaction between instructors and trainees, the impact of training experiences on other related experiences, the influence of peer culture among those being trained, and the implicit messages which the organization gives about itself in the training process. (Light, 1979, p. 552)

When an evaluation seeks information on how someone is being affected by some learning, performance, or change intervention, observation methods of data collection can be a good choice. Although we certainly engage in forms of observation daily, we will specifically focus this chapter on methods of systematic observation. By "systematic," we mean a process that is planned and purposeful and could be replicated by others if desired. This chapter will address when and how to use observation and archival data collection methods, and advantages and disadvantages of observation and archival data collection methods.

Using Methods of Observation

In the context of evaluating learning, performance, and change within organizations, observation methods of data collection are particularly helpful in evaluating employees' current competency or proficiency level, training participants' transfer of knowledge and skills, and the implementation of an organizational change initiative. For example, observation can help:

- *Understand a learner or group's level of performance before the learning intervention, specifically:*
  1. The extent to which the learner is able to perform specific tasks prior to training
  2. The context of the learner's work environment

- *Understand how and when participants are transferring their learning, specifically:*
  1. How much of the learning participants are applying to their work
  2. Content areas in which participants experience difficulty in applying their new skills and knowledge
  3. Obstacles that impede participants' ability to transfer their learning
  4. The extent to which managers and supervisors are supporting the learning, performance, or change intervention
  5. The ways in which managers and supervisors are supporting the transfer of learning

- *Understand how well an organizational change initiative is being implemented, specifically:*
  1. The extent to which the program is on schedule
  2. The extent to which the employees are actively engaged in the initiative

3. How well the program is being facilitated

4. The ways in which upper management is supporting the initiative

To conduct these observations, we could observe employees in the normal course of their work and document their activities and interactions. Observations are usually made during the typical workday, with little to no manipulation of the environment.

There are times, however, when you might wish to observe an individual in a simulated condition. Simulated activities developed specifically for evaluation purposes are best suited to situations where the behaviors being evaluated are not easily observable. For example, it is difficult to observe the effects of leadership development or sales training since the observer would have to shadow the participants over a period of hours, days, or weeks to get sufficient insights into their use of the knowledge and skills from the training program. Another example of where simulations are useful is in the area of technological system evaluations. To determine how easy it is to navigate a web site or determine how much time it takes trainees to complete a computer-based learning module, evaluators are establishing special environments in which they can observe such behaviors. Observations of simulations can occur during or immediately after the learning, performance, or change intervention. They can be designed as role plays that are videotaped, assessment centers, or usability labs.

The power of using observation methods is that it engages all of our senses, not just our sight. It enables us to take in and make sense of the entire experience through our noses (smell), eyes (sight), ears (hearing), mouth (taste), and body (touch). Unlike other data collection methods, observation data can provide us with a more holistic understanding of the phenomenon we're studying.

Observer Roles

How visible and intrusive one is when conducting an observation varies with the purpose of the observation and the evaluator's relationship to the program being evaluated. There may be times when it is prudent and effective to be a nonparticipant in the program being observed. In this case, you as the observer would have no involvement in the activities of the program being observed. Yet for some evaluations, being a partial or full participant observer is appropriate and most useful. The three most common types of observer roles are full participant observer, partial observer, and onlooker or outsider (Patton, 1987).

Full Participant Observer

Being a full participant observer is often required when observing a program in which you are currently, or have been, heavily involved. For example, if you were responsible for the company's new mentoring program that is now being evaluated, it would be impossible for you to be a nonparticipant observer. Therefore, while you are in meetings and performing other tasks related to the program being evaluated, you might also be conducting an observation. This is the most difficult role to assume since it requires that you step back from participating at certain times in order to document your observations. You might also assume this role when there are so few participants in the activity that not joining in might seem out of place or inappropriate.

Partial Observer

A variation on complete participation is observer as participant. Here you are clearly an observer, but are willing to become involved if invited or if it seems like the right thing to do. For example, one of the authors was evaluating an innovative science education program in various schools around the country. During one of her site visits, she was invited to sit among the students and several times was asked her opinion on the topic being discussed. Although her purpose was not to share her knowledge, she willingly became a part of the class since she was invited to do so and didn't think her participation would negatively affect the quality of the observation data she was collecting. She believed that staying in the back of the classroom, aloof and separate, would have created more curiosity and distraction than was warranted.

It is important to note that where you are situated during the observation often influences the likelihood that you might become a participant. Even though the evaluator sought out a seat in the back of the classroom when she first entered the room, she quickly learned that the students had designated a seat for her in the middle of the room before her arrival. She interpreted this gesture as an indicator that the students were expecting her to be at least partially involved with the class.

Nonparticipant Observer

A nonparticipant observer is just that—one who does not participate at all, but observes as an onlooker or outsider. You might choose this role when it is clear that you have no function in the process or program, or when your involvement would be an impediment or interference that could alter the interactions among participants. Nonparticipant observations are most successful when those being observed are used to being observed, such as in public schools, government and community meetings, or in certain kinds of businesses. For example, Intel, the computer chip manufacturer, routinely provides guided tours of their plants. Employees are used to visitors peering through glass enclosures as they do their work and are unlikely to alter their behavior even though they're being observed.

What to Disclose

Related to each of these roles are decisions regarding what you tell others about the observation and your purpose. Before conducting an observation, you will need to decide how you are portrayed as the observer and what you tell others about the observation as well as the overall evaluation. In portraying your role to program staff and participants, you can let program staff and participants know what is being observed and who the observer is. For example, during an evaluation that one of the authors conducted of an at-risk youth training program, both the program's staff and program participants were told the purpose of the on-site observations and what was being observed (principally, their behavior and the site's artifacts). During several observations, participants asked the evaluators questions about the evaluation. With a commitment to full disclosure, the evaluators answered all their questions truthfully and completely to the best of their ability.

When full disclosure is deemed unwise, you may choose to tell some program staff and participants about the observation, but not all. If you think that individuals' behavior would be affected by their knowing about being observed, then you might not wish to fully disclose your role as an observer or about the observation to some organization members. For example, imagine an evaluation is being conducted on how well customer service employees are using the knowledge and skills provided in a recently delivered on-line training module. The evaluator, training manager, and customer service manager are aware of the evaluator's plan to collect observation data by listening in on customer service calls. However, the customer service employees are unaware of when the evaluator is listening to their phone conversations with customers. Thus, they are unaware of the observations being made of them at the time. Since managers have done this for personnel evaluations and it's considered accepted practice, it is not generally considered a violation of privacy.

Regarding what to tell others about the purpose of the observation, you can 1) provide a full explanation of the real purpose to everyone, 2) provide partial explanations, or 3) provide covert explanations where no one is given any information. It is important that you carefully consider each of these options and their implications before conducting the observations to avoid any misunderstanding of your role and the purpose of the observation or the evaluation.

Collecting and Recording Observation Data

There are several choices to be made when considering how to collect and record observation data. Where qualitative data are required, the evaluator simply writes down detailed information in the form of a narrative, as she or he is observing. This is sometimes called qualitative observation. This method has been used extensively in case study designs and provides rich contextual information about the activities, setting, and interactions of those being observed. The data recording form would likely have spaces for the observer's name, the name of the person or group being observed, and the date, time, and location of the observation. The rest of the document recording form would be blank, leaving room for the evaluator to note observations about the room layout, interactions among participants and the facilitator, and other aspects of the environment. If the evaluator in the vignette presented at the beginning of this chapter

FIGURE 8.1   Sample Qualitative Observation Recording Form

Self-Directed Team Evaluation

Date of Observation_____ Time of Observation_____

Name of Observer _____ Location of Observation _____

Describe the following:
  Who is talking
  The subject of conversation
  Nonverbal behaviors
  Timing of events/discussions
  Location of team members around the table
  Who comes and goes
  How the agenda is followed
  How the meeting is facilitated—by whom and what processes
  What actions are agreed to and by whom
  General atmosphere of meeting
  Other

---

were to employ this approach, she might use the observation recording form in Figure 8.1.

It is important to remember that the more information is noted from the observation, the more useful the data are likely to be. If the notes are vague and general, it will be hard to interpret or make sense of what was observed later during the data analysis phase. Figure 8.2 illustrates notes that are detailed and concrete versus too general.

Although not all observations have to be quite as detailed as depicted in the exhibit, it is important to remember that observers should not interpret or judge what is being observed—the purpose of qualitative observations is to *describe*. Such interpretations are left to the data analysis phase of the evaluation. It is a good idea, however, to document personal thoughts regarding the observation on another sheet of paper or in italics or caps so that it is easily distinguishable from the descriptive observations.

Videotaping someone's performance is another useful method for collecting observation data. Here, the evaluator positions a video camera to

FIGURE 8.2   Taking Notes During an Observation

Example of Effective Note Taking

The vice-president of marketing burst through the doorway and told everyone within hearing distance that "the new product was finally launched." He went around to each employee showing the brochure and the list of preorders. As he went to each person he shook their hands and told them how they contributed to making the launch a success. He then invited everyone out for dinner next Saturday to celebrate. Nearly every person started applauding and whistling. A group of three employees yelled, "We've done it!" Two others smiled, shook their heads, and went back into their offices. The six remaining employees talked with one another for four minutes and then returned to their desks. Ten minutes later, one employee posted a sign that read, "We're #1!"

Example of Incomplete Note Taking

The vice-president of marketing came in and told everyone the product had been launched. After a brief speech, everyone went back to work.

---

record the individual's actions. The major advantage of this approach is that every detail can be captured and later reviewed. Such taping allows for a more thoughtful and detailed analysis of the person's performance. However, this approach may be perceived as more threatening to the person being taped if the intended use of the tape is not made perfectly clear in the beginning. Using video might also enhance the individual's nervousness about being taped, thus altering his or her performance. In this case, the data recorded would not be valid; the person's performance would not be indicative of her usual behavior. Before videotaping anyone, however, it is critical that the evaluator seek permission to videotape from the individuals, the organization, or both.

The use of still photographs is another way to capture observation data. The evaluator may decide to take photographs of the organization's environment, the employees' workspace, employees performing some task, or interactions between and among employees. Although this method does not provide as much detail as videotaping and it can't provide information on noise levels or auditory responses, it is fairly easy and cost-effective. One should be cautious, however, in interpreting photographs. It is important to remember that the photograph is merely an image captured at one point in time and may not be representative of the entire work environment or employees' performance. (See Torres, Preskill, and Piontek, 1996, for a longer discussion on how to use photographic methods in evaluation.)

A method that is more structured and typically provides quantitative data takes the form of a checklist or rating form. In this case, the evaluator develops a list of questions or items that will guide the observation. For example, you could use a checklist of skills the employee is expected to perform after training. Considering the case presented in the vignette again, the evaluator could have used a quantitative observation recording form such as the one in Figure 8.3.

At the same time the employee is performing the related tasks, the observer would indicate whether the individual is using the skill, or perhaps rate the individual on the level of competency being exhibited for each skill (using a Likert scale of 1 to 5, for example). Although this method cannot collect detailed information as to the "why's or how's" of a person's performance, an observation recording form might also include space for writing comments (as in Figure 8.3) that would provide additional information for helping interpret the numerical rating.

An approach that is gaining popularity is audio observing. If you've ever called an organization's technical assistance call center or customer service center, you might have heard a recording that says, "For the purposes of quality control, your call may be monitored." This technique allows the evaluator to randomly sample various phone calls to observe the ways in which the calls are handled. The observer might use a checklist or other rating form to document the extent to which the employee used certain skills or processes (see Figure 8.4).

Observing physical traces of behavior is another observation technique that has been widely used by anthropologists and sociologists over the years. Called unobtrusive measures, "physical traces are generally very indirect indicators of psychological and social processes" (Bouchard, 1976, p. 270; Webb, Campbell, Schwartz, and Sechrest, 1966, 1999). Such traces are referred to either as erosion or accretion measures, and are a result of some human activity that either accumulates (accretion) or is depleted (erosion).

FIGURE 8.3   Sample Observation Checklist

Self-Directed Team Evaluation

Name of Observer _____   Date of Observation _____

Team Being Observed _____

Location of Observation _____Time _____

Things to Observe	Comments
☒ The meeting has an agenda.	
☒ The meeting's facilitator is clearly identified.	
☒ The facilitator guides the conversation so each person is heard.	
☒ When problems arise, team members help each other resolve it.	
☒ Team members show respect for one another.	
☒ Team members stay focused on the task.	
☒ When conflict arises, there is a process for mediating it.	
☒ The team seems to understand its mission.	
☒ Team members appear willing to state their opinions.	
☒ Decisions are made collectively.	
☒ Team members appear to listen to each other.	
☒ Team members review the progress they've made.	
☒ The team works on improving their processes as well as completing tasks.	
☒ Team members appear to appreciate the input of each other.	

FIGURE 8.4   Example of Call Monitoring Observation Form

Person Evaluated_____Evaluator_____Date_____

Behaviors	Excellent	Adequate	Ineffective	N/A	
Open					
1. Create a positive impression in **greeting** the customer					*Comments:*
2. Express **interest** and **willingness** to help					
Other behaviors or actions (specify)					
Learn					
3. Respectfully **ask open questions** to understand thoroughly					*Comments:*
4. Respectfully **ask closed questions** to understand thoroughly					
5. **Encourage customer** to talk					
6. **Listen** nondefensively; attend to cues					
7. **Review relevant data** from customer's past experience					
8. **Paraphrase** or recap; demonstrate understanding					
Other behaviors or actions (specify)					
Respond					
9. **Ease tension**; empathize; acknowledge; assure; show respect					*Comments:*
10. **Compensate** for **communication difficulties** (language differences, technical jargon, etc.)					
11. **Share relevant information** or suggestions in **plain terms**					
12. **Focus on what can be done**; deal gracefully with unfulfillable requests					
13. **Act quickly** to **improvise, improve or impress**					
14. Maintain **focus** or gently **refocus** the conversation					
Other behaviors or actions (specify)					
Close					
15. **Recap;** review					*Comments:*
16. Leave **positive impression**; offer goodwill gesture, if appropriate					
17. **Thank** the customer					
Other behaviors or actions (specify)					

Examples of accretion measures include:

- Litter on the road (to determine effectiveness of antilitter campaign)
- Files and books stacked on someone's desk (to determine interests)
- Dust on library books (to determine recency and amount of usage)
- Inventories (to determine level of sales)
- Pages still glued together in a book or manual (to determine degree of usage)
- Bumper stickers on cars (to determine current social culture)
- Fingerprints or food stains on various documents (to determine usage)
- Notes made on handouts, in manuals (to determine level of engagement and interest in material)
- Nose prints on museum exhibits (to determine age and rate of visitors)
- Recycling bins on pick-up day (to determine a community's commitment to recycling)

Erosion measures, on the other hand, provide evidence of the wearing away or wearing down of something. Examples include:

- Broken windows, doors in school buildings (to determine community pride in school and students' morale)
- Worn spots in carpet or other kinds of flooring (to determine traffic patterns, rooms most used)
- Pages missing in a training manual or book (to determine use and interest)
- Materials requested or taken by employees (for example, brochures, catalogs, schedules) (to determine interest in subject matter)
- Worn computer keys (to indicate amount of computer use)
- Missing or stolen office supplies (to determine degree of loyalty toward organization)
- Wear and tear on transfer/job aids and training manuals (to determine degree of use)

- Broken equipment (to determine degree of usage or quality)

Although unobtrusive measures can provide interesting data that are often useful to evaluation studies, one must be very cautious not to over-interpret their meaning. Given the multiple interpretations one may make from these kinds of data, this method is best used in conjunction with other data gathering techniques.

Conducting Observations

The major benefit of collecting qualitative observation data is that it can provide a rich description of the program's environment, context, and participants. The observer can draw pictures of the setting that might include the room arrangement and interactions of those being observed. Narrative data can describe the activities that took place, who participated, the meanings of the activities, and the level of participants' engagement in the program's activities (see Figure 8.1). By listening to participants, the observer can note patterns in language usage, and by watching, the observer can note nonverbal behaviors. Just as important as being attuned to what is happening in the setting is to take special note of *what is not happening* that might have been expected. For example, in the beginning vignette, it was expected that team members would conclude each meeting with a check-in process where each member would reflect on their own experience with the meeting and its accomplishments. However, because the meeting ran late, the team leader skipped this—thus, the evaluator was unable to observe this particular activity.

Before collecting observation data of any type, evaluators should seriously consider the focus of the observation. In some cases, the observer might wish to concentrate on a single element of the program, such as the trainer's delivery style. In other cases, the observer might take a broader view and wish to take in the entire program as it is occurring. In an evaluation one of the authors conducted of a three-year educational reform effort, her first-year observations focused on many of the school's activities and teacher-student interactions. She took a holistic approach since there was so much to consider in the school's first few months. By the second year, however, as the school was stabilizing its procedures and policies, the teachers asked her to pay specific attention to how students were selecting their cooperative group members for various activities. They had made some informal observations and wanted the evaluator to make more systematic, formal, and longer-term observations to confirm *what* they thought was happening as well as to better understand *how* it was happening. Thus, for a period of three months, the evaluator focused her observations on this single element of the school's functioning.

Length and Number of Observations

The choice of determining how long or how many observations should be conducted is largely based on:

- What other data collection methods are being used to complement the observation data.
- The depth of information required from the observation. If the observation were the primary data collection method, one would expect to make several, possibly long-term observations so that sufficient data could be collected to make valid inferences about the program being evaluated. On the other hand, if individual interviews and surveys were being conducted in addition to the observations, fewer observations might be needed.

When planning to collect observation data, three choices need to be made:

1. How long the observation should last
2. How many observations should be made
3. How many observers should be used

When observing performance, for example, it might be necessary to make multiple observations over a period of time, at different times of the day, to ensure that what is being observed truly represents the employee's typical performance. To carry out these observations in an efficient and timely way, the evaluator might invite and train other organization members to conduct observations. The decision of how long to observe should be based on the frequency of the behavior to be observed, the complexity of what is being observed, and the context within which the observation is being made.

There is no magic formula for determining how many observations are necessary to come to a valid conclusion about a person or group's performance. However, it is true that the more observations you make, the more certain you can be that what you have observed is truly indicative of the individual's or group's behavior. The decision concerning how many observations to make is largely dependent on the budget for the evaluation and the time frame for completing the evaluation. On the plus side, using multiple observers can decrease the length of time required to conduct observations and can decrease the likelihood of a sole observer's bias. On the downside, the validity of the data may be compromised if the observers are not well trained. If one person conducts all of the observations, this will likely add days, weeks, or months to the evaluation time line. As with all methods, there are tradeoffs with the choices we make.

Location of Observations

As stated earlier, most observations are made in the natural work setting. An important consideration, however, is to make sure that you are observing the employee's actions in more than one location if that behavior is likely to occur in more than one place. For example, if you were trying to determine the extent to which an employee is using a particular software program correctly, you would merely observe the individual while she was at the computer doing her work. On the other hand, if you are attempting to gauge how well a supervisor is using her newly learned coaching skills, you would want to observe her in more than one location with more than one person to obtain a large enough sample of behaviors to develop a valid conclusion about the degree to which the skills are being used. Before collecting observation data, you should consider where the observations might take place and the level of intrusiveness the observation may require.

Timing of Observations

When to observe an individual's or group's behavior should also be carefully considered. We know that human behavior often varies with the time of day, emotional and physical state, and location. To ensure that the observation is representative of an individual's or group's performance, it is wise to conduct the observations at different times of the day or week. Doing so can increase the likelihood that what you observe is an accurate depiction of the knowledge, skills, or behaviors being observed. Alternatively, there may be times when you would want to observe different times of the day and different work shifts at the same location, over a period of days.

Ethics of Observation

Observation often evokes images of Big Brother watching over us, waiting to catch us in something we're not supposed to be doing. The observer must carefully consider how she would feel if the she were the one being observed. It is always best to step back and reexamine the extent to which observation is the best method for answering the evaluation question(s). If observation is indeed called for, it is important to protect the rights of the people being observed and that all necessary approvals be obtained before conducting any observations. For example, one of the authors wanted to observe employees who worked assembling computer boards in a large manufacturing company. To do so required obtaining permission from the plant manager and the human resources manager.

Training Observers

The quality of observation data rests largely on the ability of the evaluator to accurately note and describe or depict what is being observed. Reliability and validity issues are just as important for observation data as for any other kind of data. Thus, when several people are conducting the observations, be they employees or consultant evaluators, it is important that they be well trained on when, where, and how to conduct the observations. This can be accomplished by explaining the purpose and process of the observations and the evaluation overall, and then having observers role-play scenarios whereby they practice their observation skills and note-taking or rating skills. This process can be further enhanced by videotaping the role plays and having the observers critique themselves and their peers by using a review form or checksheet, and then debriefing what went well, what needs to be improved or changed, and what might have been misunderstood.

Advantages and Disadvantages of Collecting Observation Data

All data collection methods have inherent strengths and weaknesses; no one method is perfect. The processes for choosing data collection methods takes into account the advantages and disadvantages of each. The following are some things to consider when deciding whether to collect observation data.

Advantages

- Easily collectable—As long as access is provided to the observation site, the data are fairly easy to collect. Because there is no need to ask participants to do anything out of the ordinary, the logistics require less intrusiveness and effort than setting up focus group or individual interviews, for example.
- Allows for patterns and theories to develop—As multiple observations are conducted at various times and locations, the evaluator is able to detect certain patterns of behavior across participants. Observation provides an opportunity for the evaluator to discover what is really happening in the organization versus what someone thinks is happening. It provides another lens for looking at current realities.
- Highlights discrepancies between fact and fiction—Conducting observations provides the evaluator an opportunity to see firsthand what is happening with employees in their work environment by comparing description against fact and noting any discrepancies and systematic distortions. It also increases the ability of the evaluator to learn about things participants or staff may be unwilling to talk about in an interview.
- Increases understanding about the program's context—When in the work setting, the observer is able to note other variables that may affect the employee's performance that would not be known through an interview or test.
- Enables evaluators to see things that may routinely escape the consciousness of participants—Sometimes we are so close to what we are doing that we don't see the nuances in our work or

the work of others. Observation can make us aware of things we can't or haven't articulated.

- Complements other data collection methods—When used with other methods, observation data adds rigor to the overall evaluation and contributes to developing a holistic picture of the program or process that is being evaluated.

Disadvantages

- Threats to validity—Observation relies on the evaluator/observer to be "objective" in spite of one's own values and beliefs. It is possible that an evaluator's bias can interfere with the observation and influence the type and quality of information documented. However, using observation in conjunction with other data collection methods and using multiple observers can help minimize this potential threat to the data's validity. Searching for negative cases is another technique to minimize the observer's biases. Another threat is the reactivity of those being observed who might modify their behavior, resulting in a false representation of their knowledge or skills. Conducting multiple observations over time tends to minimize this threat as those being observed tend to get used to the observer's presence. In addition, using obtrusive measures might also be useful when reactivity is an issue.

- Threats to reliability—When using only one observer and making only one observation, the data may simply be the result of that specific observer or that specific situation. By conducting observations at different times and under varying conditions, this potential problem can be minimized. In addition, using multiple observers increases the reliability of the observations.

- Training of observers—When more than one evaluator is enlisted to conduct observations, training on how to perform the observations is essential. Observers need to be trained on what and how to observe, how to document the observations, and what role they are to play during the observation. Though this isn't a disadvantage of observation per se, the implications of people not being trained is. If observers fail to implement the observations according to a specified systematic process, the resulting data's validity may be seriously affected.

- Cost of collecting observation data—Conducting observations can be costly and time-consuming. To uncover trends in performance, for example, you might have to observe employees more than once and over some period of time. If you were to do this for more than twenty individuals, the cost might become prohibitive, depending on the resources available for the evaluation.

Observation data can provide important data for answering specific evaluation questions for many kinds of evaluations. Should you decide to conduct observations the guidelines in Figure 8.5 might be helpful.

Collecting Archival Data—Records and Documents

••

Vignette #6: Documenting Safety Training at MyNuclear Facility

James Lee, a safety coordinator, has been working in the area of nuclear safety for one of the Department of Energy's laboratories. There has been an increasing concern that employees are not following the regulated procedures for minimizing their exposure to lead during the course of their work. As a result, a Lead Exposure Control Training Program was developed and implemented with employees from two of the most vulnerable departments. In addition to conducting a survey and individual interviews, James plans to review certain records and documents before and after the training program, to determine if workers are implementing the correct procedures they learned in the training program. He develops and uses the form in Figure 8.6.

••

Additional evaluation data may come from the various records and documents that exist in an organization. These materials often provide information about dates, locations, topics of meetings, policies, procedures, frequencies, history, perceptions, and costs associated with what is being evaluated.

Before using any of the following records and documents, you should make sure to obtain any necessary approvals. It is possible that some of

FIGURE 8.5   Guidelines for Collecting Observation Data

✔ Determine what behaviors will be observed.

✔ Determine what aspects of the environment will be observed.

✔ Determine how many observations should be made.

✔ Determine the length of each observation.

✔ Determine the location of the observation.

✔ Prepare the observation recording forms.

✔ Seek all necessary permissions to conduct the observations.

✔ Train the observers.

✔ Consider how much to tell those being observed in advance, what the observer will be doing.

✔ Conduct observations.

✔ Analyze the data.

✔ Integrate with other evaluation data.

---

these materials will be considered private or confidential. It is always best to determine this *before* beginning the data collection process. It could turn out that the records you want to review are off limits, thus requiring reassessment of how you will collect certain information.

Records and documents could be those developed before, during, or after the learning, performance, and change intervention. For example, as part of the evaluation design phase, the evaluator might review an organization's newsletters, program materials, previous evaluation reports, sales figures, or other relevant records and documents to understand the program's context and history. This information could help the evaluation team determine the evaluation's rationale, key questions, stakeholders, evaluation design, and data collection methods.

During an organizational change initiative, employees might develop a document that describes how they view the organization at that point in time. For example, they could be asked to write a brief description of their organization that would include the goals of the organization, what works well and what could be improved, what they would recommend to others, how people do their jobs, and what image the organization pro-

FIGURE 8.6　Sample Record/Document Analysis Form

Data Source	Data Available Yes/No	District	Document Date	Provide Details about How Lead Exposure is Addressed or How the Workplace or Worker was (is) Affected
1. Workplace exposure assessment monitoring records				
2. Personnel air monitoring results				
3. Blood lead level test				
4. Risk assessment records				
5. Accident/ illness reports				
6. Administrative control plans				
7. Engineering control plans				
8. Safety policies and procedures manual				

jects to the outside world. These descriptions could be collected and re-viewed for specific patterns and themes relevant to the desired changes leaders wish to make.

At the end of a training program, the evaluator could collect training participant enrollment data to gauge employees' interest and need levels on the topic. If the program were aimed at reducing the amount of em-ployee turnover, the evaluator could review the turnover records over the next several months as well.

Records

Records typically provide quantitative information regarding the program being evaluated. They tend to be written artifacts that attest to an event or situation, or provide an account of an event or transaction. Examples of records include:

- Absentee, sick leave, or vacation records
- Records of grievances and complaints
- Length of service records
- Production and other output figures
- Sales records
- Employee figures
- Hot line call records or logs (problem type and frequency of report problem)
- Customer service center call records or logs
- Equipment repair records or logs
- Production schedules
- Phone records
- Sick call rates
- Turnover rates
- Participation rates
- Grades
- Accident costs and rates
- Equipment downtime
- Numbers and rates of new accounts
- Work backlog
- Overtime costs
- Election records
- Professional directories

Documents

Documents tend to provide more descriptive, qualitative kinds of information, but may also include quantitative data. Examples of documents include:

- Training manuals
- Training activities
- Evaluation plans
- Advertised program goals and objectives
- Evaluation and research reports
- Job aids
- Minutes of meetings
- Policies and procedures handbook
- Federal and state laws
- Employment ads
- Press releases
- Reward or recognition certificates/awards
- Newsletters
- E-mail correspondence
- Memos and letters
- Annual reports
- Diaries and journals
- Published speeches
- Desk calendars
- Employee files (including performance review material)
- Training course catalogs and advertisements

As described in Figure 8.6 and James's evaluation of the lead exposure safety-training program (beginning vignette), he chose to use various records and documents to understand the extent to which employees who participated in the program were using what they learned. The archival data recording form he used allows for dichotomous (yes/no) responses that can be quantified as well as open-ended comments that can provide qualitative insights into the participants' ability to transfer their learning.

The following describes three additional examples where archival data in the form of records and documents are used for collecting evaluation data.

Example #1: As part of an evaluation to determine the extent to which five division offices are implementing self-directed teams, the evaluators ask the managers to provide memos, newsletters, strategic plans, and anything else that will provide evidence that self-directed teams are being implemented. During the evaluators' site visits where they conduct individual and focus group interviews and observations, they are able to determine if what they were seeing and hearing confirms what was implied or stated in the records and documents.

Example #2 An evaluator is asked to determine the extent to which certain projects have met their contractual obligations as specified in their proposals for work. She compares the proposals' time lines, budgets, and expected outcomes with the projects' final reports and related documents.

Example #3 A nonprofit organization that is heavily dependent on volunteer workers is experiencing a significant amount of turnover. An evaluation team is established to evaluate the reasons why volunteers are resigning. In addition to conducting exit interviews with people who recently quit as well as with several managers, the evaluation team reviews attendance records, hiring documents, and other correspondence with volunteers to determine if there are any patterns related to those who stay and those who leave.

Advantages and Disadvantages of Collecting Archival Data

The strengths and weaknesses of using archival data in an evaluation include:

Advantages

- Are easily collectable—Reviewing records and documents doesn't require individuals to do anything different; the method is unobtrusive—there are minimal reactive effects.
- May provide quantitative data—Records and documents can provide data for evaluation questions that focus on quantity or frequency.
- May provide an historical context to the evaluand—When you want to understand the background or rationale for an evaluation or the evaluand, records and documents may provide important contextual information.
- Is often cost-effective—Documents can reduce costs if the data are easily accessible and are in a centralized location.
- Elicits information that cannot be collected from interviews or surveys—There are times when an interviewee or survey respon-

dent can't or won't discuss a certain topic. Various records and documents may contain such information.

- Increases perception of data's credibility—Data collected from records and documents may be perceived as more credible than data collected through interviews or qualitative observations.
- Provides a chronology of events—Records and documents can be collected over time and thus provide chronological information.
- Represents unobtrusive measures—They are less likely to disrupt the work of organization members.
- Requires minimal training on how to collect data—Teaching others about what and how to collect records and documents is relatively brief and straightforward.

Disadvantages

- Inaccessibility of data—Certain records and documents may be unavailable to the evaluator, or permission may not be granted. This is particularly true for an organization's financial data that may be restricted to certain internal and external evaluators.
- Limitations of recall—Records and documents may represent only what someone recalls of events and thus might not be accurate. For example, if minutes of a meeting were noted after the meeting, the resulting minutes may not be as complete or accurate as if they had been taken during the meeting.
- Incomplete representation of events—Records and documents may not include a complete representation of the event—certain information may be left out. Or the document could have been written for specific audiences.
- Poor writing—The quality of writing in documents varies, and some may not be completely legible or intelligible.
- Time-consuming—If there are many documents to review, the task can be tedious and costly in terms of time.
- Sample limitations—It is often difficult to know the degree to which the available records and documents represent all that exist or were ever written. It is possible that some have been discarded, destroyed, or archived in ways that are not accessible.

FIGURE 8.7   Guidelines for Collecting Archival Data

✔ Determine which records and documents will help answer evaluation questions.

✔ Determine if permission to review any of the records and documents is required.

✔ Obtain necessary permissions.

✔ Develop data recording form.

✔ Review documents—note any discrepancies or missing information.

✔ If possible, have second person review documents for confirmability.

- Errors—Some records and documents may be inaccurate owing to clerical errors.
- Political slant—Documents can be written with a particular agenda in mind, such as making a program look particularly effective when there is little data to suggest this.
- Limited to manifest content—When reviewing documents you are restricted to analyzing what is on the page. You won't always know the author's intent.
- Unrepresentative sample—Samples described in the document may not be representative of all participants.

Some guidelines to help you plan for and use archival data can be found above in Figure 8.7.

....

Keep in Mind . . .

- Observation methods may collect both quantitative and qualitative data.
- It's important to determine what role the observer will play and the associate level of intrusiveness the evaluation context can accept.
- Observation data can be collected through videotaping, photographs, checklists or rating forms, audiotapes, and unobtrusive measures.
- Archival data may be readily available in the organization.
- Consider the wide variety of records and documents that can be reviewed for the evaluation.

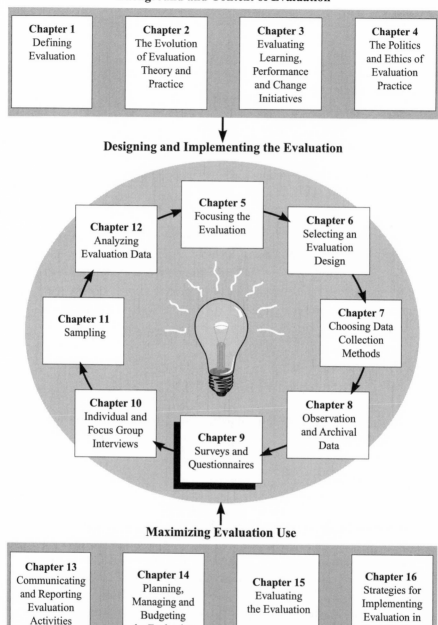

Background and Context of Evaluation

Chapter 1
Defining
Evaluation

Chapter 2
The Evolution
of Evaluation
Theory and
Practice

Chapter 3
Evaluating
Learning,
Performance
and Change
Initiatives

Chapter 4
The Politics
and Ethics of
Evaluation
Practice

Designing and Implementing the Evaluation

Chapter 5
Focusing the
Evaluation

Chapter 6
Selecting an
Evaluation
Design

Chapter 12
Analyzing
Evaluation Data

Chapter 7
Choosing Data
Collection
Methods

Chapter 11
Sampling

Chapter 8
Observation
and Archival
Data

Chapter 10
Individual and
Focus Group
Interviews

Chapter 9
Surveys and
Questionnaires

Maximizing Evaluation Use

Chapter 13
Communicating
and Reporting
Evaluation
Activities
and Findings

Chapter 14
Planning,
Managing and
Budgeting
the Evaluation

Chapter 15
Evaluating
the Evaluation

Chapter 16
Strategies for
Implementing
Evaluation in
Organizations

Surveys and Questionnaires

- Types of Surveys
- Guidelines for Constructing Surveys
- Format Considerations
- Pilot-Testing the Items and Surveys
- Summary of Steps in Survey Construction
- Logistics with Survey Design and Administration
- Handling Nonresponse Bias
- Managing the Data Collection Process
- Electronic Surveys

....

Vignette #7: The Wonderful World of Surveys at MyCommunity Associates

Sarah Mendelson, manager of human resource development at MyCommunity Associates, wanted to understand how well the new volunteer orientation training program was preparing volunteers to do their work. After talking with several managers, she developed a thirty-item survey. Since she wanted the participants to express their opinions about the training, most of the survey questions were open-ended. The survey was given to three sets of participants at the end of the daylong training workshop. They were asked by the trainers to drop it in a box on their way out of the building. When the surveys were collected from the box, Sarah learned that although nearly eighty surveys had been distributed, only ten people had completed and returned the surveys. Another thirty surveys that were placed in the box were completely blank, and the remaining forty were missing.

....

Surveys and questionnaires are frequently used methods for gathering information within organizations. In fact, we've often heard learning, performance, and change professionals say, "Let's do an evaluation to determine the effectiveness of the program." Although this is a great first step, all too often the response has been, "Great, let's give them a survey!" without first considering what needs to be known and whether a survey is the most appropriate method. As a result, surveys and questionnaires may be the most overused and underdeveloped evaluation method.

Surveys consist of a predetermined set of questions that can be distributed by mail, fax, e-mail, or handed to individuals. Though they are typically self-administered, they can also be read to respondents (see Chapter 10 on individual and focus group interviews). Although the word *survey* generally refers to the method of data collection, the word *questionnaire* refers to the actual instrument. For clarity and consistency purposes, however, we will use the word *survey* throughout this chapter to denote both the method and the instrument, since this term is most frequently used in organizations.

Surveys make three assumptions: (1) the respondent can read (when in text form), (2) the respondent is both willing and able to provide truthful responses, and (3) if the respondent must search for the information, he or she will go through whatever records are necessary to provide a response. Regarding the first assumption, if the respondent cannot read, he or she would have to be willing to ask someone else to read and record his or her responses. With the second assumption, an item may require that the respondent not be afraid or embarrassed to provide an honest response. In addition, there is an assumption that the respondent can remember the needed information. Finally, with the third assumption, respondents must find it worth the time to search for the needed information. As the evaluator, you need to ask yourself whether the respondents are able and willing to do what is required to respond in a way that provides valid and useful information.

Given these assumptions, it is important to consider whether a survey is the best method for addressing the key evaluation questions. If you are gathering closed-ended responses to a small number of items from many different people in several locations, you may want to use a mailed survey. If, on the other hand, you are trying to gather information from people who have difficulty reading, you may want to use a data collection method that does not require reading. Or if people in the organization have received numerous surveys in the past months and feel "oversurveyed," you may want to consider another approach to data collection. Although a survey may collect useful information, it is not always the best method.

Advantages of Using Surveys

Using surveys as an evaluation data collection method offers several advantages. These include:

- Administration is comparatively inexpensive and easy even when gathering data from large numbers of people spread over wide geographic areas.
- The same questions are presented in the same manner to all respondents, with no interpretation on the part of the evaluator, thus reducing the chance of evaluator bias.
- Many people, particularly from the United States and western European countries, are familiar with surveys.
- Some respondents may feel more comfortable responding to a survey than participating in an interview.
- Tabulation of closed-ended responses is an easy and straightforward process.
- The use of surveys may increase the likelihood of obtaining a representative sample.

Disadvantages of Using Surveys

As with any data collection method, there are certain limitations to using surveys:

- Although you can distribute surveys to many people in several geographic locations, survey recipients may not complete and return the surveys. As a result, surveys often result in low response rates, which threaten the external validity of the findings and the confidence one might have in using the results.
- Although the same questions are presented in the same manner, the items may not have the same meaning to all respondents,

leading to problems with reliability and validity of the information.

- Because surveys depend on the respondents being able to read and answer in the language used in the survey, their use may limit the size or diversity of the sample.
- Given the lack of personal contact with the respondent, you may not really know who completed the survey. If another person completes the survey, the results may lack internal validity.
- The data from surveys are limited in that you are unable to probe for additional details from the respondents.
- Good survey questions are hard to write—they take significant time to develop and hone.

For any evaluation, you must decide whether the benefits of surveys outweigh the costs (both in terms of resources as well as disadvantages). However, you can identify creative methods for overcoming certain limitations. For example, if you find that critical data are needed but missing from a survey, you might consider conducting telephone or focus group interviews to supplement and expand on the survey data. Or you can provide incentives as a means for increasing the response rate.

Types of Surveys

Surveys are commonly used to evaluate learning, performance, and change initiatives because they can assess a wide variety of knowledge, skills, behaviors, attitudes, and opinions. The most frequently used types are:

- Postcourse reaction forms
- Behavioral or skill measures (or transfer-of-training measures)
- Employee satisfaction or organizational climate surveys
- Knowledge tests

Postcourse Reaction Surveys

Perhaps the most commonly used method for evaluating learning and performance activities or events involves the feedback forms that are of-

TABLE 9.1   Reaction dimensions used in reactionnaires (n = 77)

Dimension Used	Number	Percentage (%)
Recommendation for program improvement	64	83.1
Overall evaluation	63	81.2
Planned action/transfer expectation	61	79.1
Instructor/facilitator	59	76.6
Program objectives/content	54	70.1
Program material	44	57.1
Instructional activities	38	49.4
Program time/length	34	44.2
Delivery methods/technologies	32	41.6
Training environment	25	32.5
Logistics/administration	13	16.9
Other: prior knowledge	9	11.7
Other: perceived gain	6	7.8
Other: expectation met	5	6.5

SOURCE: From Lee, S. H. 1998. "Making Reaction Evaluation a More Useful Tool in Evaluation of Corporate Training Programs: Reactionnaire Dimensions and Design Criteria." Ph.D diss., Indiana University, Bloomington. Reprinted with permission.

ten distributed at the end of a day or program. Typically, these include items asking for feedback on the quality of the instructional methods, facilities, materials, and instructors or facilitators. In a study of seventy-seven training reaction evaluations collected from U.S. corporations, Lee found that the following dimensions were represented on over 50 percent of the forms he reviewed: (a) recommendations for program improvement, (b) overall evaluation, (c) planned action/transfer expectations, (d) program objectives/content, and (e) program materials (1998; see Table 9.1).

All too often we have found that postcourse reaction forms are developed without much thought or concern, and as a result are so poorly designed that they provide useless data. In many cases, we have seen them used more symbolically as a means for managers and employees to say, "Yes, we do evaluate our learning, performance, and change initiatives." In such cases, the forms end up in a drawer or a garbage can and are rarely entered into a database or used in any tangible way. When this happens, we lose an important opportunity to collect useful information.

In most cases, postcourse reaction forms are distributed at the end of a learning, performance, or change workshop or session. To encourage everyone to respond, the facilitator may want to distribute the forms before the last portion of the session. To encourage honest responses, the facilitator should also consider leaving the room while participants complete the forms. It is important to understand that although reaction forms can provide immediate and helpful feedback for program improvement purposes, these kinds of surveys may not necessarily substitute for other measures of effectiveness or impact of the learning, performance, and change initiative (see Chapter 3).

Behaviorial or Skill Measures

Another way of using surveys to evaluate learning, performance, and change initiatives gathers ratings of trainees' behaviors. Such surveys can be distributed to trainees, their managers, their subordinates, their peers, or some combination of one or more of these groups. If surveys are gathered from all of these groups, the results can be presented to individuals in the form of 360-degree feedback. When gathered and presented for individuals or groups, 360-degree feedback data can be used before the learning, performance, and change initiative as one way to determine needs (see Ravishankar and Russ-Eft, 1995, for more details on this method used as a needs assessment).

Behavior surveys may also be used after a learning, performance, and change intervention under assumptions similar to using knowledge tests. By using such surveys after the initiative, you are assuming that participants did not possess these skills and behaviors prior to the initiative. When using a post-only survey, one option for comparing prior knowledge is to ask respondents to rate their pretraining skill level retrospectively and then rate the current skill level (see Chapter 6).

Other times, behavioral or skill surveys are used both before and after a learning, performance, and change initiative as a way to determine the impact of the intervention. As with knowledge tests, you will need to decide whether to administer such measurements immediately after training or some days, weeks, or months later. This decision will depend on the evaluation questions; namely, are you interested in determining immediate or longer-term changes?

Employee Satisfaction or
Organizational Climate Surveys

It is possible that your evaluation includes questions focusing on the impact a learning, performance, or change effort has had on employee satisfaction or the organization's climate. A survey may provide the most effective means for gathering this information. Here, you would need to decide whether to purchase a commercially available survey or whether you would want to develop one specifically for your organization. You would also need to decide on the frequency of data gathering (such as before and after the intervention or periodically) and the timing of each survey.

Knowledge Tests

Another commonly used method for evaluating learning and performance is some form of knowledge test. In some cases, the knowledge test takes the form of a certification exam. In other cases, particularly in computer-based training programs, the knowledge test can be embedded into the program to allow branching or skipping through sections of the material, or enabling the learner to exit the course and obtain some certification (assuming correct completion). Such tests can be an appropriate method for evaluating learning and performance initiatives if you are interested in knowing whether the trainees learned what was intended from the intervention. Although knowledge tests can be used both before and after the program, they typically are only used after training. Using tests only after the course or workshop assumes that participants begin the program as "blank slates" or with no knowledge of the topic beforehand. You need to decide whether such an assumption is warranted. In addition, you need to decide whether you want to administer the tests at the end of training to measure immediate recall or whether you want to wait for some period to test long-term retention. Note that knowledge tests typically don't provide sufficient information on how the learning and performance initiative might be improved. You might also want to check with your organization's legal department or management to make sure that knowledge tests or other kinds of exams are allowed.

Guidelines for Constructing Surveys

There are several issues to consider when designing a survey. What follows are several guidelines that may help guide your work.

Anonymity and Confidentiality

Issues of anonymity and confidentiality must be decided for each method of data collection. In the case of surveys, an anonymous response means that no one (even you as the evaluator) can identify who provided the survey data. Anonymity is difficult to assure when using surveys, particularly when there is a need to follow up on nonrespondents or when the survey is administered via the Internet or an organization's intranet.

However, confidentiality can sometimes be provided to survey respondents. Confidentiality means that you may be able to identify the respondents and their responses, but you guarantee that this information will be given to no one else. If you do promise confidentiality to respondents, then you must consider all aspects of the evaluation, including data collection, data analysis, and reporting in making this promise. In data collection and analysis, you may want to use an identifying number rather than the person's name. In such cases, you should inform potential respondents about the identifying number and its purpose in the cover letter. When communicating and reporting the findings you must also take care to avoid the use of names or other identifying information. It is important to remember that violating a promise of anonymity or confidentiality is considered a breach of professional ethics (see Chapter 4).

Types of Survey Questions

One of the first decisions to make when creating a survey involves the types of questions to be asked. These include questions that are (a) open-ended, (b) fill-in-the-blank, (c) dichotomous or two-choice questions, (d) multiple-choice, (e) rating scales, and (f) ranking. The following four factors should be considered when choosing among the various question formats:

1. *Who will be answering the questions?* If the respondents have limited reading and writing ability, then they may not be able to effectively com-

municate their ideas, particularly to an open-ended question. Also, many respondents may not be interested in writing extensive responses to open-ended questions.

2. How much time will respondents be able and willing to spend? If people must respond quickly, they may not be willing to provide detailed responses. Or if the respondents have just completed an eight-hour training workshop, they will probably not want to devote much time to completing a survey. On the other hand, if the survey is given to people at the beginning of the training session, they may be more willing to complete a long survey (especially if accompanied by coffee and doughnuts). The only drawback to providing the survey at the beginning of the event is that some participants may rate things too early based on initial impressions and not go back to review their ratings at the end of the day.

3. How many respondents will be involved? If you plan to gather data from only ten people, you may want to use some open-ended questions, since the data analysis task will be more manageable with a small sample. If, on the other hand, you plan to gather data from 1,000 people, you may want to use closed-ended questions, since they can be more easily tabulated (see Chapter 11 on sampling).

4. How much is known about the range of possible answers, and do you want to provide them to the respondent? If you already know what the alternative responses are for a particular question, you may want to provide them in a multiple-choice-type question. For example, you may want to ask a preference question, such as: "Which of the three exercises did you prefer?" Since you probably are not interested in using this item to test respondents' recall of the exercises, you would simply list the three exercises.

The following section describes each of the six question types.

1. Open-ended questions. Open-ended questions ask respondents to write a response using their own words, preferably in complete sentences. Examples of several open-ended questions can be seen in Figure 9.1.

Open-ended questions are particularly effective when you are uncertain as to the entire range of alternative answers, or you wish to obtain examples, stories, lists, or descriptions. Respondents' answers to open-ended questions often result in useful insights into their experiences, attitudes, values, and beliefs. A truly open-ended question should cause the respondent to stop and reflect. Although these questions may appear easy

FIGURE 9.1   Examples of Open-Ended Survey Items

▶   What did you hope to learn from this workshop?

▶   What are three things you learned today that you plan to use tomorrow back on the job?

▶   How did employees' performance change as a result of the web-based course?

▶   If you were going to recommend this workshop to a colleague, what would you say?

▶   Please describe how a particular activity helped you learn one of the concepts covered in this program.

▶   What obstacles might you encounter when you try to apply this process in your organization?

---

to construct, they require some effort to make sure that the results will be useful.

Although open-ended questions may result in rich and insightful information, they pose some challenges. First, it is important to carefully consider what needs to be known—and then to carefully word the question. For example, you should avoid asking vague and throwaway questions such as, "What did you like best/least about this program," or "What would you change?" These questions are so generic or all encompassing that respondents often skip them or provide one-word answers that are difficult to interpret. Open-ended questions also require a significant effort during the data analysis stage. Since they produce text, these responses need to be analyzed differently than quantitative data (see Chapter 12 on data analysis). Another common problem in using open-ended questions is that respondents misinterpret the question because a set of choices is not available to guide their responses. Of course, the better worded the question is, the less likely this is to happen. One more concern is that when a survey includes many open-ended questions, as illustrated in the vignette presented at the beginning of this chapter, a lower response rate may be obtained since most people do not like having to write a lot on surveys (Preskill and Mullen, 1988).

Given these challenges, limiting the number of open-ended questions to those where such information is critical is always a good idea. When

FIGURE 9.2   Examples of Fill-in-the-Blank Survey Items

- The first step when confronting an unconscious person is _____
  _____.

- One of the four critical steps in selling is _____
  _____.

- _____is the best word to describe this workshop.

- My plant location is _____.

---

considering the use of open-ended questions, you need to ask yourself two important questions: "Is it necessary to ask this as an open-ended question?" and "Are the alternative responses well known and, therefore, better presented as a multiple-choice, rating, or ranking question?"

2. Fill-in-the-blank questions. Fill-in-the-blank questions typically ask the respondent to insert a word or number in a blank spot within a statement. Figure 9.2 above shows examples of fill-in-the-blank-type questions.

Note that a fill-in-the-blank question is a variant of the open-ended question. In this case, however, you are asking for a limited number of words as a response.

Fill-in-the-blank questions have many of the benefits of open-ended questions: They are easy to construct and use; they allow for a range of alternative answers; and they can provide a richer source of information than a closed-ended question. Indeed, fill-in-the-blank questions are useful for identifying alternatives that can be used later in multiple-choice questions.

The limitations of these kinds of questions are also similar to open-ended questions: They involve time and effort for the respondent to create the response; they require a greater analysis effort than for closed-ended questions; and the respondent may misinterpret them.

3. Two-choice questions. This type of item, also known as dichotomous questions, allow for choosing between two alternatives, such as those shown in Figure 9.3.

Unlike open-ended questions, two-choice questions enable a rapid response and permit fast and economical computer data analysis. They are most appropriate for questions that seek facts and when individuals have a clear-cut position, opinion, or view.

FIGURE 9.3   Examples of Two-Choice or Dichotomous Survey Items

- Would you recommend this course to a colleague?
    _____Yes
    _____No

- My organization could be called a learning organization.
    _____True
    _____False

- Employees value each other's opinions in this organization.
    _____Agree
    _____Disagree

Sometimes, however, there are disadvantages to providing only two responses options. Two choices, such as "yes-no" or "true-false," may not provide enough information to answer the evaluation's key questions. In the example described in Figure 9.3, we do not know whether the person would recommend the course to one colleague or all colleagues. We do not know whether the recommendation would go to only certain kinds of people. We also do not know *why* the person would make the recommendation. Is it because of the course content, the instructor, or the food?

When considering two-choice questions, you need to decide whether this type of question is appropriate or whether there are some other reasonable options. If so, then they must be stated as well. Furthermore, you also need to decide whether to include the response options "Don't know," "No answer," or "Not applicable." If these choices are not included, you may have some respondents leaving certain questions blank, and you will not be able to determine whether there was some reason for their nonresponse or whether the person simply skipped the question, either intentionally or by mistake. If respondents feel that they have to choose one point on the scale without having the option of not applicable, for example, they may provide invalid data because their response does not really reflect their opinion or attitude.

4. Multiple-choice questions. Multiple-choice questions provide respondents with several choices from which they are to select one or more responses. Figure 9.4 shows three examples of multiple-choice questions.

FIGURE 9.4   Examples of Multiple-Choice Survey Items

- After the workshop, who provided you with the greatest assistance in applying what you learned back on the job? (Check only one.)

  _____ Trainer/facilitator
  _____ My peers
  _____ My supervisor
  _____ Other. Please specify _____

- Of the following teaching/training methods, which ones do you prefer? (Check all that apply.)

  _____ Lecture
  _____ Computer-based
  _____ Video
  _____ Group activities
  _____ Demonstration

- What is your organization's primary activity? (Check only one.)

  _____ Manufacturing
  _____ Education
  _____ Financial, real estate, insurance
  _____ Government and military
  _____ Health care
  _____ Retail, wholesale, distributor
  _____ Utilities, communications, transportation
  _____ Hospitality (food, lodging)
  _____ Other, please specify:_____

As with the two-choice questions, multiple-choice questions can be answered quickly and easily. Similarly, computer data entry and analysis is quick and straightforward.

To obtain valid information, however, the questions and their alternatives must be carefully worded. Furthermore, the full range of alternatives must be provided. One approach to obtaining a list of alternatives involves asking the question as an open-ended question or a fill-in-the-blank question first, with a limited number of respondents. You can then develop a list of the choices to use in surveying a large number of respondents later on.

With multiple-choice questions, you also need to decide whether it is reasonable to restrict the responses to the choices given. In addition, you must state clearly whether the respondent should *check only one* or *check all that apply.* As with two-choice questions, you should consider including a response option for "Don't know," "No answer," or "Not applicable."

5. Rating scale questions. A variant of the multiple-choice question is the rating scale. We will discuss the Likert-type scale, behaviorally anchored scales, and behavior-observation scales separately below.

5a. Likert-type scales. Renee Likert (1932) developed a scaling method in which the low end of the scale represents a negative response and the high end represents a positive response. Such a scale allows responses of varying degrees to each specific survey item. Examples of Likert-type scales can be seen in Figure 9.5.

As is shown in Figure 9.5, the scales either have an odd or even number of choices. With an odd-numbered scale, there is a midpoint, which allows the respondent to choose a middle ground. Clearly, with the even-numbered scale, such a midpoint does not exist. In this case, the respondent has to choose one side or the other of the scale. The choice of which to use depends on whether you wish to "force" respondents to one side of the scale or the other. When you believe that respondents have an opinion, then an even-numbered scale may be appropriate. If, on the other hand, you wish to provide them with the neutral option of the midpoint, then you would choose an odd-numbered scale. However, keep in mind that there will always be respondents who will automatically choose the midpoint.

When responding to a Likert scale, some people feel compelled to put a mark somewhere in between numbers on the scale (for example, between the 2 and the 3). When this happens, you will have to make one of the following choices before entering the data:

1. Make an arbitrary decision to score all the ratings in the same way (such as the higher of the ratings). You could, however, be accused of "manufacturing" the data.
2. Create a "new" point on the scale that is halfway between two of the ratings (such as 3.5). You are also "manufacturing" the data, but with potentially less impact on the results.

FIGURE 9.5   Examples of Likert-type Scale Survey Items

1. How satisfied are you with how much you learned today?

Very Dissatisfied −2	Dissatisfied −1	Neither Satisfied nor Dissatisfied 0	Satisfied +1	Very Satisfied +2

2. Using this new process will increase my productivity.

Very Strongly Disagree 1	Strongly Disagree 2	Disagree 3	Neither Agree nor Disagree 4	Agree 5	Strongly Agree 6	Very Strongly Agree 7

3. How satisfied are you with the registration process?

Very Dissatisfied 1	Dissatisfied 2	Satisfied 3	Very Satisfied 4

4. The facilitator gave clear instructions for the group activities.

Strongly Disagree 5	Disagree 4	Neither Agree nor Disagree 3	Agree 2	Strongly Agree 1

3. Do not enter any data for this item. Consider it missing data or invalid data. You can still use the rest of the survey items if the items are completed appropriately (preferred method).

You may also encounter times when respondents mark two ratings. You can adapt the above options in these cases. We believe that ethical practice dictates choosing the third option and strongly recommend that you carefully consider the implications for interpreting a response that is different from that which was requested.

One decision you will have to make when using Likert-type scales involves the number of response options. The examples in Figure 9.5 show four, five, and seven Likert-scale-response options. Interestingly, research conducted by one of the authors (Russ-Eft, 1986) found that increasing the number of options from three to five options or from five to seven options increases the variability of responses. That is, rather than having many people responding with a 4 on a five-point scale, people responded with a 5 or a 6 on a seven-point scale. The variability failed to increase, however, when moving from seven to nine options. Even when respondents were provided a wider range of options, they tended to confine their responses to only seven options. What this means is that respondents' answers are likely to cluster in one part of a scale as the number of options increases. The implication from her research is to limit Likert scales to no more than seven points.

Another decision involves whether to include descriptions for each point on the scale. This decision primarily depends on the number of options that you want to provide, the availability of nonoverlapping descriptions for each response, and participants' experiences with completing surveys. If you can provide descriptions for each point on the scale, it will help respondents know what their response really means—it decreases the amount of ambiguity inherent in the scale. However, certain words have vague or similar meanings. Therefore, even though you provide a descriptor, different respondents may interpret the word differently. Thus, choosing specific words for the response options on a Likert-type scale can prove difficult. Figure 9.6 shows several different descriptors.

Another important consideration for choosing scale descriptors is making sure that the descriptors reflect the dimension being explored in the question. Consider an item where the stem of the question reads, "Indicate the extent to which you agree with the following statements," and the descriptors are "Extremely satisfied" to "Extremely Dissatisfied." Although the question seeks a level of agreement, the scale is measuring satisfaction. Inconsistency between the question stem and the response scale jeopardizes the validity of the answers.

A final decision involves the numerical value assigned and the direction of those numbers. According to Likert (1932) that decision is arbitrary, but the assignment must be consistent so that "favorable" is at one extreme and "unfavorable" is at the other extreme. Specifying numeric val-

FIGURE 9.6   Examples of Likert Scale Descriptors

Agree	Tend to Agree	Don't Know	Tend to Disagree	Disagree
Excellent	Very Good	Good	Fair	Poor
Very Important	Important	Neither Important nor Unimportant	Unimportant	Very Unimportant
Much Higher	Slightly Higher	About the Same	Slightly Lower	Much Lower
Far Too Little	Too little	Enough	Too Much	Far Too Much
Very dissatisfied	Dissatisfied	Neither satisfied nor dissatisfied	Satisfied	Very satisfied
Always	Often	Sometimes	Seldom	Never
Very High	High	Moderate	Low	Very Low
None	Very mild	Mild	Moderate	Severe
Never	Rarely	Sometimes	Usually	Always
Very Great Degree	Great Degree	Some Degree	Very Little Degree	None at all
Definitely	Probably	Not Sure	Probably Not	Definitely Not
A Great Deal	Above Average	Average	Not Too Much	Hardly Any
Very ineffective	Ineffective	Neither effective nor ineffective	Effective	Very effective
Not Important	Somewhat Important	Important	Very Important	Extremely Important
Not at all	To a Little Extent	To Some Extent	To a Great Extent	To a Very Great Extent
Much worse than expected	Worse than expected	As expected	Better than expected	Much better than expected

ues along with the descriptors simplifies data entry, since statistical analyses require numerical data.

Likert-type scales are frequently used because they can be highly reliable and they can be adapted to measure many different phenomena. At the same time, as with any survey question, care must be taken to word them clearly and carefully and to consider the various choices in developing the scales. This will be discussed in a later section in this chapter.

5b. Behaviorally anchored scales. Behaviorally anchored rating scales were introduced by Smith and Kendall in 1963. The notion is that various levels on the scale are "anchored" into performance categories for a specific job category or position. Figure 9.7 (see opposite page) provides an example of a behaviorally anchored scale.

One advantage of this kind of rating scale is it is based on actual behavioral data. A second advantage is that it provides concrete examples for the respondents. That can, however, pose problems for some respondents who have difficulty matching their observations to the examples of behavior that are presented.

If using this kind of scale for observing someone's performance, the instructions should direct the respondent to mark only one response. Yet in Figure 9.7, what would that person mark when a prospect qualifies for two or three programs and the recruiter indicates that all of those are desirable? Thus, when using a behaviorally anchored rating scale, it is important to think about and possibly use a pilot to determine some of the issues that may arise for respondents.

5c. Behavior observation scale. An alternative to the behaviorally anchored rating scale is the behavior observation scale (Latham, Saari, and Fay, 1979; Latham and Wexley, 1981) (see Figure 9.8 on page 244).

This scale uses components of the behaviorally anchored and the Likert-type scales. Specifically, it uses the behavioral items from the behaviorally anchored scale, but it also uses the scale or rating options from the Likert-type scale. One major advantage to the behavior observation scale is that an extensive data collection effort is not required to determine the scale options, and it is based on a systematic analysis of the job. Another advantage is that it provides a listing of behaviors in concrete and explicit terms.

6. Ranking questions. Ranking is an effective question format when you want respondents to compare several things. The procedure asks the respondent to rank order the components of a list, as in Figure 9.9 (page 245).

FIGURE 9.7   Example of Behaviorally Anchored Survey Item

Sales Skills

Skillfully persuading prospects to join the military; effectively overcoming objections; closing skills.

Rating	Description
6	When prospect did not qualify for preferred program, recruiter talked the person into an alternate program, emphasizing available training.
5	When talking with a high school senior, recruiter mentions the names of others from that school who have enlisted.
4	When prospects qualify for only one program, recruiter conveys that it is a desirable program.
3	The recruiter states that the prospect can try for the preferred program but because it will not be open for another month suggests taking a second choice.
2	The recruiter insists on showing brochures and files, even though the prospect indicated wants to sign up now.
1	When prospect states an objection to the military, recruiter ends the conversation.

Ranking questions can be extremely helpful for identifying something as "best" or "worst." Nevertheless, a weakness of this format is that it results in only a ranking. That is, you only know that one thing is considered better or worse than another, and you have no information as to whether the respondent thinks that all the activities are "good" or "bad," for example. Moreover, ranking questions can be difficult to answer. An indication of the difficulty can be seen when respondents give the same rank to multiple choices (for example, give a #1 to two or more of the choices). A general rule of thumb is to limit the number of items to be ranked to ten.

An alternative to ranking is the paired-comparison technique. In this case, the respondent is given only two things to rank at a time. Through successive pairings, one can obtain a ranking of the choices. Figure 9.10 (page 245) shows what this would look like.

Paired comparison items are relatively easy for the respondent to answer and they result in more reliable and valid data than simple ranking. How-

FIGURE 9.8   Examples of Behavior Observation Scale

→   Skillfully persuades prospects to join the military.

Almost Never				Almost Always
1	2	3	4	5

→   Effectively communicates the organization's vision.

Very Ineffective				Very Effective
1	2	3	4	5

→   Answers the phone stating the organization's name.

Almost Never			Almost Always
1	2	3	4

→   Gives regular feedback to employees.

Not at all			To a Very Great Extent
1	2	3	4

ever, as the list of items to be ranked increases, the number of pairings also increases dramatically. For example, with three items, the respondent would receive only three pairs to compare; however, with ten items, the respondent would have to compare forty-five items. To determine the number of pairings that would be necessary, you would calculate: $0.5 N (N - 1)$, where N equals the number of items. So, if you had eighteen items to be ranked, you would take half of eighteen, which is nine, and multiply that by eighteen minus one, which is seventeen. Nine times seventeen equals 153

FIGURE 9.9   Example of a Ranking Survey Item

Please rank the following list of today's activities in terms of their helpfulness in learning the program's content where,

1 = the activity that was most helpful in learning the content, and
4 = the activity that was least helpful in learning the content.

_____ Picture This
_____ Leaning on Friends
_____ Unwelcome News
_____ Sticking Together

FIGURE 9.10   Example of Paired-Comparison Survey Item

We would like to know which of today's four activities were most helpful in learning the program's content. For each pair of activities, indicate with an "X" the activity that was *most helpful* in learning the content.

1. Indicate which was most helpful:
    _____Picture This
    _____Leaning on Friends

2. Indicate which was most helpful:
    _____Picture This
    _____Unwelcome News

3. Indicate which was most helpful:
    _____Sticking Together
    _____Picture This

4. Indicate which was most helpful:
    _____Leaning on Friends
    _____Unwelcome News

5. Indicate which was most helpful:
    _____Unwelcome News
    _____Sticking Together

6. Indicate which was most helpful:
    _____Sticking Together
    _____Leaning on Friends

pairs—respondents would have to rate 153 pairs of items. When considering this approach keep in mind that the analysis of such pairings can be relatively complicated. (See Guilford [1954] and Preskill and Wentling [1984] for more details on the use of this method.)

Question Construction

The next step involves the actual writing of the survey question. In order to obtain valid information, it is important to word each question carefully. The following are some suggestions and cautions that can help you develop effective questions.

- *Use terms that respondents will understand.* Although some terms may seem to be common, they may not be part of the respondents' vocabulary. For example, "human performance improvement" may be understood by you and others in your department but may not be clear to other people in the organization. If you think that some of the potential respondents may not understand a certain word, it is a good idea to choose another word or phrase, explaining the concept in simpler terms.
- *Avoid the use of acronyms.* You, your colleagues, and many employees may understand that "EAP" means "Employee Assistance Program," but you may be administering the survey to new employees who may have never encountered such a program. Always spell out the words of an acronym. Never assume anything.
- *Avoid using double negatives.* This is caused by phrasing the question in a negative way. As can be seen in the following example, the evaluator has created a question respondents may find difficult to answer:

Do you believe that trainees should *not* have to pay for their own training? (Check one.)
☐ Yes
☐ No

By using the negative in the question, a response of "No" actually means, "Yes, I believe that trainees should pay for their own training." You can remove the problem by rewording the question, as follows:

Do you believe that trainees should pay for the training themselves? (Check one.)
☐ Yes
☐ No

- *Avoid wording that suggests answers or biased responses in one direction* such as:

Isn't it true that our organization's new-hire orientation training should be improved? (Check one.)
☐ Yes
☐ No

This problem can be more subtle, as shown in the following example. Here the writer believes that training should occur at least weekly and fails to provide the option "None." As a result, few respondents will indicate that no safety training should be provided, whereas if such a response option were listed, some respondents may select that option.

How many times a week should safety training be provided? (Check only one.)
_____Once a week
_____Twice a week
_____Three times a week

- *Avoid leading or loaded questions.* A leading or loaded question is one that would lead the person to respond differently if the question had a different wording. This is a more subtle form of a biased question. Actually, any form of question could be considered leading or loaded; it could be loaded on one side or the other or it could be loaded evenly. The following is one example.

You are not alone if you think that the organization is not doing enough to support employee's professional development. Do you think the cap on tuition reimbursement be increased to $1,500 per year?
☐ Yes
☐ No

- *Avoid "double-barreled" questions that ask for more than one piece of information in the question.* Such a question may result in the respondent answering one part of the question and not the other.

The following kind of question is a common example of this problem:

Was this seminar *interesting* and *useful*? (Circle one.)

Yes   No

If you think that "interesting" and "useful" mean the same thing, then one of the two words should be eliminated. Otherwise, these should be made into two separate questions:

Was this seminar interesting?   Yes   No
Was this seminar useful?   Yes   No

As is probably clear by now, if we don't take the time to consider how survey items are worded, we are likely to obtain data that are either invalid or not usable. In the study conducted by Lee referred to earlier, he identified nine common errors on the seventy-seven reaction forms he studied. As can be seen in Table 9.2 on the next page, the most common error that showed up on nearly 78 percent of the surveys reviewed was the use of "double-barreled questions," whereas 36 percent had "leading" questions.

Some might say that the development of good survey questions is as much an art form as it is a science. With this in mind, we offer Figure 9.11 to illustrate the creation of a survey item.

Format Considerations

It is important to consider the respondent population when developing the format or layout of survey questions. If employees have responded to past surveys using a particular format, you may decide to use that same format to avoid any confusion. On the other hand, the same format may lead to boredom and a lower response rate.

Figure 9.12 shows two different format options. The first example is one that is commonly used in surveys. Note that it requires the respondent to remember the scale and the responses. In contrast, the second one makes the scale more visible to the respondent.

A survey's format should be both simple and interesting. The following are some general formatting suggestions:

TABLE 9.2   Common Errors of Question Items in Reactionnaires (n = 77)

Guidelines Used for Assessment	Number	Percentage (%)
Double-barreled questions	60	77.9
Leading/loaded questions	28	36.4
Already know answer	16	20.8
Use non-neutral wording	13	16.9
Response category not mutually exclusive	13	16.9
Do not use simple, clear, and short words (KISS principle)	13	16.9
Not single purpose	12	15.6
Do not avoid jargon, slang, and abbreviations	4	5.2
Do not avoid negative and double-negative questions	1	1.3

SOURCE: From Lee, S. H. 1998. "Making Reaction Evaluation a More Useful Tool in Evaluation of Corporate Training Programs: Reactionnaire Dimensions and Design Criteria." Ph.D diss., Indiana University, Bloomington. Reprinted with permission.

- If the survey is paper-based rather than electronic and it is longer than one page, use an attractive cover page. This may include the organization's logo and a title for the survey.
- For a mailed survey, use colored paper so that it stands out on someone's desk. Be careful, however, not to choose a color that is too bright or dark, thus making the survey difficult to read.
- Consider whether you want to include a letter from you or from an executive sponsor for the evaluation, such as the president or chief executive officer of the organization.
- Space items so that they do not appear cramped or crowded. It's almost always better to have more space between items and more pages than fewer pages but difficult-to-read items.
- Include clear, brief general instructions for completing the survey.
- Group items into logical sections; for example, by topic areas.
- Group items that have the same question format or response options.
- Include smooth transitions between sections on the survey.
- Provide clear directions at the beginning of each question or format change. (list continues on page 252)

FIGURE 9.11   The Creation of a Survey Item

Stage 1:   Shouldn't there be a change in our existing sales training program?
　　　　　　　____Yes
　　　　　　　____No

? This question begs for an affirmative answer

Stage 2:   Should there be changes in the existing sales training program?
　　　　　　　____Yes
　　　　　　　____No

? What kinds of changes would be needed?

Stage 3:   Should there be more sales training?
　　　　　　　____Yes
　　　　　　　____No

? Does 'more' say what is intended?

Stage 4:   Should there be more frequent sales training?
　　　　　　　____Yes
　　　　　　　____No

? Only one alternative is stated.

Stage 5:   Should there be more frequent sales training, or is the existing sales training adequate?

　　　　　　　____Yes, sales training should be more frequent
　　　　　　　____No, existing sales training is adequate

? What if less sales training is desired?

Stage 6:   Should there be more frequent sales training, less frequent sales training, or is the current frequency of sales training adequate?

　　　　　　　____Should have more frequent sales training
　　　　　　　____Should have less frequent sales training
　　　　　　　____Current frequency of sales training is adequate

? What if no sales training is desired?

FIGURE 9.11 *(continued)*

Stage 7:   Should there be more frequent sales training, less frequent sales training, no sales training, or is the current frequency of sales training adequate?
____Should have more frequent sales training
____Should have less frequent sales training
____Should have no sales training
____Current frequency of sales training is adequate

? Sales training for which groups?

Stage 8:   Should there be more frequent sales training for new hires and experienced staff, less frequent sales training, no sales training, or is the current frequency of sales training adequate?
____Should have more frequent training
____Should have less frequent training
____Should have no sales training
____Current frequency of sales training is adequate

? This is a "double-barreled question."

Stage 9:   Should there be more frequent sales training for new hires, less frequent training for new hires, no sales training for new hires, or is the current frequency of sales training adequate?
____Should have more frequent training
____Should have less frequent training
____Provide no sales training
____Current frequency of sales training is adequate

? This is excessively wordy.

Final Question
Stage 10:   For new hires, there should be:
____more frequent sales training
____less frequent sales training
____no sales training
____the current frequency of sales training

CAUTION: Now the question is ready for pilot-testing and further revision and refinement.

FIGURE 9.12   Example of More and Less Interesting Survey Formats

---

Answer the following questions by indicating one number between one and seven that best reflects what you do.

1 = Not at All
7 = To a Very Great Extent

To What Extent Do You:
1. Run effective meetings?   _____
2   Model effective meeting management?   _____
3. Focus attention on a few important issues?   _____

Obtaining the same information with a more interesting format.

Answer the following questions by circling the number that best reflects what you do.

What Extent Do You:	Not At All		To Some Extent				To A Very Great Extent
1. Run effective meetings?	1	2	3	4	5	6	7
2. Model effective meeting management?	1	2	3	4	5	6	7
3. Focus attention on a few important issues?	1	2	3	4	5	6	7

- Avoid placing threatening questions at the beginning of the survey. Threatening questions can include demographic questions that some respondents may think will identify them personally.
- Avoid putting the most important questions at the end of the survey.
- Number the items and pages.
- Place an identification code on each page of the survey so those pages can be identified if they are separated.
- Make sure to proofread, proofread, and proofread the survey before mailing it out.

Pilot-Testing the Items and Surveys

Once you have carefully examined all the items to ensure clear wording and instructions, it is important to pilot-test the survey to identify any weaknesses that may have been overlooked. The respondents selected for the pilot test should be representative of the eventual target sample. In some cases, you may select a few people from your target population to participate in the pilot test. If you do so, you will need to consider whether to include them as part of the final sample. One reason for including them in the final sample is that they are members of the target population. However, a reason to exclude them is that the pilot test may have made them more sensitive to the issues raised in the survey and thus influence their final responses.

Note that if your evaluation is being supported by a contract with any federal government agency, you must follow strict limitations on the number of people in your pilot test. Specifically, any question that is asked of more than nine people must go through a clearance process by the Office of Management and Budget (OMB Clearance). Such restrictions do not apply for evaluation work conducted under a federal grant or in other kinds of organizations. Nevertheless, you should keep pilot testing to a reasonable number. We suggest that you use more than one or two people and probably fewer than ten people.

You or someone else familiar with the evaluation and its purpose should conduct the pilot test. The rationale is that you are the person most familiar with the objectives of the evaluation. Therefore, you are in the best position to determine during the pilot test whether each question is being understood and the response is providing useful information. One approach to pilot-testing involves being physically present while the respondent completes the survey. In such cases, you are able to observe the respondents' reactions to each question and any problems they appear to have in responding to the survey. These observations may lead you to revise the survey. Another approach involves sending the form to respondents and having them complete the form while you are on the telephone.

In both of these cases, you should record the amount of time that it takes each respondent to complete the survey. Sometimes you may even want to time specific questions. During the pilot testing, the respondent should be asked to comment on the content and wording of the questions. In addition, it might also be helpful to ask respondents to: (1) read and explain the question, (2) explain the reasons for his or her choices, and (3) describe other answers that could be given. These probes may reveal incorrect assumptions or alternative rationales that were never anticipated.

Summary of Steps in Survey Construction

The following list presents a twelve-step process for constructing a survey.

1. Use a variety of sources for possible items, such as available reports, correspondence, and previous surveys.
2. Use potential respondents' language rather your own.
3. Try to avoid using "and/or" in an item. If you use one of these words, you may be asking two questions at the same time.
4. Try to include three to four items to measure the same variable (especially for a test).
5. Keep the survey as short as possible. A lengthy survey can lead to a high nonresponse rate.
6. Include brief instructions where needed. Try to clarify what respondents are supposed to do.
7. Use consistent wording and formatting as much as possible. For example, you might write, "To what extent does your supervisor do the following: completely, somewhat, not at all" throughout the survey; or "How often does your supervisor do the following: all the time, sometimes, not at all" throughout the survey. It is not a good idea to use a mixture of the two.
8. Make sure that the format is conducive to your chosen method of data entry, such as hand tabulation, computer entry, or optical scanning.
9. Conduct a pilot test with a group similar to the potential participants. The purpose of the pilot is to remove or revise confusing and unnecessary items.

10. If feasible, use more items than necessary for the pilot study. You can then eliminate items that do correlate with any other items or are confusing to participants.

11. In some cases, you may want to conduct some statistical analyses of the pilot data, such as correlations, interitem reliabilities, and factor analyses. These analyses help to identify items that should be modified or eliminated. (See Chapter 12 on analyzing evaluation data.)

12. Revise the survey and, if necessary, administer a second pilot test.

Logistics

Survey Administration

Once you have developed the final survey, you must decide how you want to distribute it. You have three basic choices: (1) distribute the surveys in one or more group sessions, (2) send them to individuals through the mail (either regular mail, inter-office, or via e-mail), or (3) administrate them via the Internet. The following describes some procedures that can be used.

1. Group administration. One major advantage of group administration is that it ensures that all surveys are completed and returned. In addition, a group session can help overcome fears and questions about completing the surveys. This method typically requires less of your time for administration and follow-up; the administration is conducted at one time and, in most cases, you have all the participants there and will not have to spend time following up on nonrespondents. The following provides some recommendations for administering a survey to a group in a specially scheduled session. You can adapt these steps for a regularly scheduled meeting:

A. Prepare a list of the survey participants, along with needed contact information.

B. Prepare the surveys for distribution.

C. Schedule the meeting(s) in a separate, quiet room. Depending on the room size and on the number, availability, and location of the participants, you can plan to assemble all the participants at one time, or you can divide the group into smaller groups. Note that at the time of the meeting, the room will need to be equipped with tables, chairs, pencils or pens, surveys, and envelopes for returning the surveys to you or the data collection person.

D. Announce the meetings to managers or supervisors of the participants. The announcement should ask for the managers' or supervisors' cooperation. It should state the purpose, date, and time of the meeting(s). (See Figure 9.13 for an example of such an announcement.)

E. Send out announcements of the meeting(s) to the evaluation study participants. The announcements should state the purpose, date, time, and location of the meeting(s). (See Figure 9.14 for a sample announcement.)

F. Administer the survey. On the day of the meeting, arrive at least a half-hour early to check the room facilities. As mentioned previously, the room should have tables and chairs for all participants. At each seat, place a survey, an envelope, and a pencil or pen. After the participants arrive, begin with a greeting and instructions on how to complete the surveys. In some cases, you may want to reinforce the instructions printed on the survey by reading them aloud to participants.

G. Do not circulate while survey participants are working. Remain quietly seated unless someone raises his or her hand. Then, go to that person, answer the question, and return to your seat. In some cases, especially if you are asking the survey participants to rate the quality of your own facilitation or instruction, you may want to leave the room.

H. Whether you remain in the room or not, you should provide instructions as to what participants should do with the completed survey. You may ask each respondent to put his or her survey in an individual envelope and seal it, or you may tell respondents to place the survey in a specified envelope or box when they leave.

2. Mail, e-mail distribution, or Internet administration. Some situations require that you mail or e-mail the surveys to participants or request that they go to a particular website to complete a survey. For example, you may

FIGURE 9.13   Announcement for Group-Administered Survey—
Manager/Supervisor

DATE: July 1
TO: Roberta White
FROM: Sam Jones, Training Specialist
RE: Study of Training Effectiveness

Masquerade, Inc. is committed to offering effective training for all its employees.
As our president, Lee Smith, has stated, "We want training that truly makes a
difference." Therefore, to determine the effectiveness of the "Effective
Presentations" training program, we are undertaking an important evaluation
with those who have participated in this program.

One of the employees in your department, Sally Greene, has been selected to
participate in this evaluation. Her participation will involve no more than thirty
minutes to complete the attached survey, which will be administered to a large
group of training participants on *July 26* from *9:30 to 10:00 A.M. in the Operations
meeting room.*

We hope that you will communicate to Sally how important her participation is
so that we may continually improve and refine our training program's
effectiveness. We greatly appreciate your support.

---

want to distribute surveys to individuals who are in many different locations. Or since it is difficult to schedule a meeting with the selected people, you may decide to mail it.

You will need to weigh the benefits and costs of the mailed, e-mail, or
Internet, survey method to make your final decision about its administration. The following provides some steps to follow when using a mailed
survey method.

A.   Prepare a list of the survey participants, along with needed ad-
     dress and contact information.
B.   Prepare the surveys for distribution.
C.   For a mailed survey, prepare return envelopes. Making it easy
     for participants to return the surveys helps to ensure that partic-
     ipants will return the forms. If the surveys will be returned
     through the U.S. mail, be sure that the self-addressed envelopes

FIGURE 9.14   Announcement of Group-Administered Survey—Participant

---

DATE: July 2
TO: Sally Greene
FROM: Sam Jones, Training Specialist
RE: Evaluation of Training

Masquerade, Inc. is committed to offering effective and ongoing training to all employees. Therefore, we want to determine the effectiveness of the "Effective Presentations" training in which you recently participated.

You have been selected to participate in this important evaluation. Your participation will take no more than 30 minutes to complete two survey forms. We will be administering the surveys in the Operations meeting room on July 26 from 9:30 to 10:00 A.M. Please contact *Debbie Dagwood* if you cannot attend or need to reschedule.

You do not need to prepare anything for this session. We will provide all the materials at the time.

We look forward to your participation and your willingness to help Masquerade, Inc. provide its employees with the best training possible.

---

have the correct postage. Postage stamps, rather than metering, should be used to give the impression of a more personal approach. Depending on the availability of resources, you might want to consider using certified, special delivery, or overnight mail, since each of those makes the survey seem more important and can increase the response rate. Be sure to include a fax number for returning the surveys, since some participants may prefer this option.

D.   Compose a cover letter to accompany each survey. The cover letter should state the study's purpose and give the participants instructions on completing and returning the surveys. Statements as to the importance of completing and returning the survey, including an indication of official sponsorship, how the person was chosen to participate, and how the results will be used, can help to improve the response rate. (See Figure 9.15 for an example.)

FIGURE 9.15   Cover Letter for Mailed Survey

July 2

Mr. Robert White
All-Round Tires, Mfg.
1425 Palm Avenue
Anytown, Anystate 11111

Dear Mr. White,

Masquerade, Inc. is committed to offering effective and ongoing training to all its employees and vendors. Thus, to make certain that this training truly meets their needs, we are undertaking an important evaluation. The results of this study will be used to make any necessary changes to the "Effective Presentations" training program in which you recently participated.

Enclosed is a survey that asks specific questions about your experience with and opinions about the training. We would greatly appreciate your taking a few minutes to complete the survey and return it in the enclosed self-addressed, stamped envelope within the next couple of days.

Keep in mind that your responses are strictly confidential. The results will focus on the responses from all those participating rather than on specific individuals.

If you have any questions, please contact *Debbie Dagwood at 999-0000*. Thank you for your time and cooperation.

Sincerely,

Sam Jones
Training Specialist

Enclosures

SJ:cfr

E. For mailed surveys, prepare envelopes for mailing. Use the list of names with accurate addresses, created in the first step. Prepare a mailing envelope for each survey participant, with name and address information on the outside of the envelope. Place all the forms with the self-addressed, stamped envelope and the cover letter into the mailing envelope. Be sure that the name on the cover letter matches the name on the envelope. Double-checking the letters and envelopes is always a good idea. If you are using an identification number on the survey, be sure to check that the correct number has been placed on the survey. Then place the envelopes in the mail (with the correct postage if being sent in the U.S. mail).

F. Create a survey tracking form to record each participant's name and the date was the survey sent and when it has been received. See Figure 9.16 for an example of a survey tracking form. In this example, the evaluator is surveying not only the training participants but also each participant's manager and three of the participant's employees both before and after training.

G. Record the receipt of forms as received. Even if you do not have identifying information on the forms, you can count the forms to determine how many participants have responded. This will be important for reporting the survey's response rate.

Methods for Increasing the Response Rate of Mailed Surveys

Certainly careful wording and formatting of the survey will increase the chances the survey is completed and returned. However, additional procedures described previously for group administration and mail survey administration will help to increase the response rate. The following are some additional suggestions for encouraging potential participants to respond.

A. *Importance of the survey.* The survey or the survey's cover letter should emphasize that the future direction of the program being evaluated depends on each individual's response and that each response is really needed. Furthermore, without each respondent's help, the organization will not have the best information for making important decisions.

FIGURE 9.16 Survey Tracking Form

Participant's name	Pretraining Surveys										Posttraining Surveys									
	Date Sent					Date Received					Date Sent					Date Received				
	Self	Mgr	Emp1	Emp2	Emp3	Self	Mgr	Emp1	Emp2	Emp3	Self	Mgr	Emp1	Emp2	Emp3	Self	Mgr	Emp1	Emp2	Emp3

B. *Keep it short.* Ask only questions that are needed for the evaluation and base these on the key evaluation questions. This is the time to winnow out the "nice to know" from the "need to know." A shorter survey will also likely result in more people willing to complete it.

C. *Additional "interesting" questions,* especially at the beginning, can help an otherwise uninteresting survey. This is particularly the case when you have a survey that is longer than one page. In such cases, adding a couple of questions that lead to a higher "interest level" more than compensates for the additional length.

D. *Handwriting.* Handwritten signatures, names, addresses, or postscripts urging a prompt reply can partially redeem an otherwise impersonal survey.

E. *Appearance of the survey.* Items and choices should not be crowded together, even if such spacing results in more pages for the survey.

F. *Incentives.* A variety of incentives have been shown to be effective in increasing the response rate to mailed surveys. Depending on the group being surveyed, incentives can include dollar bills, coupons for food or other items, restaurant certificates, a promise of the results, a donation to a favorite charity, candy, cookbooks, personal care items, raffle tickets, movie tickets, child care, a meal, and phone cards. You must decide on the importance of stimulating responses through an incentive as well as on the appropriateness of the incentive.

G. *Deadlines.* Care should be taken with the use of deadlines as a motivation to respond. A deadline implies that the responses cannot be used after a certain fixed date. Rather than indicating a fixed date, you should recommend that the respondent try to complete the survey within a day or two or within a week or two, depending on the urgency of the survey data. Also, describing the nonresponse follow-up procedures as well as the importance of the response may motivate respondents to return the survey promptly.

H. *Follow-up procedures.* Systematic follow-up procedures can help improve the response rate to mailed surveys. These procedures include the following:

One week prior to mailing the survey: Send a postcard or a letter to the respondents alerting them to the upcoming survey and indicating its importance.

One week after mailing the survey: Send a postcard or a memo reminder. Or you may insert an article in the organization's newsletter describing the evaluation and the forthcoming survey.

Three weeks after mailing the survey: Send a letter, along with another copy of the survey.

Three weeks after the second survey mailing: If possible, call those who have not responded, and encourage them to complete the survey (see Dillman, 1978).

Handling Nonresponse Bias

In spite of our most valiant efforts to increase the number of responses, it is rare to obtain a 90 percent to 100 percent response rate. Some numbers of survey recipients do not respond because of fear, disinterest, or preoccupation with tasks that they consider a higher priority. Others do not respond because they never receive the survey (possible mail problems) or they are unable to complete the survey (because of illness or a language barrier, for example). As an evaluator, you should make advance plans for how you will deal with nonrespondents.

One option is to do nothing. In this case, you plan to analyze the data from the respondents and draw conclusions based on those responses. This is a reasonable option if there are only a few nonrespondents. Remember, however, that if only 20 percent of the recipients return the survey, you have no way of knowing whether the other 80 percent would have responded similarly to those who did respond.

Another option is to undertake a nonrespondent check. Using previously gathered information about the sample participants (such as demographic information on department, location, and position), you compare the respondent group with the nonrespondent group using appropriate statistical tests. If there are no significant differences between the groups, you can assume that the nonrespondents (had they responded) would have responded in a manner similar to the respondents.

Another option is to undertake a nonrespondent follow-up. In this case, you follow up with a random sample of nonrespondents, typically by phone or in person. In this case, you ask a few of the critical survey questions of these nonrespondents. Such a follow-up provides the data needed to determine whether the nonrespondents do, in fact, respond in the same way as the original pool of respondents. Furthermore, you have the data needed to make statistical adjustments to your results if you find that the nonrespondents answer differently from the respondents.

Managing the Data Collection Process

Keeping track of the survey responses comprises a major task for any data collection effort, but it is particularly important when undertaking an evaluation using a survey with many participants. Only by keeping track of the respondents will you be able to know whether, when, and with whom you will need to follow up. In addition, if you are undertaking a pretraining and posttraining survey, for example, you will want to make sure that participants complete surveys before and after training. Otherwise, specific kinds of comparisons will be impossible to carry out (see Chapter 12 on data analysis).

One approach to keeping track of the survey responses is to use a survey tracking form as described earlier and presented in Figure 9.16. At the same time you keep track of the survey responses, another task is to make an immediate check on any problem questions. You can do this by examining each survey when it is returned for indications that respondents were confused or unable to respond. If you find such problems in the surveys, you will need to decide whether you should undertake some follow-up questioning of respondents to clarify the problems or whether to use the respondents' data at all.

Another task is to make final plans for handling nonrespondents. Although the tracking can help to identify the individuals with whom you will need to follow up, it can also help determine if there are characteristics that are common to the nonrespondents. For example, many of the nonrespondents may come from the same location. This nonresponse may result from some situation in that location (for example, a strike or layoff at that facility) or from lost mail. Alternatively, if the nonrespondents did come from the same location, you may want to find out whether there are some organizational issues affecting the respondents' lack of participation. If there are some common characteristics, you may be able to determine an appropriate kind of intervention to encourage responses.

Electronic Surveys

Evaluators are increasingly using computers to administer surveys (Buchanan and Smith, 1999; Mehta and Sivadas, 1995; and Schaefer and Dillman, 1998). These surveys can be sent via e-mail or can appear on a web site. Using computers for survey purposes simplifies distribution and data collection (Pettit, 1999; Watt, 1999) and appears to yield results similar to paper-based surveys (Smith and Leigh, 1997; Webster and Compeau, 1996). Once the electronic version of the survey has been created, the survey can be administered to hundreds or thousands of people without additional costs. At the very least, you eliminate both printing and mailing costs. Responses to electronic surveys can be gathered more quickly because mailing delays do not occur. Furthermore, if the version has been created properly, the respondents enter their own data into the survey database, eliminating costs and time for data entry. In a recent example, one of the authors undertook a survey in Canada by posting it to a web site. After potential respondents completed a short demographic survey—with the option of using English or French—those who met the qualifications were asked to continue with the full survey. The entire data collection and data entry effort was completed in a two-week period, as compared with a similar data collection effort using paper-and-pencil forms in the United States that lasted six weeks.

The use of electronic surveys, whether via e-mail or a web site, should be determined based on the population being surveyed. The major question to ask is whether the people selected for the sample regularly use e-mail or the Internet. If so, then the next considerations involve the length and complexity of the survey. If the survey is long and contains numerous skip patterns, you may experience a lower than desired response rate.

Suggestions for improving the response rate include:

- Follow the same presurvey notification and follow-up processes as for mailed surveys.

- Use e-mail for the presurvey and postsurvey notifications, rather than postcards or letters.
- In the prenote, indicate a nonelectronic way of requesting a paper-and-pencil version, such as a return postcard. Then when receiving such a notice from a respondent, send that person a paper-and-pencil version.
- Personalize the e-mail messages sent to each respondent rather than using a group message or group address. Indeed, be sure to avoid sending such group messages. A respondent may inadvertently send his or her survey responses to the entire group.
- Be aware that browsers and servers possess encryption systems. You can ensure the security of the responses by using this technology.
- Be aware that an e-mail survey may not look the same on each respondent's screen. Differences will occur owing to differences in browsers and in computer configurations. Because of these differences, Schaefer and Dillman (1998) predicted that the use of web sites, rather than e-mail, will become the preferred option for survey administration.
- Be sure to develop a method for validating the identity of the user and preventing multiple submissions (Miller, 1999).

In spite of the many advantages of electronic surveys, there are some issues to consider. With electronic surveys, you cannot guarantee, because you may not have control over, who has access to the information systems. In addition, how often they are disseminated through an organization's intranet should be carefully considered. When an organization attempts to survey its members repeatedly on a particular topic, employees might tire of the survey and find ways to avoid participating. The following is a true story.

In response to the company's concern about the quality of its customer service, it decided to monitor how employees felt about the level of customer service being provided. To do this, an on-line survey was developed and implemented for a period of two years. Every day, when employees opened their e-mail, they were presented with a series of questions they had to answer before their e-mail could be opened. After responding for quite a long time, one employee says she really didn't care how she responded . . . she just wanted to get to her e-mail. After about six months, she discovered that if she pushed ALT PF 10, her response would be automatically entered, as "everything was perfect." She could then read and respond to her e-mail without further ado. When she called the survey administrator and asked to be taken off the list to which the survey was sent, she was told that it was mandated by "corporate" and everyone was required to participate. When the fourth-quarter results were published, she had to wonder. They read:

Percent of Good/Satisfactory Ratings

Production Services	99.57%
Electronic Mail	99.91%
Test Application Services	99.56%
Overall	99.68%

This employee couldn't help but believe that others had also found the ALT PF 10 remedy.

Keep in Mind . . .

- Surveys are an effective method for collecting data, but avoid overusing them.
- Surveys are deceptively simple-looking; allocate sufficient time and resources for their development and pilot testing.
- Consider using various kinds of questions, such as open-ended, fill-in-the-blank, two-choice, multiple-choice, rating scales, and ranking.
- Only ask the "need-to-know" questions; limit the number of "nice-to-know" questions.
- Consider using electronic surveys when appropriate to reduce data collection and data entry time and costs.

Background and Context of Evaluation

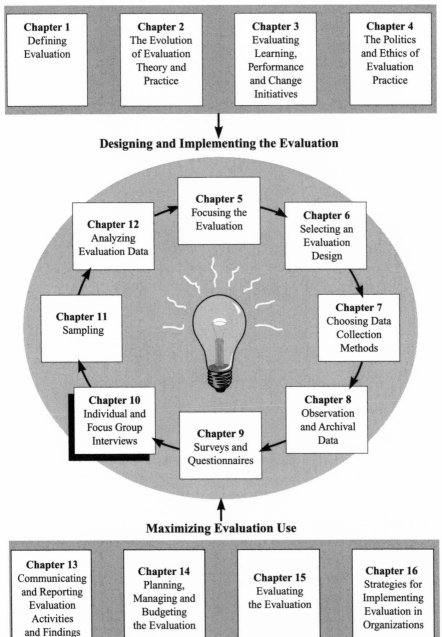

Chapter 1
Defining
Evaluation

Chapter 2
The Evolution
of Evaluation
Theory and
Practice

Chapter 3
Evaluating
Learning,
Performance
and Change
Initiatives

Chapter 4
The Politics
and Ethics of
Evaluation
Practice

Designing and Implementing the Evaluation

Chapter 12
Analyzing
Evaluation Data

Chapter 5
Focusing the
Evaluation

Chapter 6
Selecting an
Evaluation
Design

Chapter 11
Sampling

Chapter 7
Choosing Data
Collection
Methods

Chapter 10
Individual and
Focus Group
Interviews

Chapter 8
Observation
and Archival
Data

Chapter 9
Surveys and
Questionnaires

Maximizing Evaluation Use

Chapter 13
Communicating
and Reporting
Evaluation
Activities
and Findings

Chapter 14
Planning,
Managing and
Budgeting
the Evaluation

Chapter 15
Evaluating
the Evaluation

Chapter 16
Strategies for
Implementing
Evaluation in
Organizations

Individual and Focus Group Interviews

- Types of Interviews
- Determining Which Interview Approach to Use
- Advantages of Individual and Focus Group Interviews
- Disadvantages of Individual and Focus Group Interviews
- Guidelines for Constructing Individual and Focus Group Interview Guides
- Guidelines for Conducting Individual and Focus Group Interviews
- The Interviewer's Role
- Selecting and Training Interviewers
- Managing the Interview Process
- Computer-Aided Interviewing

••

Vignette #8: Getting the Most from Interviewing at MyFuture Electronics

Sandy Gutierrez, manager of information technology at MyFuture Electronics, Inc., wanted to better understand the organization's learning needs regarding the development, management, and use of information. After writing down several questions that she wanted answered, Sandy invited thirty-five employees from different departments to a focus group interview (she sent them each an e-mail invitation promising refreshments if they were to attend). At the scheduled time, twenty-five of the thirty-five employees showed up. After the interview, however, Sandy expressed some disappointment in that only a few people seemed to talk. She wondered if those who had been quiet really felt the same as those who had been more willing to express their thoughts and opinions. As a result, she wasn't quite sure what to do—should she act on the information she had obtained from the few?

....

Because of the perceived ease of conducting individual and focus group interviews, they are frequently used methods for gathering evaluation information within organizations. In this chapter, we discuss different types of interviews, advantages and disadvantages of using the interview method to collect evaluation data, and guidelines for conducting effective interviews.

Types of Interviews

In this section, we describe three types of interviews: (1) individual, in-person interviews, (2) telephone interviews, and (3) focus group interviews.

Individual In-Person Interviews

The in-person interview is sometimes called a face-to-face interview. In organizations, such interviews typically take place in the interviewee's office or in some other location where the interviewee is comfortable speaking. In-person interviews allow the interviewer to meet, talk with, and observe the interviewee often in their normal surroundings. Individual in-person interviews typically last from thirty minutes to three hours.

Telephone Interviews

In contrast to the in-person interview, the telephone interview takes place with the interviewee in his or her office, while the interviewer remains in his or her office. Telephone interviews are often the method of choice when the interviewee is unable to meet face-to-face because of scheduling limitations or when interviewees are in a different geographic location. As a result, telephone interviews avoid the costs and delays caused by extensive travel on the part of the interviewer. However, since the interviewer is not physically present, the interviewer cannot gain insights into the organizational setting through personal observation. Telephone interviews typically last between ten and thirty minutes.

Focus Group Interviews

The major difference between the in-person and a focus group interview is that the in-person interview involves only one interviewee, whereas a focus group interview involves multiple interviewees. Thus, a focus group interview typically consists of six to twelve participants who share a common experience and can collectively address a set of questions (Krueger, 1994; Stewart and Shamdasani, 1990). Keeping the size of the group to a manageable number increases the likelihood that all participants will have an opportunity to speak. As illustrated in the vignette, when you have too many people in a focus group, it may be difficult to gain full participation from each person. When this happens, you potentially lose out on gaining important information.

The interaction among focus group participants can have both positive and negative effects. On the one hand, as group members interact, they may stimulate new ideas and memories. On the other hand, the influence of other group members can be viewed as problematic, if one person dominates or the group reverts to a "group-think" mentality. It is the interviewer's responsibility to keep the interview on track and to encourage everyone to offer his or her experiences, thoughts, and opinions.

To ensure that participants feel safe and comfortable talking with one another, it is usually wise to structure the focus group interviews so that people of similar position, experience, tenure, or need are within the same group. Focus group interviews are generally scheduled for one and a half to three hours.

Determining Which Interview Approach to Use

To determine whether the interview method should be used as an evaluation data collection method, you should consider 1) if an interview approach is an appropriate method given the organization's context and its population, and 2) which interview approach will best address the evaluation key questions. For example, if you are conducting extensive interviews with a small number of individuals in one or only a few locations, you may want to use the in-person interview. If, on the other hand, you are trying to gather information from many people in different locations, you may want to consider conducting a telephone interview. If groups of people are located in certain sites and you want the interaction of a group, then you might choose the focus group interview method.

Advantages of Individual and Focus Group Interviews

There are several advantages of using individual and focus group interviews as an evaluation data collection method. These include:

- Individual or focus group interviews typically provide more in-depth information than other methods. Interviews often result in stories, examples, and qualitative descriptions that would otherwise go unrepresented.
- Both types of interviews allow the interviewer to make a personal connection with the interviewee, which might enhance the quality and quantity of the data provided.
- The interviewer can gather and record personal impressions regarding the interviewee and, possibly, the setting, which may contribute further information to the evaluation.
- Since questions are read or spoken to the interviewee by the interviewer, individual and focus group interviews are particularly useful when gathering data from people for whom reading and writing may be difficult.
- Unlike the survey method, the interviewer knows who the interviewees are and thus can ensure greater participation.
- Both types of interviews can uncover unexpected information.
- Once individuals have agreed to participate in an interview, most are likely to complete the entire interview as compared with a survey.
- In comparison to focus group interviews, individual interviews allow the interviewer to have greater control over the situation, thus ensuring that all the questions are addressed.
- Focus group interviews provide opportunities for participants to interact with one another in ways that may enrich the depth and quality of the data. Participants often motivate each other in ways that result in new ideas and insights.
- Focus group interviews allow for the gathering of data from a large number of people at a relatively low cost.

Disadvantages of Individual and Focus Group Interviews

Although there are many good reasons to use the interview method described on the previous page, there are inherent limitations. These include:

- Although the same questions may be presented in the same manner during individual interviews, interviewees may not interpret them in the same way, and thus may respond quite differently to the questions.
- Both individual in-person and focus group interviews can be relatively expensive methods of data collection as compared with a mail survey, particularly when gathering data from people in diverse locations (which requires travel expenses).
- Qualitative data collected from interviews will take longer to transcribe and analyze than survey, checklist, or test data.
- Some groups within an organization, such as executives, may refuse to participate in a focus group interview. In such cases, you might need to conduct an individual in-person or telephone interview with these individuals.
- Both individual and focus group interviews require skilled and trained interviewers. In contrast, after the difficult work of developing the survey has been completed, a mailed survey can be handed to an administrative person or a mailing house for distribution and follow-up.
- Both types of interviews can be difficult to schedule.

Guidelines for Constructing Individual and Focus Group Interview Guides

The following two sections describe three types of interview questions and discuss the importance of pilot-testing the interview guide.

Types of Interview Questions

As you consider using an interview approach, you need to think about how structured you want the interview to be. For example, you might wish to conduct the interview using an unstructured approach. Here, you may develop one or two questions to guide the interview, but the interview resembles more of a conversation that meanders through certain topics of interest to the interviewee. An unstructured interview may be particularly appropriate when all of the interview questions are not known and preliminary conversations will help identify the most critical or pertinent issues.

A second type of question format is the semistructured approach, whereby the interviewer develops a set of questions to guide the interview process in a consistent manner with all interviewees. However, the semi-structured interview allows for probing, rephrasing of the questions, and asking the questions in a different sequence than laid out on the interview guide. As such, it appears informal and conversational, yet its purpose and direction are clear to the interviewees. This approach is most commonly used for in-person individual and focus group interviews.

The third type of interview is the structured approach. This method is often used for telephone interviews, whereby the interviewer asks each question in the exact order listed on the interview guide of all interviewees. The interviewer using the structured method rarely probes for details or more information, and only sometimes is willing to rephrase a question. Structured interview guides often include rating scales or multiple-choice items. This method is most effective for reducing interviewer bias when several interviewers are used.

Once you have chosen the type of interview that is best suited for your evaluation, one of the next tasks is to develop the interview guide (for semistructured and structured interviews). Many of the suggestions that appear in Chapter 9 on the wording of questions are also relevant for constructing an individual or focus group interview guide.

Pilot-Testing the Interview Guide

Pilot-testing the interview guide can help identify questions that may be confusing to or misinterpreted by interviewees. Conventional pilot-testing has typically consisted of interviewers conducting a small number of interview sessions. Interviewers can then determine if specific items need further clarification or rewriting.

A second approach to pilot-testing is behavior coding, in which an observer views, live or by tape, the pilot interviews. Here, the observer notes the interviewee's reactions to the interviewer and his or her questions. Items that elicit a response that varies from the intended question or seem to be confusing to the interviewee are then modified for the final interview guide.

Guidelines for Conducting Individual and Focus Group Interviews

This section focuses on the recruiting of interview participants and suggestions for scheduling the interviews.

Recruiting Participants

Regardless of the type of interview, the interviewer will need to make some initial contact with potential interviewees. This initial contact can be extremely important in securing their cooperation and participation. The following are some guidelines to facilitate this process.

- Either in a letter or by phone, briefly describe the purpose of the evaluation and what will be done with the information. Your goal is to stimulate potential participants' interest in the evaluation (see Figures 10.1 and 10.2 for examples of recruiting scripts).
- For both individual and focus group interviews, you may need to ask some qualifying questions during the recruitment stage. For example, you may want to include only those who have experienced a layoff in their department. If so, such qualifying questions should be asked early in the recruiting call and certainly prior to making arrangements for the individual or focus group interview.
- For all interviews, assure the person, if you can, that the information will be kept confidential.
- If you can offer an incentive for their participation, then do so. However, be aware that cash payment for participating in inter-

FIGURE 10.1   Example of a Recruiting Script for an In-Person Interview

Hello, my name is Cathy Mansfield. I'm calling from the Organizational Development and Performance Department of Santa Fe Concepts, Inc. Jake Richards, the site coordinator for the training program you participated in last month, gave me your name. He said that you might speak with me about your experience with the course, "How to Learn on the Web." We are looking at ways to improve the course and thus are conducting an evaluation of its design and effectiveness. We want the course to be both educational and visually engaging.

I would like to schedule an interview with you during the week of October 10. Our conversation should take about thirty minutes, and I would be happy to come to your office. Would you be willing to participate? *If Yes*, What day and time works best for you? *If No*, Okay, thanks anyway.

Name   _____

Department: _____

Address: _____

                      _____

Phone: _____

Date/day and
time: _____

Or

Reason for
refusal: _____

                      _____

Thank you for your time. *(Hang up)*

views may be considered income and therefore taxable. This could create problems if the payment is to a public agency or to certain kinds of organizations. In these and other cases, you may wish to provide certificates, small gift items, or the like.

- Arrange a time for the interview. For an in-person or telephone interview, this should be at the earliest mutually acceptable time. For a focus group interview, suggest one or more possible times if multiple group sessions will be conducted.

FIGURE 10.2   Example of a Recruiting Script for a Focus-Group Interview

Name:	Follow Up: Faxed Info, call back
Department:	"Service Plus" Date/Time:
Address:	Phone: Fax:

Hello, my name is Ben Viejo and I'm calling from the instructional technology department. I understand that you recently participated in a web-based training program on customer service skills called "Service Plus."

[*IF YES*] We are conducting an evaluation to determine how effective the course was in helping participants service their customers. We would like to invite you to attend one of four focus group interviews that we will be conducting in the boardroom on the 10th floor. The purpose of the interview will be to understand your experiences as you've tried to apply what you learned back to the job.

[*IF INTERESTED*] We are scheduling focus groups at four different times.
Tuesday, May 20, from 11:00 to 1:00
Tuesday, May 20, from 3:00 to 5:00
Wednesday, May 21, from 11:00 to 1:00
Wednesday, May 21, from 3:00 to 5:00

Which of these times and dates would be best for you? [*Check the selected time and date.*]

Time:	Tuesday, May 20	Wednesday, May 21
11:00–1:00		
3:00–5:00		

[*Let them know that lunch will be provided during the 11:00–1:00 time slot and refreshments will be served during the 3:00–5:00 time slots.*]

Thank you for agreeing to participate. We will fax you a confirmation within the week. Can you please give me a fax number? Is this your correct title and address? [*Read them the title and address that is listed.*] If you have any questions, please feel free to call Sally Jones at 555-5555.

[*If person is not interested thank them for their time and move on. If they're not sure, schedule a follow-up call.*]

- State the beginning and ending time and the anticipated length of the interview. You should be sure to give some reasonable time that you will not exceed (unless at the urging of the intervie-wees).
- For both individual in-person and focus group interviews, iden-tify the location for the meeting. Be sure that the setting pro-vides a private and quiet environment. For the individual inter-view, don't assume that the person's office is the best place.
- Leave a telephone number, e-mail address, or other contact in-formation where you can be reached, if necessary, before the in-terview.

When inviting people to be interviewed, you want to provide them enough information to make them want to participate, but we recom-mend that you not provide the complete list of interview questions ahead of time. Though giving them an overview of the questions is fine, provid-ing them the interview guide might affect the validity of their responses during the interview if they've developed "canned" responses in prepara-tion for the interview. Of course, there may be situations where providing the list of interview questions would be appropriate. For example, you may want to interview people in English who have limited English-lan-guage proficiency. Giving them the interview questions in advance may make them more comfortable and able to respond during the interview.

Scheduling the Interviews

Trying to arrange an interview sometimes feels like climbing Mount Everest. With people's hectic schedules, it is often a good idea to schedule the interviews at least four weeks in advance. Even then, there are in-evitable scheduling or logistical problems that prevent collecting inter-view data in a timely and efficient way. Some of the most common prob-lems and their solutions are summarized below.

- Sometimes it's difficult to reach the individual. First, call the person and leave a voice-mail message. If calling does not yield a response, try using e-mail and fax. If the person still does not re-spond, try contacting colleagues to determine why this person might not be responding. He or she may be on vacation or on a business trip, for example. In addition, you can ask the colleagues to have the person return your call. If none of these procedures works, you may want to substitute this person with another interviewee of the same type.

- If a potential interviewee is hesitant to participate, reexplain the evaluation purpose and emphasize the importance of their participation. Be sure to let them ask questions, and try to address any concerns they may have. Be careful not to annoy the person or goad them into participating. When the person refuses, try to find out why they do not wish not to participate.

- If the person is concerned about confidentiality, provide reassurance that only the evaluation team will see the notes or the transcripts of specific individual or focus group interviews. Indicate that quotes from an interview that are included in a report will not be attributed by name. However, there may be times when an individual may be asked permission to use a specific quote in a final report.

- Since delays typically occur in conducting the interview, make an appointment for the earliest possible date.

- Since individual and focus group interviewees may or may not remember the specifics of why you want to interview them or the time of the interview, call, fax, or e-mail each person to remind them of the scheduled time, place, or both. In some cases, you may want to do all three, just to make sure that the participant received the information and remembers the appointment.

- Either before or during an interview, the participant may raise concerns about answering certain questions. The interviewer should assure the person of the right to refuse to answer any particular questions.

- Sometimes a participant really does not have time to be interviewed. In other cases, unexpected schedule changes occur. When this happens, participants tend to be polite and even apologetic about the cancellation. If an interviewee breaks an appointment, for whatever reason, try to reschedule the interview as soon as possible. The interviewer should volunteer to change the location or timing of the interview to make it more convenient if necessary. In the case of focus-group interviews, if another group meeting is possible, then reschedule the participant for another time.

- Ordinarily, individuals have the right to refuse to take part in an evaluation. The interviewer may encounter a person who regards the individual or focus group interview an invasion of privacy. Although this situation is rare, it can occur. If an interviewer encounters a person who refuses to participate or to answer a question, the above approaches can be used. In the case of a firm and final refusal, the interviewer must record the refusal. If the person refuses to participate at all, then seek an appropriate replacement interviewee or focus-group participant, if available (see Chapter 11 on sampling).

The Interviewer's Role

The interviewer often becomes a participant in the study by inadvertently influencing responses through the manner in which questions are asked or responses are acknowledged. Such influences caused by the interaction between the interviewer and the interviewee must be recognized, defined, and minimized to maintain the data's validity and trustworthiness.

Regardless of the type of interview, interviewees may want to portray themselves in an "acceptable" manner. In some cases, they may respond in a way that seems appropriate, socially acceptable, or politically correct to the interviewer. Thus, interviewer affect, question sequence, and even the ordering of information within the question can lead interviewees to respond in a particular way. Therefore, interviewers should be careful not to communicate information to interviewees that would bias their responses, and should in most cases not express their personal views.

The interviewer should, however, try to develop rapport by using a friendly, relaxed, and nonjudgmental approach. Developing rapport does not, however, imply that the interviewer should agree with what the interviewee says. Rather, the interviewer should understand and be sensitive to what is being expressed. The following are some suggestions for developing rapport.

- Remain neutral, but not monotonous, in delivering questions. Try to avoid giving positive or negative verbal or nonverbal reactions.
- Do not agree or disagree with the interviewee, either verbally or nonverbally. Raised eyebrows, indicating disagreement with the interviewee, can substantially alter later responses. The interviewer's response should be to affirm understanding of what the interviewee is saying—not agreement or disagreement with it.
- Note that with in-person and focus group interviews, the act of writing what the interviewee has said provides one of the most important indications that you consider the information meaningful and important. Recording responses in writing or on audiotape increases the likelihood that the interviewee will continue to talk.
- Maintaining eye contact with the interviewee indicates interest in the comments of the interviewee.
- If you feel that you must say something to maintain rapport, paraphrase what the interviewee said.

Creating a relaxed atmosphere for the in-person or focus group interview is critical. A receptive, attentive, and interested interviewer can achieve such an atmosphere. In addition, the interviewer should be familiar with the questions so that they can be asked without hesitancy. In some cases, the interviewer may want to work toward memorizing the guide so that he or she can direct attention to the interviewee, rather than to the guide.

Facilitating the Interview

The following guidelines may be useful to consider when preparing for and conducting the interviews.

- The beginning of the individual or focus group interview should include a brief introduction to the purpose of the evaluation, how the respondents were chosen to participate, and an indication of how the information from the interviews will be used. Figure 10.3 (page 283) shows the introduction to a telephone interview, and Figure 10.4 (page 284) presents an example of a focus group introduction.

- Recognizing that the interviewee may have some anxiety regarding the interview, it's usually a good idea to begin with easy or nonthreatening questions. Such questions will enable the interviewee and the interviewer or facilitator to become comfortable with the setting and the process.

- Because focus group participants do not tend to arrive at the same time, it is helpful to prepare a one-page survey for those who come early. The questions should be relevant to the focus group topic, and the facilitator can then ask participants to report on their responses to one or more of the questions at the beginning of the session. This survey could focus on collecting necessary demographic information on the participants. In either case, these surveys should be collected at the end of the focus group interview, because they provide additional, useful data. Make sure to collect surveys from all participants regardless of the time they arrived.

- Ask the questions as they are written on the interview guide if using a more structured interview approach. In general, changes should be limited. It is important to keep the wording of the questions the same for each interviewee. Realistically, however, there will be circumstances when the interviewer will decide that a given question or part of a question is inappropriate. If so, the question may be altered to make it more relevant. If such a change or omission is needed, note what was said or write "omitted" by the question.

- When using a semistructured or structured approach, avoid immediate rephrasing of a question if an answer is not immediately forthcoming. Although an initial silence may lead you to feel that the question has not been understood, allow the interviewee a few moments to come up with an answer or to request clarification. If no answer comes, repeat the question verbatim. If there is still no answer or if the interviewee does not appear to understand the question, try to clarify the question by rewording it. Note, however, if you do reword a question, try to record your exact words in brackets on the interview guide.

FIGURE 10.3   Example of an Introduction for a Telephone Interview

---

Participant ID# _____

Hello, my name is Mary Javier, and I called you a few weeks ago about participating in an evaluation we're conducting on the Leadership Counts training program at Wieviel Enterprises. When we last spoke, you suggested that this would be a good time for the interview. As we discussed during our earlier conversation, the interview should take no longer than 30 minutes. In addition, everything you say will be treated confidentially and no one but the evaluation team will have access to your responses. All of the data collected for this evaluation will be aggregated, and your name will not be used in the final reporting. Is this still a convenient time for you?

If YES, continue with questions.
If NO, when would be a good time to talk?

Date   _____

Time   _____

- Ask all questions on the interview guide, unless you know that an item is inappropriate or irrelevant for specific interviewees. When you are not certain whether a question applies, either ask the question anyway or begin by asking a preliminary, clarifying question (and record it in brackets).
- Be sure to keep track of the time as you are conducting the interview. If you are running out of time, you may need to decide which are the most important questions to ask.
- Recognize that all interviews require some flexibility. Sometimes it's not possible to go in a particular order if interviewees answer other questions in the process of answering one question.

When posing multiple-choice questions in a structured interview, keep in mind the following:

- Do not change the wording of the questions, unless to paraphrase in semistructured interviews.

FIGURE 10.4   Example of an Introduction for a Focus-Group Interview

---

Thank you so much for coming today. My name is Sandra Schmidt. I am part of the evaluation team that has been asked to evaluate the "Creating Passion in the Workplace" initiative that your organization has implemented over the last several months. We greatly appreciate your taking the time to participate in this focus group interview.

For the next ninety minutes, I will be asking you several questions about your opinions and experiences with the program. It's very important that you provide honest and candid feedback since the organization wants to use what they learn from this evaluation (1) to improve the program where needed and (2) to understand the ways in which the program is or is not successful. Rest assured, there are no wrong answers. We are conducting group interviews such as this with employees in each of the company's seven regional offices.

As you answer each question, I will try to note the essence of what you're saying on these flipchart pages. Since it's very important that I capture what you say accurately, please let me know if I've represented your thoughts in a meaningful way. If not, I will certainly correct it. I will also be tape-recording our conversation so that I can be sure to capture everything you say. If any of you would not like to be tape-recorded, please let me know at this time.

All of the information you provide today will be treated confidentially. We will not be using any names in our evaluation report. However, so that we can follow each person's comment, we've given you each a number (on your name tent) and will use that number next to your comment on the flipchart pages. This will just tell us how many different people provided the various responses.

At your table, we've provided paper and a pencil for you to use to note anything you'd like to say while others are talking (just so you don't forget!). Please feel free to get up and help yourself to the refreshments.

Do you have any questions or concerns about what we're going to do here today?

Okay, let's get started! Let's first have each person introduce him or herself.

- For multiple choice or rating scale questions, read the alternative responses clearly enough so that the interviewee can hear them. Repeat the alternatives if necessary.
- If an interviewee does not know the meaning of a word used in a question, define the word.
- If an interviewee gives a reply other than the choices available or one that supplements or explains it in any significant way, record the reply next to the question, for later use in the analysis.
- At the conclusion of the interview, you should ask each interviewee if he or she has any questions or anything else they'd like to offer. Thank the interviewees for their cooperation and indicate that the interview was useful and worthwhile.

Confidentiality of Interviewees' Responses

Anonymity is nearly impossible when conducting individual and focus group interviews. Confidentiality can, however, be provided to interviewees for in-person and telephone individual interviews. Confidentiality means that the interviewer may know who the interviewees and their responses are, but they do not divulge their responses to anyone else. When reporting the findings no identifying information is provided without permission.

However, in a focus group interview setting, interviewers cannot guarantee complete confidentiality since participants may choose to relay what they've heard to others outside of the focus group. Nevertheless, the interviewer should clearly explain that the evaluators regard the information as confidential and should request that participants treat what they hear as confidential. Confidentiality can also be promised by explaining that the interview transcripts, notes, and tapes will not be made available to others outside of the evaluation team.

Asking Probing Questions

Sometimes interviewees' responses do not seem to fit the question or, alternatively, seem to lead to additional important information. In such situations, asking the interviewee additional questions can improve the quality and quantity of the data. These questions are called probes and are designed to clarify, explain, and focus the comments of the interviewee to specific questions. The interviewer should consider using probing questions when:

- The response only partially answers the question
- No response is given
- The response seems irrelevant to the question
- The response is inconsistent with previously given responses
- More information would provide examples or critical incidents to further enhance the original response
- The interviewer can use one or more of the following probing methods
  - *Asking for further clarification.* Probes can be useful after vague or impersonal responses. When probing a response to a certain question, you may want to use the technique of implying that you failed to understand the response. You might ask the question, "Can you tell me a little more about this? I'm not sure that I understand what you mean." This kind of probe is useful when an answer appears to be inconsistent with previous statements or the response is not clear. The interviewer might also say, "Think of a particular example—an example from your own experience. Can you tell me more about that?" After a response that seems significant but somewhat vague, the interviewer could ask, "How did you feel about that?"
  - *Repeating the question.* Sometimes, repeating the question for the interviewee is a useful technique, particularly if the interviewee's answers have strayed from the topic of the question or if the answers indicate a misinterpretation of the question's meaning.
  - *Summarizing the interviewee's reply.* Repeating what was said is one way of making sure that you have understood the interviewee's reply. Repeating the response allows the person to indicate the degree of accuracy of what you think you heard. For example, you might say, "What you are telling me is . . ." This provides an opportunity to elaborate on their response and to obtain confirmation that what they said is what you

heard. Always keep in mind that the interviewer's interpretation may tend to "lead" the interviewee's later responses.

It is important to note that a seemingly nonresponsive answer can mean different things under various circumstances. It might mean that the interviewee is thinking about an answer, wants to evade answering the question, does not know how or in what context to respond, or really does not understand the question. When receiving such a response, the interviewer should use whichever of the above-mentioned probes is appropriate to determine the reason behind the seeming nonresponse and to try to obtain the needed information.

It should be pointed out that probes might not always be effective. Some people just do not remember specific examples or great detail. Another area in which probes may be ineffective is with questions that require highly personal or introspective answers. Some people may not have reflected on the interview topic and may not be able give a detailed reply to the particular question.

The most effective use of probes can be made only when you know the specific objectives of each question you will be asking. Only by knowing what you are after can you recognize an inadequate response. For this reason, it is important that you review the interview guide and the evaluation's key questions thoroughly.

Valuing Silence

Often interviewers feel that they must keep the interviewees occupied with a steady stream of questions. However, it is important to build in opportunities for the interviewee to contemplate a question and formulate a response. Once a question has been asked, the interviewer should allow the interviewee a few seconds to think about the question before beginning some comment or going on to the next question. Because the interviewee has not previously reviewed the questions, as has the interviewer, the person may need some time before answering.

Being silent, while ostensibly "doing nothing," can improve the quality of the interaction. An expectant pause not only allows the interviewee time to reflect on a question but also tends to encourage him or her to be more spontaneous, candid, and thoughtful. A typical pattern in which silence is useful is when the interviewee answers quickly, pauses, and finally makes a modified and sometimes more revealing statement. Occasionally silence during questioning helps create an introspective mood. Such a mood tells the interviewee that the interviewer appreciates a thoughtful response and is willing to wait to hear what the interviewee has to say.

There are, however, two cases in which silence may be misused. Verbal silence contradicted by signs of interviewer anxiety or impatience (for example, squirming, checking one's watch, fiddling, or tapping fingers) is likely to be interpreted by the interviewee as an interruption. Such silence will not encourage contemplative answers. Also, too much silence might cause the interviewee to feel pressured or embarrassed, thereby dampening their willingness to be forthcoming. The interviewer must learn the signs that indicate how much silence is most productive and monitor those signs continuously.

Managing the Unexpected

Overall, most individual and focus group interviews go smoothly and are completed in a professional manner. However, there are occasions when the interviewer is in the uncomfortable position of hearing about and feeling a need to respond to problems that are not necessarily related to the evaluation. The interviewer may encounter an interviewee with problems that might be better handled by an employee assistance program (EAP) counselor, social worker, or friend. The interviewer should not be expected to deliver any service or follow-up on personal problems discovered in the interview setting. If the interviewee is upset about some problem and the interviewer knows of a service or agency that could help in solving that problem, it would be appropriate to mention it as a possible source of assistance. If no appropriate referral is known, offering the interviewee some general sympathy and encouragement is often enough. The interviewer should not inform any staff or agency of a personal problem that is revealed during an individual or focus group interview. Such information is privileged, and to divulge it to any outside person or agency is a violation of confidentiality. Although unlikely, the interviewer may also learn of some illegal activity in the course of the interview. If it is secondhand information, the interviewer should advise the person to talk with an appropriate authority. If the interviewee mentions his or her involvement in some illegal activity, the interviewer may need to consult with a lawyer or at least another evaluator to determine the appropriate course of action. (You may want to refer to the *Program Evaluation Standards* [*Joint Committee on Standards for Educational Evaluation*, 1994] or the *Guiding Principles for Evaluators* [American Evaluation Association, 1995] as mentioned in Chapter 4.)

In rare circumstances, an interviewee may decide to terminate an interview or want to leave a focus group before it is completed. First, the interviewer should determine whether the person is objecting to a certain question (which he or she has a right to do). If that is the case, the interviewer should indicate that the interviewee does not need to answer the question. If the interviewee still wants to terminate participation, the interviewer should determine whether the interviewee is simply tired or ill or has some other work or appointment. In a focus group interview situation, the interviewer should invite the person to leave, thank the person for his or her participation, and continue with the rest of the interview. In the case of an individual interview, the interviewer should ascertain whether the interviewee would consent to continue the interview at another time or on another day. If the interviewee wishes to end the interviewing process and not resume later, the interviewer should thank the person for his or her time before leaving. If appropriate, the interviewer should then arrange for another person who meets the same criteria to be interviewed.

Recording Individual and Focus Group Interview Responses

There are several choices to be made with regard to how the interview data will be documented for later analysis and interpretation. In all cases, consider the extent to which you can promise confidentiality of the transcripts, tapes, or notes.

Audio- or videotape recording. Using an audio- or videotape recorder can be an effective means for documenting individual and focus group interview data. Each interviewee, however, must agree to the tape recording. Indeed, in some states, it is illegal to record a telephone conversation without the person's permission. In any case, ethical practice demands that the interviewer obtain permission to tape-record the interview. Furthermore, it is advisable to obtain a tape recording of the interviewee affirming permission for the taping when recording an in-person or telephone interview. If the person seems anxious or reluctant to be recorded, you can offer to place the equipment in an unobtrusive location or to turn it off and take notes instead. Even if you are taping the individual or focus group interview, you should not rely on it as the only record of the interview. Notes should also be taken if possible. Otherwise, if the taping equipment were to fail, no data would be available.

Handwritten or computer written notes. Responses to all questions should be recorded in such a manner that they can be recalled and rewritten just as they were given by the interviewee—that is, as nearly verbatim as possible. This is not difficult in most cases, especially since the interviewer exercises some control over the pace of the session. Writing quickly and using abbreviations of responses is generally necessary during the session. With experience, interviewers typically develop an effective system of shorthand to faithfully capture the meaning and tenor of each response. In any case, it is important to write up the interview soon after it is over so that limited data loss occurs and so that others involved in the data analysis can read the transcripts.

For many questions, the interviewee may provide detailed examples or stories that can be tape-recorded easily but cannot be completely written down during the interview. For example, stories may be too lengthy to record verbatim or you may be unable to fully describe the tone or inflections with which the interviewee gave an answer. In these situations, it's a good idea to jot a quick note or even a single word. Even without a recorder or in case the equipment fails, the remainder of the answer can be filled in immediately after the interview has ended.

When taking notes during the individual interview, try to ensure that your notes summarize everything that the interviewee has said. In particular, *do not* omit what seems to be peripheral or overly descriptive. These stories often tell a great deal about the interviewee and may be useful in ways that do not appear obvious at the time. By leaving out some of the details, we may inadvertently lose the richness that interviews provide. Furthermore, omitting such details gives a distorted impression of the interview's content and of the interviewees' character and concerns.

As mentioned above, the degree of emotion or emphasis that the interviewee expresses is part of the response. However, it is a difficult thing to record during the session. If the interviewee becomes overly emotional—cries, becomes very animated and enthusiastic, raises his or her voice in discussing some topic, and so on—this can be noted in a word or two. Make it very clear when something is your impression or conclusion and not part of the interviewee's comments by placing brackets around your impressions or comments.

It is also good practice to avoid summarizing or paraphrasing the interviewee's answers. Summarizing or paraphrasing a response results in a loss of information. In some instances, this can distort the interpretation of the interview data, since the summarized response obscures the interviewee's own answer. For example, consider the following:

Verbatim recording	*Summarized recording*
"I have a hard time getting to the training programs. My car is pretty old. I don't like to drive after dark. And, I'm afraid to take a bus at night."	The employee rarely goes to the company training programs.

In addition to distorting the meaning of the response, the summarization fails to provide details of the response that may be crucial to its interpretation. In the example given above, the summary fails to include the actual words used by the interviewee, some elements of the response, or any indication of the length of the response.

Whenever possible, include all your probes, comments, and explanations in your notes. Any such statements made by the interviewer should be recorded on the interview guide at the point in the session where they were made. These statements should appear in brackets or parentheses to differentiate them from the interviewee's statements. This ensures that later interpretations are more accurate, because you will know which statement prompted which response.

Provide a response or explanation for each question in the interview guide. Each question should be either answered by the interviewee or have some explanation as to why it was not answered. Questions might not be asked because the interviewer skipped them, either intentionally or by mistake.

Completing the interview transcript. If using a tape recording of the interview, make a thorough check of the tape to ascertain that the recording is complete and understandable. If the entire tape or portions of the tape are missing or difficult to understand, your handwritten notes should be used to complete the transcript.

The final versions of the interview transcript must be written accurately and legibly. Although having typed copies of the final copies of the notes will ensure legibility, it is not always possible or desirable to wait until a computer is available to do the transcription, particularly when a tape-recording is not available or is difficult to understand. In these cases, the transcription should be done as soon after the interview as possible, preferably within the succeeding twenty-four hours. If possible, the transcription of one interview should be completed before the next interview is conducted. Alternatively, the day's interviews may be written up after all have been completed, but this tends to cause confusion about precisely what was said in which interview. To whatever extent possible, the interviewer should avoid delays, because data loss increases with time.

In addition to the transcript available through the tape-recording or the interview notes, you may also have materials that were created during the interview. Particularly in the case of focus-group interviews, you may use flip charts to gather responses or ideas. These, too, must be transcribed.

Selecting and Training Interviewers

In some cases, you will be conducting an evaluation in which you will employ others to conduct in-person, telephone, or focus group interviews. This may occur when data collection must take place with many people in a short amount of time. Alternatively, you may be conducting an evaluation using a team approach. Whatever the circumstances, you should be sure that all interviewers are carefully selected and trained.

The role of the interviewer is crucial to the data collection process. He or she exerts control over the quality and quantity of data collected, particularly with more complex and extensive interview guides. Interviewees are likely to make judgments about the study and the staff conducting the study based on their personal contacts with the interviewers. For these reasons, the selection, training, and supervision of such staff can represent a major responsibility.

Interviewers may include "outside" contracted professionals, departmental staff, evaluation staff, or some combination of these. The following describes certain advantages and disadvantages associated with using each group.

The main advantage of contracting outside interviewers is the previous experience of these people. Such interviewers usually possess strong technical skills, can gain the confidence of interviewees because of their perceived objectivity, and can dedicate their full time to the completion of data collection. An experienced interview supervisor can easily coordinate day-to-day activities and can serve as a liaison to the lead evaluator. In addition, such a team can usually obtain additional trained personnel when needed. Disadvantages associated with contracted professionals include increased expense, some loss of knowledge when the data-collection team disperses at the end of the project, and lack of in-depth knowledge of and experience with the program or the organization.

The principal advantage of using departmental staff is that they may gain new and more systematic insights into the nature of the program, any areas for improvement, and any impact the program may have on various groups (thus providing for individual, team, and organizational learning opportunities). In addition, interviewing affords them an opportunity to expand their firsthand knowledge about evaluation and the program being evaluated. Because of this knowledge of the program and the people involved, they may also have easy access to interviewees. Furthermore, using departmental staff can reduce data collection costs. Disadvantages of asking departmental staff to conduct the interviews include real or perceived lack of objectivity, lack of interviewing skills, little commitment to the evaluation, and little time to devote to the data collection effort.

Critical Interviewer Skills

Deciding on criteria and procedures for interviewer selection is an important task. The following criteria can be applied to the selection of appropriate contract personnel or departmental staff.

- *Acute observation skills* are an indispensable characteristic of the good interviewer. The interviewer needs to listen carefully and openly to what is stated by the interviewees and must avoid hearing only those things he or she expects to hear.
- *Ability to deal with the unexpected* is a core competency. The interviewer must be able to effectively handle the variety of unexpected challenges that arise in the in-person, telephone, or focus group interview setting.
- *Neutrality* in conducting an evaluation study is essential. If the interviewee senses that the interviewer has an agenda or expects a certain kind of response, the interviewee may not respond honestly, which will then affect the validity of the data. However, the interviewer should be able to express empathy, where appropriate.
- *Interviewing experience* is desirable, though not critical. This includes familiarity with asking a series of questions and handling in-depth probes. Experience may come from related types of interview situations (for example, counseling, clinical, or journalistic interviews).
- *Willingness and ability* to follow the prescribed procedures is a must. The interviewer must be willing and able to complete interviews and the written summaries on schedule and in sufficient detail.
- *Educational background*, including bachelor's level training in the behavioral or social sciences or experience in social science or educational research, should be sought whenever possible. Equivalent paid or volunteer experience may be substituted for academic training.
- *Availability* for the entire period of the data collection effort is clearly necessary.

Interviewer Training

Once selected, the evaluator should prepare interviewers for the data collection task. Ideally, all interviewers should meet as a group in a central place so that they receive the same training. If the group cannot meet at one time and place, two alternatives are available. Training may be done in smaller groups where interviewers are clustered (such as in an organization's regions). The problem with decentralized training is that the reliability of the results may suffer if the content or processes of the various sessions are not consistent.

If in-person, decentralized training is judged infeasible, other media (such as video, web, or telephone conferencing, training manuals, videotapes or audiotapes with illustrative individual or focus group interviews) may be developed and combined with telephone consultation and close supervision. Regardless of the training mode chosen, two agenda items should be included in interviewer preparation: orientation and materials.

Orientation. A thorough orientation to the study—its scope, intent, and possible uses of the evaluation's findings—should be an early part of the agenda. Knowledge of the evaluation's key questions allows the interviewer to ensure that these are addressed. In particular, such knowledge may help the interviewer develop appropriate probes to clarify a point. To minimize the unintended biases of interviewers, several training methods can be used. These methods include critical observations and group discussions to develop an awareness of how interviewer effects manifest themselves and how these effects can be minimized. In addition, demonstration and practice interviews will prove helpful.

Demonstration interviews. The interviewer should be given an opportunity to observe a demonstration session conducted by the evaluator or an experienced interviewer who was involved in the development of the interview guide. The interview may involve interviewees who meet the criteria for inclusion in the study, or interviewees may be role-played by staff members. It is advisable to have all observers take notes as if they were conducting the interview. The notes serve as a basis for later discussions regarding the nature of responses, probing, coding decisions, and issues of interpretation.

Practice interviews. After observing the demonstration interview, trainee interviewers should practice interviewing and recording responses under supervision. Individual interviewers can be paired with each other for practice. Focus group interviewers can lead a small group of staff or other interviewers. After they become comfortable with the interview guide, practice with "real" interviewees is advisable. It is important to include some practice with unexpected responses and situations.

Materials. All written materials for use in the data collection process should be distributed and reviewed. Typically, these materials include the following:

A general *interviewer's handbook* containing sections about the evaluation's purpose and key questions (or the entire evaluation plan), types of interviewees, time schedules, suggested responses to anticipated queries or problems, interviewee privacy and confidentiality, data handling, staff to be contacted and circumstances under which to seek staff help, and other related issues.

Individual and focus-group instruments for each type of interviewee involved in the evaluation.

Related materials, including documents such as introductory letters, follow-up telephone call guidelines, interview handouts, and financial and travel policies and forms.

Managing the Interview Process

Keeping track of who is being interviewed and when is an important part of the management process. It might be advisable to develop an interview management plan to carefully monitor this phase of data collection (see Chapter 14 on planning, managing, and budgeting the evaluation).

Keeping Records of Contacts

Each contact with a interviewee, whether a letter, initial telephone call, follow-up call, or confirmation call should be recorded in some form of a "project log." For each contact you should record:

- The date of the contact
- The type of the contact (for example, letter, initial telephone call)
- The person contacted (name and position)

- The purpose of the contact
- A brief statement of the content of the contact

This information should be filed according to the interviewee's name for easy access.

Interview Logistics

The specific logistics of each interview effort will differ. As a result, you may want to create a week-by-week or day-by-day plan. Nevertheless, the following will need to be a part of any plan.

- Confirming participation. You will want to send some confirmation via e-mail, fax, letter, or postcard of the scheduled time for the in-person, telephone, or focus group interview.
- Assembling materials. For each interview, you will need to gather all of the appropriate materials. These may include: interview guides, surveys, flip charts, markers, adhesive tape, video or audio recorders, batteries, microphones, and tapes.
- Labeling materials. At the conclusion of each interview, you should label the tape, surveys, and flip charts with the date, location, and the name of the interviewee or group.

Computer-Aided Interviewing

Computers are not only being used for surveys but they are also becoming an important part of conducting individual and focus group interviews. The following will discuss some aspects of computer use in individual and focus group interviews.

Computer-assisted telephone interviewing (CATI) systems were first developed in the 1970s. Here the interviewer is led through the interview guide, and the interviewer can enter the responses directly into the computer. Some advantages of CATI systems are that the computer can provide:

- Complex skip and branching patterns in the questioning
- Rotation of choices to present to the interviewee
- Insertion of the response from a previous question.
- Access to previous historical data on the interviewee.

The major disadvantage is that the interviewer may seem somewhat constrained and stiff. Skilled interviewers can easily overcome such problems.

In recent years, some advances have occurred in computer-aided interviewing. In-person interviews can now use laptop computers to enable computer-assisted personal interviewing (CAPI). This has now advanced so that the computer can provide the questions orally. For example, Turner, Ku, Rogers, Lindberg, Pleck, and Sonenstein (1998) conducted a study comparing the use of audio computer–assisted self-interviewing (audio-CASI) or audio-computer-assisted self-administered interviewing (audio CASAI) with the traditional self-administered questionnaire. This audio-CASI or audio-CASAI approach presents interviewees with questions that have been digitally recorded and stored on a laptop computer. In addition, the questions are presented on the screen in visual form. The interviewee can then simply type the response into the computer.

Computers can be used in focus-group interviews as well. The interviewer can use a form of groupware to poll the individuals in the focus group for their responses to certain questions. In these cases, individuals can respond without seeing other participants' responses until and unless the interviewer wants to show those responses.

··

Keep in Mind . . .

- Interviews provide an excellent way of gathering in-depth information.
- The three types of interviews are (1) individual in-person interviews, (2) telephone interviews, and (3) focus group interviews.
- The interviewer plays a critical role in facilitating the interview, maintaining confidentiality, asking probing questions, managing unexpected situations, and recording responses.

- Interviewers should be selected based on their acute observation skills, their ability to deal with the unexpected, their ability to remain neutral, and their willingness to follow the prescribed procedures.

Background and Context of Evaluation

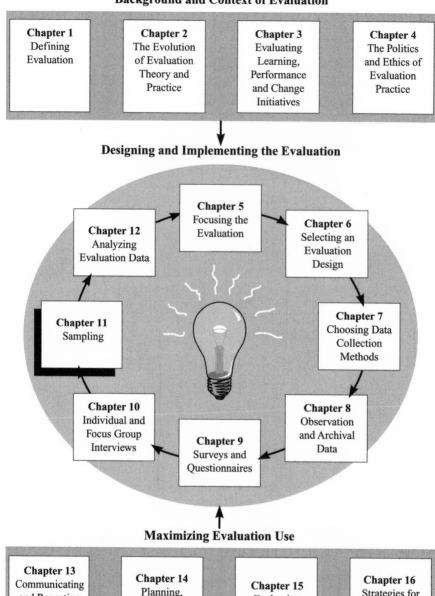

Chapter 1
Defining
Evaluation

Chapter 2
The Evolution
of Evaluation
Theory and
Practice

Chapter 3
Evaluating
Learning,
Performance
and Change
Initiatives

Chapter 4
The Politics
and Ethics of
Evaluation
Practice

Designing and Implementing the Evaluation

Chapter 12
Analyzing
Evaluation Data

Chapter 5
Focusing the
Evaluation

Chapter 6
Selecting an
Evaluation
Design

Chapter 11
Sampling

Chapter 7
Choosing Data
Collection
Methods

Chapter 10
Individual and
Focus Group
Interviews

Chapter 9
Surveys and
Questionnaires

Chapter 8
Observation
and Archival
Data

Maximizing Evaluation Use

Chapter 13
Communicating
and Reporting
Evaluation
Activities
and Findings

Chapter 14
Planning,
Managing and
Budgeting
the Evaluation

Chapter 15
Evaluating
the Evaluation

Chapter 16
Strategies for
Implementing
Evaluation in
Organizations

chapter 11

Sampling

- Approaches to Sampling
- Sampling Procedures
- Issues to Consider When Selecting a Sample

••

Vignette #9: Selecting a Sample at MyDepartment of Labor

Joan Cushing, a trainer with MyDepartment of Labor, was asked to conduct an evaluation of a new software application that was being delivered via computer-based training. To evaluate the program's effect on trainees' knowledge of the software's functions, she decided to develop and use a knowledge test with the pretest-posttest control group design. The next time the course was offered, over forty employees signed up, but there were only twenty spaces available. Therefore, she decided to select the first twenty people who registered to be the trainee group, and assigned the next twenty people to the control group. Since she didn't want to deprive the control group employees the benefit of taking the course, she offered the program to these employees one month later.

••

The term "sample," according to *The American Heritage Dictionary*, refers to "a set of elements drawn from and analyzed to estimate the characteristics of a population." Thus, in the vignette above, Joan selected some people from the organization (called a sample) with the hopes of being able to generalize these results to all the people in the organization (called the population). As mentioned in Chapter 6, the method of sampling can directly affect the data's internal and external validity. This chapter will discuss various strategies for drawing a sample and will highlight each method's strengths and weaknesses.

Why Sample?

Sampling is undertaken when it is difficult or not feasible to involve the entire population in the evaluation. Reasons for this include:

- Time constraints—you do not have the time to interview a large number of individuals.
- Cost constraints—you do not have the travel budget to visit various places to collect data.
- Limited accessibility—some people within the population are difficult to reach.
- Accuracy may be compromised—for example, if you cannot find qualified interviewers to conduct all of the interviews, the quality of the data may be less than desired.

In the following sections, we describe several sampling approaches. But first, it's important to consider the following issues when choosing a sampling method.

- Budget—how much money is available for travel, hiring consultants, interviewers, postage, audiotapes, and other materials.
- Size of the population
- Geographical location(s) of the population
- Availability of a sampling frame (a list of all those in the population)
- The data collection method(s)
- How much variance there is in the population

Approaches to Sampling

A fundamental question to ask before selecting a sampling approach is: *Do you want a sample that represents the total population so that you may generalize the study's findings?* If the answer is "Yes," then you will want to draw a probability sample, whereby participants are randomly selected. This means that each person has an equal chance of being selected. If generalization is not a goal, or if you wish to select specific kinds of individuals to participate in the various data collection activities, then you would be interested in a nonprobability sampling procedure.

Nonprobability sampling. Depending on the evaluation's purpose and key questions, you may wish to use one of the following nonprobability sampling methods: convenience sampling, purposive sampling, and snowball sampling. It is important to remember that these sampling approaches do not provide information that can be generalized to larger populations with much confidence. This is because the sample is not randomly selected, and thus the sample may include some unknown bias that could affect the validity or usefulness of the findings.

1. Convenience sampling. Within many organizations, it is sometimes difficult, if not impossible, to draw a random sample. Thus, we often resort to selecting members of the population that are most accessible. For example, in the beginning vignette, Joan was not in a position to determine who would or would not receive the training program since the organization's commitment is to provide just-in-time training to all its employees. Therefore, Joan used a convenience sampling method whereby the first twenty people who signed up for the computer-based training course became her sample.

The drawback of this approach is that Joan won't know if the first people to register for the course represent certain characteristics that could bias the outcome of the evaluation. For example, do these first twenty people learn particularly well from computer-based programs, or are they extremely motivated individuals who always try new things first? Their comfort with technology or their high level of motivation could affect their level of engagement in the course and as a result produce more positive posttest results than might be found if the sample were randomly selected from the organization's total population.

Another example of convenience sampling is when people agree to participate in a focus group interview or return a survey. It is possible that the people who agree to provide information for an evaluation are those who feel strongly about an issue. Although these individuals may supply extremely interesting and useful information, we have no way of telling if their perspectives are representative of the larger population.

2. Purposive sampling. A purposive sample involves the selection of specific individuals because of their position, experience, knowledge, or attitudes. For example, let's say you wanted to evaluate senior managers' opinions of the organization's newly implemented performance management system. Since you were particularly interested in these managers' perceptions, you would only select senior managers to participate in the study.

Another example of purposive sampling can be found in Lackey's (2000) study of the role of Chief Learning Officers (CLOs) in North American organizations. She initially sought respondents with the title of "Chief Learning Officer (CLO)," through notices on Internet lists as well as through professional networking. Persons who had identified themselves as Chief Learning Officers or leaders of organizational learning, either in the literature or on the Internet, were then contacted. To establish their fit with her research questions, she selected her final sample by the extent to which they represented the following criteria: 1) they had been in the CLO position for at least one year, 2) they were from profit as well as nonprofit organizations, and 3) they worked in various types of industries and services. In addition, she wanted to make sure that the sample included females as well as males. In the end, she was able to conduct in-depth interviews with fourteen Chief Learning Officers. Because Lackey was specifically interested in studying people who were in CLO positions, a purposive sample was deemed most appropriate. However, because her sample was not randomly selected, she was limited in her ability to generalize the findings beyond those interviewed.

3. Snowball sampling. A third type of nonprobability sampling is the snowball sample. In this case, one contacts certain organizations, departments, or individuals and asks them for suggestions as to who might be in a position to provide the necessary information. It is a particularly useful approach when a list of names is difficult or impossible to obtain. For example, if you were interested in studying the background and experience of those involved in mentoring new employees, you might obtain a list of mentors from a local organization that you know has a mentorship program and arrange to interview a sample of these individuals. As you concluded your interview with each person, you would ask him or her for the names and phone numbers of mentors in other organizations.

Robbins (2001) provides another example of using the snowball sampling technique. In his study of mapping how knowledge is processed within an organization during a crisis, he explored through interviews and documents the chain of events that led to a resolution of specific problems. After identifying a particular episode to explore, he contacted one of the key participants who appeared to be most knowledgeable about the situation. He then conducted an interview with the individual seeking details on the sequence of events and other people involved in the episode. From the names provided by the first contact, he selected others to interview. As a result of this process, he was able to interview five to nine individuals for each episode he explored.

Probability sampling. As explained earlier, a probability sample ensures that every member of the population has an equal chance of being selected for the sample. It is usually applied when one seeks to generalize the findings of the evaluation to the larger population. An advantage of drawing a random sample is that a sampling error can be estimated. The sampling error is the difference between the *sample* results and the results if one had conducted the evaluation with the entire *population*. By knowing the sampling error, one can determine the precision of the results obtained from the sample that can then affect the level of confidence decision makers may have in the findings. The following paragraphs describe different types of probability sampling methods.

1. Simple random sampling. With this approach, you merely take the whole population and randomly select those who will be part of the sample. For example, if we wanted to pilot-test a new knowledge management system with a small group of the organization's employees, and wanted to make sure that everyone had an equal opportunity of being selected, we could draw a random sample. In this case, we aren't concerned about individuals' position or location—we just want whoever is randomly selected.

Although simple random sampling is fairly straightforward and easy to understand, it is not frequently used in an organizational context for several reasons. First is the difficulty in obtaining a complete and accurate list of the population. If the population consists of customers, clients, vendors, or others external to the organization, it may be difficult to acquire a list of names and addresses. Furthermore, many employees may have left the organization since the original contact was made. Second, the clerical effort that is required to number each person on the list to draw a sample may be very time-consuming if the population is large. Third, if an organization's records are incomplete (for example, there is an address, but no phone number), this will make it even more difficult to contact individuals. Finally, it may not be appropriate to select some individuals and not others. The politics and the ethics of the situation must be considered for each evaluation.

2. Stratified random sampling. This is an extension of simple random sampling that involves dividing the population into a set of subpopulations, such as regions, personnel levels, or departments. These subpopulations are called strata. Simple random sampling then takes place within each stratum.

Using stratified random sampling allows one to control for problems that may result in random oversampling or undersampling of some strata (for example, different departments within an organization). The stratification ensures that each stratum or subpopulation is sampled and thus represented. This approach enables the evaluator to analyze the data of different subgroups and to compare and contrast the findings for each group. So, in the example of pilot testing the knowledge management system, if we used a simple random sampling approach it could possibly lead to a sample that fails to include certain departments, particularly if they contain only a few people. If the findings were favorable showing that the knowledge management system was being well used, some might then argue that the system shows good results only for particular kinds of people. It is important, therefore, to identify variables to use in the stratification that may affect the results or be of concern to decision makers. These might include job functions, departments, locations, and regions of the country or the world.

Another type of stratification is *proportional stratified sampling,* which involves the *purposive* oversampling of some strata and the undersampling of others. This might also be used when some departments have only a few staff members. You might want to begin by selecting a variable to be sampled, such as the number of people in each grade or personnel level within the organization. You would then decide what percentage of each level you would like to sample, for example, 20 percent. The next step would be to randomly select 20 percent of the individuals at each grade or level to participate in the evaluation. For statistical analysis purposes, it's important to have at least twenty people in each stratum.

3. Cluster sampling. This type of sampling, which is also called multistage or hierarchical sampling, refers to a situation in which you first sample some larger unit and then you sample within the larger unit. It is particularly useful for reducing costs and the time required to survey people across many different locations. For example, we might want to evaluate how various field offices are using the results of evaluations they've conducted. We therefore select six of the twelve most profitable field offices and within each office, draw a random sample of employees to interview. The major disadvantage with cluster sampling stems from potential confusion that arises when trying to keep clear the units or clusters of analysis.

Sampling Procedures

The following are general guidelines for drawing a probability sample:

1. Identify the population of interest.
2. Create a list of all the members of that population.
3. Decide whether you will use any stratification with or without proportional sampling or clustering. If you decide to stratify the population, you must decide on the stratum levels, the proportions, or the type of clustering.
4. Decide on the method for selecting the random sample.

One method for drawing the random sample uses a *physical mixing* and *drawing of names*. For example, you could list each person in the population on separate pieces of paper and then put these pieces of paper into a box. After mixing up the pieces of paper, you would pull names out of the box until you reached the desired sample number. The only problem with this method is that it can be awkward and laborious if the population and sample is large. In addition, such physical mixing may not actually lead to an equal probability of selection if that mixing is not thorough enough or if the paper sizes or weights are not all equal.

Another method for selecting the random sample would be to use a *random number generator on a computer*. In this case, you would assign each person on the list a unique number. Then if the computer selects that person's number that person would be part of the sample. A table of random numbers that can be found in most research and statistics books is also an effective way for randomly selecting a random sample. A possible variation to this is to use an existing random number already assigned to each employee (for example, their phone extension). If you want a 10 percent sample, randomly select a number from a random number generator and select employees with an extension that ends in that number.

A third method is called *systematic sampling*. In this case, every nth member is drawn from a list of the population (for example, every third name in the client database). This method is considered a form of random sampling when there are no patterns in how the population is listed. Thus, as long as you do not think that the list contains some organizing feature, such as every fourth person is from a particular department, you begin the sampling process by randomly selecting the starting point. Then you would choose every nth person, depending upon the number and percent of the population that you want to select, such as every tenth person on the list.

Issues to Consider When Selecting a Sample

Although the process for selecting those who will participate in an evaluation is not particularly difficult, there are several issues to consider beforehand.

Representativeness

A sample is representative of a population, or capable of being made representative, if two conditions are met. First, there are well-defined rules for random selection of the sample from the population. These rules include a definition of the population, a description of the type of sampling method being used, and a description of the sampling method. Second, a sample member must represent every population member in some fashion. In some cases, however, where sample members represent different numbers of population members, as with oversampling or undersampling, one may want to use weights during the data analysis process to make the results representative.

If you want to make some estimate about the entire population (that is, population estimate), you will need to use a more rigorous sampling method than if your focus is on exploring relationships among variables. For example, you may undertake an evaluation to determine the percentage of employees in the United States who receive more than fifteen hours of training each year. In this case, you would be concerned about the representativeness of the sample. Therefore, you could oversample from some strata, such as part-time employees, and still achieve representativeness by weighting the data differentially. Such representativeness is necessary for external validity (generalizability). For other types of evaluations, however, such careful attention to representativeness is not as critical. In these cases, the members of the sample may represent variation across the population, although not according to any particular quantitative rule. For example, an evaluation might focus on a question such as, "Do employees who attend more hours of training have better on-the-job performance?" If you were interested in answering this question, you might want to make sure that some part-time employees were included in the sample, but you would not need to deal with weighting the data.

Sample size.   In determining a sample's size, we need to ask, "How many is enough?" Clearly, the larger the sample, the more likely it will represent the total population. The sample's size depends on several factors.

- *The rarity of a specific characteristic or event*—If the variable or characteristic is rather rare, then a larger sample should be used. For example, if the probability of a safety violation at a particular plant is low, you would have to sample a larger part of the population or a larger sample of archival data.
- *Available resources*—If there is sufficient time, personnel, and money, then you might draw a large random sample. For example, with more resources, you have the ability to collect and analyze more data.
- *The degree of precision that is needed*—If the evaluation involves determining whether training led to improved safety at a nuclear power plant, then you may want to draw a larger sample so that you can be more accurate in determining whether the benefits outweigh the potential side effects.
- *The desire to generalize the findings*—If generalization is not a goal, then the number depends on the key evaluation questions, how many methods are being used to collect data, and what decision makers believe would be sufficient in order to use the findings. If generalization is a goal of the evaluation, then you would likely choose a probability sampling method.

It is important to remember, however, that a large sample size does not necessarily result in a representative sample. As can be seen in Figure 11.1, if the population you wanted to study is comprised of 300 people, you would only need data from 168 people to have a 95 percent confidence level in the results. With the confidence level at 95 percent, there's only a 5 percent chance that your results would be due to error. Thus, if you found that 75 percent of the employees responded in a certain way, these results would be precise within plus or minus 5 percent (or between 70 percent and 80 percent). In contrast, you may decide on a lower level of precision, leading to a sample of seventy-three people. Although you could still have a 95 percent confidence level in the results, the results would be less precise. In the previous example, where 75 percent of the employees responded in a certain way, the results would be precise within plus or minus 10 percent (or between 65 and 85 percent).

The relationship of sample size to credibility for particular audiences is more difficult to predict. A specific sample size may appear too small to certain decision makers and stakeholders, regardless of the actual level of precision. For example, you may have a population of 400 employees in the organization. According to Figure 11.1 (opposite), you would need data from a sample of 196 for a high level of precision. If you were concerned that responses from certain departments might be underrepresented, you may intentionally treat each department as a stratum. To do so would then require sampling from each department. If we assume that each of the four departments has 100 people, you would have to select 80 employees from each department for a total of 320 people. At this point, you may decide that it would be better to include all employees rather than drawing a sample.

Sampling Errors

Both sampling and nonsampling errors can occur when drawing any sample. One example of a sampling error would be the procedure used to interview whoever answers the telephone on a single call to a phone number. This is a common method used in telephone surveys. If no one answers, the random-digit-dialer proceeds to select another number. The reason that this provides a source of sampling error is because those who are easy to reach on the phone tend to differ from the population as a whole. Similarly, if you used a phone book from which to select names it would eliminate anyone who either has an unlisted number or doesn't have a telephone.

Nonsampling error can arise from a variety of sources. One important source is that of nonresponse or missing data. Missing data can arise because of an inability to contact a person or because of a person's refusal to participate or to answer specific questions. In the case of a refusal to participate, you should focus on using whatever (ethical) means are necessary to achieve cooperation and participation. Usually, some personal contact and explanation of the purpose of the study is all that is needed to obtain the participation of nonrespondents. Suggestions for dealing with missing data because of nonresponse appear in Chapter 12.

FIGURE 11.1   Determining a Sample Size (confidence level = 95%)

Population	Required Precision + or - 5%	Required Precision + or - 10%
Total Number of People	Sample Size	Sample Size
50	44	33
75	63	42
100	80	49
150	108	59
200	132	65
300	168	73
400	196	78
500	217	81
1,000	277	88
3,000	340	93
5,000	356	94
10,000	369	95

Another source of nonsampling error arises because of response errors. In this case, the respondent lies or provides an inaccurate account. Respondents either may not tell the truth when asked sensitive or personal questions, or may provide an inaccurate account because they don't remember. Suggestions for enhancing the data's quality can be seen in Chapters 9 and 10. An additional source of nonsampling error results from processing the data. Processing errors can occur when entering the data into the computer or computing the analyses by hand, where there is a high likelihood of hitting wrong keys or losing track of where one is in the entry process. These kinds of errors suggest the need for a thorough checking and rechecking of the accuracy of the data entry process.

••

Keep in Mind . . .

- You draw a sample when you cannot collect data from the entire population.
- You need to decide whether to draw a *random* or a *nonrandom* sample and then choose from a variety of methods for selecting individuals or groups.
- You need to decide on the desired level of representativeness and the size of the sample.

Background and Context of Evaluation

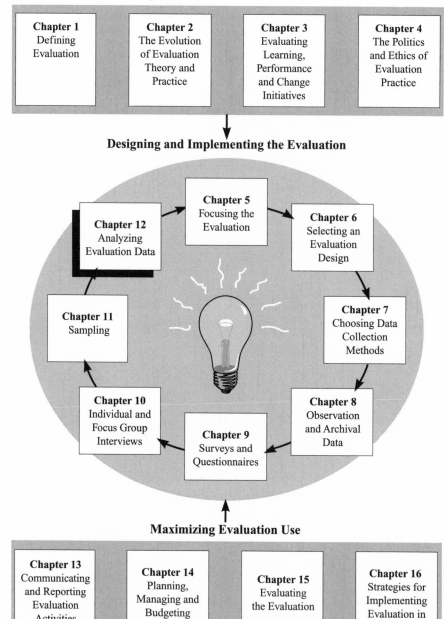

| **Chapter 1** Defining Evaluation | **Chapter 2** The Evolution of Evaluation Theory and Practice | **Chapter 3** Evaluating Learning, Performance and Change Initiatives | **Chapter 4** The Politics and Ethics of Evaluation Practice |

Designing and Implementing the Evaluation

Chapter 5 Focusing the Evaluation

Chapter 6 Selecting an Evaluation Design

Chapter 7 Choosing Data Collection Methods

Chapter 8 Observation and Archival Data

Chapter 9 Surveys and Questionnaires

Chapter 10 Individual and Focus Group Interviews

Chapter 11 Sampling

Chapter 12 Analyzing Evaluation Data

Maximizing Evaluation Use

| **Chapter 13** Communicating and Reporting Evaluation Activities and Findings | **Chapter 14** Planning, Managing and Budgeting the Evaluation | **Chapter 15** Evaluating the Evaluation | **Chapter 16** Strategies for Implementing Evaluation in Organizations |

Analyzing Evaluation Data

- Basic Considerations for Analyzing Data
- Approaches to Qualitative Data Analysis
- Approaches to Quantitative Data Analysis
- Economic Analyses of Learning, Performance, and Change Interventions
- Potential Problems in Analyzing Data

••

Vignette #10: Doing the Right Thing with Data at MyLearning and Associates

After administering surveys and conducting interviews with trainees after a workshop, trainer Tom Wells reflects: Well, finally, we have the satisfaction ratings and the in-person interview transcripts from all fifty trainees. What options do I have for analyzing the data? Well, I could count the number of people who rated that they were "very satisfied," and then pick out one or two quotes from these interviews. That would be fast and easy. On the other hand, I could undertake a more thorough analysis of all the data. I could do a qualitative analysis of the interview transcripts to determine in what ways people are using what they learned back on the job, what factors are supporting their use of the skills, and what factors are preventing them from using what they learned. Maybe there is a way to determine whether the satisfaction scores correlate with use of the skills on the job.

••

Tom is faced with making decisions about how to analyze the data that have been collected as part of the program's evaluation. Just picking the easiest and fastest way to analyze the data may not be the best tactic. Al-

313

though it surely is a way to wrap things up quickly, it may also produce invalid results and could garner serious criticism. In this chapter, we describe various approaches for analyzing both quantitative and qualitative data collected during an evaluation. First, we provide some basic considerations regarding the data's analysis. In the next two sections, we present decision trees to aid you in identifying the most appropriate analyses based on the type of data collected. In addition to some commonly used qualitative and quantitative analysis techniques, we discuss issues related to conducting economic analyses and the use of computer software to facilitate the data analysis process.

Basic Considerations for Analyzing Data

In this section, we deal with using the evaluation's key questions as a guide to data analysis, choosing and communicating data analysis methods so that stakeholders will understand, types of data, levels of data, and the robustness and sensitivity of data.

Using the Evaluation's Key Questions as a Guide

The first consideration in analyzing evaluation data involves a review of the evaluation's purpose and key evaluation questions. Once having collected the data, you may be tempted to explore something interesting that wasn't part of the original purpose or key questions. Such explorations should be planned and executed only after the key questions have been addressed. In order to ensure that you have answered all of these questions, you may want to create a matrix that links or shows the relationship between the key questions, the available data, the proposed analyses, and possible problems with the data or the analyses (see Chapter 14 for some examples).

Considering Stakeholders' Understanding of Data Analysis Methods

When choosing methods of data analysis, it is also important to consider the stakeholders' level of technical expertise when it comes to understanding the results of quantitative data analyses. With the availability of statistical software, it is not uncommon for statistical analysis procedures to be used that few or none of the evaluation staff fully understand. Of primary importance, however, is the comprehensibility and clarity of the results. Thus, although you should not choose a particular analysis procedure just because a stakeholder may or may not be familiar with the approach, you should consider how you would communicate the purpose of the analysis and its results. This may mean that you will need to analyze the same data in more than one way to tailor the communicability of the findings to different groups. For some stakeholders, a quote from one or two interviews can provide a good summary of the data. In other cases, frequencies, percentages, and simple two-way tables and graphs are as much as some stakeholders want to know and can use. Information such as the standard deviation and standard error, as well as correlations, may also provide key insights into the results. Some stakeholders may even be comfortable with multiple regression analyses, analysis of variance, analysis of covariance, discriminant analysis, and factor analysis procedures. In such cases when the stakeholder group comprehends statistics, such complex analyses (when appropriately used) can lend greater credibility to the evaluation.

The use of procedures that do not require or assume analytical sophistication on the part of the stakeholders has the advantage that the results are more easily communicated, are clearly relevant to the information needs of the program, and are based on methods that are available and uncontroversial. The validity of the results is usually higher, because there are fewer assumptions involved in the proper use of the methods. Certainly, credibility is higher when results can be clearly presented and articulated. On the other hand, more sophisticated procedures may increase the precision and generalizability of results. This can occur when statistical procedures can correct for effects resulting from characteristics that differ between the evaluation sample and the general population. Advanced analysis procedures may also produce insights into complex relationships among variables that would not otherwise be apparent. Such insights can increase the usefulness of the evaluation's findings. When these more complex analyses are truly appropriate for the data, you need to take steps and time to develop and present simplified, understandable explanations of their meaning.

Types of Data (Quantitative and Qualitative)

This consideration focuses on whether the data are quantitative (numerical) or qualitative (that is, descriptions of incidents, actions, and processes). Quantitative analyses, as compared with qualitative analyses, usually involve less personnel time, are almost always performed using computers, and often result in substantially lower data analysis costs. In some cases and for some stakeholders, "hard numbers" are seen as more credible than the text-based analyses of qualitative data, even if they are not any more valid. On the other hand, the power of individuals' words from a qualitative analysis often "speak" more loudly to some stakeholders.

Analysis of qualitative data, on the other hand, can be more expensive and time-consuming than quantitative analyses because of the amount of time it takes to read, categorize, and code transcripts that result from interviews or observations and open-ended items from surveys. In addition, the process of analyzing qualitative data usually requires a greater level of training or expertise on the part of the persons analyzing the data to obtain valid and credible results.

Levels of Data

We use numbers in a variety of ways. Many times, we use numbers in a mathematical or statistical way, such as balancing our checkbook, whereby we are adding and subtracting. In other cases, numbers are associated with objects and are not necessarily mathematical in nature. For example, telephone numbers or zip codes are not usually values that are added, subtracted, multiplied, or divided. When you are collecting quantitative data, it is important to consider the level of data they represent.

- *Nominal data.* Numbers are often used to name, distinguish, or categorize groups or objects. For example, you might distinguish different organizations from each other by giving them numbers (as in Organizations 1, 2, and 3) or different departments in the same organization (as in Departments 1, 2, and 3). With nominal level data, all you can say is that one piece of information fits into one category and not another. For example, person A is in Department 1, person B is in Department 2, and so on. Sometimes such data are referred to as "frequency data," "attribute data," or "categorical data." Examples of nominal data include gender, political affiliation, job category, and geographic region.

- *Ordinal data.* In this case as with nominal data, the data are distinguishable, but they can also be placed in some order. An example would be a ranking of potential staff in terms of their "leadership" qualities, a ranking of salespeople according to their revenue generation, or a listing of preferred learning methods. In these cases, the items or objects would be ranked first, second, and so on—lower numbers would reflect the highest levels on the scale. With an ordinal scale you can say that one object is bigger or better or more of something than another, but you cannot say *how much* bigger or better or more.
- *Interval and ratio data.* As with ordinal level, data are distinguishable and can be ordered. With interval and ratio data, however, you can use mathematical operations of adding and subtracting. The only difference between the two types of scales is that a ratio scale includes a true zero point, whereas an interval level uses an arbitrary zero point. This means that numbers on an interval scale cannot be related to each other as ratios or multiples. For example, when using a Fahrenheit scale (interval scale) as in the case of a thermometer, we cannot say that 100 degrees is twice as hot as 50 degrees. However, in measuring weight or height that uses a ratio scale, we can say that a person is twice as heavy or twice as tall as another. For most practical purposes in data analyses, these two levels are treated in similar ways.

In the case of Likert scale data, which are theoretically ordinal data, many people treat the numbers on the scale as if they were interval data, especially when analyzing the data. The rationale for doing so is that robust statistical tests are able to treat the data as interval, and if the data are normally distributed the level of data they represent is less important.

Data Robustness and Sensitivity

Robustness of the data denotes the strength of the assumptions needed for a particular quantitative analysis to produce valid results. For example, some statistical analyses are based on the assumption that the groups were randomly selected from a single population and the members in the groups were assigned randomly to the various groups. Other statistical analyses, such as calculating an average, do not require such rigorous assumptions. Thus, robust methods:

- Are undertaken with very few assumptions
- Can be used validly in many different situations
- Are usable when the assumptions are violated in varying degrees
- Tend to be less sensitive to small effects
- Are likely to be replicable

When using any statistical analysis, the evaluation team needs to understand the assumptions of the analysis, the ways of testing those assumptions, and the direction in which results would tend to be biased if the method is used when the assumptions are not strictly met.

Approaches to Qualitative Data Analysis

Although the analysis of most survey, test, or checklist items is straightforward when you know what kinds of statistical analyses you wish to conduct, the same is not necessarily true for the analysis of qualitative data that result from interviews, open-ended survey items, qualitative observations, drawings, photographs, and some archival data. Yet the richness and insights from qualitative data are often worth the labor involved in their analysis. Before we discuss how to analyze qualitative data, we wish to make a few points:

1. Qualitative data analysis is a systematic and rigorous process that should lead to results as credible and valid as quantitative analysis procedures.
2. Analysis of qualitative data requires time and a willingness to reflect on the data and their meaning.
3. When you list all of the responses to a survey item, this is called "listing." It is *not* analysis.

We make these points to emphasize that qualitative data, when analyzed appropriately, provide extremely useful and valid results.

Often referred to as "content analysis" or "thematic analysis," qualitative data analysis is a process for identifying themes and patterns in the data and then coding and categorizing these themes in an effort to understand and explain the phenomenon being evaluated. It is a way of organizing and making sense of qualitative data.

To illustrate how this is accomplished, consider the following example. In a study on the status of evaluators' perceptions of evaluation use (Preskill and Caracelli, 1997), respondents to a survey were asked what they thought constituted the misuse of evaluation findings. The question read, "How would you define evaluation misuse?" From the survey respondents' answers to these questions, various categories of misuse were developed. The situations they described were then coded with a number representing each of these categories. For example, one category was labeled "To Withhold or Selectively Use Evaluation Findings." Responses that were sorted into this category included:

- Stakeholders select some results for decisionmaking and ignore others.
- Selective use to support predetermined conclusion or course of action.
- Selection of findings for public dissemination that conform to desired outcomes, and hiding or burying negative findings.
- Omitting relevant findings of the evaluation so that only the findings that support an independently reached conclusion are presented.
- When stakeholders knowingly pick and choose data to report on the basis of "as needed" or "for convenience" to pursue their own agendas.
- Submitting only a part of a full evaluation report to funders of a program.

In developing these categories and describing each one through the examples provided by the respondents, the authors were able to more fully describe what represents misuse, which was one of the goals of their study.

Case Study Analysis and Cross-Case Analysis

As described above, qualitative data consist of interview responses, written observations, photographs, drawings, and text-based archival data. Before the analysis process begins, it's important to decide how you want to organize and represent the findings. The guiding question here is, *Do you want to present a case study analysis or a cross-case analysis?* A case study analysis involves preparing a case description for each site or person in the evaluation. In contrast, a cross-case analysis would involve grouping or categorizing responses or observations from several sites or people. It is possible to do both by starting first with a case study analysis and then comparing the cases if necessary or desired.

A case study consists of a specific and bounded description of persons, groups, processes, events, programs, or organizations. The case is based on data collected from observations, archival records, transcriptions, notes from interviews, responses to questionnaires, photographs, or drawings. The critical feature of the case is that it provides enough information for the reader to vicariously experience what was being evaluated (that is, the case).

Several steps of analysis are involved in analyzing data for a case study. The first step consists of assembling the raw data. The second step consists of writing a case record. The case record assembles and organizes the raw data into a manageable form by removing redundancies and organizing the information chronologically or thematically. This step should be undertaken only if there is so much raw data that it needs to be condensed. The final step is that of writing the case study itself, either from the raw data or from the case record. Case studies can be further analyzed by examining patterns or themes within or across cases or over time. They can also be used for developing explanations of certain outcomes.

If preparing a cross-case analysis, you can, but are not required to, develop a case study analysis as the first step. You can also begin the cross-case analysis using the raw data. The decision rests with the evaluation's key questions, how you want to present the findings, and the amount of data that you have. If you want to present individual case data or you have redundant data, you may want to begin with the creation of one or more individual case studies prior to the cross-case analysis. Regardless of whether you are undertaking a case study or a cross-case approach, the following section will help you decide among alternative analysis techniques. For example, one of the authors conducted an evaluation that collected data from seven cities. A case analysis was developed for each site and then a cross-case analysis compared and contrasted each of the individual sites.

Deciding How to Analyze Qualitative Analysis

Figure 12.1 shows a decision tree to help determine which approach you might use for developing categories or themes from the data. These include deriving categories from:

- The theoretical literature
- An existing framework or schema
- The current data set

As you will note, regardless of which approach you employ, the methods for actually sifting through the data and making sense of the patterns and themes is similar. The following paragraphs will provide a brief description of each technique.

Deriving categories from the theoretical literature. With this approach, you are undertaking the analysis to determine whether the data collected support a particular theory. Two frequently used frameworks for such an analysis are *grounded theory* and *analytic induction.*

Grounded theory involves an iterative process of examining the data and the theory concurrently. One technique involves "open coding," in which the analyst underlines key phrasing and pulls these together in some organized fashion. This can be done as a line-by-line analysis, by considering sentences or paragraphs, or using the entire document. Here's where the analyst starts to perceive themes within the data. By generating themes, you are organizing the data. At this point, you may also want to apply the "constant comparative method," which involves comparing the theoretical literature with the data. (Glaser and Strauss, 1967; Strauss and Corbin, 1990).

Whereas open coding breaks down the data into discrete events, axial coding "puts those data back together in new ways by making connections between a category and its subcategories" (Strauss and Corbin, 1990, p.

FIGURE 12.1   Decision Tree for Qualitative Analysis

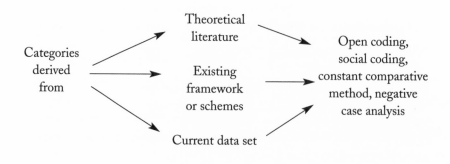

97). With axial coding, the task involves identifying the relationship among separate pieces of data. This may focus on the conditions that gave rise to a particular category or subcategory, such as the context, the actions or strategies by which it is handled, and the consequence of those actions. For example, in an evaluation conducted by one of the authors, one of the evaluation questions addressed the quality of a school's environment. In analyzing the interview data, two themes emerged using open coding. One concerned the issue of student discipline and the other addressed the physical environment of the school. One of the subcategories within the category of school discipline was that of student fighting. This was related to one of the subcategories within physical environment that dealt with the layout of the school and the teachers' inability to know where students were. The relationship drawn here involved axial coding. Note that although open coding and axial coding are described as separate methods, in practice the analyst alternates between the two.

As for naming the categories or subcategories, the analysts can use a label from the technical literature. For example, in the customer service literature, one might adopt the phrase "emotional labor" to describe situations in which the customer service person had to hide his or her feelings to serve the customer. Alternatively, one might use "in vivo codes" or categories (Glaser, 1978; Strauss, 1987). In this case, the labels would come from the respondents' own words.

Another approach to linking theory with data involves *analytic induction*. As with grounded theory, analytic induction is an iterative process. Thus, the techniques of open coding, axial coding, and the constant comparative method can be used. In addition, you may want to employ negative case analysis. Here, you formulate an explanation or theory about some situation or phenomenon and compare the data to that explanation. If the data fit, then you go to the next case. You continue with this comparison until you find a negative case. At that point, you have two options. Either you can change the explanation to include the case or you can decide to focus on some other situation or phenomenon within the cases. Either way, your purpose is to develop an explanation that can handle all of the known cases.

Deriving categories from an existing framework or schema. In some cases, you are not interested in linking the data to a particular theory. Rather, you may want to organize the data around some preexisting framework, rubric, outline, agenda, or structure. For example, you might develop categories related to the program or organization's goals, the evaluation's key questions, or the program's objectives. This is a useful and straightforward approach for analyzing qualitative data if such schema are available and relevant to the evaluation. One has to be cautious, however, not to limit or force the data into the categories provided by the framework. The preexisting framework is merely a starting point.

Deriving categories from the current data set. There are times when the data analysis process should not be guided by some preexisting schema or theoretical literature. When you want to see how the data can be organized without any overarching framework, then you would use content analysis to inductively review the text and develop specific categories. With this approach, the categories emerge from the data. This approach is particularly appropriate when no other framework exists for developing the categories, when imposing a preexisting schema could limit the full range of findings, or when using a preexisting framework could be criticized for biasing the results. When using this approach it is often a good idea to engage more than one analyst so that a level of inter-rater agreement can be determined. If the inter-rater agreement is high, then it is safe to assume that the analysis and subsequent categories and reporting of findings are valid.

Guidelines for Good Category Construction

The number of categories used to code and sort the data is largely based on the chosen method of analysis, the amount of data, the complexity of the data, the study's comprehensiveness, and the evaluation's purpose and focus. Whereas in some evaluations you might develop five or six categories, other studies might result in ten or twelve categories or more. It cannot be overstated that *qualitative data analysis stands or falls on the quality of the categories and the procedures used for coding the data.* The following are some general guidelines for analyzing qualitative data:

- Determine who will be involved in analyzing the qualitative data.
- Do not try to guess what respondents mean, especially on surveys where only one or two words are provided.
- Make sure the categories reflect the chosen method of analysis (that is, theoretical literature, existing framework or schema, or current data set).
- Attempt to create categories that are mutually exclusive so that a piece of data goes into one or another category but not into both.
- Keep careful notes about the decisions you make about why a certain kind of response goes in one category and not another.
- Develop a means for highlighting useful quotations you might wish to include in the final report.
- Determine what you will do with comments such as "okay" or "good" if they don't fit into any of the categories.
- Develop a miscellaneous category for data that don't fit into any of the categories but that are relevant to the study's purpose.

Procedures for Analyzing Qualitative Data

Once you have considered these guidelines and are ready to begin analyzing the qualitative data, consider the following procedures:

1. Read and reread the data—Get to know your data intimately. Compose notes or questions in the margins about what occurs to you as you read. You might also highlight certain information that you want to go back to or use in your final report.
2. Make notes (decision rules) regarding how you decide what kind of information goes in each category as well as characteristics of that category. Try out these themes with others on the evaluation team.
3. Compare and contrast data with expectations, standards, or other frameworks.
4. Develop codes for each category. A code is the name, acronym, or number that is associated with the category.
5. Assign codes to data.
6. Sort data into the established coded categories.
7. Revise codes, categories, or both as necessary.
8. Whenever possible, ask a colleague to code at least a portion of the data to determine inter-rater agreement or reliability.
9. Count frequency of codes, if desired.
10. Look at the substance of the data within each category and examine how categories relate to each other.
11. Write up your findings relating them to the evaluation purpose and key questions.
12. Consider displaying the data through diagrams, tables, matrices, and graphs.
13. If you've also collected quantitative data, determine how you will integrate both sets of data.
14. Knowing when the analysis is over is important. Though it is often tempting to keep analyzing and reanalyzing the data, you know it's time to stop when new data no longer generate new insights, or there are no more data to analyze.

Cautions When Analyzing Qualitative Data

- Make sure you have a good chunk of time to devote to the analysis—this process is hard to accomplish in twenty-minute spurts.

- Stop coding the data when you feel tired and distracted. Take a break and return to it another time.
- When a piece of information doesn't immediately seem to fit a particular category, the impulse may be to throw it into the miscellaneous category. This could be a sign that you are tired or that the categories are not working particularly well.
- Be very careful not to begin inferring what you think respondents meant when there isn't enough data to support these inferences. It is better not use data that are unintelligible or lacking clarity than to make unfounded assumptions.

Using Qualitative Data Analysis Computer Software

The analysis of qualitative data is a conceptually challenging task, and just the sheer amount of text to enter, read, and code is sometimes overwhelming. Although there is no getting around reading and coding the data yourself, computer software programs to assist in some parts of the process are becoming increasingly available. As anyone who has transcribed audiotapes will attest, this is time-consuming, tedious, and expensive. Voice recognition software, however, will soon help eliminate this task.

Today we have software that can aid in the categorization, coding, and sorting processes once the text has been entered into a computer. A content dictionary provides one method for automating the classification task. In this case, the analyst assigns a word or phrase to a certain category. The computer program then searches for that word or phrase and assigns the data to the category. Qualitative data analysis software provides tremendous help when dealing with large amounts of text, but it is not a replacement for a human being to develop the conceptual framework and categories for the data.

For small numbers of cases (transcripts), a word-processing program can often suffice for data entry purposes. For larger amounts of data where the number of transcript pages exceed 500 pages, you might consider purchasing a qualitative data analysis software package, such as NUD*IST (Non-Numerical Unstructured Data Indexing, Searching and Theory-building), QSR-NVivo, ATLAS.ti, or Ethnograph. Scolari, the software division of Sage Publications, sells each of these.

Approaches to Quantitative Data Analysis

This section describes various statistical techniques for analyzing quantitative data. Given that this is not a statistics book, we will not provide specific formulas or calculation procedures for these tests. However, evaluators must understand the choices that need to be made when determining which quantitative data analysis procedure is appropriate, given the level of data, the population from which the data came, and the evaluation's key questions. For example, quantitative data consists of numbers that represent nominal-, ordinal-, interval-, or ratio-level data. As is true with qualitative data analysis, the evaluation's key questions should guide certain data analysis decisions. Regardless of the evaluation question, the type of data (qualitative or quantitative), or the level of the data, it is often useful to calculate a frequency distribution of the data (see Figure 12.2 for an example). A frequency distribution is simply the number of responses of a certain type. In most cases, it gives you a thorough understanding of the data and their characteristics. In some cases, however, a frequency distribution can illuminate a missing link in a chain of reasoning leading to a decision. For example, finding that customer service representatives spend more time in dealing with angry customers than in handling routine calls may suggest the need for system changes to allow for the extra time that angry customers require, at the same time not neglecting questions from other customers. This may result from a review of customer satisfaction data using ratings of "very good," "good," "neutral," "poor," and "very poor." You might have found these results by analyzing the data on customers providing ratings of "poor" and "very poor."

It is common to present frequency distributions as bar charts or pie graphs rather than tables (see Figure 12.3). You can make such charts more useful by considering the order of the categories. Thus, by placing similar frequencies in adjacent positions, you can more easily see which is larger. Another common option is to present both the frequencies and the percentages that those frequencies represent.

One type of frequency distribution that should be presented—but as an appendix—is a distribution of the frequencies of all responses on a survey. These frequencies, along with the percentages or percentiles, may not be of interest to many readers, but will be critical for those who are interested in the details (see Figure 12.2).

FIGURE 12.2   Example of Frequency Distribution of Responses to Each
Question

Item	Response	Frequency	Percentage
How well did participants understand the reasons for the merger?	Extremely well	13	14%
	Very well	29	31%
	Moderately well	45	48%
	Not well	4	4%
	Not at all well	2	2%
How well did participants perform the required process?	Extremely well	9	10%
	Very well	33	35%
	Moderately well	43	46%
	Not well	7	8%
	Not at all well	1	1%
How well are employees prepared for reorganization?	Extremely well	10	11%
	Very well	32	34%
	Moderately well	37	40%
	Not well	11	12%
	Not at all well	3	3%

Beyond the frequency distributions, Figure 12.4 provides a diagram to help decide which statistical analyses to use. The first question to ask is what kind of information you want from the data or what kind of question you are asking of the data. As shown in the diagram, you may want to do one or more of the following:

- Describe the data
- Search for or specify relationships
- Predict a relationship between two or more variables (a predictor and a criterion)
- Test for significant differences between two or more variables

Note that this chart is not all-encompassing, but it does provide some of the more common statistical procedures. The following paragraphs will

FIGURE 12.3   Example of a Pie Chart

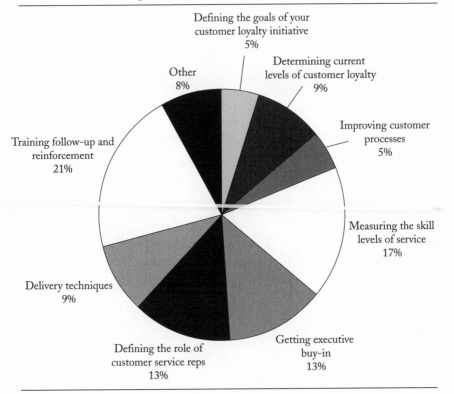

walk you through this decision tree and the resulting statistics and analyses.

Describing the Data

Beyond the frequency distributions, you may want to describe the data by providing two types of values. One is a value that can be viewed as "representative" of all the data. Such a value is called a "measure of central tendency." The other value indicates how much variation or dispersion exists in the data. This value is called a "measure of dispersion or variability." The following describes the various measures of central tendency and dispersion or variability that can be used to describe the data. Any reporting of the data should include descriptions of: (1) the total number of people in the population, (2) the number of people in the sample, (3) the

330

FIGURE 12.4   Example of Frequency Distribution of Responses to Each Question

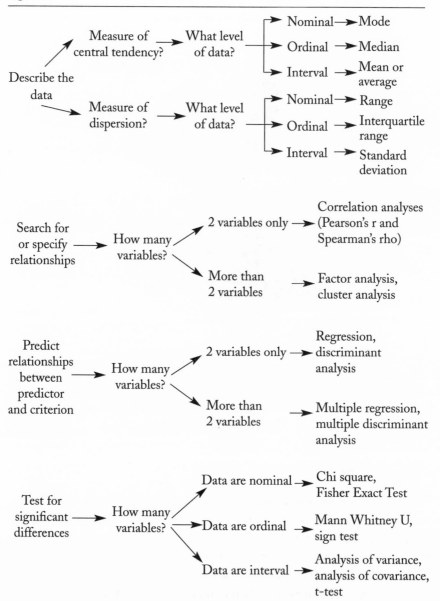

number and percentage of respondents, (4) the number and percentage of missing responses, (5) any recordings or rescorings that were performed in translating responses into numerical scales, (6) a measure of central tendency, and (7) a measure of dispersion.

1. Measures of central tendency. To best describe a set of data, you will need to ask yourself about the level of the data—whether they represent nominal, ordinal, or interval/ratio-level data. If the data are nominal, you should use the mode as the measure of central tendency. The mode refers to the most frequent value. If the data are ordinal, you would use the median or the middle-most value as the measure of central tendency. The median can be found at the 50th percentile. If the data are interval- or ratio-level data, you should use the mean or the average as the measure of central tendency. In cases where the frequency distribution is symmetrical and contains one mode, the same value will appear for the mode, the median, and the mean.

In some situations, you may want to use the mean when reporting ordinal data. Statistics texts often state that one should not make inferences based on means of ordinal variables. For example, on a Likert-type scale with ratings of "very good," "good," "neutral," "poor," and "very poor," such texts may imply that one should avoid assigning them the numbers and calculating means, because "very good" may be closer to "good" than "good" is to "neutral." Thus, when using ordinal scales, one cannot assume equal intervals between the response options. Although one must consider such precautions, they should not be taken as grounds for avoiding the use of means or averages in examining and reporting the data. You should describe the procedures for assigning number values to the response options. For example, you may assign the values of 2, 1, 0, -1, -2 or alternatively, you may assign the values of 5, 4, 3, 2, 1. Then you should examine the distribution of the responses to the categories to determine whether the data appear to be normally distributed. In the report, you should note that the conclusions refer to the numbers assigned to the ratings.

Upon examining the distribution of responses, you may find that the response distribution is skewed. If the distribution is skewed, then the median value will be somewhere between the value for the mode and the value for the mean. With such skewed distributions, you may want to consider using the median as the measure of central tendency since it provides a better reflection of the data. A common example of the use of the median is the value often cited for home prices in a community, even though housing prices represent ratio-level data. A graph of these prices would reveal a skewed distribution, such that many homes would be priced at the lower end of the scale and only a few homes would be priced at the top end of the scale. The mean value would tend to be higher than many of the home values, because its calculation would be affected by the few homes at the top of the scale. Thus, the median home value would provide a better indicator of the area's home prices.

If you have ordinal-level data, you can use the mode and the median. If you have interval- or ratio-level data, you can use the mode, the median, and the mean.

2. Measures of variability. In addition to the measure of central tendency, you should also calculate and report a measure of variability. This value describes the degree to which the data cluster together or are spread apart. To decide which of the measures to use, you need to identify the level of the data, as with the measure of central tendency. Thus, if the data are nominal, you should use the range. The range refers to the difference between the highest and the lowest values. If the data are ordinal-level data, you should use the semi-interquartile range. The semi-interquartile range (or Q) refers to one-half of the range of the middle 50 percent of the values. Finally, if the data are interval- or ratio-level data, you should use the standard deviation. In addition, if they are ordinal-level data and normally distributed, you can use the standard deviation. The standard deviation (or SD) is the square root of the mean or average of the squared deviations from the overall mean. The standard deviation provides three advantages: (1) it allows for comparing different distributions in terms of their variability; (2) it provides a precise measure of the location of data points within the distribution; and (3) it provides the basis for more advanced statistical tests.

If you have ordinal-level data, you can report both the range and the semi-interquartile range. If you have interval or ratio data, you can report the range, the semi-interquartile range, and the standard deviation.

Exploring Relationships

When you are considering exploring relationships among variables in the data, the question is one of determining whether there is a relationship between two variables or among several variables. As one example, you may be interested in whether a relationship exists between ratings of satisfaction with a training course and the extent to which trainees use their newly learned skills on the job. As another example, you may want to know whether certain dimensions or factors emerge from a fifty-item needs assessment instrument administered to managers and supervisors. Your interest here is learning whether three major factors encompass most of the data. You can then use this information to reduce the number of items in the instrument. In this second example, you are interested in examining the relationships among the fifty different items. After deciding that you are searching for or specifying relationships within the data, you then must determine whether you want to examine the relationship (1) between two variables, as in the first example or (2) among more than two variables, as in the second example.

1. Relationship between two variables. With the first example, you are asking whether a relationship or a "correlation" exists between one variable and another. Using that example, a positive correlation would indicate that respondents who give high ratings of satisfaction tend to use the skills on the job. A negative correlation would indicate that respondents who give high ratings of satisfaction do not tend to use the skills on the job. A zero correlation would indicate that no relationship exists between satisfaction and skill use. Note that a correlation does not mean that there is a cause-and-effect relationship. So, in the case of a positive correlation between satisfaction and skill use, we cannot say that the high satisfaction "caused" the skills to be used nor can we say that the skill use "caused" high satisfaction. What we can say is that those people who were highly satisfied with the workshop also tended to use the skills.

At this point, you may be wondering what level of a correlation is considered "good" or "significant." The issue of a statistically significant correlation will be determined by the size of the sample and by referring to a statistics book. Correlations run from +1.0 as the highest positive correlation to 0 as indicating no correlation to -1.0 as the lowest negative correlation. Typically, then, a correlation from +0.7 to +1.0 or -0.7 to -1.0 is considered a high correlation. In contrast, a correlation from +0.3 to 0.0 or from -0.3 to 0.0 is considered a low correlation. One way to decide whether the correlation is important is to consider the amount of variance accounted for. You can determine this by squaring the correlation.

So, with a correlation of +0.3, which may be statistically significant with a large sample, the amount of variance accounted for is +0.3 times +0.3, which equals +0.09. Thus, the correlation of +0.3 accounts for only 9 percent of the variance. In this case, many other factors affect the relationship. Therefore, one would be hard pressed to say that this correlation has much practical significance.

To determine the appropriate correlation statistic, you need to ask whether data are nominal, ordinal, interval, or some combination of these. For example, if both variables represent nominal data, you would use a contingency coefficient (C), which can be calculated from a chi square analysis. (A chi square analysis compares observed frequencies with expected frequencies.) If both variables represent ordinal data, you would use the Spearman's rho (or the Spearman rank order coefficient, or r_s). If both variables represent interval data, you would use the Pearson's r (or the Pearson product moment coefficient). Analyses involving some combination of interval-, ordinal-, and nominal-level data require less commonly used correlational analyses that can be found in advanced statistics books or can be computed by a statistical consultant.

2. More than two variables. In some cases, you may want to examine the relationships between and among more than two variables. In the example above of the fifty-item needs assessment instrument, you may want to determine whether the items on this assessment instrument fall into certain groups or represent certain factors.

Again, you would need to determine the level of the data. If the data are at the interval or ordinal levels, you can use factor analysis. Note that, although some texts indicate using factor analysis only with interval-level data, you can use factor analysis with rank-order correlations. Factor analysis is a statistical method used to reduce the number of dimensions or items required to account for similarities. In other words, factor analysis identifies which items may be grouped conceptually together on the instrument, and which ones might be redundant, and therefore unnecessary.

The factor analysis would start with a correlation or covariance matrix of all of the items. In the case of the fifty-item assessment instrument, this would result a correlation matrix that would show the correlation coefficient of each item with every other item. The results might reveal that the assessment really consists of five major factors, with most of the items loading onto one of those factors and a few of the items not loading onto any factor. With this information, you could reduce the length of the instrument in the following ways: (1) on factors with many items (more than five, for example), you can eliminate some of the items based on the strength of the factor loadings; and (2) you can eliminate all of the items that do not load onto any of the major factors. This process helps finetune the instrument so that it produces valid results.

If the data are nominal, you can use a contingency analysis, which is derived from a chi-square test. For more details on this or analyses involving some combination of interval, ordinal, or nominal levels, you should consult an advanced statistics book or a statistical consultant.

Predicting Relationships

Rather than simply search for or specify a relationship between or among variables, you may want to make some kinds of predictions from the data. For example, you may want to determine whether you can predict customer satisfaction ratings (criterion variable) based on the scores obtained from a knowledge test given at the end of the customer service training program (predictor variable). After deciding that you want to predict relationships, then you must determine whether you want to predict a relationship (1) between two variables (as between a predictor and a criterion) or (2) among more than two variables (as between a set of variables and a criterion).

1. Two variables. When you have only two variables and you want to predict a criterion variable from a predictor variable, you would compute a regression analysis. In this case, you might imagine plotting the relationship between the two variables on a scatterplot. A regression analysis determines the equation for the best fitting line that minimizes the deviations between the various data points and the line. Having calculated that regression line, you can predict the criterion variable (in the example, customer satisfaction ratings) based on the predictor variable (in this case, end-of-the-course test scores). Let us say that the test gives you a score between 0 and 100. Having the information from the regression analysis, you can take any score on the test and provide a prediction of the customer service rating.

Discriminant analysis, similar to regression analysis, is used to generate a set of weighting functions (or discriminant functions). These are then used to classify observations (such as people) into one of several groups. The purpose for such classification can be (1) to determine whether two or more groups are significantly different in their profiles, (2) to maximize the discrimination among the groups, and (3) to develop rules for placing new cases into one of the groups.

2. More than two variables. In many cases, you may have more than two variables. Let us take the example of the knowledge test given at the end of customer service training. You may have other variables in addition to test scores, such as attendance records, records of completed assignments, and attitude ratings about the course. Here, you want to predict how well customer service staff will use the skills gained in a training workshop (that is, criterion variable). To do so, you would use multiple regression.

Multiple regression is a technique for predicting some criterion score from some combination of predictor variables and assigning weight to each predictor variable based on its relative contribution to predicting the criterion. It is an iterative technique that starts with the variable having the largest partial correlation with the criterion. Other variables are added one at a time to determine whether they significantly improve the ability to predict the criterion. Similar to multiple regression, multiple discriminant analysis uses multiple variables to create the discriminant functions to classify people, objects, or events.

Testing for Significant Differences

Some evaluation questions might indicate a need to determine if there are significant differences between two or more groups or the same group at different times. For example, you may want to compare a group that participated in an asynchronous web-based training program with those who participated in a traditional classroom training session covering the same content. After determining that this is the main question, you would next need to identify the level of data: nominal, ordinal, or interval.

1. Nominal level. In the example above with nominal data, you may want to compare the two groups in terms of their preferred training method—asynchronous web-based training or traditional classroom. The variable of preferred training method is at the nominal level, and the data would consist of the number of people indicating their preference for one of those methods. In this case, a chi-square would be the appropriate statistic. This statistic tests whether two or more variables can be regarded as independent. An alternative to the chi-square is Fisher's Exact Probability Test. This latter test is appropriate when you have two variables each having two groups (or a two-by-two table) and one of the expected values is less than five.

2. *Ordinal level.* You may be comparing two groups using ordinal-level data, such as rating scales. When the data are skewed and are not normally distributed, the Mann-Whitney would be appropriate. Another alternative when you have pairs of data, such as pre- and post-ratings, is the Sign test. This is a relatively straightforward test, since you simply subtract each of the pairs and count the numbers of plus and minus signs to determine whether this number could have been obtained by chance.

3. *Interval level.* Finally, you may be comparing groups using interval-level data or ordinal-level data with normally distributed data. Analysis of variance (ANOVA) is one of the most powerful and versatile statistical techniques for these kinds of data. It tests for group or treatment differences (such as trained and control groups) by breaking down the total sums of squared deviations from the grand mean across all groups into that variance due to error and that variance due to the group differences. ANOVA is appropriate when comparing two groups on one factor, such as comparing a trained and control group on their posttraining test scores. If you think that some variable or variables may account for differences between the groups, you may want to use an analysis of covariance, or ANCOVA. For example, you may have pretraining test scores from the two groups. The ANCOVA would enable you to adjust for the pretraining differences.

Instead of comparing two groups, you may want to compare the same group over time, such as a group several times before training and several times following training. In this case, you would use an ANOVA with repeated measures. If you want to compare two or more groups on more than one factor, such as posttraining satisfaction as well as knowledge, you would use a multiple analysis of variance, or MANOVA. An advanced statistics book or a friendly statistician can help you decide which of these analyses is most appropriate. Once having determined that there is a significant difference, you can use some form of paired comparison (or posthoc test) to identify the specific factors or items yielding significant differences.

Economic Analyses of Learning, Performance, and Change Interventions

If you have evaluation key questions that focus on the allocation of resources, you may want to consider some form of economic analysis. Economic analyses require that learning, performance, and change interventions be viewed as if they were production processes in which resources (for example, staff, facilities, materials, and equipment) are applied to raw materials (for example, trainees) to produce products (such as employees who can perform job functions). The relationship between the resources and outputs can provide information to help choose among alternatives. The following paragraphs describe three interrelated types of economic analysis: *cost analysis, cost–effectiveness analysis,* and *cost–benefit analysis.*

Cost Analysis

Cost analysis consists of identifying all the components contributing to the total cost of a program. All of the resources required by a program are identified, and their dollar value is calculated. Some of the costs that need to be considered include:

- Trainee costs, such as salary and benefits, travel costs, and value of reduced productivity as a result of absence from the job.
- Instructor costs, such as instructor salary and benefits and travel costs.
- Materials or instructional development costs.
- Facilities costs.

The results of cost analysis are most useful for selecting among several alternatives in cases where all alternatives display approximately equal effects or benefits. In such cases, cost data may be sufficient for decision-making. Using the results, decision makers can choose the least expensive alternative.

Estimation of costs is a component of both cost-effectiveness analysis and cost-benefit analysis. These latter two techniques permit comparisons of outputs as well as costs to be used in making choices among programs, methods, or strategies. The estimation of an alternative's cost will be the same in either cost-effectiveness or cost-benefit analysis. It is the analysis of the outputs that differs.

Cost-Effectiveness Analysis

This type of analysis focuses on the direct outcomes, effects, or impacts of a program. Outcomes, effects, or impacts may be measured by assessing changes from before to after the program. The amount of change is then compared to the cost of producing it, resulting in a ratio of cost to effect.

The cost-effectiveness ratio compares the value of resources used as expressed in dollars (cost) to the number of units of effectiveness achieved (effect). These units of effectiveness may include such things as:

- Increased output
- Time savings
- Reduced errors
- Improved customer satisfaction
- Improved work habits
- Improved work climate
- New skills

Note that a cost-effectiveness analysis does assign dollar values to costs but does not assign particular dollar values to measures of effectiveness. For example, it may cost $500,000 in process changes and training to yield a certain level of increased output. Based on the cost and effect information, the decision maker must decide whether the effect is worth the cost or which of two programs producing comparable kinds of effects is most efficient.

Cost-Benefit Analysis

In conducting a cost-benefit analysis, a dollar value is assigned to the many effects of a program, as well as to the costs for the program. This permits a comparison of the costs and effects using the same scale. Cost-benefit analysis uses a single dimension of monetary value as the measure of both cost and effects; this is in contrast to cost-effectiveness analysis in which only the costs are expressed as a monetary value.

As an example, let us assume that a customer-service training program showed $500,000 of benefits for the year (in terms of increased sales revenue) and $250,000 of program costs. Thus,
Benefit/cost ratio = Program benefits / Program costs
Benefit/cost ratio = $500,000 / $250,000
Benefit/cost ratio = 2:1

This example shows that two dollars are returned as benefits for every dollar spent on the training.

Clearly, you can encounter some difficulty in determining the dollar value of the benefits. With increased sales revenue, the dollar benefits are obvious. With improvements in customer satisfaction or in teamwork, however, the dollar benefits may not be calculated so directly.

Return on Investment (ROI)

Having gathered the data needed for a cost-benefit analysis, you can also determine the ROI. An advantage to using ROI is that many executives understand this calculation.

Let's use the example above to calculate the ROI. Thus,
ROI = (Net program benefits / Program costs) X 100%
ROI = ($500,000 − $250,000) / $250,000 X 100%
ROI = 100%

This calculation means that the costs were recovered and an additional 100 percent of the costs were returned as benefits.

Time value of money. Two other approaches for calculating ROI—Net Present Value (NPV) and Internal Rate of Return (IRR)—take into account the time value of money. These two methods are used in many organizations by financial analysts to weigh investment decisions. They recognize that money obtained today is more valuable than the same money received in the future. Thus, money used to implement training is spent first, but the results of this investment are not realized until later. To compare training costs and benefits on an equal footing, it is necessary to calculate their value as if they occurred at the same point in time. For more details on these methods, you might wish to consult an advanced accounting textbook.

Limitations to Economic Analyses

Determining the "monetary" effects of a learning, performance, or change initiative may be a difficult process. Raters may disagree over the value of some benefits, and some benefits may be overlooked entirely. If disagreement arises in placing a value on the benefits, you may be limited to conducting a cost analysis or cost-effectiveness analysis.

Another concern is related to the goals of the initiative. Although one can measure the effects of a program without knowing its goals, effectiveness can only be determined in relation to some objective or standard. To measure whether progress is being made toward achieving specific goals, these goals must be precisely stated. Thus, the effectiveness part of the cost-effectiveness or cost-benefit ratio must represent the actual impact, not merely whether certain activities were conducted. For example, in the customer service training example, one would have to state that the goal was increased sales revenue.

A final concern relates to the purpose of the analysis. An economic analysis represents one type of impact evaluation, and it requires an assessment of effectiveness. Such an assessment of effectiveness is best undertaken after a program has been well established. Under these conditions, the effects of the program can be more easily isolated from other variables that could affect results, such as an improved economy or recently implemented bonuses for increased sales revenue.

Quantitative Computer Software Analysis Tools

As with qualitative data analysis, there are also computer software tools to help you analyze quantitative data. The most widely used tools for quantitative analyses involve BMDP (or Biomedical Data Processing), SAS/STAT, and SPSS (or Statistical Package for the Social Sciences). In addition, EXCEL provides some basic statistics. Each of these provides the results of almost all quantitative analyses and statistics. Given the availability of these tools and their ease of use, you can focus your efforts on deciding on the most appropriate analyses rather than on their intricacies and calculations.

Potential Problems in Analyzing Data

The last step in any data analysis effort is to consider potential problems with the data and the analysis procedures. The sources of potential problems are numerous, but we can list a couple of the major categories of problems. You should determine the likelihood of these problems and proceed accordingly. Probably the best advice is to consult an expert who has a strong statistical analysis background.

Problems with data analysis can generally be traced to actions taken during earlier phases in the evaluation. These include (1) focusing the evaluation and (2) collecting the data. These will be discussed in turn.

The first of these problem areas is the most complex. If the evaluation does not have a proper focus or the focus changes in midstream, then the data and the analyses may not yield useful results. Another problem involves the extent to which the program processes, the moderating variables, and the potential effects can be identified. A complete system analysis for something as complex as an organizational intervention or initiative is merely an ideal. It can only be approximated through continued refinement. Since it is impossible to undertake such a complete system analysis, every observed relationship can be explained by numerous alternative relationships and explanations. The development of a logic model will help you anticipate and account for the most plausible of these alternative explanations. For example, you may be comparing trained and control groups. You would want to make sure that the groups were similar in terms of types of people and level of experience. You may not, however, be able to control for the type and amount of managerial support experienced by members of the two groups.

The second problem area, associated with data collection, is that of missing data or nonresponses. If more than 20 percent of the intended responses are missing, ignoring that fact and proceeding with the data analysis may yield inaccurate conclusions. Therefore, you should provide some caveats indicating potential problems with the analyses.

If possible, however, you should undertake one of the following methods to adjust the data for nonrespondents or missing data. The basic approach for solving the nonresponse problem involves estimating values for the missing data, assessing the bias introduced by filling in estimates to replace missing data, and then conducting analyses using the estimated data. There are three basic methods for dealing with this bias: (1) stratification of the entire sample (including respondents and nonrespondents) and replacement of missing data within each stratum, (2) a regression approach that uses the relationships between variables to provide predictions of the missing data, and (3) a follow-up of a sample of the nonrespondents to use the nonrespondent data to represent all of the nonrespondents. (Advanced statistics and methodology texts will provide you with further details on these approaches.)

We fully recognize that these approaches may seem daunting given the need to produce evaluation results quickly in a real-world organizational setting. At the very least, however, you should make efforts to follow up with a sample of the nonrespondents, or carefully review the data of the very last respondents (who are likely to be similar to nonrespondents) to make sure that their responses are not significantly different (statistically or practically) from those who did respond. The critical issue here is the resulting amount of confidence you and the stakeholders may have in the findings. If key decisions are to be based on the evaluation results, then basing those decisions on a 30 percent response rate, for example, could not only be foolish, but it could be detrimental to the organization, its employees, and its customers or clients.

....

Keep in Mind . . .

- The evaluation's key questions and the level of analytic sophistication of the stakeholders should guide decisions regarding appropriate data analyses.
- Qualitative data analysis consists of linking data with theory, creating empirically derived categories, and applying codes to qualitative data.
- Quantitative data analysis focuses on describing the data, searching for or specifying relationships among variables, predicting relationships among variables, or testing for significant differences among variables.
- Economic analyses consist of cost analysis, cost-effectiveness analysis, cost-benefit analysis, and return on investment.

PART THREE

Maximizing Evaluation Use

Background and Context of Evaluation

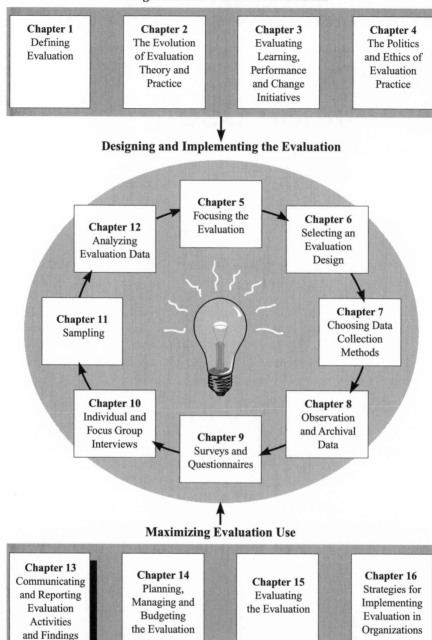

| Chapter 1 Defining Evaluation | Chapter 2 The Evolution of Evaluation Theory and Practice | Chapter 3 Evaluating Learning, Performance and Change Initiatives | Chapter 4 The Politics and Ethics of Evaluation Practice |

Designing and Implementing the Evaluation

Chapter 12 Analyzing Evaluation Data

Chapter 5 Focusing the Evaluation

Chapter 6 Selecting an Evaluation Design

Chapter 11 Sampling

Chapter 7 Choosing Data Collection Methods

Chapter 10 Individual and Focus Group Interviews

Chapter 8 Observation and Archival Data

Chapter 9 Surveys and Questionnaires

Maximizing Evaluation Use

| Chapter 13 Communicating and Reporting Evaluation Activities and Findings | Chapter 14 Planning, Managing and Budgeting the Evaluation | Chapter 15 Evaluating the Evaluation | Chapter 16 Strategies for Implementing Evaluation in Organizations |

Communicating and Reporting Evaluation Activities and Findings

ROSALIE T. TORRES

- Purposes of Communicating and Reporting
- Audiences for Communicating and Reporting
- Timing of Communicating and Reporting
- Content for Communicating and Reporting
- Formats for Communicating and Reporting

••

Vignette #11: Communicating and Reporting Decisions for MyFuture Unlimited

A large international youth development organization, MyFuture Unlimited, has received a major foundation grant to pilot and evaluate an after-school program that it has developed. The program focuses on diversity awareness, social responsibility, and service to the community. Based on the results of this primarily formative evaluation, the program will be revised in preparation for regional and then national dissemination.

A Collaborative Working Group (CWG), consisting of representatives from several youth development partner organizations as well as parents, participated in the development of the program over the previous two years. In addition to three new organizations, three of the organizations represented in the CWG will participate in the pilot implementation. The director of program development at MyFuture Unlimited has met with the MyFuture Unlimited research and evaluation staff to discuss how they will carry out the pilot and its evaluation. They decide to form an evaluation team, which will have overall responsibility for the evaluation portion of the work. The team consists of:

- The MyFuture Unlimited director of program development
- The MyFuture Unlimited director of research and evaluation
- A MyFuture Unlimited program evaluator
- Two MyFuture Unlimited staff developers
- Representatives from each of the six pilot sites

In one of their early meetings the evaluation team identified the following individuals and groups as stakeholders for the evaluation of the pilot program:

- MyFuture Unlimited program development staff
- MyFuture Unlimited president
- MyFuture Unlimited managing director
- Collaborative working group
- Executive directors of the pilot sites
- Program directors and staff of the pilot sites
- Youth participants at the pilot sites
- Parents of youth at the pilot sites
- Sites that will use the program in the future
- Youth and parents of future sites
- Evaluators working in youth development/community service settings
- Curriculum and staff developers working in the youth development field

The evaluation team has begun their work to design the evaluation and decide on the various data collection methods they will use. Given the dates by which they plan to have findings available, they have established a rough schedule for when most of the evaluation activity will need to take place.

••

Communicating and reporting about an evaluation's activities and findings can easily be seen as one of the most critical aspects of an evaluation, particularly if the objective of the evaluation is learning. As with almost every aspect of an evaluation endeavor, careful planning is the key to success. The vignette just presented suggests that effective communicating and reporting addresses several interrelated dimensions at the outset of the evaluation:

- Audiences—Who are the individuals and/or groups that would benefit from knowing about the evaluation and its findings? Who are the individuals and groups that need to be involved for the evaluation to be successful?
- Purposes—What purpose is the communication meant to serve?
- Timing—When is the best time for communications about the evaluation to take place?
- Format and content—What format is best to use, given the purpose (that is, content), the audience, and the timing of the communication?

You will notice that consideration of the communicating and reporting *format* appears last in the list above. Oftentimes we are most familiar with particular frequently used formats (for example, comprehensive written reports, executive summaries) and too readily assume they are the best ones to serve our purposes. As will be discussed later in this chapter, there are a variety of formats for communicating and reporting, and the best choice depends on the audience, the purpose, the timing, and the resources available. Another dangerous and limiting assumption is that the best time for communicating and reporting is at the end of the evaluation—when all the data have been collected and analyzed, and the findings compiled. Although this is clearly an important time to communicate, it is not the only time, nor should it be the first time. The central theme of this chapter is that the most effective communicating and reporting takes place throughout the life cycle of the evaluation endeavor. This chapter guides you through the necessary considerations about audience, purpose, timing, and format to develop and carry out successful communicating and reporting. The chapter is organized according to the following essential steps:

1. Think about what *purposes* your communicating and reporting can (and should) serve.

2. Review and identify the evaluation stakeholders and think about the purposes for which they should be considered a communicating and reporting *audience*.

3. Determine the best *timing* of your communicating and reporting to serve the purposes you have identified for each audience.

4. Choose the best *format*—based on purposes (that is, *content*), audiences, and timing.

Purposes of Communicating and Reporting

Communicating and reporting serves two general purposes: communicating about the evaluation itself and reporting the evaluation findings. Although the reporting of evaluation findings most often involves some written communication and interaction with evaluation audiences, the most important communication takes place long before findings are available. The success of an evaluation is never entirely dependent on the technical expertise of the evaluator. It requires the cooperation, support, and expertise of others who provide needed time, access, and information. For example, in addition to the cooperation of those who will provide data directly, we also often need information from others about access and logistics to carry off the data collection activities.

The more collaborative an evaluation is, the more meaningful it tends to be. As has been suggested in other chapters, involving stakeholders in (a) decisionmaking about the evaluation's overall purpose and design, (b) the development of its data collection methods, (c) the logistical arrangements necessary to carry out the evaluation, (d) the analytic frameworks that will be used, as well as the choice, (e) timing and content of communicating and reporting activities—are essential to making the evaluation logistically feasible, relevant, and useful for those it is meant to serve. This collaboration and decisionmaking requires ongoing communication between and among evaluators and stakeholders.

Collaborative decisionmaking about the evaluation involves individuals who represent the various stakeholder groups. As this chapter's vignette shows, sometimes such a group will be established as an "evaluation team" with a specific charge to advise, or design and carry out, the evaluation. Additionally, various persons immediately or peripherally involved with the evaluation will need to be kept informed about upcoming evaluation activities (for example, all the employees within an organization would need to know about an upcoming survey). Additionally, some general communication that an evaluation is being planned or taking place, as well as periodic reports about the progress of an evaluation, may also be necessary. Keeping evaluation stakeholders informed is good professional practice—it can reduce the possibility of unforeseen reactions by individuals or groups who find out about an evaluation through other means, and it can help build support for the evaluation activities and interest in its findings.

Once data have been collected and analyzed, the reporting of findings typically becomes the focus of communications between evaluators and stakeholders. Indeed, reporting evaluation findings is usually seen as the general end toward which any evaluation is striving. Yet reports of evaluation findings have been criticized on two major fronts: (1) they tend to be available too late—that is, after the time when they would have been useful; and (2) they are not easily accessible to audiences—for example, lengthy reports shrouded in academic or statistical jargon. The most effective evaluations include ongoing communications of findings in formats accessible to a variety of audiences. One format that will be discussed later in the chapter, "working sessions," includes key evaluation audiences in a presentation and discussion of findings during which the entire group participates in interpreting the findings and developing recommendations. Figure 13.1 summarizes the different purposes that communicating and reporting serves in an evaluation.

Audiences for Communicating and Reporting

In the vignette, the evaluation team has begun their work to develop the evaluation plan. As part of the plan they want to address how they will communicate and report the evaluation's activities and findings to the various stakeholders. As a group, they've brainstormed questions they want to address:

- How will these different groups be involved?
- What will they need to know?
- When?

FIGURE 13.1   Communicating and Reporting Purposes

- Collaborative decision making about evaluation design and activities
- Informing those directly involved about specific upcoming evaluation activities
- Keeping those directly and indirectly involved informed about the progress of the evaluation
- Presentation, and possibly the collaborative interpretation, of initial or interim findings
- Presentation, and possibly the collaborative interpretation, of complete or final findings

- What's the best way to communicate with them?
- What findings will the different stakeholders be most interested in?
- What resources do we have for communicating and reporting?

In Chapter 5, you learned how to identify the evaluation stakeholders—individuals or groups who have some interest in the evaluation. All stakeholders are potential audiences for some communication or report about the evaluation. By considering each stakeholder or stakeholder group in terms of the purposes just described, as well as the time and resources you have available, you will be able to determine if a stakeholder is also a communicating and reporting audience. In some cases not all stakeholders (for example, future program participants who could be said to have an interest in the evaluation) will be communicating and reporting audiences for your evaluation. Typically, the most primary stakeholders (program participants, managers, or funders who commissioned the evaluation) are the communicating and reporting audiences.

The resources available may also define the audiences for the evaluation findings. That is, more removed stakeholders—for example, staff in other organizations who run programs similar to the one being evaluated—might have an interest in the evaluation findings. But because of limits in time, funding, or both, you may not able to take an active role in making the findings available to them (such as at a conference or in a trade journal). Figure 13.2 summarizes these points about communicating and reporting audiences.

FIGURE 13.2   Communicating and Reporting Audiences

- All evaluation stakeholders are potential communicating and reporting audiences.
- Consider each stakeholder in terms of the purposes in Figure 13.1 to determine if they are also a communicating and reporting audience.
- Consider what resources are available for communicating and reporting findings.
- The most primary stakeholders are usually the most primary communicating and reporting audiences.
- Other audiences may depend upon having time and resources to collaborate about evaluation activities and/or to make evaluation findings available to them.

Once you determine the communicating and reporting purposes and audiences, you are ready to build a communicating and reporting plan. Figure 13.3 shows an example of such a plan based on this chapter's vignette.

Let's consider the audiences identified in Figure 13.3 and the communicating and reporting purposes indicated for each audience. The seven audiences identified are:

- Evaluation team (MyFuture Unlimited staff members [youth development program director, research and evaluation director, evaluator]; representative from each pilot site)
- MyFuture Unlimited program staff
- MyFuture Unlimited president and managing director
- Staff at pilot sites (not on the evaluation team—executive director, program directors, and staff)
- Parents and youth at the pilot sites
- Foundation (funders)
- Members of the collaborative working group

These audiences were identified from among the stakeholders listed in the vignette because: (a) they are directly involved in the development of the program, its implementation as a pilot, and/or the evaluation; and/or (b) they have a vested interest in the outcome of the pilot and the evaluation.

FIGURE 13.3   Example of Communicating and Reporting Plan

Communicating and Reporting Plan for Evaluation of: Youth Development After School Program

Purpose	Possible Formats	Timing/Dates	Notes
Audience(s): *Evaluation team (MyFuture Unlimited: program development director, R&E director, evaluator; representative from each pilot site)*			
☑ Include in decision making about evaluation design/ activities	Working sessions	Ongoing at bimonthly meetings	
☑ Inform about specific upcoming evaluation activities	Working sessions	Ongoing at bimonthly meetings	
☑ Keep informed about progress of the evaluation	Working sessions	Ongoing at bimonthly meetings	
☑ Present initial/ interim findings	Working sessions	End of January	
☑ Present complete/ final findings	Working sessions	End of August	
☐ Document the evaluation and its findings			
Audience(s): *Other MyFuture Unlimited development staff for the pilot program*			
☑ Include in decision making about evaluation design/activities	Working sessions, e-mails/memos with attachments to get feedback on instruments	As needed	Periodically include in ET meetings
☐ Inform about specific upcoming evaluation activities			
☑ Keep informed about progress of the evaluation	Emails, Memos	Quarterly	
☑ Present initial/ interim findings	Working sessions	End of January	

FIGURE 13.3 *(continued)*

Purpose	Possible Formats	Timing/Dates	Notes
☑ Present complete/ final findings	Working sessions	End of August	
☐ Document the evaluation and its findings			

Audience(s): *MyFuture Unlimited senior management (president and managing director)*

Purpose	Possible Formats	Timing/Dates	Notes
☐ Include in decision making about evaluation design/ activities			
☐ Inform about specific upcoming evaluation activities			
☑ Keep informed about progress of the evaluation	E-mails, Memos	Quarterly	
☑ Present initial/interim findings	Working sessions	End of January	
☑ Present complete/ final findings	Working sessions	End of August	
☑ Document the evaluation and its findings	Comprehensive final report	By September 15	

Audience(s): *Staff at pilot sites not on the Evaluation Team (executive director, program directors & staff)*

Purpose	Possible Formats	Timing/Dates	Notes
☑ Include in decision making about evaluation design/activities	Personal discussions/ meetings	Early April	Pilot staff survey
☑ Inform about specific upcoming evaluation activities	Verbal presentation/at site staff meeting	September and as needed throughout year	
☑ Keep informed about progress of the evaluation	Written memo	By February 15	Based on written interim report to funders

(continues)

FIGURE 13.3 *(continued)*

Purpose	Possible Formats	Timing/Dates	Notes
☑ Present initial/ interim findings			
☑ Present complete/ final findings	Executive summary		Based on comprehensive final report to funders
☐ Document the evaluation and its findings			

Audience(s): *Parents and youth at the pilot sites*

Purpose	Possible Formats	Timing/Dates	Notes
☑ Include in decision making about evaluation design/ activities	Personal discussions/ meetings	Early April	Pilot parent survey
☑ Inform about specific upcoming evaluation activities	Article included in site newsletter	Early September	Overview of the pilot program and its evaluation
☐ Keep informed about progress of the evaluation			
☑ Present initial/interim findings			
☑ Present complete/final findings	Article included in site newsletter	Late August	
☐ Document the evaluation and its findings			

Audience(s): *Foundation (funders), Members of the CRG (Collaborative Working Group)*

Purpose	Possible Formats	Timing/Dates	Notes
☐ Include in decision making about evaluation design/activities			
☐ Inform about specific upcoming evaluation activities			

FIGURE 13.3 *(continued)*

Purpose	Possible Formats	Timing/Dates	Notes
☑ Keep informed about progress of the evaluation	Written interim report	By February 15	Combine report of methods (evaluation progress) and findings in one report
☑ Present initial/ interim findings			
☐ Present complete/ final findings			
☑ Document the evaluation and its findings	Comprehensive final report including executive summary	By September 15	

Other stakeholders such as youth and parents at future sites were not included as audiences for this evaluation of the pilot program because the evaluation team realized that they would be more appropriate as audiences later when the program was disseminated nationally after an outcome evaluation had been completed. Additionally, the evaluation team recognized that other evaluation stakeholders, such as evaluators and youth development staff working in other settings, might be interested in the findings as well as learning about the evaluation effort itself. However, they concluded that their present budget would not support the time for developing a conference presentation or journal article.

As shown in Figure 13.3, four of the audiences will be involved in *decisions about the evaluation's design and activities*. They are the evaluation team, members of MyFuture Unlimited development staff, staff at the pilot sites, and parents at the pilot sites. The evaluation team (including representatives from each pilot site) will be responsible for the overall design of the evaluation; MyFuture Unlimited and pilot staff and parents will be asked to provide feedback on draft evaluation instruments (for example, written surveys) and procedures for administering the instruments. MyFuture Unlimited senior management (president and managing director), the foundation who funded the pilot and its evaluation, and members of the collaborative working group will not provide input into the evaluation design—primarily because they have entrusted this work to the evaluation team and must prioritize the work with which they become directly involved.

Only the evaluation team and those who will be asked to provide evaluation data will be *specifically informed about upcoming evaluation activities* (staff, parents, and youth at the pilot sites). Instead, most of the other evaluation audiences—MyFuture Unlimited development staff and senior management, the funders, and the collaborative working group—will be *kept informed about the progress of evaluation,* as will staff at the pilot sites.

In this case example, *initial/interim findings* will be presented to all of the audiences with the exception of parents and youth at the pilot sites. The evaluation team reasoned that this audience would be most interested in complete findings available at the end of the evaluation, and that taking the time necessary to develop an interim report appropriate for parents and youth would jeopardize staying on schedule with other activities during this busy time in the middle of the evaluation. It should be noted that one must be very careful about what is shared as interim findings, and that stakeholders clearly understand that the current findings are only *interim*. In other words, they should be cautioned that the direction of findings could shift before the final report is written, and some initial findings may be more or less supported as additional data come in.

All evaluation audiences will be provided with the final evaluation findings. Additionally, three audiences—MyFuture Unlimited senior management, the funder, and the CRG—will receive a full report of the evaluation, including a complete description of the data collection instruments, procedures, and analytic methods used. In the next sections, information on the timing, content, and formats for communicating and reporting is presented. The end of the chapter returns to further consideration of this example plan.

Timing of Communicating and Reporting

Generally speaking, the more often the communication, the better. Early in the evaluation, communicating with audiences will necessarily focus on decisionmaking about the evaluation. Later the topic of your written and verbal communications will shift to carrying out the evaluation's data collection activities, and ultimately to the evaluation findings. In many cases overall timing is roughly, if not directly, tied to the life cycle of the program, department, organization, or issue that is the subject of the evaluation. Often there will be an impending decision that the evaluation is meant to inform. If such a deadline exists, it establishes the time line for the evaluation activities that must come before. Most of us are familiar with developing a project schedule by working backward from an established deadline when the project must be complete. The same process applies to determining the timing for communicating and reporting.

Within any general timeframe that you establish for the evaluation, there may be considerable discretion about when different communications take place. If you are conducting a collaborative evaluation, you will be in regular communication with many of those individuals and groups with the most need to know about any particular evaluation activity or findings. For instance, specific dates for delivering many of the communications and reports will not necessarily have to be explicitly established for the evaluation team at the outset. These dates will fall into place as a matter of course in your ongoing work with the team.

Specific dates and sufficient lead time will need to be established for communicating with and reporting as needed to wider audiences. For example, sometimes you will want to arrange a meeting to discuss upcoming evaluation activities, or determine if this can be done as part of an already scheduled meeting (for example, a department or organization's regularly scheduled staff meeting). Lead time is necessary not only for (a) planning and scheduling, but also for (b) preparing the communication or report, and (c) possibly involving others in reviewing, if not helping to develop, it. Although technology has increased the speed of our communications dramatically, some time must be allowed for the receipt and reading of e-mails and faxes. Although delivery is almost immediate, these electronic communications are becoming so commonly used that it can no longer be assumed they will garner the immediate attention of recipients, as perhaps they once did. Figure 13.4 summarizes key aspects of the timing for communications and reports.

FIGURE 13.4   Communicating and Reporting Timing

- Overall timing for communicating is roughly tied to the life cycle of the program, department, organization, or issue that is the subject of the evaluation.
- Evaluation, communicating, and reporting time lines are typically worked out with the objective of making findings available at a specified time.
- Collaborative evaluations inherently provide for ongoing communication with key audiences.
- Communicating and reporting to wider audiences typically requires additional lead time.
- Communications and reports, particularly comprehensive written reports, often take more development time than many evaluators anticipate.

Content of Communicating and Reporting

Naturally, the content of your evaluation's communications and reports will primarily be tied to the purposes each is meant to serve. The most important criteria for success is that the content be presented in such a way that it can be readily understood and easily assimilated by the audience for whom it is intended. This section outlines four major considerations for effective written communications, particularly those reporting evaluation findings. They are: (1) writing in a clear, jargon-free style; (2) using tables and figures; (3) communicating qualitative and quantitative findings; and (4) communicating negative findings.* Guidelines for each strategy are shown in Figure 13.5.

Writing in a Clear, Jargon-Free Style

Clear, easily understood written communications is the goal of most any professional whose job involves paperwork. It is especially important in writing evaluation communications and reports. Misunderstood communications can result in lost time and missed deadlines. In the case of reports of evaluation findings—complex, confusing, or jargon-ridden reports can result in lack of understanding at the very least, and at the

---

*For further detail in each of these areas as well as additional considerations when developing the content of communications and reports, see Torres, Preskill, and Piontek (1996).

worst, misinterpretation of findings. When considering the guidelines in Figure 13.5 remember that appropriate writing styles for audiences will vary, depending on their backgrounds and familiarity with the subject matter.

It is important, however, to also strive for writing that is understandable. In combination with a well-chosen format, clear and jargon-free writing should result in a communication or report that its intended audience is able to quickly and easily assimilate. Most evaluation audiences are busy people—whether they are coworkers, funders, or parents. Almost any audience conceivable is the recipient of numerous communications daily—all vying for their attention. It is important that evaluators make the most of the time any audience member is able to afford our communications. The following sections further describe how to maximize the effectiveness of communications and reports.

Using Tables, Graphs, Charts, and Illustrations

Using tables and figures is one of the easiest ways to make complex information easily understood. Tables, graphs, and charts usually represent numerical data. Figures typically represent concepts or qualitative data in a graphic illustration. Both serve the important function of reducing information so that it is more easily assimilated and understood. A related type of display for data or findings can be done with an exhibit such as the figures and table shown in this chapter. These exhibits contain text describing and summarizing the main ideas of the chapter—a similar approach could be used in a lengthy evaluation report or even in a memo about data collection procedures.

The use of tables to present numbers, text, or both in columns and rows for showing relationships and trends are familiar to most people who are likely to be involved with conducting an evaluation. Similarly, graphs and charts representing quantitative findings and showing trends are familiar to most of us—if not in our work arenas, certainly they are prevalent in the news media. For this reason, and because other sources provide further guidance that might be needed (for example, see American Psychological Association, 1994; Torres, Preskill, and Piontek, 1996), it will not be given detailed treatment here. It is worth emphasizing, however, that when representing quantitative data in tables, charts, and

FIGURE 13.5   Guidelines for Effective Communicating and Reporting
Content

Writing in a Clear, Jargon-Free Style
- Avoid jargon and technical terms that your audience may not understand.
- Check the clarity of long sentences.
- Limit the use of passive voice.
- Use word processing tools for spelling, grammar, and writing style.
- To improve your writing—write and rewrite.
- Use collaborative writing to stimulate creativity.
- Allow sufficient time for writing several drafts, getting feedback, and proofreading.

Using Tables, Graphs, Charts, and Illustrations
- Think about the essence of the message and the type of presentation that will describe it most effectively.
- Keep your tables and figures simple, considering whether more than one table or figure is needed to communicate a particular set of findings.
- Check and recheck the accuracy of quantitative data in tables, charts, and graphs.
- Make each table and figure self-explanatory by providing titles, keys, labels, and footnotes.
- For a report, construct tables and figures first, then write the text to further explain the table/figure.
- Do not overuse color.
- Allow sufficient time for developing tables and figures.

Communicating Qualitative and Quantitative Findings
- Develop a framework that can guide the integration of qualitative and quantitative findings.
- Form teams of evaluators to provide expertise in both qualitative and quantitative data collection, analysis, and reporting.
- Determine the primary audiences' preferences for different types of data when deciding if one type should take center stage over another.
- Even in short reports and summaries or within limited time for verbal presentations, selectively present qualitative data to convey the richness and significance of overall findings.

Communicating Negative Findings
- Situate the evaluation within an organizational learning context.
- Involve stakeholders in the evaluation's design, data collection, and analysis activities.

FIGURE 13.5 *(continued)*

- Communicate as much as possible with stakeholders throughout the evaluation.
- Keep in mind stakeholders' perspectives and position them as problem-solvers, rather than culprits.
- Facilitate stakeholders to interpret findings themselves.
- In a written report, present positive findings first.
- Use language like "issue or concern areas" rather than "negative findings."

graphs two things are foremost: accuracy and self-sufficiency. Tables, charts, and graphs should be checked and rechecked to ensure their accuracy. They should also contain enough information in their titles and labels (and if necessary, footnotes) so that they can be understood and interpreted without accompanying verbal or written explanation. Busy individuals sometimes only scan reports, bypassing text and reviewing the tables and other graphics to glean the essential information. Making tables complete and self-explanatory will help assure that under these circumstances, data are interpreted accurately.

Illustrations may be a less familiar way to represent data or findings, particularly qualitative data. However, including a graphic illustration depicting the major constructs and interrelationships revealed in a qualitative study can be a powerful adjunct to written accounts. Further, a graphic illustration is often a necessary element of any verbal presentation of qualitative findings—which in their text form are typically difficult to summarize in the time available for a verbal presentation. Fortunately, most word-processing programs include drawing features that make the creation of illustrations relatively easy.

Communicating Qualitative and Quantitative Findings

When communicating qualitative and quantitative findings it is usually a good idea to combine both types of findings to support a broader theme. As described in Chapter 12, your objective should be to use a framework that reflects the evaluation's key questions or what has emerged from the data. In either case, the challenge is to present both quantitative and qualitative findings in a way that is clear.

Qualitative findings typically require more "space" to report—either in a written communication or a verbal presentation. The content of your communication about quantitative and qualitative findings will typically depend on the format being used. That is, a comprehensive final report is the place where you will be able to include the fullest presentation of the qualitative findings—interview quotes, graphic illustrations, and so on. Shorter communications like executive summaries or newsletter items will necessarily include a summary of key findings. Remember, though, qualitative findings can be particularly powerful in communicating the meaning of your results for those who are experiencing them directly or would be most likely impacted by the implications of the findings. It is often possible, even within a limited space or time, to selectively present interview quotes or graphic illustrations to help convey the data's richness and significance of findings.

Communicating Negative Findings

Evaluations can be threatening because, inherently, they create the possibility that negative findings about a particular program or organization will emerge. Like positive findings, these can be seen as a reflection of the work of particular groups or individuals. The objective of any evaluation is not to identify persons or groups who are performing poorly, but rather, for most program evaluations, it is to make known what otherwise would not be known for the purposes of continuous improvement. The learning and improvement purposes of the evaluation should be stressed early on and throughout the evaluation—and most especially at the time findings are reported.

Evaluation audiences who have been involved throughout the evaluation are more likely to find negative findings truly helpful and to view them as issue or concern areas than they are to find them threatening. By the time evaluation findings are available, key audiences should see themselves as problem solvers rather than possible culprits. This role can be further solidified by engaging key audiences in interpreting findings, and then based on their interpretations developing plans for corrective action.

Formats for Communicating and Reporting

By now you have probably concluded that for any one evaluation endeavor you are likely to need a number of different communicating and reporting formats to serve the various purposes and audiences identified. Beyond the requirement or need for a comprehensive final report, evaluators and evaluation teams usually have lots of discretion in choosing formats for communicating and reporting. The guiding principle is to choose the format (and delivery method) that maximizes access and audience engagement. The most engaging formats are those that actively involve the evaluation audiences rather than positioning them as static recipients of information. Figure 13.6 shows various formats in terms of the extent of audience interaction they afford.

Timing is a consideration in choosing a communicating and reporting format as well. In any given situation, some formats will take more time and resources to use (for example, expertise, funding, access to technology) than others. To meet particular communicating and reporting deadlines, speed and simplicity may determine your choice of format. Information explaining each format shown in Figure 13.6 and examples of *when* to use it are provided in the following sections. Figure 13.7 lists further guidance on *how* to use each format.

Working Sessions

Working sessions are facilitated meetings with primary audiences that can be used for almost any aspect of the evaluation—its design, to draft evaluation instruments, or to present and interpret findings. The main feature of working sessions is that they bring key audiences together, allow their perspectives to be voiced, and provide the opportunity for consensus about some aspect of the evaluation or its findings. Participants have the chance to reflect, share their perspectives, and engage in dialogue with each other in a constructivist learning environment. That is, by the end of the meeting it is quite possible for individuals to have new, shared understandings and convictions that have been informed through the group process and would not otherwise have been possible with the same speed and efficiency.

FIGURE 13.6   Communicating and Reporting Formats by Degree of
Interaction with Audience

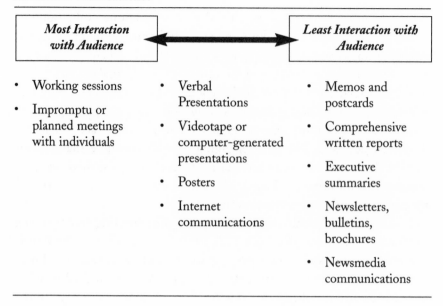

Working sessions are an ideal format for the evaluation team to work
on overall design, instrument development, or any other aspects of the
evaluation that require the input and perspectives of several individuals.
They can be a useful approach at the beginning of the evaluation for
building consensus and ownership. They are also particularly well suited
for presenting evaluation findings to audiences and then facilitating dialogue to interpret findings and action plans.

Impromptu or Planned Meetings
with Individuals

At different times throughout an evaluation it will undoubtedly be necessary to have meetings with individuals to get the input of key audience
members, follow up with those unable to attend working sessions, or

FIGURE 13.7   Guidelines for Using Different Communicating and
Reporting Formats*

MOST INTERACTIVE

Working Sessions
- Use with primary audiences to design the evaluation, draft evaluation instruments, and present and interpret findings.
- Carefully plan what each working session is designed to accomplish.
- To increase access/efficiency, consider conducting working sessions as part of other regularly scheduled meetings. Balance this with considerations for getting the necessary time for the working session.
- Provide sufficient background information at the beginning of the working session, and always close it with a clear outline of what is to follow.
- Follow up with audience members who were not able to attend.

Impromptu or Planned Meetings with Individuals
- Use with individuals unable to participate in working sessions and to pursue "teachable moments."
- Plan ahead to know how you will handle both prearranged and impromptu personal discussions.
- Make sure the content of communications with individuals is the same as what has been communicated to others involved in the evaluation. Similarly, if "new" information about some aspect of the evaluation develops during a personal discussion or meeting, make sure you also communicate this information to other audiences.

POTENTIALLY INTERACTIVE

Verbal Presentations
- Use as part of working session or any other meeting format to communicate about the evaluation purposes, design, data collection procedures, or findings.
- Take the audience's perspective when planning your presentation.
- Focus the presentation on a few selected topics, particularly when time for the presentation is limited.
- Plan ways to warm up and involve the audience.
- Incorporate visuals to make information more understandable, pique interest, and stimulate discussion.
- Use handouts to support your presentation and increase audience understanding.

* Adapted from Torres, Preskill, and Piontek (1996).   *(continues)*

FIGURE 13.7 *(continued)*

- Practice your presentation and use effective presentation techniques.
- Check the working order of any audio-visual or computer equipment you will use.
- Get evaluative feedback about your presentation so that you can continuously improve.

Videotape or Computer-Generated Presentations

- Use to create a stand-alone, widely distributable, visual communication— typically about evaluation findings.
- Establish the presentation's purpose and criteria for the selection of program events and activities to be included, making sure the presentation includes sufficient background information (about the object of the evaluation, the evaluation purpose, and so on).
- Carefully consider the intended audience(s) when determining the length of the presentation.
- Obtain permission from program participants prior to videotaping.

Posters

- Use to create a visual display of information about the evaluation and/or its findings that can be viewed once or remain in an accessible place over a period of time.
- Keep the format of posters simple and easy to read from a distance.
- Include visuals and color to help get your message across.

Internet Communications

- Use to communicate about the evaluation and make reports easily accessible to a very broad audience at minimal cost.
- Check out your audiences' access and practices with respect to the Internet prior to establishing it as a mainstay for communicating and reporting.
- As with any report of evaluation findings, carefully check its accuracy and possibly have key stakeholders review it before posting it on the Internet.
- Allow sufficient time for setting up "chat room" and LISTSERV® exchanges so that any technical glitches can be resolved.

LEAST INTERACTIVE

Memos and Postcards

- Use to deliver short communications about evaluation activities, reminders, updates, and summaries of interim or final findings.
- Carefully edit the contents of short communications using feedback from key audiences.
- Familiarize yourself with the most effective means of delivery of short communications to intended audiences. Consider intraorganizational mail, regular post, and faxes.

FIGURE 13.7   *(continued)*

Comprehensive Written Reports
- Use to fully document an evaluation and its findings.
- Carefully consider the need for a formal written report at the outset of the evaluation. Budget adequate time to produce the report.
- Consider the use of alternative formats designed to make the most important information easily accessible to the reader.
- Involve key audiences in the preparation and review of the report.

Executive Summaries
- Use to overview the evaluation and its findings for audiences who do not need or want a comprehensive final report.
- Include a copy of the executive summary at the front of each final report to reach those who, despite their best intentions, will not read the entire final report.
- Format the executive summary for easy assimilation of its contents.
- Include sufficient, clearly written information to make the executive summary a stand-alone document.

Newsletters, Bulletins, and Brochures
- Use these existing communication channels to reinforce or introduce information about the evaluation and its findings.
- At the outset of the evaluation, identify what newsletter, bulletins, and brochures different evaluation audiences receive. Investigate the appropriate channels for including information about the evaluation and determine production schedules.
- Maximize the use of the space you will be allowed by focusing on the most important information for each audience.

Newsmedia Communications
- Use newsmedia communications to reach the general public and members of particular industries or professions.
- Carefully consider any reporting plan that includes newsmedia communications.
- Initiate contact with the media only after key stakeholders have had a chance to read and reflect on evaluation findings.
- If your evaluation is likely to garner newsmedia attention, be prepared with a summary of the evaluation to provide reporters.
- Be cooperative with news personnel, but answer only those questions that you feel it is appropriate to answer at the time.
- If possible, avoid reporters who appear to have a single agenda and may fail to represent evaluation findings accurately.

communicate with some persons individually at their request. Personal discussions about evaluation activity, findings, or both can occur at any time or place—particularly when an audience member or other stakeholder initiates them. It is important to recognize that when you are responding to any question about the evaluation, you are engaging in communication about it. For this reason you must give some of the same care and forethought to the communication that occurs in personal discussions or individual meetings as you do to planned written communications.

You should anticipate what will be communicated in either planned meetings or impromptu discussions, making sure the messages are the same as what has been shared with other evaluation participants and audiences. Without some forethought you may be unduly influenced by the exigencies of the moment and the limitations of your own selective recall. It is particularly important to avoid discussing evaluation findings before they are fully available. Yet it is not uncommon for evaluators to be stopped "in the hall" and asked what they are finding while the evaluation is still in progress. In these situations, an appropriate planned response can be helpful; for example, explaining that not all of the data have been collected and it is the evaluation team's policy not to describe partial findings that may be misleading. Given the experience with early, inaccurate reporting of results during the 2000 U.S. presidential election, most persons will likely be well satisfied with this explanation, despite their understandable desire to know how the findings are coming along.

Impromptu or planned meetings with individuals can also provide an opportunity to pursue "teachable moments" about some aspect of the evaluation that might not present themselves in a group meeting. Perhaps an individual has concerns about the evaluation that she wants to share in a one-on-one setting. You will have the opportunity to explain its purpose, allay fears, and otherwise articulate the benefits of the evaluation process.

Verbal Presentations

Like working sessions and individual meetings, verbal presentations can be used for communicating and reporting in most any phase of an evaluation. They can be part of working sessions or other meetings where evaluation activities or findings need to be addressed. As shown by their middle position in Figure 13.6, verbal presentations can vary in the extent to which they are interactive with the audience.

Typically, the more time available for the presentation, the more opportunity for audience interaction there is. Regardless of the time available, it is important to make the presentation of information easy to understand and assimilate for your audience—whether it is about the evaluation purpose, design, data collection procedures, or findings. This is especially important for "executive briefings," where your objective is to present key findings within a limited amount of time. Typically, these busy audience members will not have read the entire evaluation report beforehand. Therefore, as difficult as it is to summarize months of evaluation work and a host of evaluation findings into just a few minutes, it must often be done. High-level decision makers will often make decisions based on these extremely short briefings. Even if, in such cases as this, verbal presentations allow for only minimal audience interaction, they need not be static or devoid of meaning. The presentation can include selected interview quotes or tables, charts, and graphs containing key pieces of information. Additionally, resources for the production of colorful overhead transparencies or animated computer presentations (possibly including audio) are becoming standard within many organizations.

In other cases, your audiences will expect and appreciate a more extended opportunity to ask questions and voice their concerns or reactions. Verbal presentations that include substantial opportunity for audience participation may actually be working sessions. Verbal presentations with a question-and-answer period about any aspect of the evaluation might be used either with audiences who are (a) directly involved and likely to most impacted by the evaluation process or its findings, and (b) less directly involved with the evaluation, but have a need (or right) to know about it.

Videotape or Computer-Generated Presentations

Videotape or computer-generated presentations are sometimes used to create stand-alone, widely distributable, visual communications about an evaluation—typically to report findings. The major determinant for use of this format is usually cost. Most organizations would need to contract for the services required to produce a videotape, although computer-generated presentations including video and sound are increasingly within the technical capability of many organizations.

These kinds of presentations can be particularly useful when you want to provide a visually engaging presentation to numerous audiences who are not in the same location—for example, in the case of a multisite evaluation with national or international sites or audiences. In addition, videotaped presentations can also be used with local audiences and with new staff members. For local audiences you can incorporate some interaction by including question-and-answer or discussion periods during or at the end of the presentation.

Although videotape presentations are widely used in a variety of contexts, some people might associate them with sales and marketing efforts. For this reason it is important to consider whether your intended audiences will perceive such a presentation as credible. It may be wise to limit the extent to which the presentation has a commercial look or feel.

Posters

Posters or other visual displays of information about the evaluation or its findings can be (a) viewed by audiences once at a single event, (b) reused at additional events, or (c) placed where there will be accessible to audiences over a period of time (for example, in the hall or entry area of any organization frequented by the widest array of possible audiences). Poster "sessions" are sometimes held at conferences where presenters can discuss their displays with conference members who visit them. Posters are typically used in settings or as part of events that have a broader purpose than providing information about a particular evaluation, but some group or groups of evaluation audiences frequent the settings or events. As another example, they might also be included as part of a school's "open house" event when parents and students visit at the beginning of the school year.

A poster display can include any amount or type of information about the evaluation, and it can be interactive or static. A representative for the evaluation can be present to orient audiences and answer specific questions. Poster displays are sometimes accompanied by computer-generated presentations that audiences can access on their own or with the help of a presenter. In either case, posters or other public displays of information about an evaluation are typically designed to be understood and assimilated by audiences without the aid of a presenter. That way, use with a presenter is optional at any given time.

Internet Communications

The possibilities for evaluation communicating and reporting via the Internet are ever increasing; it is hard to imagine any evaluation taking place without use of the Internet. In addition to e-mail exchanges, downloadable text files containing evaluation reports and summaries can be made part of any organization's web site. Using the Internet allows you to communicate about the evaluation at any time via e-mail, and to make reports easily accessible to a broad audience at minimal cost. E-mail can be used to schedule meetings, to keep audiences informed about evaluation activities, to answer questions, to carry on "conversations" with a group of individuals, and to send drafts of written communications and reports and solicit feedback. Any evaluation communication or report can be part of a text file attached to an e-mail. In this way, e-mail is simply serving as a mode of delivery in the same way the postal service does, albeit faster.

Written reports can be posted on web sites for access by anyone with Internet access. Although this would primarily be a one-way form of communication, your organization could invite audiences to contact you via e-mail or telephone with questions they might have about evaluation findings and reports.

Greater interaction can be arranged through inviting evaluation audiences to participate in "chat room" or LISTSERV® conversations about evaluation procedures and findings. Chat rooms engage audiences in on-line conversations at a specified time about a specified topic. LISTSERV® is a system that makes it possible to create, manage, and control electronic "mailing lists" on an organization's network or on the Internet.

Your organization's computer or management information systems department will be able to advise you if it has the capability to set up a LISTSERV® where members can exchange information and carry on text-based "conversations" about any aspect of the evaluation—which are then retrievable by any other member of the group. Obviously, this communicating format would be particularly useful in multisite or crossnational evaluations, and when ongoing exchange about evaluation processes and procedures is desirable.

Memos and Postcards

Short communications written in memo style and delivered internally within organizations or via fax to outside organizations can be used throughout the evaluation for keeping audiences abreast of evaluation activities, soliciting feedback, requesting participation in working sessions, and reporting interim or final findings in summary form. Memos are designed for easy access and assimilation. Postcards can be used to send reminders and updates. They are usually limited to a single message and can include a graphic and/or catchy typeface on bright paper to draw attention.

Comprehensive Written Reports

Comprehensive written reports are the most traditional and frequently used format for communicating about an evaluation and its findings. In their most conventional form, they are written in an academic style and adhere to the standards of social science research reporting. The objective is to give a full accounting of the evaluation purpose, design, methods, findings, and recommendations such that a reader otherwise uninformed about the program or the evaluation could judge for him- or herself the relevance of the design, the appropriateness of data collection methods and analysis methods, and the validity of conclusions and recommendations. Many evaluation audiences—particularly funders, external evaluation clients, and others familiar with traditional evaluation approaches—will expect such a report. The typical components of a comprehensive written report are shown in Table 13.1.

In some situations a program or organization may benefit more from time spent in working sessions where key audiences are presented the

TABLE 13.1   Typical Sections and Contents of Comprehensive Written
Evaluation Reports

Report Section	Contents
Introduction	• Purpose of the evaluation • Brief description of the program • Evaluation stakeholders/audiences • Relationship between/among organizations involved and those serving in evaluator roles • Overview of contents of the report
Program Description	• Program history, background, development • Program goals/objectives • Program participants and activities
Evaluation Design and Methods	• Evaluation questions • Data collection methods (including participants and schedule) used to address each question • Analysis methods for each type of data collected
Findings/Results	• Results of analyses of quantitative and/or qualitative data collected (usually represented in tables, charts, graphs, illustrations, and text)
Conclusions and Recommendations	• Conclusions drawn about the evaluation results • Recommendations for action based on these conclusions

evaluation findings and have an opportunity to reflect on and interpret them, and then themselves engage in action planning. This is preferable to receiving a written evaluation report from an evaluator who has interpreted the findings and developed recommendations in isolation from those most likely to be impacted by the recommendations or those expected to carry them out.

One option for increasing the relevance and participation in the compilation of a comprehensive final report is to make it a collaborative effort of the entire evaluation team, rather than relying primarily on the one or two individuals on the team who have the most evaluation expertise. Another option is to write the evaluation report after working sessions to interpret findings and develop action plans have been conducted. The report would then include the interpretations and recommendations of the working session participants.

Finally, alternative formats for comprehensive written reports are another option for increasing their usefulness. For instance, information about methods can be included in an appendix, and findings and recommendations can be presented in terms of each evaluation question. In this case, the report is organized around the evaluation questions, not the traditional elements of a social science research report. Use of wide margins, headers, bullets, and boxes can also increase the likelihood that the contents will be read and understood.

Executive Summaries

Typically, comprehensive written reports are accompanied by an executive summary that focuses primarily on the evaluation findings. It includes only enough background and methodological information to orient the reader. Obviously, many evaluation audiences will benefit most from reading an executive summary rather than a lengthy report. In fact, many key audiences who are busy, frequently only read the executive summary—even when they are the ones for whom the comprehensive report was primarily intended.

Being shorter, executive summaries have the advantage of being deliverable in numerous ways. They can be written in a memo style and faxed or attached to an e-mail. They can be produced on eye-catching paper and formatted with bullets and boxes for easy assimilation of text.

Newsletters, Bulletins, and Brochures

Newsletters, bulletins, and brochures are existing communication channels that can be used to reinforce or introduce information about the evaluation and its findings. For example, seeing evaluation findings summarized in a school newsletter would reinforce the findings for teachers who had earlier participated in a staff meeting where findings were presented and discussed. On the other hand, some parents might be learning about the evaluation for the first time when they read of it in the school newsletter.

For many readers, these documents have the advantage of already being part of an information stream that they regularly receive and incorporate in their work or professional lives. Recognize, however, that space will usually be limited and may allow for only a "summarized version" of the executive summary.

Newsmedia Communications

Relatively few evaluations are the subject of newsmedia communications—particularly those that are conducted as part of learning, performance, and change efforts within organizations. Those most likely to be considered newsworthy for the public are large-scale, government-funded evaluations of public institutions (such as school districts or particular educational or social service programs). More narrowly focused evaluations may be newsworthy for specific industry or professional groups. The chief advantage of newsmedia communications is their ability to reach a vast number of audience members.

Newsmedia communications include press releases and interviews with program or evaluation staff carried on radio, television, in newspapers, or the Internet, and is typically focused on evaluation findings. Newsmedia communications may be initiated by program (or evaluation) staff or by news organizations. Press releases are usually brief accounts of some aspect of the evaluation and are written by someone involved with the program or evaluation and submitted to a news organization. It may be published as is or excerpted. If the release creates enough interest, a reporter may contact the organization for an in-depth interview.

News media personnel may also contact program or evaluation staff for an interview about an evaluation if, for example, they have obtained a copy of an evaluation report, feel it is newsworthy for their particular audience(s), and would like further information. In these situations, unwelcome attention may be drawn to a particular evaluation—especially if the interviewee finds that their words or the evaluation findings are reported in a misleading way. With most newsmedia, communications there are no guarantees about what will show up on the newspaper page, computer screen, or air. The newsmedia is a one-way communication system and should be approached with caution.

Returning to the Case of MyFuture Unlimited

Now that we have reviewed various formats that can be used for different purposes throughout an evaluation, let's conclude by returning to our consideration of the communicating and reporting plan shown in Figure 13.1 and developed for the evaluation vignette at the beginning of the chapter. The evaluation team will be involved in working sessions throughout the evaluation for its design, development of instruments and procedures, and consideration of findings.

Other MyFuture Unlimited development staff will be invited to the working sessions where their input and perspectives are needed to develop the evaluation design and to draft evaluation instruments. Sometimes they will be sent e-mails with file attachments containing draft instruments for their review before the working session. After instruments are developed, they will be piloted with staff, parents, and youth at pilot sites. To get feedback on the instruments, different members of the evaluation team will conduct individual meetings with pilot-version participants.

The two groups who need to be informed about specific upcoming evaluation activities will be contacted in different ways. Staff at pilot sites will learn about evaluation activities as part of their regular staff meetings when a member of the evaluation team makes a verbal presentation and answers questions about the evaluation. Parents and youth at pilot sites will be informed via the site newsletter.

MyFuture Unlimited development staff not on the evaluation team, as well as MyFuture Unlimited senior management, will be kept abreast of the progress of the evaluation through quarterly e-mails or memos. For this purpose, staff at pilot sites will receive a written memo that will also include a report of interim findings. This same memo will be sent to funders and members of the collaborative working group, which was involved in the development of the pilot program.

The evaluation team's working sessions where interim and final findings are presented will also include MyFuture Unlimited development staff and senior management. Based on the outcomes of these sessions, the evaluation team will write a comprehensive final report and executive summary, which will be available to others but is primarily intended for MyFuture Unlimited senior management, the funders, and members of the collaborative working group. A summary of the evaluation's completed findings will be included in the August newsletter for parents and youth at the pilot sites.

The evaluation team's next task is to investigate how they can make a copy of the full report and executive summary available on the web sites of MyFuture Unlimited and the pilot program sites. They have received inquiries from evaluators and program staff in other organizations who learned about the evaluation and want to know more. Now that the work of this evaluation year is over, they can turn their attention to making information about the evaluation available to other stakeholders. Yet they want to avoid the time and expense of producing multiple copies of the final report and mailing them out. They are pleased that putting the report and executive summary on the Internet will make this information available to anyone with Internet access.

Keep in Mind . . .

1. Think about what *purposes* your communicating and reporting can (and should) serve.
2. Review and identify the evaluation stakeholders and think about the purposes for which they should be considered a communicating and reporting *audience*.
3. Determine the best *timing* of your communicating and reporting to serve the purposes you have identified for each audience.
4. Choose the best *format*—based on purposes (that is, *content*), audiences, and timing.

Background and Context of Evaluation

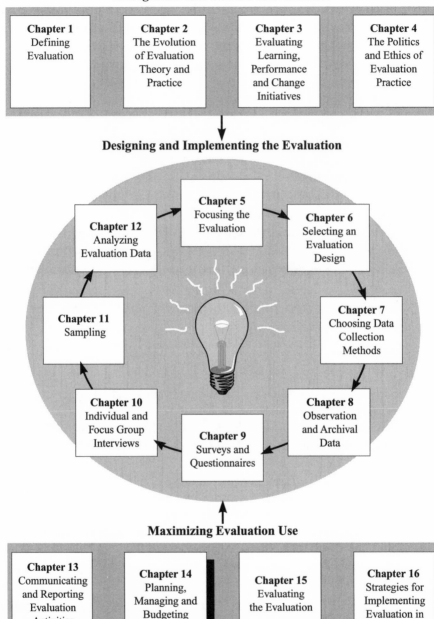

| **Chapter 1**
Defining
Evaluation | **Chapter 2**
The Evolution
of Evaluation
Theory and
Practice | **Chapter 3**
Evaluating
Learning,
Performance
and Change
Initiatives | **Chapter 4**
The Politics
and Ethics of
Evaluation
Practice |

Designing and Implementing the Evaluation

Chapter 5
Focusing the
Evaluation

Chapter 6
Selecting an
Evaluation
Design

Chapter 12
Analyzing
Evaluation Data

Chapter 7
Choosing Data
Collection
Methods

Chapter 11
Sampling

Chapter 10
Individual and
Focus Group
Interviews

Chapter 9
Surveys and
Questionnaires

Chapter 8
Observation
and Archival
Data

Maximizing Evaluation Use

| **Chapter 13**
Communicating
and Reporting
Evaluation
Activities
and Findings | **Chapter 14**
Planning,
Managing and
Budgeting
the Evaluation | **Chapter 15**
Evaluating
the Evaluation | **Chapter 16**
Strategies for
Implementing
Evaluation in
Organizations |

Planning, Managing, and Budgeting the Evaluation

- Planning the Evaluation
- Managing the Evaluation
- Developing an Evaluation Budget

....

Vignette #12: Planning an Evaluation at MyBank, Inc.

Chuck Yazzi, an organization development specialist at MyBank, Inc., invited seven stakeholders to a meeting in an effort to begin the process of focusing the evaluation of a new teller training process. Soon after the stakeholder group had discussed the background and history of the new teller training program and had developed several evaluation key questions that would guide the evaluation, the group started asking the following questions:

- Who was going to collect the data?
- From whom would we collect data?
- What would be the evaluation's timeframe?
- How much will the evaluation cost?
- What will we do if we encounter obstacles in the data collection process?

It soon became clear to Chuck that an evaluation plan was needed. This would help to ensure that the evaluation could be conducted with clearly defined roles and responsibilities and that the evaluation process could be implemented in a timely and well-organized way.

....

By this point, it has probably become abundantly clear that evaluating learning, performance, and change initiatives requires considerable planning and resources, just like any other kind of work activity. In this chapter, we provide guidelines on how to effectively plan, manage, and budget the evaluation. We first discuss how to think about and design various kinds of planning tools, and then describe how to develop an evaluation budget.

Planning the Evaluation

Although we advocate that evaluation should be ongoing and integrated with how work is accomplished, we recognize that there are better times than others to conduct an evaluation. If the organization or program is unstable owing to recent reorganization efforts or if changes in structure or personnel are imminent, an evaluation might not produce useful or valid information. Under these circumstances it is possible that employees' concerns, fears, anxieties, or even excitement might influence how they would respond to providing evaluation data or being available to participate in an evaluation. It is possible that if they do respond, their answers will reflect the tenuous situation versus how they really think and feel about the program being evaluated. For example, in an evaluation one of the authors conducted for a large insurance company, she noted some hesitation on the part of clerical staff that was participating in a focus group interview. The purpose of the evaluation was to determine how the organization might expand its career development system. Question after question seemed to elicit little response and it was clear that the participants were uninterested in the topic. Finally, she asked the group why they seemed so hesitant to speak. After a brief silence, one woman raised her hand and said, "We're all nervous about the rumors we've heard that the company is going to lay off a bunch of folks. It's hard to concentrate on your questions when we don't even know if we'll be here next week." To put it mildly, the evaluator was quite taken aback. None of the evaluation's stakeholders had mentioned the potential layoff situation. Yet, it was clearly affecting how the focus group participants were responding to the interview questions. As a result, the focus group interview concluded shortly thereafter.

Certain times of the year also make evaluation more challenging. For example, the weeks before and after major holidays are often busy times for organization members (both professionally and personally). Other times include peak vacation and holiday weeks, and whenever the organization is engaged in its budgeting process. It's not that evaluation work can't take place during these times, but that it might be more difficult for people to participate in, conduct, and actively support the evaluation.

Another consideration is how quickly the stakeholders need the evaluation results to make decisions. As part of the focusing phase, the timeframe for the evaluation should have been discussed and negotiated. We say negotiated because in today's volatile workplaces, there is little patience for efforts that take more than a few days. Learning, performance, and change professionals need to balance the need for timely information with what can be reasonably supplied. It probably does more damage to quickly collect data without thoughts about design or use than to lobby for more time. Just as we must help organization members understand the value and need to carefully design learning, performance, and change interventions, we must help them understand the necessary time requirements for collecting valid data. Hence, if we rush to collect data without serious consideration of the questions, methods, and potential use of findings, we may inadvertently provide data that lead to faulty decision-making, or evaluation findings that are not useful for taking action.

Managing the Evaluation

Even with the most simple and straightforward evaluations, there is a need to carefully plan for how, when, and by whom the evaluation will be conducted. Managing the evaluation entails:

- Monitoring the evaluation project's tasks and personnel
- Staying on schedule or negotiating schedule changes
- Monitoring the evaluation's budget
- Staying on budget or negotiating changes
- Keeping the client and stakeholders informed of the evaluation's progress and any problems that occur

Developing various project or management plans can help ensure that the evaluation is implemented as planned, that people responsible for various tasks do indeed carry out their responsibilities, and that any potential obstacles can be considered ahead of time. What follows are ex-

FIGURE 14.1   Sample Data Collection Management Plan A

Key Questions	Customers	Employees	Records and Documents
1. What organizational factors affect employees' ability to provide high-quality customer service?	Survey	Focus Group Interviews	X
2. How effective was the training program in increasing employees' ability to provide high-quality customer service?	Survey	Focus Group Interviews	X
3. How consistent is the service being provided to customers?	Survey	Focus Group Interviews	X
4. How satisfied are customers with the level of customer service being provided?	Survey	Focus Group Interviews	X

amples of various kinds of management plans, each providing a slightly different piece of information. We recommend that you consider developing at least one time line and one data collection plan for each evaluation project, though you may develop others as needed.

The Data Collection Management Plan A in Figure 14.1 links the evaluation questions to the methods that will be used to answer each question.

The advantage of this plan is that it guarantees that each of the key questions will be addressed by at least one data collection method. In the example, you can see that all four questions will be answered through three data collection methods. By using more than one method we can have greater confidence that the data are valid; that is, that the evaluation truly represents the knowledge, opinions, and attitudes of the respondents (see Chapter 6).

The Data Collection Management Plan B in Figure 14.2 provides information on who is responsible for each task. This is a particularly useful plan if there are multiple individuals responsible for various tasks and there are many details to be tracked in implementing the evaluation. It

FIGURE 14.2   Sample Data Collection Management Plan B

Patient Focus Group Interviews	Personnel Responsible
• Obtain list of patient names for each region	• Division staff
• Draw random sample within each region (20%)	• Evaluators
• Divide sample into 2 groups —1 for focus groups and 1 for survey	• Evaluators
• Explore incentives to focus group interview and survey participants	• Evaluators
• Determine dates and times for focus groups	• Program managers, evaluators
• Identify location for focus group interviews	• Regional managers
• Write letter of invitation to focus group interview	• Evaluators
• Mail letter of invitation	• Division staff
• Confirm focus group interview date/time	• Division staff
• Obtain refreshments for focus group interviews	• Regional office staff
• Conduct focus group interview	• Evaluators
• Send thank you notes for participating in focus group interviews	• Division staff

Patient Survey

• Write cover letter for survey	• Evaluators
• Code surveys for follow-up purposes	• Evaluators
• Type addresses on envelopes	• Division staff
• Obtain postage for surveys	• Division staff
• Stuff surveys	• Division staff
• Mail surveys	• Division staff
• Track returning surveys	• Evaluators
• Follow-up phone interviews w/ non-respondents	• Evaluators

Program Manager Individual Interviews

• Obtain list of program manager names for each region	• Division staff
• Determine dates/times for interviews	• Evaluators
• Identify location for interviews	• Program managers
• Write letter of invitation to interview	• Evaluators
• Address and stuff envelopes	• Evaluators
• Obtain postage	• Evaluators
• Mail letter of invitation	• Evaluators
• Call to confirm interviews	• Evaluators
• Conduct interviews	• Evaluators
• Send thank you notes for participating in interviews	• Evaluators

FIGURE 14.3   Sample Evaluation Management Plan C

Key Questions	Data Collection Method	Personnel Respondents	Responsible	Date(s)
1. What do future trainees know about how to negotiate contracts?	Pretest	All trainees	Instructor	5/1
2. One month after training, what do the trainees know about negotiating contracts?	Posttest	All trainees	Instructor	8/1
3. To what extent are trainees using negotiation strategies correctly?	Observation	25% of trainees (randomly selected)	Evaluation team	7/15–8/1
4. What supports or obstacles are trainees experiencing when using what they learned about negotiation in the workshop?	Individual interviews	25% of trainees— selected based on test scores	Evaluation team	8/15–30

helps those involved with implementing the evaluation know what they're responsible for so they can plan their schedules accordingly. In addition, naming the personnel responsible adds an element of accountability in case certain tasks are not completed in a timely way. It might also help in identifying personnel that will need to be hired or consulted, which will ultimately affect the evaluation budget.

The Data Collection Management Plan C depicted in Figure 14.3 also lists the evaluation questions and the methods associated with each question, but it adds information regarding the data sources, personnel responsible for the collection of data, and the dates of implementation. Consequently, this plan includes information that will be helpful for organizing the tasks for each phase of the data collection process. For example, knowing that you will be observing a random sample of trainees helps you prepare an observation guide (or protocol) and a method for randomly selecting trainees.

The Data Collection Management Plan D shown in Figure 14.4 (page 388) includes types of information similar to that presented in Figure 14.3 but in a slightly different format.

We have never known an evaluation to go according to plan—there are always surprises and unanticipated events. Plans E and F illustrated in Figures 14.5 and 14.6 help the evaluation team to anticipate what problems might occur during the evaluation process, and to plan for how they might deal with, or manage, such occurrences.

Management Plan E outlines the evaluation phases and areas that might be of concern. For each area of concern, the evaluation team brainstorms about possible problems that could challenge the evaluation's effectiveness. For each of the potential problems, the team determines possible solutions or actions that could be taken in case the area of concern surfaces. The value of this plan is its proactive nature, which prepares the evaluation team for potentially problematic situations. Plan F also helps identify possible problems but these focus on issues with the proposed data analyses.

Data Collection Plan G in Figure 14.7 allows one to see the full scope of how much data will be collected. This helps the evaluator or evaluation team prepare a time line and other task outlines.

There is no right or wrong plan. It is important that all the necessary management plans be developed to smoothly guide the evaluation's design and implementation. For some evaluations, this might mean developing a time line and a simple data collection plan. For more comprehensive and complex evaluations that employ an evaluation team, several different plans might be needed. There are several program management software programs available to aid this process (for example, Microsoft Project).

Developing an Evaluation Budget

For external evaluators, developing a budget is a necessary requirement of their practice. Oftentimes a client organization will say, "What can you do for X dollars?" Or they may ask the evaluator to develop a budget after the focusing meeting, as part of developing a proposal. Even internal evaluators who perform evaluation as part of their job should calculate all of the costs associated with conducting an evaluation. There may be times when an evaluation calls for monetary incentives, travel, or hiring consultants to assist in specific evaluation activities, which may require

FIGURE 14.4   Sample Evaluation Data Collection Management Plan D

Method	Key Questions Addressed	Timeline	Data Sources	Instrument	Personnel Involved
Individual Interview	1, 2, 4, 5	January	VPs, program directors	Individual interview guide	Evaluator
Focus Group Interviews	1, 2, 3, 4, 6	February–March	Home office employees	Focus group interview guide	Evaluator, note taker
Survey	1, 2, 3, 5, 6	April–May	Field employees	Survey	Evaluator, clerical staff
Document Review	5, 6	January–May	Logs, e-mail messages, newsletters	Document review form	Evaluator

the request of additional operational funds. It is important to remember that evaluation, just like any other project, activity, or work task, requires personnel and material resources. If the appropriate resources are not allocated to planning and conducting the evaluation, the results may produce data that are invalid or not useful for decisionmaking and action.

An evaluation budget should consider each of the following categories of costs and represent between 10 percent to 20 percent of a program's overall cost (Fink, 1995). For example, if a program cost $100,000 to design, develop, and deliver, the budget for evaluating that program could range from $10,000 to $20,000. This is not a hard and fast rule, but is offered as a general guideline. Though we provide several different kinds of costs, it is likely there are other costs not listed here that might be incurred in your evaluation. The value of having a budget is that it forces stakeholders to agree on the value of the evaluation and to clearly see the resources needed to effectively support the evaluation, and it allows the evaluation team to negotiate various evaluation activities if the cost is perceived to be too high. We have identified seven major categories of costs that should be considered for every evaluation.

FIGURE 14.5   Sample Evaluation Management Plan E

Evaluation Phase	Area of Concern	Problems to Anticipate	Possible Solutions
Focusing the evaluation	• Employees are oversurveyed.	• Stakeholder insists on using a survey.	• Provide alternative methods that will gather similar kinds of information
	• Client wants to know the program's return on investment.	• No predata are available; expected change in behaviors is near impossible to quantify with dollar value.	• Ask client what she hopes to learn from the evaluation. Ask, "What will convince you that the program worked? Will evidence of transfer of learning suffice?"
Carrying out the evaluation (the data collection phase)	• Accessibility of data sources	• Employees may not be willing to provide information.	• Seek upper management support to encourage participation
	• Poorly designed instruments have been used in the past.	• Previously developed surveys won't yield useful information.	• Redesign survey • Pilot-test new survey
	• Client wants the evaluation to include everyone in the organization.	• Budget and resources will not permit including total population in the evaluation.	• Sample using relevant criteria

FIGURE 14.6   Sample Data Collection Management Plan F

Evaluation Questions	Data Collection Method	Proposed Data Analyses	Potential Problems
To what extent did participants understand the processes in establishing a customer account?	Knowledge test	Percent of correct answers overall. Percent of correct answers for each item	Calculations may be inaccurate if done by hand.
To what extent did those who didn't complete the on-line training differ from who did complete the on-line training?	Completion Data (Records): •Position •Time with organization •Department within organization	Multiple regression analyses associated with completion Descriptive statistics (percentages)	Regression analysis may be difficult to explain to others. Neither analysis will explain why they differ just how they differ

FIGURE 14.7   Sample Data Collection Management Plan G

	Focus Groups with Clients	Focus Groups with Volunteers	Phone Interviews with Clients	Phone Interviews with Volunteers	Record and Document Reviews	Phone Interviews with Doctors
Boise	7	4			X	4
Sacramento	3	5			X	3
Rockford	2	3			X	1
New Orleans	4	2			X	4
Miami			16	9	X	3
Charlotte			10	6	X	3
Portland			24	9	X	4
Totals	16	14	50	24		22

1. Personnel/Professional Staff

The costs associated with personnel may be up to or more than 70 percent of the overall evaluation budget. To calculate the personnel costs for the evaluation, it is important to estimate the number of days or hours that will be spent on designing, implementing, and communicating and reporting the evaluation processes and findings. In determining personnel costs, be sure to consider all those who might be providing some form of assistance or those who have direct responsibility for various tasks, and what kind or level of compensation will be necessary. It is particularly useful to first develop a list of tasks, indicate who will be responsible for implementing that task, compute the number of hours or days on each task, and then assign a dollar figure based on an hourly or daily rate (this could be depicted in a management plan). Typical categories of personnel or professional staff are:

- Evaluator(s) fee/salary (this may include salary and benefits)
- Clerical support (this may include salary and benefits)
- External consultant fees (depending on the size and complexity of the evaluation, a consultant might be hired to do the following:
  - Design, layout, desktop publishing, proofreading (for data collection instruments and reports)
  - Data collection (for conducting individual and focus group interviews, observation, and so on)
  - Data translation (from one language to another)
  - Data entry or transcription
  - Data analysis
  - Presentations to senior management

2. Materials, Supplies, and Equipment

The following costs include anything that is necessary for collecting and analyzing data and reporting the findings.

Supplies
- Markers
- Flipchart paper and easels
- Audio and videotapes
- Computer disks

- Letterhead and envelopes
- Posterboard (for presenting the findings)
- Data analysis software
- Overhead transparencies

Refreshments
- Beverages
- Snacks or meals

Equipment Purchase or Rental
- Audiotape recorder and microphone
- Computer
- Video recording equipment
- Projector

Incentives (for surveys and individual and focus group interviews)

3. Communications

These costs are associated with communicating with evaluation respondents or members of the evaluation team.

- Postage (for example, surveys, letters, postcards)
- Telephone
- Fax

4. Printing and Reproduction

These costs are related to any duplication and report preparation activities.

- Duplication (for example, surveys, letters, interview guides, invitations, thank-you notes)
- Communicating and reporting
  - Laminating
  - Binding

5. Travel

These costs are usually incurred when traveling to locations to collect data or to attend evaluation team meetings.

- Transportation (airplane, car, taxi, shuttle, parking, gas)
- Hotel
- Meals (while traveling)

6. Facilities

There are times when it is desirable or necessary to rent a room to conduct focus group or individual interviews at a convenient or "safe" location. Alternatively, you may want to rent a special focus group interview facility to use special seating arrangements and equipment (such as two-way mirrors and videotaping).

- Room rental (at a hotel or other facility to conduct focus group interviews)
- Personnel and other support

7. Overhead and/or general administrative costs

These costs are associated with your own organization. As a contractor, through a university or consulting group, you will need to include these costs when providing a cost estimate to external clients and, in some cases, internal clients.

8. Miscellaneous or Contingency Costs

You may want to include a budget item for miscellaneous or contingency costs. These costs can be related to unforeseen changes in the evaluation plan, unexpected travel, and additional expenditures for materials. If the evaluation plan changes extensively, you may need to renegotiate the evaluation contract.

Although budgeting for an evaluation is not an exact science, with practice, one becomes more adept at estimating its cost. Once these costs

FIGURE 14.8   Sample Budget

EVALUATION BUDGET

The following budget constitutes the evaluator's fixed fees and the costs associated with conducting the evaluation (which may be variable).

Personnel

• Josie Anderson, Lead Evaluator	$10,300
• Mike Glosser	5,700
• Janine Hernandez	3,500
• Clerical support (10 hrs per week/20 weeks/$15 hr.)	3,000
	Personnel $22,500

Travel

Travel for Data Collection

Omaha—2 nights/3 days (Anderson & Glosser)

• Airfare	$340
• Hotel	720
• Taxi/Rental Car	150
• Airport Parking	60
• Meals	200
• Tips	10
	$1,480

Texarkana—2 nights/2 days (Glosser & Hernandez)

• Airfare	$368
• Hotel	720
• Taxi/Rental Car	150
• Airport Parking	60
• Meals	200
• Tips	10
	$1,508

Bend—2 nights/3 days (Anderson)

• Hotel	$360
• Taxi/Rental Car	225
• Airport Parking	30
• Meals	120
• Tips	10
	$745

Travel for Meetings

Data Analysis Meeting with Evaluation Advisory Group

• Airfare	$340
• Taxi/Rental Car	50
• Airport Parking	20
• Meals	10
	$420

Final Report Presentation

• Airfare	$340

FIGURE 14.8 *(continued)*

• Taxi/Rental Car	50		
• Airport Parking	20		
• Meals	<u>10</u>		
	$420	Travel	**$ 4,573**

Communications
Telephone
• Phone interviews	$658		

Postage
• Surveys (n=246)	$200		
• Invitations to focus group interviews (n=327)	120		
• Thank you letters (n=385)	125		
• FedEx or other overnight mail service	<u>200</u>		
	$645	Communications	**$1,303**

Materials, Supplies, and Equipment
Refreshments for Focus Group Interviews
• First line supervisors	$500		
• Managers	175		
• Vendors	<u>25</u>		
	$700		
Tapes and batteries	$100		
Poster Board for presenting findings	$50	Materials, etc.	**$850**

Printing and Duplication
• Data Analysis Meeting and Final Report Preparation	$300	**Printing & Duplication**	**$300**

Miscellaneous
• Unexpected costs (e.g., unanticipated travel, supplies)		**Miscellaneous**	**$2,000**
		Total Cost for Evaluation	**$31,526**

••

Keep in Mind

- When planning an evaluation, be sure to consider organizational context and stakeholder's timeframe for making decisions.
- Every evaluation should have at least one or more management plans.
- When developing a budget for the evaluation, carefully consider all of the costs involved.

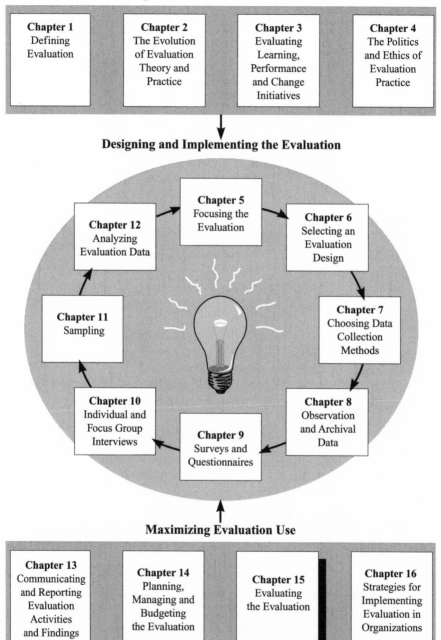

Background and Context of Evaluation

Chapter 1
Defining
Evaluation

Chapter 2
The Evolution
of Evaluation
Theory and
Practice

Chapter 3
Evaluating
Learning,
Performance
and Change
Initiatives

Chapter 4
The Politics
and Ethics of
Evaluation
Practice

Designing and Implementing the Evaluation

Chapter 12
Analyzing
Evaluation Data

Chapter 5
Focusing the
Evaluation

Chapter 6
Selecting an
Evaluation
Design

Chapter 11
Sampling

Chapter 7
Choosing Data
Collection
Methods

Chapter 10
Individual and
Focus Group
Interviews

Chapter 9
Surveys and
Questionnaires

Chapter 8
Observation
and Archival
Data

Maximizing Evaluation Use

Chapter 13
Communicating
and Reporting
Evaluation
Activities
and Findings

Chapter 14
Planning,
Managing and
Budgeting
the Evaluation

Chapter 15
Evaluating
the Evaluation

Chapter 16
Strategies for
Implementing
Evaluation in
Organizations

Evaluating the Evaluation

- Focusing the Evaluation
- Implementing the Evaluation
- Managing the Evaluation
- Communicating and Reporting the Evaluation's Activities and Findings

....

Vignette #13: Evaluating the Evaluation at MyUtilities.com.

Dorothy Smith, the evaluation specialist at MyUtilities.Com, felt that there were some aspects of the evaluation of the reorganization effort that went really well and others that proved problematic. She thought that a thorough review of what went well and what could have been better would help in designing and implementing future evaluations. She wondered how to proceed.

....

Every evaluation should be planned to provide not only needed information about the program but also information concerning the evaluation itself. In some cases, programs, products, or processes are evaluated on a periodic basis, for example, every other year. Even when a program is only evaluated once, the learning from that evaluation can and should be applied to future evaluations. Such evaluation reviews can be useful in establishing successful evaluation systems by determining the effectiveness of each evaluation activity and phase. Evaluation that looks inward on its own practice is called *metaevaluation* (Scriven, 1991).

397

Metaevaluation is an excellent means for judging the value and soundness of an organization's evaluation processes and systems. It can provide insights and learning about what works and doesn't work within the context of a particular organization. With this in mind, metaevaluation is just one more method for ensuring that the evaluation is contributing to various stakeholders' needs for decisionmaking and change.

The following are three possible approaches for conducting a metaevaluation:

- The evaluator or evaluation team can take responsibility for carrying out the metaevaluation. Although this is certainly in line with the goal of learning from evaluation, which is fundamental to individual, team, and organizational learning, it is not without problems. It's important to recognize that when evaluating your own evaluation, the credibility of the results may be challenged since the evaluation team has a significant stake in the outcome and will likely be seen as biased. Furthermore, they may be so close to the evaluation that they may not always be able to see the forest for the trees. One way to address this potential predicament is to invite one or two organization members or an external consultant to be part of the metaevaluation team, thus creating a system of checks and balances.
- In some circumstances, the evaluator or evaluation staff may want to ask the program staff to provide a critique of the evaluation. Engaging the staff in the metaevaluation may increase the use of the evaluation findings and support for future evaluations since it becomes clear that the evaluation process is intended to add value to the organization. If this option is implemented, the staff may be asked to critique (a) the ways in which the evaluation was conducted, (b) the communication aspects of the evaluation, (c) the credibility and accuracy of the findings as they were reported, and (d) the likelihood that the results will be used. A drawback of this approach is that it requires more staff time—time they may not have or be willing to provide.

- Evaluation experts from universities or consulting firms could also be asked to conduct a metaevaluation. A peer group of evaluators could examine the (a) evaluation report and (b) evaluation process from memos, e-mail messages, data collection instruments, project management plans, and other related documents. Though this approach may increase the metaevaluation's credibility, it is limited by the experts' unfamiliarity with the program and organizational context. As a result, their criticisms may be of less value. It should be noted that metaevaluation conducted by external evaluators is relatively rare in organizations.

In the following sections, we discuss areas to consider when conducting a metaevaluation.

Focusing the Evaluation

As was explained in Chapter 5, how the evaluation is initiated and developed is critical to ensuring the ultimate usefulness of the results. Thus, reviewing the beginning stages of the evaluation may provide helpful insights into what went well and what could be modified for future evaluations.

Revisiting the Rationale and Purpose of the Evaluation

Once the evaluation has been completed, it is a good time to go back and determine the extent to which the evaluation reflected what was known about the program and what the evaluation was intended to do, as evidenced by the evaluation's rationale and purpose. The following questions might be useful in this exploration:

- Was there anything that should have been discussed regarding the background, history, and purpose of the evaluation that was not and thus influenced the direction of the evaluation?
- Did the purpose flow naturally from the evaluation's rationale?
- To what extent was the problem (evaluation issue) evaluable?

Identifying the Stakeholders

If we consider that evaluation is to serve the needs of organization members so that they may use the information to make decisions and take action, then we have to ensure that the evaluation has involved individuals or groups that can provide input into the evaluation and are in a position to use the findings. As discussed earlier, such stakeholders might include program staff, clients, customers, board members, students, community members, and others. Questions to ask during this phase of the metaevaluation include:

- To what extent were all the relevant stakeholders identified and invited to participate?
- To what extent were the stakeholders' intended uses of the evaluation findings discussed?
- To what extent did the stakeholders contribute to or hinder the completion of the evaluation?
- In what ways could greater cooperation from the stakeholders have been obtained?
- What did stakeholders learn from being involved in the evaluation?

Evaluation of Key Questions

At the end of each evaluation, you should review the extent to which the key questions were addressed as well as their comprehensiveness. The major issue here is whether the evaluation actually addressed the key questions and yielded the necessary information. The following questions can guide you in this phase of the metaevaluation:

- To what extent were the key questions clear and comprehensive enough to address the evaluation's purpose?
- To what extent were the key questions responsive to the stakeholders' needs for information?

- To what extent were all of the key questions addressed by the data collected? If they were not answered, why not?
- To what extent did the findings indicate that other key questions should have been asked?

Implementing the Evaluation

Even with the best of evaluation designs, there will be obstacles or surprises that are difficult to anticipate. Therefore, it's important to reflect on the various stages of the evaluation's implementation.

Evaluation Design

We are often confident that a particular design will work with an organization or group of people, but one thing we've learned about evaluation is that it's never predictable. So, although we may think that a pretest-posttest control group would provide highly credible findings, we may find that when we implement the evaluation, this design won't work because of organizational politics or logistical problems. Therefore, it's important that we learn from our experiences in ways that help us discern what the best design is not only for a particular set of evaluation questions, but for a particular organization's context. This next set of questions can be asked at this stage of the meta-evaluation:

- Why was the particular design(s) chosen?
- What problems, if any, were encountered in implementing the chosen design?
- What implications did these problems have on the evaluation findings?
- What implications are there for choosing a design for future evaluations?

Sampling

Given today's dynamic organizations, a specified sampling approach may be difficult if not impossible to achieve, as we discussed in Chapter 11. You may have randomly assigned people to particular groups only to have some people leave the organization and drop out of the sample. Alternatively, other people may be hired by the organization, and you are asked to include them in the intervention. The metaevaluation should examine the following questions regarding the sample:

- Why was this particular sampling method chosen?
- What problems, if any, were encountered in implementing the chosen sampling method?
- What implications did these sampling problems have on the evaluation findings?
- What implications are there for deciding on a sampling method for future evaluations?

Data Collection Methods and Instruments

Knowing which methods will collect useful information often comes from experience. However, even after many years of conducting evaluations, we've found that some methods that work with certain populations don't always work with others. Thus, it's important to reflect on how the chosen methods worked in obtaining information to answer the key evaluation questions. Consider asking the following questions during the metaevaluation:

- How successful was each method in obtaining the desired information?
- What issues were encountered in implementing certain methods?
- What was the response rate for each method?
  - What was done to reach the desired sample size?
  - Did the number in the sample match the projected sample size? If no, why not?

• What might be done in future evaluations to obtain the desired sample size?

Examining a Specific Method. Information kept on which methods are particularly effective may reveal those that could be used in the next phase or in the next evaluation. For example, in an evaluation undertaken by one of the authors, a response rate of over 95 percent was obtained to a questionnaire within one week by:

• Including a letter from the president of the organization stressing the importance of an immediate response.
• Sending the questionnaires by overnight mail, even to locations outside the United States.
• Including prepaid overnight envelopes for the questionnaire returns.

In another evaluation effort, where thirty-minute interviews were conducted, a response rate of over 85 percent was obtained within one month by:

• Scheduling the interviews on the phone
• Confirming with fax (before the use of e-mail)
• Faxing the questions a few minutes in advance (respondents were non–native English speakers)
• Allowing interviewees to complete the interview entirely on the phone or partly on the phone and partly by fax

Reviewing the data collection process can help you develop future successful efforts. A statement indicating recommended changes to data collection efforts should be included in the metaevaluation report. This statement can then be used as the basis for implementing changes in future data collection plans.

Comparing the Results from Different Types of Data Collection Procedures. Another kind of analysis involves a comparison of the response rates and the results using different types of data collection procedures. You may find, for example, that in-person interviews yield a 100 percent response rate as compared with a 30 percent response rate for e-mailed surveys. Thus, although more expensive to conduct, the in-person interviews may yield more representative results. You then have information to make future decisions about the cost benefits of certain data collection approaches within the organization.

The quality of the data collection instruments will also directly affect the extent to which the findings are believed to be both credible and useful. Therefore, a careful analysis of each data collection instrument and the ways in which respondents answered the questions should be included in a metaevaluation. Questions to be asked include:

- How did respondents answer each question? For example,
  - Were there many "I don't know" responses?
  - To what extent were items skipped?
  - Were there many responses to the "other" category for multiple-choice items? What did these other responses indicate?
  - Did respondents appear to understand the directions for how to complete each item?
  - To what extent did respondents provide legible and useful information for the open-ended items?

Respondents' Comments. Comments made by respondents should also be included in the metaevaluation. These include (1) written notes made by respondents on surveys, observation checklists, or archival records, and (2) verbal comments made during the individual or focus group interviews. All of these comments, suggestions, and questions should be noted and reviewed. In some cases, these may be highlighted in the metaevaluation report and used as guides for future evaluations.

Analyzing the Level and Type of Nonresponse. Examining the level of nonresponse is critical to making a determination as to whether the data collection instruments and methods yielded trustworthy information. If the nonresponse level is high, then the results may simply reflect an unusual subsample of the original population. One example is the U.S.

Census. Despite special efforts, homeless people tend to be underrepresented in the Census. When data are collected within organizations, it may be that certain populations will be underrepresented or will display a high nonresponse level. These may be unskilled workers, those with limited English language proficiency, or even people who fear some retribution from the evaluation.

If the nonresponse level is high, you should definitely examine whether the nonrespondents come from a certain function, level, or geographic location within the organization. Such an examination can prove useful even when the nonresponse level is not very high. In any case, it may point out some important reasons for the nonresponses. For example, you may have collected information from e-mail messages and web-based surveys. Upon examination of the data, you may discover certain pockets within the organization that have limited access to computers and the web. You can then decide whether to use these methods with certain populations in any future evaluations.

Data Analysis and Recommendations

Using appropriate data analysis methods is of paramount importance in any evaluation. Data analysis involves looking for patterns and themes in the data and sometimes reducing the data to numerical statements that describe or explain respondents' knowledge, skills, attitudes, or opinions. If qualitative data are not adequately analyzed or if the wrong statistics are used with quantitative data, then the resulting interpretations, judgments, and recommendations may not only be weak but they may be wrong. Therefore, in a metaevaluation, the following questions are worth considering:

- To what extent were the appropriate methods of data analysis used?
- To what extent did the analyses reflect the key evaluation questions?
- To what extent did various stakeholder groups understand the analysis methods?

- To what extent did the analyses lead to reasonable interpretations, judgments, and recommendations?
- To what extent did the recommendations address the key evaluation questions?
- To what extent do the findings support the recommendations?

Managing the Evaluation

The entire evaluation process should be reviewed relative to the various project management plans that were developed for the evaluation. This would include any roles and responsibility plans, data collection plans, budgets, and the time line. Discrepancies in what was planned versus what happened should be noted and discussed as a means to inform future evaluations. In addition, documents such as e-mail messages, memos, interim reports, and logs or journals should be reviewed for further insights into how the evaluation was managed. Questions for the metaevaluation to address include:

- To what extent did the evaluation team members carry out their responsibilities as outlined in the plan? What problems, if any, were there?
- To what extent did the evaluation meet its projected budget?
- What implementation issues arose when carrying out the various project management plans?

Communicating and Reporting the Evaluation's Activities and Findings

For the evaluation results to be used, the findings must be clearly communicated and disseminated to stakeholders and others as identified in the evaluation plan. As discussed in Chapter 13, it is critical that various aspects of the evaluation and the findings be disseminated in ways that facilitate learning from the evaluation process as well as the findings. The metaevaluation might address the following questions:

- How often were stakeholders apprised of the evaluation's progress? To what extent was this sufficient?
- How was the progress of the evaluation communicated with stakeholders? How effective were these modes of communication?
- How were the findings of the evaluation reported? To what extent were these methods successful?
- To what extent were the stakeholders provided assistance in interpreting the findings?
- To what extent was the report disseminated in a timely fashion so that the results could be used?
- To what extent were alternative courses of action discussed with stakeholders?
- What steps were taken to use the findings for decisionmaking and action?
- What obstacles, if any, were encountered in trying to implement the recommendations?
- What changes regarding communicating and reporting the evaluation's activities and findings should be considered for future evaluations?

Tracking the Dissemination of Information. After the basic reporting on the evaluation has been completed, members of the evaluation staff should assume responsibility for monitoring the dissemination process. Records should be kept of all requests for the evaluation reports, for specific information about the evaluation, for questions concerning information in the reports, and ways in which the results have been used. Such record-keeping can provide an invaluable resource for identifying dissemination patterns. It can also aid in an examining the ways in which the evaluation results are used as described below.

Tracking the Use of Evaluation Results. Part of evaluating the evaluation involves monitoring where the reports go, who uses the findings, and how the recommendations are implemented. Unless some follow-up is undertaken, you will not really know whether the information was useful and used. To understand how the evaluation's results or recommendations have been applied, the following questions could be asked of all stakeholders, including those who specifically requested the evaluation and its subsequent reports:

- What reports, data, and information have you received from the evaluation?
- How credible are the results?
- In what specific ways have you used the evaluation results?
- What barriers, if any, have you encountered in trying to use the findings or implement the recommendations?
- What questions do you have about the reports or the information that you have received?
- What other kinds of information about the program could you use? How would you use this information? By what date would you need this information?
- What was learned from participating in the evaluation process?

The results of this monitoring and evaluation effort, along with recommendations for future evaluation efforts, should be included in the metaevaluation report.

In addition to the questions provided in this chapter, we strongly recommend that you review the *Program Evaluation Standards* (Joint Committee on Standards for Educational Evaluation, 1994) and the *Guiding Principles for Evaluators* (American Evaluation Association, 1995; see Chapter 4). They provide additional criteria for assessing the quality of an evaluation.

....

Keep in Mind . . .

- Evaluating the evaluation, or metaevaluation, is a way to learn from each evaluation.
- The evaluation team, the program staff, or some external evaluator can conduct a metaevaluation.

- At the very least, the metaevaluation should examine the evaluation's rationale and purpose, identification of stakeholders, key questions, design, sampling, data collection methods and instruments, data analysis and recommendations, management and budgeting, and communicating and reporting activities.

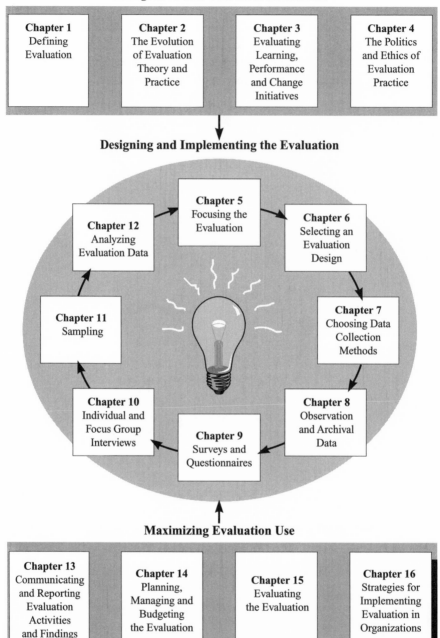

Background and Context of Evaluation

| **Chapter 1** Defining Evaluation | **Chapter 2** The Evolution of Evaluation Theory and Practice | **Chapter 3** Evaluating Learning, Performance and Change Initiatives | **Chapter 4** The Politics and Ethics of Evaluation Practice |

Designing and Implementing the Evaluation

Chapter 5 Focusing the Evaluation

Chapter 6 Selecting an Evaluation Design

Chapter 12 Analyzing Evaluation Data

Chapter 7 Choosing Data Collection Methods

Chapter 11 Sampling

Chapter 10 Individual and Focus Group Interviews

Chapter 9 Surveys and Questionnaires

Chapter 8 Observation and Archival Data

Maximizing Evaluation Use

| **Chapter 13** Communicating and Reporting Evaluation Activities and Findings | **Chapter 14** Planning, Managing and Budgeting the Evaluation | **Chapter 15** Evaluating the Evaluation | **Chapter 16** Strategies for Implementing Evaluation in Organizations |

Strategies for Implementing Evaluation in Organizations

- Gaining Commitment and Support for Evaluation Work
- Using Participatory and Collaborative Approaches
- Understanding the Evaluation Context
- Engaging in Evaluation Professional Development
- Choosing an Evaluator Role

As we've emphasized throughout this book, evaluation offers important opportunities to understand the process and impact of learning, performance, and change initiatives. Yet because some organizations have little experience with the kinds of evaluation we have described or have had negative experiences with evaluation, it may be difficult to convince others of its value. In this final chapter, we describe five strategies for increasing the viability of evaluation in your organization. They are gaining commitment and support for evaluation work, using participatory and collaborative evaluation approaches, understanding the evaluation context, engaging in evaluation professional development, and choosing an evaluator role. We've included questions that may help you think about steps you can take to address each strategy.

Gaining Commitment and Support for Evaluation Work

In spite of all the reasons why evaluation should be embraced, we fully understand that in some organizations, getting members to approve of

411

and engage in evaluation may be challenging. Yet for evaluation to be successful, there must be a certain level of commitment from the general employee population as well as from management. This commitment must be visible, tangible, and consistently communicated throughout the organization. We have found that all too often, management wants the organization to conduct more evaluations, but fails to provide adequate time and resources to pursue these studies. The organization's leadership must do more than pay lip service to evaluation. Managers and supervisors should: 1) demonstrate that evaluation leads to more informed decisions and actions, 2) reinforce and reward employees' use of evaluation knowledge and skills, and 3) integrate evaluation into the organization's daily work—make it an expected part of everyone's job. This support can take the shape of a manager affixing his or her signature to a cover letter for a survey, an e-mail message from someone in a leadership position stating that the evaluation is important and timely, or involving leaders in the evaluation process. Regardless of how this commitment is communicated, it is important to consider whose buy-in is needed and whose name and involvement would add credibility to the evaluation. When evaluation is fundamental to how the organization accomplishes its goals, then even changes in leadership, politics, or the organization's direction will do little to diminish its value.

The following questions might help you determine whose commitment and support is necessary for the evaluation's success:

1. Who is interested in the evaluand's success or failure?
2. Who has influence over the evaluand?
3. Who would need to support the evaluation for employees to know that the evaluation was important?
4. Who would add credibility to the evaluation?

Using Participatory and Collaborative Approaches

As we've suggested several times, evaluation is often most effective when it engages multiple internal and external customers and uses a participatory and collaborative approach. Evaluation is about gaining a greater understanding of the evaluand and involves judgments about merit, worth, and value. Since results should be used for action, you should involve numerous stakeholders who are in decisionmaking positions. A participatory and collaborative approach provides opportunities for:

- Ensuring that all voices are heard
- Using processes throughout the evaluation that emphasizes inclusion
- Addressing a diverse set of evaluation questions
- Increasing the credibility of the data and results
- Learning not only about the program being evaluated, but about evaluation theory and practice as well
- Sharing the workload
- Engaging in individual and team reflection
- Surfacing individuals' values, beliefs, and assumptions about the evaluand and evaluation

Employing a participatory and collaborative approach can be a powerful means for creating individual, team, and organizational learning.

Consider the following questions as you think about using a collaborative and participatory evaluation approach:

1. To what extent are teams currently used in the organization? In general, how effective are these teams?
2. To what extent would the organization be open to using a collaborative approach?
3. What are the advantages and disadvantages of using a team approach?
4. How could a participatory and collaborative approach benefit the evaluation and the organization?
5. What kinds of support would be needed to implement a participatory and collaborative approach?
6. If the organization and its members won't support a participatory or collaborative approach or the evaluation does not warrant such an approach, what alternative approaches will effectively address the evaluation's purpose and key questions?

Understanding the Evaluation Context

The success of evaluation work can be significantly affected by various organizational characteristics. Therefore, before beginning an evaluation, the evaluator should find out as much as possible about the organization's attitudes and experiences with evaluation, the organization's business, and issues surrounding the evaluand. What follows are five things for the evaluator to know at the onset of an evaluation. Having this information ahead of time will make the evaluation run more smoothly and result in a greater likelihood of the results being used.

- *Knowing when to conduct an evaluation*

In large part, the success of evaluation is based on an organization's infrastructure; that is, the strength of the underlying foundation or framework for supporting learning within the organization. An organization's infrastructure can strongly influence the extent to which organization members learn from evaluation and use their learning to support personal and organizational goals. The elements of the organization's infrastructure include culture, leadership, communication, systems, and structures (Preskill and Torres, 1999a). The nature of these components provides the footing on which evaluation efforts can be undertaken and sustained. Specifically, these components will facilitate or inhibit learning from evaluation to varying degrees, depending on how they operate within the organization.

In some cases, you may want to assess where the organization is in terms of its readiness for evaluation. For example, Preskill and Torres (2000) (see Appendix A) have developed the *Readiness for Organizational Learning and Evaluation (ROLE)* instrument, which measures an organization's readiness for learning from evaluation. A survey such as this helps determine the organization's strengths and weakness for supporting evaluation work. Based on the results of using this or other diagnostic instruments, you might wish to involve certain individuals in the evaluation process, design the process in a particular way, or work on shoring up certain parts of the organization before conducting the evaluation.

There are also times in an organization or program's life when evaluation may be more or less successful. Immediately before or after a merger, during a period of staff reduction, or in times of serious financial strain, evaluation might not be timely, unless it is directly related to one of these situations. When to conduct an evaluation is ultimately tied to the purpose and key questions. Thus, evaluation might occur before, during, or sometime after a learning, performance, and change intervention.

* *Knowing how the results may be received and used*

A good tactic for avoiding misuse and the lack of use of evaluation findings is to begin the focusing phase of the evaluation with several "what–if" statements that the evaluation team and other stakeholders can respond to. For example, you could pose the following questions for discussion: "What if the evaluation results show that trainees are not using what they learned back on the job?" What if the results indicate a drop in retention?" What if the results show a 300 percent increase in productivity?" Asking these kinds of questions helps stakeholders prepare for a variety of results. If they are seriously concerned about any of the answers, they could then have the option of not pursuing the evaluation before significant resources had been allocated and used.

* *Knowing the organization's "business" and financial situation*

Even the most successful evaluations will have little impact if the results and recommendations are not closely tied to the specific work of the organization. Understanding the business context means being aware of the organization's challenges and successes and how these might affect the evaluation process and the use of the results. This awareness may translate into inviting certain individuals to participate in the evaluation and the evaluation's focus and key questions, as well as the evaluation's time line and budget.

* *Knowing the external pressures on the organization*

Organizations are subject to myriad external pressures—pressures that one day pull them in one direction and the next in another direction. As such, organizations may be responding to new government regulations, increasing customer demand, soaring competition, or to a board of directors who want more control. As a result, managers and leaders are often caught between a rock and a hard place. For the evaluator, this means asking questions about these forces and inquiring how they might affect the design or implementation of the evaluation and the use of its results. It is possible that answers to these questions will imply involving certain individuals in the evaluation, focusing on a certain issue, or delaying an evaluation until a more opportune time.

- *Knowing where evaluation expertise lies*

It is unfortunate that so much talent goes untapped in today's organizations. Perhaps it's always been that way, but it seems even more so with the increasing number of external consultants. This is not to say that consultants don't provide invaluable services—they do. However, we often forget that right in our midst are people who have years of experience and a diversity of perspectives. In terms of evaluation, this means it is important to know who has specific knowledge and skills that can aid in the evaluation process. One person might be a great group facilitator who can keep meetings focused and productive. Or there might be a person who could use desktop publishing software to design the survey. Another person might know statistics and could help with quantitative data analyses. Another might be quite adept at writing survey items. Identifying and involving these people in the evaluation will likely keep the costs lower, enhance team and organizational learning, and increase the buy-in to the evaluation process and its results.

Questions that can guide your thinking about understanding the organization's context include:

- What is going on in the organization that makes this evaluation timely (or not)?
- How well prepared is the organization and its members to conduct an evaluation?
- What needs to happen to prepare organization members for the evaluation and the possibility of surprising results?
- What impact might the evaluation and its findings have on the evaluand, the unit, or the organization?

- What is the current "business" and financial situation of the organization, and what impact might this have on the evaluation?
- What external pressures might support or impede the evaluation?
- Who has areas of expertise that can be invited to work on the evaluation?

Engaging in Evaluation Professional Development

Good evaluation work is the result of both practice and education. Our observations over the years have led us to believe that learning, performance, and change professionals tend to learn about evaluation on the job, or from an evaluation workshop. Increasingly, however, university human resource development, organization development, management development, instructional and performance technology, and adult learning undergraduate and graduate programs are including evaluation courses in their curriculum.

Other valuable resources for learning about evaluation are the various professional organizations. The American Evaluation Association (AEA) (www.eval.org), and other national evaluation associations are excellent ways to become acculturated into the evaluation field. The AEA has local affiliates in several states that hold meetings and workshops throughout the year. Organizations like the Society of Industrial/Organizational Psychology have special-interest groups committed to the study and practice of evaluation. In terms of workshops, in addition to what AEA's local affiliates offer, there is the Evaluator's Institute (www. evaluatorsinstitute.com), which offers workshops on various evaluation topics and is endorsed by the AEA.

Ask any evaluator how they learned their craft, and most would say they learned the most when working with an experienced evaluator. Evaluators' interest in mentoring and apprenticeship is leading to the development of such opportunities via various national evaluation associations and societies. If you know someone in your organization or community from whom you'd like to learn more about evaluation, you should contact him or her to explore the possibility of an apprenticeship. There is nothing like learning in the trenches.

Resources also exist for locating practicing evaluators throughout the world. These are available from such organizations as American Evaluation Association, the Canadian Evaluation Society, the Australasian Evaluation Association, the European Evaluation Society, the National Science Foundation, Western Michigan University, the Kellogg Foundation, and the World Bank.

The importance of evaluation knowledge and skills cannot be overemphasized. While *you* don't have to have all of the necessary knowledge and skills, as a collective, evaluation team members must have what is needed to carry out a reliable, valid, and useful evaluation process.

Questions to consider regarding your own and others' professional development in the area of evaluation include:

- What are my strengths and weaknesses regarding evaluation theory and practice? What are knowledge and skills of others with whom I work?
- What kinds of professional development resources (for example, education, training, consultants, organizations) are available in my community?
- Should I become a member of a professional evaluation association or society? Should I attend one of the professional association conferences?
- How can I begin to develop an evaluation resource library?

Choosing an Evaluator Role

As the evaluation field has grown and become more pluralistic, it has broadened its views on what role an evaluator should play. Evaluators need to determine what role is appropriate, given the evaluation context and topic, what role the organization will accept, what role are they good at, and what role will support the greatest use of the evaluation findings. In some cases (though increasingly rare), the evaluator may assume the aloof, value-free social scientist role. If there is great concern about objectivity and being unbiased with regard to the program, then an external evaluator who approaches the evaluation this way might be called for. In other situations, where the goal is learning from the evaluation process as well as the results and is highly participatory, the evaluator may assume the role of coach, mentor, or facilitator. Your choice of role is an important decision, since it will influence your relationships with those involved in the evaluation, the process you use to carry out the evaluation, and the extent to which you work with the organization to design and implement the evaluation and its findings. The following questions might help you make this decision:

- What experience does the organization have with evaluators and evaluation? How has this experience influenced the role they expect from an evaluator?
- What role do I wish to take, given my experience with evaluation, my position within the organization, and the perceptions of others of my evaluation knowledge and skills?
- What are the advantages and disadvantages of assuming these different roles?
- What role will lead to a more credible evaluation and use of the evaluation results?

It is generally agreed that the future success of organizations will be dependent on their ability to build core competencies within a context of collaboration. Technology and quick and easy access to information will help create web-like structures of work relationships that will facilitate their working on complex organizational issues. As such, evaluation can be a means for a) collectively identifying information needs, b) gathering data on critical questions, and c) providing information that, when used, becomes part of the organization's knowledge base for learning, decision making, and action.

To develop support for evaluation as a knowledge-creating enterprise, we must create a market for it. If we think about evaluation as a means for learning and attaining knowledge, then it becomes integrated into every organizational effort—from product development to program design to process reengineering to systemic change. The following strategies may assist you in introducing or expanding evaluation practice within your organization:

- Stress the organizational benefits that may accrue because of evaluation—provide specific examples.
- Link evaluation work to the organization's mission.
- Involve stakeholders throughout the process and communicate often with them.
- Emphasize the use of findings and building learning capacity throughout the evaluation process.
- Start with small projects involving only a few stakeholders, then widely disseminate your findings using multiple communicating formats.
- Link evaluation work to knowledge development and management.
- Connect evaluation to other learning systems within the organization.

As organizations have been forced to respond to an increasingly competitive environment that is volatile and unpredictable, and as they are likely to continue being pressured to do things better, faster, and cheaper, they are looking at evaluation as a means to help them determine how best to proceed. It is our sincere hope that this book has not only inspired you to do more evaluation work within your organization, but that you will use evaluation to better understand the process and impact of learning, performance, and change interventions.

Appendix A:
The Readiness for
Organizational Learning and
Evaluation Instrument (ROLE)[1]

Directions

Before you begin responding to the items, please check one of the two boxes below to indicate whether you will be thinking about the organization as a whole, or your department /unit as the focus for your ratings. Base this decision on the entity with which you are most familiar. For example, if you are part of a large department it probably makes sense to respond in terms of your department. On the other hand, if you are very familiar with the organization as a whole, you can respond in terms of the organization.

☐ 1. I will be thinking about the entire organization.
☐ 2. I will be thinking about my department/unit.

For each of the items below, circle the number that best represents *your opinion based on your experiences,* and not on how you think other individuals would answer, or your organization's official policy or intent.

Culture

Collaboration and Problem Solving

	Strongly Disagree				Strongly Agree
1. Employees respect each other's perspectives and opinions.	1	2	3	4	5
2. Employees ask each other for information about work issues and activities.	1	2	3	4	5

---

[1]2000 Hallie Preskill & Rosalie T. Torres. This instrument is based on *Evaluation Inquiry for Learning in Organization,* Thousand Oaks, CA: Sage, 1999.

421

	Strongly Disagree			*Strongly Agree*	

3. Employees continuously look for ways to improve processes, products, and services. 　1　2　3　4　5

4. Employees are provided opportunities to think about and reflect on their work. 　1　2　3　4　5

5. Employees often stop to talk about the pressing work issues they're facing. 　1　2　3　4　5

6. When trying to solve problems, employees use a process of working through the problem before identifying solutions. 　1　2　3　4　5

7. There is little competition among employees for recognition or rewards. 　1　2　3　4　5

8. Employees operate from a spirit of cooperation, rather than competition. 　1　2　3　4　5

9. Employees tend to work collaboratively with each other. 　1　2　3　4　5

10. Employees are more concerned about how their work contributes to the success of the organization than they are about their individual success. 　1　2　3　4　5

11. Employees face conflict over work issues in productive ways. 　1　2　3　4　5

12. Employees generally view problems or issues as opportunities to learn. 　1　2　3　4　5

Risk Taking

13. Mistakes made by employees are viewed as opportunities for learning. 　1　2　3　4　5

14. Employees continuously ask themselves how they're doing, what they can do better, and what is working. 　1　2　3　4　5

15. Employees are willing to take risks in the course of their work. 　1　2　3　4　5

16. Employees are committed to being innovative and forward looking. 　1　2　3　4　5

17. Employees are confident that mistakes or failures will not affect them negatively. 　1　2　3　4　5

Participatory Decision Making

18. Employees generally trust their managers or supervisors. 　1　2　3　4　5

19. Managers and supervisors view individuals' capacity to learn as the organization's greatest resource. 　1　2　3　4　5

20. Employees use data/information to inform their decision-making. 　1　2　3　4　5

	Strongly Disagree			Strongly Agree	

21. Asking questions and raising issues about work is
    encouraged.   1   2   3   4   5
22. Employees are not afraid to share their opinions even if
    those opinions are different from the majority.   1   2   3   4   5
23. I feel safe explaining to others why I think or feel the way
    I do about an issue.   1   2   3   4   5
24. Employees are encouraged to take the lead in initiating
    change or in trying to do something different.   1   2   3   4   5
25. Managers and supervisors make decisions after
    considering the input of those affected.   1   2   3   4   5
26. In meetings employees are encouraged to discuss
    the values and beliefs that underlie their opinions.   1   2   3   4   5
27. Employees are encouraged to offer dissenting opinions
    and alternative   1   2   3   4   5

Leadership

28. Managers and supervisors admit when they don't know
    the answer to a question.   1   2   3   4   5
29. Managers and supervisors take on the role of coaching,
    mentoring and facilitating employees' learning.   1   2   3   4   5
30. Managers and supervisors help employees understand
    the value of experimentation and the learning that can
    result from such endeavors.   1   2   3   4   5
31. Managers and supervisors make realistic commitments
    for employees (e.g., time, resources, workload).   1   2   3   4   5
32. Managers and supervisors understand that employees
    have different learning styles and learning needs.   1   2   3   4   5
33. Managers and supervisors are more concerned with
    serving the organization than with seeking personal
    power or gain.   1   2   3   4   5
34. Managers and supervisors are open to negative
    feedback from employees.   1   2   3   4   5
35. Managers and supervisors model the importance of
    learning through their own efforts to learn.   1   2   3   4   5
36. Managers and supervisors believe that our success
    depends upon learning from daily practices.   1   2   3   4   5

	Strongly Disagree				Strongly Agree

37. Managers and supervisors support the sharing of knowledge and skills among employees.   1   2   3   4   5

38. Managers and supervisors provide the necessary time and support for systemic, long-term change.   1   2   3   4   5

39. Managers and supervisors use data/information to inform their decision-making.   1   2   3   4   5

Systems and Structures

Open and Accessible Work Environment

40. There is little bureaucratic red tape when trying to do something new or different.   1   2   3   4   5

41. Workspaces are designed to allow for easy and frequent communication with each other.   1   2   3   4   5

42. There are few boundaries between departments/units that keep employees from working together.   1   2   3   4   5

43. Employees are available (i.e., not out of the office or otherwise too busy) to participate in meetings.   1   2   3   4   5

Rewards and Recognition Systems and Practices

44. Employees are recognized or rewarded for learning new knowledge and skills.   1   2   3   4   5

45. Employees are recognized or rewarded for helping solve business/organizational problems.   1   2   3   4   5

46. The current reward or appraisal system recognizes, in some way, team learning and performance.   1   2   3   4   5

47. Employees are recognized or rewarded for helping each other learn.   1   2   3   4   5

48. Employees are recognized or rewarded for experimenting with new ideas.   1   2   3   4   5

Relationship of Work to Organizational Goals

49. Employees understand how their work relates to the goals or mission of the organization.   1   2   3   4   5

50. Employees' performance goals are clearly aligned with the organization's strategic goals.   1   2   3   4   5

51. Employees meet work deadlines.   1   2   3   4   5

Communication of Information

Availability

52. Information is gathered from clients, customers, suppliers or other stakeholders to gauge how well we're doing.   1   2   3   4   5

53. Currently available information tells us what we need to know about the effectiveness of our programs, processes, products, and services.   1   2   3   4   5

54. There are adequate records of past change efforts and what happened as a result.   1   2   3   4   5

Dissemination

55. There are existing systems to manage and disseminate information for those who need and can use it.   1   2   3   4   5

56. Employees are cross-trained to perform various job functions.   1   2   3   4   5

57. Employees have access to the information they need to make decisions regarding their work.   1   2   3   4   5

58. Employees use technologies to communicate with one another.   1   2   3   4   5

59. When new information that would be helpful to others is learned or discovered, it gets disseminated to those individuals.   1   2   3   4   5

Teams

60. My department/unit currently operates via (or is transitioning towards) a team-based structure.

   ☐ Yes, this is true.
   ☐ No, this is not true.

61. Employees are provided training on how to work as a team member.

   ☐ Yes, this is true.
   ☐ No, this is not true.

62. My work is sometimes conducted as part of a working group that is or could be identified as a "team."

   ☐ Yes, this is true. (Continue with item 63)
   ☐ No, this is not true. (Go to item 71)

		Strongly Disagree				Strongly Agree

Respond to items 63–70 based on your experiences as a team member.

63. When conflict arises among team members, it is resolved effectively.   1 2 3 4 5

64. Team members are open and honest with one another.   1 2 3 4 5

65. Team meetings are well facilitated.   1 2 3 4 5

66. Team meetings address both team processes and work content.   1 2 3 4 5

67. Team meetings strive to include everyone's opinion.   1 2 3 4 5

68. Teams are encouraged to learn from each another and to share their learning with others.   1 2 3 4 5

69. Teams accomplish work they are charged to do.   1 2 3 4 5

70. Teams are an effective way to meet an organization's goals.   1 2 3 4 5

Evaluation

Please use the following definition of *evaluation* when responding to the items below:

> Evaluation is a process of systematic inquiry to provide information for decision-making about some object—a program, project, process, organization, system, or product. Use of the evaluation results might lead to making refinements to the program or to offering new services or products.

71. The integration of evaluation activities into our work has enhanced (or would enhance) the quality of decision-making.   1 2 3 4 5

72. It has been (or would be) worthwhile to integrate evaluation activities into our daily work practices.   1 2 3 4 5

73. Managers and supervisors like (or would like) us to evaluate our efforts.   1 2 3 4 5

74. Evaluation helps (or would help) us provide better programs, processes, products and services.   1 2 3 4 5

75. There would be support among employees if we tried to do more (or any) evaluation work.   1 2 3 4 5

76. Doing (more) evaluation would make it easier to convince managers of needed changes.   1 2 3 4 5

77. This would be a good time to begin (or renew or intensify) efforts to conduct evaluations.   1 2 3 4 5

Strongly   Strongly
Disagree   Agree

78. There are evaluation processes in place that enable
    employees to review how well changes we make are
    working.   1   2   3   4   5

Additional Information

79. Which of the following best describes your job category? (Check one.)

    ❒ First-Line Supervisor
    ❒ Middle Manager
    ❒ Senior Manager
    ❒ Administrative
    ❒ Production
    ❒ Sales
    ❒ Non-Managerial Professional
    ❒ Technical
    ❒. Customer Service
    ❒ Other

80. Which of the following best describes your organization? (Check one.)

    ❒ Manufacturing
    ❒ Business Services
    ❒ Transportation/Communication/Utilities
    ❒ Health Services
    ❒ Wholesale/Retail Trade
    ❒ Finance/Insurance/Banking
    ❒ Education Services
    ❒ Government (Local, State, Federal)
    ❒ Non-Profit
    ❒ Other

81. How long have you worked for this organization? (Check one.)

    ❒ Less than 6 months
    ❒ 6 months – 1 year
    ❒ 1–3 years
    ❒ 4–6 years
    ❒ 7–10 years
    ❒ More than 10 years

The Readiness for Organizational Learning and Evaluation Instrument (ROLE)[2]

Developed by Hallie Preskill, Ph.D., and Rosalie T. Torres, Ph.D.[3]

Purpose

This instrument is designed to help an organization determine its level of readiness for implementing organizational learning and evaluation practices and processes that support it. The instrument's results can be used to:

- Identify the existence of learning organization characteristics
- Diagnose interest in conducting evaluation that facilitates organizational learning
- Identify areas of strength to leverage evaluative inquiry processes
- Identify areas in need of organizational change and development.

In sum, the organization may use the results to focus its efforts on improving or further strengthening areas that will lead to greater individual, team, and organizational learning.

Background and Rationale

In an effort to respond to internal and external demands for growth and success, many organizations have adopted the goal of becoming a learning organization. Organizational learning is "a continuous process of organizational growth and improvement that (a) is integrated with work activities; (b) invokes the alignment of values, attitudes, and perceptions among organizational members; and (c) uses information or feedback about both processes and outcomes to make changes" (Torres, Preskill & Piontek, 1996, p. 2). Evaluation conducted in support of organizational learning provides a means for (a) developing a community

---

[2]Based on the book, *Evaluative Inquiry for Learning in Organizations*,1999.

[3] Hallie Preskill, Professor, University of New Mexico, College of Education, Organizational Learning & Instructional Technologies, Albuquerque, NM 87131 (505) 277–6015, hpreskil@unm.edu.

Rosalie T. Torres, Director of Research and Evaluation, Developmental Studies Center, 2000 Embarcadero, Suite 305, Oakland, CA. 94606 (510) 533–0213, tcgrtt@aol.com.

of inquirers, (b) harnessing the knowledge capital of its members, and (c) addressing problematic issues that face the organization. It can serve as a catalyst for learning and action on organizational issues (Preskill & Torres, 1999, p. 43). Implementing organizational learning and evaluation efforts, however, is not an easy task. It requires that the organization carefully assess how prepared its structures, policies, procedures, and members are to support organizational learning and evaluation practices.

Description of the Instrument

The items on the instrument reflect the research on organizational learning and evaluation processes and practices. The results from this body of research suggest that an organization must have certain elements of its infrastructure in place if it is to truly support and encourage organizational learning. Research on the use of evaluation findings has also shown that the organization's culture and context significantly influence the extent to which evaluation findings are used to support learning and decision making.

The ROLE consists of 78 items grouped into six major dimensions. These include: (a) Culture, (b) Leadership, (c) Systems and Structures, (d) Communication, (e) Teams, and (f) Evaluation. Within four of these dimensions are eight subcategories (see Table 1). Three additional questions are included to provide information about the respondent and the organization. As individuals respond to each item, a picture begins to emerge that describes the extent to which organizational learning and evaluation practices and systems are present in the organization. Reliability data for the instrument are shown in Table 1 (see also Preskill, Torres, & Martinez-Papponi, 1999)[4].

Respondents are asked to respond to (a) 75 Likert scale items on a scale of 1 to 5, with 1 meaning "Strongly Disagree," and 5 meaning "Strongly Agree;" (b) three yes/no items; and (c) three multiple choice items. In administering the instrument with organization members, it is important to emphasize that there are no right or wrong answers. What matters most is their opinion based on their experiences. Use of the instrument is most effective when its items are answered honestly and the organization treats individuals' responses confidentially. We recommend that the results for all respondents be aggregated and reported in

[4]The authors are grateful for the support of Brenda Martinez-Papponi (University of New Mexico) and Vic Battistich (Developmental Studies Center) in analyzing the data for this instrument's validation study.

summary form. The instrument can be administered to single or multiple departments within an organization or to the entire organization.

Analysis

The instrument data should be entered in a database and mean scores calculated for each dimension and subcategory.

Interpretation of Results

If a department or organization were to score low in one or more of the dimensions, this would indicate that learning from evaluation might not be supported or allowed to succeed. Likewise, it would indicate that the department or organization isn't prepared to engage in other kinds of organizational learning practices. These kinds of results can help the organization determine where to focus its improvement efforts if its goal is to become a learning organization.

Example

Let's say a training department administered the instrument to its 50 employees. The aggregated results for the six dimensions from the survey are shown below. In interpreting the results, the department's management might conclude that it's leadership, culture, and systems of communication are doing pretty well – at least in terms of supporting organizational learning principles. On the other hand, the unit's systems and structures, its use of teams, and use and/or support of evaluation are less likely to facilitate organizational learning. Based on these results, the department decides to devote further effort to examining the results of the subcategories in the systems and structures dimension (open and accessible work environment, rewards and recognition systems and practices, and relationship of work to organizational goals). At the same time they begin looking at ways in which teamwork and evaluation efforts can support organizational goals.

Dimensions with Mean Scores of *3.5 or Above*	Dimensions with Mean Scores *Below 3.5*
Leadership (3.55)	Systems and Structures (2.60)
Communication (3.90)	Teams (3.45)
Culture (3.50)	Evaluation (2.95)

References

Preskill, H., and R. T. Torres. *Evaluative Inquiry for Learning in Organizations.* Thousand Oaks, Calif.: Sage, 1999.

Preskill, H., R. T. Torres, and B. Martinez-Papponi. "Assessing an Organization's Readiness for Learning from Evaluative Inquiry." Paper presented at the American Evaluation Association annual conference. Orlando, Florida, November 1999.

Torres, R. T., H. Preskill, and M. Piontek. *Evaluation Strategies for Communicating and Reporting: Enhancing Learning in Organizations.* Thousand Oaks, Calif.: Sage, 1996.

Table 1. Reliability Data for the ROLE Instrument

Dimension/Subcategory	Number of Items	Coefficient alpha
Culture		
-Collaboration and Problem Solving	12	.88
-Risk taking	5	.85
-Participatory Decision Making	10	.89
Leadership	12	.93
Systems and Structures		
-Open and Accessible Work Environment	4	.73
-Rewards and Recognition System and Practices	5	.89
-Relationship of Work to Organizational Goals	3	.66
Communication of Information		
-Availability	3	.79
-Dissemination	5	.80
Teams	8	.91
Evaluation	8	.84
All Likert Scale Items	**75**	**.97**
		(Cronbach's Alpha)

The Readiness for Organizational Learning and Evaluation Instrument (ROLE)

Mean Scores

Culture	Leadership	Systems & Structures	Communi-cation	Teams (if answered "yes," to items If answered 60–62) "no", skip this column)	Evaluation
Collaboration & Problem Solving	28.	*Open & Accessible Work Environment*	*Avail-ability*	63.	71.
1.	29.	40.	52.	64.	72.
2.	30.	41.	53.	65.	73.
3.	31.	42.	54.	66.	74.
4.	32.	43.	**Subtotal Mean**	67.	75.
5.	33.	**Subtotal Mean**		68.	76.
6.	34.	*Rewards & Recog Systems & Practices*		69.	77.
7.	35.	44.	*Dissemination*	70.	78.
8.	36.	45.	55.		
9.	37.	46.	56.		
10.	38.	47.	57.		
11.	39.	48.	58.		
12.		**Subtotal Mean**	59.		
Subtotal Mean		*Relationship of Work to Org. Goals*	**Subtotal Mean**		
Risk Taking		49.			
13.		50.			
14.		51.			
15.		**Subtotal Mean**			
16.					
17.					
Subtotal Mean					
Participatory Decision Making					
18.					
19.					
20.					

21.					
22.					
23.					
24.					
25.					
26.					
27.					
Subtotal Mean					
Total Mean Score	**Total Mean Score**	**Total Mean Score**	**Total Mean Score**	**Total Mean Score**	**Total Mean Score**

References

Alkin, M., R. Daillak, and P. White. *Using Evaluations: Does Evaluation Make a Difference?* Beverly Hills, Calif.: Sage, 1979.

Allee, V. *The Knowledge Evolution: Expanding Organizational Intelligence.* Boston, Mass.: Butterworth-Heinemann, 1997.

Alliger, G. M., S. I. Tannenbaum, W. Bennett, H. Traver, and A. Shotland. "A Meta-Analysis of the Relations among Training Criteria." *Personnel Psychology* 50, no. 2 (1997): 341–358.

American Evaluation Association. "Guiding Principles for Evaluators." In *Guiding Principles for Evaluators. New Directions for Program Evaluation* 66, edited by W. R. Shadish, D. L. Newman, M. A. Scheirer, and C. Wye. San Francisco: Jossey-Bass, 1995.

American Psychological Association. *Publication Manual of the American Psychological Association,* 4th ed. Washington, D.C.: Author, 1994.

Andrews, F. M., L. Klem, P. M. O'Malley, W. L. Rodgers, K. B. Welch, and T. N. Davidson. *Selecting Statistical Techniques for Social Sciences: A Guide for SAS Users.* Cary, N.C.: SAS Institute Inc., 1998.

Argyris, C., and D. A. Schon. *Organizational Learning II: Theory, Method, and Practice.* Reading, Mass.: Addison-Wesley, 1996.

Baldwin, T. T., and J. K. Ford. "Transfer of Training: A Review and Directions for Research." *Personnel Psychology* 41, no. 1 (1988): 63–105.

Baldwin, T. T., R. J. Magjuka, and B. T. Loher. "The Perils of Participation: Effects of Choice of Training on Trainee Motivation and Learning." *Personnel Psychology* 44 (1991): 51–65.

Bartel, A. P. "Return-on-Investment." In *What Works: Assessment, Development, and Measurement,* edited by L. J. Bassi and D. Russ-Eft. Alexandria, Va.: American Society for Training and Development, 1997.

Bassi, L. J., G. Benson, and S. Cheney. "The Top Ten Trends." *Training and Development* 50, no. 11 (1996): 28–42.

Bernthal, P., and W. C. Byham. "Interactive Skills Training for Supervisors: Penske Truck Leasing Company." In *In Action: Measuring Return on Investment,* vol. 1, edited by J. Phillips, pp. 23–32. Alexandria, Va.: American Society for Training and Development, 1994.

Bickman, L. "The Function of Program Theory." In *Using Program Theory in Evaluation,* edited by P. J. Rogers, T. A. Haccsi, A. Petrosino, and T. A. Huebner. *New Directions for Program Evaluation* 33. San Francisco: Jossey-Bass, 1987.

Bloom, B. S., M. D. Engelhart, E. J. Furst, W. H. Hill, and D. R. Krathwohl. *Taxonomy of Educational Objectives: Handbook I. Cognitive Domain.* New York: David McKay, 1956.

Bouchard, T. J., Jr. "Unobstrusive Measures." *Sociological Methods and Research* 4, no. 3 (1976): 267–300.

Brinkerhoff, R. O. "An Integrated Evaluation Model for HRD." *Training and Development Journal* 42, no. 2 (1988): 66–68.

———. *Achieving Results from Training.* San Francisco: Jossey-Bass, 1989.

Brinkerhoff, R. O., and M. U. Montesino. "Partnerships for Training Transfer: Lessons from a Corporate Study." *Human Resource Development Quarterly* 6, no. 3 (1995): 263–274.

Buchanan, T., and J. L. Smith. "Using the Internet for Psychological Research: Personality Testing on the World-Wide Web." *British Journal of Psychology* 90 (1999): 125–144.

Bushnell, D. S. "Input, Process, Output: A Model for Evaluating Training." *Training and Development Journal* 42, no. 3 (1990): 41–43.

Campbell, D. T. "Reforms as Experiments." *American Psychologist* 24 (April 1969): 409–429.

Campbell, D. T., and J. C. Stanley. *Experimental and Quasi-Experimental Designs for Research.* Boston: Houghton Mifflin, 1963.

Chen, H. T. *Theory-Driven Evaluations.* Newbury Park, Calif.: Sage, 1990.

———. "Current Trends and Future Directions in Program Evaluation." *Evaluation Practice* 15, no. 3 (1994): 229–238.

Clement, R. W. "Testing the Hierarchy Theory of Training Evaluation: An Expanded Role for Trainee Reactions." *Public Personnel Management Journal* 11 (1982): 176–184.

Collins, D. B. "Performance-Level Evaluation Methods Used in Management Development Studies from 1986–2000." *Human Resources Development Quarterly,* in press.

Cook, T. D., and D. T. Campbell. *Quasi-Experimentation: Design and Analysis Issues for Field Settings.* Boston: Houghton Mifflin, 1979.

Cousins, J. B., and L. E. Earl. "The Case for Participatory Evaluation." *Educational Evaluation and Policy Analysis* 14, no. 4 (1992): 397–418.

———. *Participatory Evaluation in Education.* London: Falmer Press, 1995.

Cousins, J. B., and K. A. Leithwood. "Current Empirical Research on Evaluation Utilization." *Review of Educational Research* 56 (1986): 331–364.

Cousins, J. B., and E. Whitmore. "Framing Participatory Evaluation." *New Directions for Evaluation* 80 (1998): 5–23.

Covert, R. W. "A Twenty-Year Veteran's Reflections on the *Guiding Principles for Evaluators.*" *New Directions for Evaluation* 66 (1995): 33–46.

Cronbach, L. J., S. R. Ambron, S. M. Dornbusch, R. D. Hess, R. C. Hornik, D. C. Phillips, D. F. Walker, and F. F. Weiner. *Toward Reform of Program Evaluation.* San Francisco: Jossey-Bass, 1980.

Denzin, N. *The Research Act: A Theoretical Introduction to Sociological Methods.* New York: McGraw-Hill, 1978.

Dillman, D. A. *Mail and Telephone Surveys: The Total Design Method.* New York: Wiley, 1978.

Dixon, N. M. "The Relationship Between Trainee Responses on Participant Reaction Forms and Posttest Scores. *Human Resource Development Quarterly* 1, no. 2 (1990): 129–137.

Dobbs, K. "Trainers' Salaries 1999." *Training Magazine* 36, no. 11 (1999).

Erickson, P. R. (1990). "Evaluating Training Results." *Training and Development Journal* 44, no. 1 (1990): 57-59.

Faerman, S. R., and C. Ban. "Trainee Satisfaction and Training Impact: Issues in Training Evaluation." *Public Productivity and Management Review* 16, no. 3 (1993): 299–314.

Fetterman, D. M. "Empowerment Evaluation." *Evaluation Practice* 15, no. 1 (1994): 1–15.

———. "Empowerment Evaluation: An Introduction to Theory and Practice." In *Empowerment Evaluation: Knowledge and Tools for Self-Assessment and Accountability,* edited by D. M. Fetterman, S. J. Kaftarian, and A. Wandersman. Thousand Oaks, Calif.: Sage, 1996.

Fink, A. *Evaluation for Education and Psychology.* Thousand Oaks, Calif.: Sage, 1995.

Fiol, C. M., and M. A. Lyles. "Organizational Learning." *Academy of Management Review* 10 (1985): 803–813.

Fornier, D. M. "Establishing Evaluative Conclusions: A Distinction Between General and Working Logic." *New Directions for Evaluation* 68 (1995): 15–32.

Forss, K., B. Cracknell, and K. Samset. "Can Evaluation Help an Organization to Learn?" *Evaluation Review* 18, no. 5 (1994): 574–591.

Foxon, M. J. "A Process Approach to Transfer of Training. Part 2: Using Action Planning to Facilitate the Transfer of Training." *Australian Journal of Educational Technology* 10, no. 1 (1994): 1–18.

Gable, R. K. *Instrument Development in the Affective Domain.* Boston: Kluwer-Nijhoff Publishing, 1996.

Garavaglia, P. L. "Applying a Transfer Model to Training." *Performance and Instruction* 35, no. 4 (1996): 4–8.

Gilley, J. W., and A. Maycunich. *Organizational Learning, Performance, and Change: An Introduction to Strategic Human Resource Development.* Cambridge, Mass.: Perseus, 2000.

Gist, M. E., A. G. Bavetta, and C. K. Stevens. "Transfer Training Method: Its Influence on Skill Generalization, Skill Repetition, and Performance Level." *Personnel Psychology* 43 (1990): 501–523.

Gist, M. E., C. K. Stevens, and A. G. Bavetta. "Effects of Self-Efficacy and Post Training Intervention on the Acquisition and Maintenance of Complex Interpersonal Skills." *Personnel Psychology* 44 (1991): 837–861.

Glaser, B. *Theoretical Sensitivity*. Mill Valley, Calif.: Sociology Press, 1978.

Glaser, B. G., and A. L. Strauss. *The Discovery of Grounded Theory: Strategies for Qualitative Research*. Chicago: Aldine, 1967.

Government Performance Results Act of 1993. Pub. L. No. 103-62, § 1101 et seq., 107 Stat. 328.

Greene, J. C. "Stakeholder Participation in Evaluation Design: Is it Worth the Effort?" *Evaluation and Program Planning* 10 (1987): 375–394.

———. "Stakeholder Participation and Utilization in Program Evaluation." *Evaluation Review* 12, no. 3 (1988): 91–116.

Greene, J. C., and V. J. Caracelli. "Defining and Describing the Paradigm Issue in Mixed-Method Evaluation." In *Advances in Mixed-Method Evaluation: The Challenges and Benefits of Integrating Diverse Paradigms*, edited by J. C. Green and V. J. Caracelli. *New Directions for Evaluation* 74. San Francisco: Jossey-Bass, 1997.

Guba, E. G., and Y. S. Lincoln. *Effective Evaluation*. San Francisco: Jossey-Bass, 1981.

———. "The Countenances of Fourth-Generation Evaluation: Description, Judgment, and Negotiation." In *The Politics of Program Evaluation*, edited by D. J. Palumbo. Newbury Park, Calif.: Sage, 1987.

———. *Fourth-Generation Evaluation*. San Francisco: Jossey-Bass, 1989.

Guilford, J. P. *Fundamental Statistics in Psychology and Education*. New York: McGraw-Hill, 1954.

Hamblin, A. C. *Evaluation and Control of Training*. London: McGraw-Hill, 1974.

Hargrove, R. *Mastering the Art of Creative Collaboration*. New York: McGraw-Hill, 1998.

Hatry, H. P. "Where the Rubber Meets the Road: Performance Measurement for State and Local Agencies." *New Directions for Evaluation 75* (1997): 31-44.

Hays, William L. *Statistics*, 5th ed. Ft. Worth, Tex.: Harcourt Brace College, 1994.

Helfert, Erich A. *Techniques of Financial Analysis*, 6th ed. Homewood, Ill.: Irwin, 1987.

Helgeson, S. *The Web of Inclusion*. New York: Currency/Doubleday, 1995.

Hesketh, B. "Dilemmas in Training for Transfer and Retention." *Applied Psychology: An International Review* 46, no. 4 (1997): 317–386.

Hilbert, J., H. Preskill, and D. Russ-Eft. "Evaluating Training." In *What Works: Assessment, Development, and Measurement,* edited by L. J. Bassi and D. Russ-Eft. Alexandria, Va.: American Society for Training and Development, 1997.

Holton, E. F., III. "The Flawed Four-Level Evaluation Model." *Human Resource Development Quarterly* 7, no. 1 (1996): 5–21.

Honea, G. "Evaluation, Policy, and Ethics: Mixing Oil and Water?" Paper presented at the annual meeting of the American Evaluation Association, Chicago, November 1991.

House, E. R. *Professional Evaluation.* Newbury Park, Calif.: Sage, 1993.

Industry Report. *Training Magazine* 33, no. 10 (October 1996): 37–79.

Industry Report. *Training Magazine* 37, no. 10 (October 2000): 45–94.

Jacobs, R. L., M. J. Jones, and S. Neil. "A Case Study in Forecasting the Financial Benefits of Unstructured and Structured On-the-Job Training." *Human Resource Development Quarterly* 3, no. 2 (1992): 133–139.

Joint Committee on Standards for Educational Evaluation. *Standards for Evaluations of Educational Programs, Projects, and Materials.* New York: McGraw-Hill, 1981.

———. *The Personnel Evaluation Standards.* Newbury Park, Calif.: Sage, 1988.

———. *The Program Evaluation Standards,* 2d ed. Thousand Oaks, Calif.: Sage, 1994.

Jordan, G. "Using the Logic Chart and Performance Spectrum in Corporate Performance Management: A DOE Case Study." Paper presented at the annual meeting of the American Evaluation Association, Atlanta, November 1996.

Kaufman, R., and J. M. Keller. "Levels of Evaluation: Beyond Kirkpatrick." *Human Resource Development Quarterly* 5, no. 4: 371–380.

Kaufman, R., J. Keller, and R. Watkins. "What Works and What Doesn't: Evaluation Beyond Kirkpatrick." *Performance and Instruction* 35, no. 2 (1995): 8–12.

King, J. A. "Research on Evaluation Use and Its Implications for Evaluation Research and Practice." *Studies in Educational Evaluation* 14 (1988): 285–299.

———. "Involving Practitioners in Evaluation Studies: How Viable Is Collaborative Evaluation in Schools?" In *Participatory Evaluation in Education,* edited by J. B. Cousins and L. M. Earl, pp. 86–102. London: Falmer Press, 1995.

Kirkpatrick, D. L. "Techniques for Evaluating Programs." *Journal of the American Society of Training Directors (Training and Development Journal)* 13, no. 11 (November 1959a): 3–9.

———. "Techniques for Evaluating Programs—Part 2: Learning." *Journal of the American Society of Training Directors (Training and Development Journal)* 13, no. 12 (December 1959b): 21–26.

———. "Techniques for Evaluating Programs—Part 3: Behavior." *Journal of the American Society of Training Directors (Training and Development Journal)* 14, no. 1 (January 1960a): 13–18.

———. "Techniques for Evaluating Programs—Part 4: Results." *Journal of the American Society of Training Directors (Training and Development Journal)* 14, no. 1 (January 1960b): 28–32.

———. *Evaluating Training Programs: The Four Levels.* San Francisco: Berrett-Koehler, 1994.

Kraemer, H. C., and S. Thiemann. *How Many Subjects? Statistical Power Analysis in Research.* Newbury Park, Calif.: Sage, 1987.

Kraiger, K., J. K. Ford, and E. Salas. "Application of Cognitive, Skill-Based, and Affective Theories of Learning Outcomes to New Methods of Training Evaluation." *Journal of Applied Psychology* 78, no. 2 (1993): 311–328.

Krueger, R. A. *Focus Groups: A Practical Guide for Applied Research,* 2d ed. Thousand Oaks, Calif.: Sage, 1994.

Lackey, R. "The Role of the Chief Learning Officer: Implications for Theory and Practice." Ph.D. diss., University of New Mexico, 2000.

Latham, G. P., L. M. Saari, and C. H. Fay. "BOS, BES, and Baloney: Raising Kane with Bernardin." *Personnel Psychology* 33 (1980): 815–821.

Latham, G. P., and K. N. Wexley. *Increasing Productivity Through Performance Appraisal.* Reading, Mass.: Addison-Wesley, 1981.

Lee, S. H. "Making Reaction Evaluation a More Useful Tool in the Evaluation of Corporate Training Programs: Reactionnaire Dimensions and Design Criteria." Ph.D. diss., Indiana University, Bloomington, 1998.

Levine, M., and N. Rosenberg. "An Adversary Model of Fact Finding and Decision Making for Program Evaluation: Theoretical Considerations." In *Program Evaluation in the Health Field,* vol. 2, edited by H. C. Schulberg and F. Baker. New York: Behavioral Publications, 1979.

Levitan, S. A., and G. Wurzburg. *Evaluating Federal Social Programs.* Kalamazoo, Mich.: W. E. Upjohn Institute for Employment Research, 1979.

Leviton, L. C., and E.F.X. Hughes. "Research on the Utilization of Evaluations." *Evaluation Review* 5, no. 4 (1981): 525–548.

Light, D., Jr. "Surface Data and Deep Structure: Observing the Organization of Professional Training." *Administrative Science Quarterly* 24 (1979): 551–559.

Likert, R. "A Technique for the Measurement of Attitudes." *Archives of Psychology* 140 (1932): 1–55.

Limerick, D., and B. Cunnington. *Managing the New Organization.* San Francisco: Jossey-Bass, 1993.

Lincoln, R. E., and D. O. Dunet. "Training Efficiency and Effectiveness Model (TEEM)." *Performance and Instruction* 34, no. 3 (1995): 40–47.

Love, A. J. *Internal Evaluation: Building Organizations from Within.* Thousand Oaks, Calif.: Sage, 1991.

Mabry, L. "Circumstantial Ethics." *American Journal of Evaluation* 20, no. 2 (1999): 199–212.

Madaus, G., M. Scriven, and D. Stufflebeam. *Evaluation Models: Viewpoints on Educational and Human Services Evaluation.* Boston: Kluwer-Nijhoff, 1983.

Mager, R. F. *Preparing Instructional Objectives*. Palo Alto, Calif.: Fearon Press, 1962.

Mathison, S. "Evaluation." In *Encyclopedia of English Studies Language Arts*, edited by A. C. Purves. Champaign, Ill.: NCTE and Scholastic, Inc., 1994.

McLagan, P. A. "As the HRD World Churns." *Training and Development* 53, no. 12 (1999): 20–30.

McLaughlin, J. A., and G. B. Jordan. "Logic Models: A Tool for Telling Your Program's Performance Story." *Evaluation and Program Planning* 22 (1999): 65–72.

McLaughlin, M. W. *Evaluation and Reform: The Elementary and Secondary Education Act of 1965*. Cambridge, Mass.: Ballinger, 1975.

McLinden, D. J., M. J. Davis, and D. E. Sheriff. "Impact on Financial Productivity: A Study of Training Effects on Consulting Services." *Human Resource Development Quarterly* 4, no. 4 (1993): 367–375.

Mehta, R., and E. Sivadas. "Comparing Response Rates and Response Content in Mail Versus Electronic Mail Surveys." *Journal of the Market Research Society* 37 (1995): 429–439.

Merriam, S. *Case Study Research: A Qualitative Approach*. San Francisco: Jossey-Bass, 1988.

Mertens, D. M. *Research Methods in Education and Psychology*. Thousand Oaks, Calif.: Sage, 1998.

Miller, E. "Research on the Web" (letter to the editor). *APS Observer* (July/August 1999): 4.

Morell, J. A. "Evaluation: Status of a Loose Coalition." *Evaluation Practice* 11, no. 3 (1990): 213–219.

Morris, M. "Research on Evaluation Ethics: What Have We Learned and Why Is It Important?" *New Directions for Evaluation* 82 (1999a): 15–24.

———. "You Got a Problem with That? Exploring Evaluators' Disagreements About Ethics." Paper presented at the annual conference of the American Evaluation Association, Orlando, Fla., November 5, 1999b.

Morris, M., and R. Cohn. "Program Evaluators and Ethical Challenges." *Evaluation Review* 17, no. 6 (1993): 621–642.

Morris, M., and L. R. Jacobs. "You Got a Problem with That? Exploring Evaluators' Disagreements About Ethics." *Evaluation Review* 24, no. 4 (2000): 384–406.

Mosier, N. R. "Financial Analysis: The Methods and Their Application to Employee Training." *Human Resource Development Quarterly* 1, no. 1 (1990): 45–63.

Newcomer, K. E. "Using Performance Measurement to Improve Programs." *New Directions for Evaluation* 75 (1997): 5–14.

Newman, D. L., and R. D. Brown. "Violations of Evaluation Standards." *Evaluation Review* 16, no. 3 (1992): 219–234.

———. *Applied Ethics for Program Evaluation*. Thousand Oaks, Calif.: Sage, 1996.

Noe, R. A. "Trainees' Attributes and Attitudes: Neglected Influences on Training Effectiveness." *Academy of Management Review* 11, no. 4 (1986): 736–749.

Noe, R. A., and N. Schmitt. "The Influence of Trainee Attitudes on Training Effectiveness: Test of a Model." *Personnel Psychology* 39 (1986): 497–523.

O'Dell, C., and C. J. Grayson. *If Only We Knew What We Know*. New York: Free Press, 1998.

Owen, J. M. "Institutionalising Evaluation Culture in an Organization." Paper presented at the annual American Evaluation Association meeting, Orlando, Fla., November 1999.

Owen, J. M., and F. C. Lambert. "Roles for Evaluation in Learning Organizations." *Evaluation* 1, no. 2 (1995): 259–273.

Owens, T. R. "Educational Evaluation by Adversary Proceeding." In *School Evaluation: The Politics and Process*, edited by E. R. House, pp. 295–305. Berkeley: McCutchan, 1973.

Palumbo, D. J. "Politics and Evaluation." In *The Politics of Program Evaluation*. Newbury Park, Calif.: Sage, 1987.

Patton, M. Q. *Utilization-Focused Evaluation*. Beverly Hills, Calif.: Sage, 1978.

———. *Utilization-Focused Evaluation*, 2d ed. Newbury Park, Calif.: Sage, 1986.

———. *How to Use Qualitative Methods in Evaluation*. Thousand Oaks, Calif.: Sage, 1987.

———. *Qualitative Evaluation and Research Methods*, 2d ed. Thousand Oaks, Calif.: Sage, 1990.

———. "Developmental Evaluation." *Evaluation Practice* 15, no. 3 (1994): 311–319.

———. *Utilization-Focused Evaluation: The New Century Text*. Thousand Oaks, Calif.: Sage, 1997.

Payne, S. L. *The Art of Asking Questions*. Princeton, N.J.: Princeton University Press, 1979.

Pettit, F. "Exploring the Use of the World Wide Web as a Psychology Data Collection Tool." *Computers in Human Behavior* 15 (1999): 67–71.

Plantz, M. C., M. T. Greenway, and M. M. Hendricks. "Outcome Measurement: Showing Results in the Nonprofit Sector." *New Directions for Evaluation* 75 (1997): 15–30.

Popham, W. J., E. W. Eisner, H. J. Sullivan, and L. L. Tyler. "Instructional Objectives." American Educational Research Association Monograph Series on Curriculum Evaluation, no. 3. Chicago: Rand McNally, 1969.

Preskill, H., and V. Caracelli. "Current and Developing Conceptions of Use: Evaluation Use TIG Survey Results." *Evaluation Practice* 18, no. 3 (1997): 209–225.

Preskill, H., and P. Mullen. "Assessing Training Needs: A Comparison of Three Methodologies." Paper presented at the meeting of the American Evaluation Association, New Orleans, October 1988.

Preskill, H., and R. T. Torres. *Evaluative Inquiry for Learning in Organizations.* Thousand Oaks, Calif.: Sage, 1999a.

―――. "Building Capacity for Organizational Learning Through Evaluative Inquiry." *Evaluation* 5, no. 1 (1999b): 42–60.

―――. *Readiness for Organizational Learning and Evaluation Questionnaire.* Albuquerque, N.Mex.: Author, 2000.

Preskill, H., and T. Wentling. "The Application of Matrix Sampling to Paired Comparisons in Survey Research." *Journal of Vocational Education Research* 9, no. 3 (1984).

Presser, S., and J. Blair. "Do Different Methods Produce Different Results?" In *Sociological Methodology*, edited by P. V. Marsden. Cambridge, Mass.: Blackwell, 1994.

Ravishankar, L., and D. Russ-Eft. "Quality Skills Needs Assessment: AER Inc." In *In Action: Conducting Needs Assessment*, edited by J. J. Phillips and E. F. Holton III, pp. 207–226. Alexandria, Va.: American Society for Training and Development, 1995.

Richey, R. C. *Designing Instruction for the Adult Learner.* London: Kogan Page, 1992.

Robbins, S. A. "How Organizations Learn from Experience: An Empirical Exploration of Organizational Intelligence and Learning." Ph.D. diss., University of New Mexico, 2001.

Rossi, P. H., and H. E. Freeman. *Evaluation: A Systematic Approach,* 3rd ed. Thousand Oaks, Calif.: Sage, 1985.

Rossi, P. H., H. E. Freeman, and M. W. Lipsey. *Evaluation: A Systematic Approach,* 6th ed. Thousand Oaks, Calif.: Sage, 1999.

Rouiller, J. Z., and I. L. Goldstein. "The Relationship Between Organizational Transfer Climate and Positive Transfer of Training." *Human Resource Development Quarterly* 4, no. 4 (1993): 377–390.

Russ-Eft, D. "Evaluability Assessment of the Adult Education Program (AEP)." *Evaluation and Program Planning* 9 (1986): 39–47.

Russ-Eft, D. "Research Methods for Advancing Performance Improvement." In *Performance Improvement Theory and Practice. Advances in Developing Human Resources* 1, no. 1, edited by R. J. Torraco, pp. 68–82. San Francisco: Berrett-Koehler, 1999.

Russ-Eft, D., S. Krishnamurthi, and L. L. Ravishankar. "Getting Results with Interpersonal Training." In *In Action: Measuring Return on Investment*, vol. 1, edited by J. Phillips, pp. 199–212. Alexandria, Va.: American Society for Training and Development, 1994.

Safire, W. "Stakeholders Naff? I'm Chuffed." *New York Times* (May 5, 1996): 26.

Salopek, J. J. "Liar, Liar, Pants on Fire." *Training and Development* 53, no. 11 (1999): 16.

Schaefer, D. R., and D. A. Dillman. "Development of a Standard E-Mail Methodology: Results of an Experiment." *Public Opinion Quarterly* 62 (1998): 378–397.

Schaie, K. W., R. T. Campbell, W. Meredith, and S. C. Rawlings, eds. *Methodological Issues in Aging Research.* New York: Springer, 1988.

Schmidt, R. E., J. W. Scanlon, and J. B. Bell. "Evaluability Assessment: Making Public Programs Work Better." *Human Services Monograph Series* 14, November 1979.

Schwandt, T. A. "The Landscape of Values in Evaluation: Charted Terrain and Unexplored Territory. *New Directions for Evaluation* 76 (1997): 25–39.

Scriven, M. "The Methodology of Evaluation." In *Curriculum Evaluation,* edited by R. E. Stake (American Educational Research Association Monograph Series on Evaluation 1, pp. 39–83). Chicago: Rand McNally, 1967.

———. "Goal-Free Evaluation." In *School Evaluation,* edited by E. R. House. Berkeley: McCutchan Publishing Co., 1973.

———. "Standards for the Evaluation of Educational Programs and Products." In *Evaluating Educational Programs and Products,* edited by G. D. Boruch. Englewood Cliffs, N.J.: Educational Technology, 1974.

———. *Evaluation Thesaurus,* 4th ed. Thousand Oaks, Calif.: Sage, 1991.

———. "Product Evaluation—The State of the Art." *Evaluation Practice* 15, no. 1 (1994): 45–62.

———. "The Logic of Evaluation and *Evaluation* Practice." *New Directions for Evaluation* 68 (1995): 49–70.

———. "The Theory Behind Practical Evaluation." *Evaluation* 2, no. 4 (1996): 393–404.

Senge, P. M. *The Fifth Discipline.* New York: Doubleday, 1990.

Shadish, W.R., Newman, D.L., Sheirer, M.A., and Wye, C. (eds.), "Guiding Principles for Evaluators." Guiding Principles for Evaluators. *New Directions for Program Evaluation,* no.66. San Francisco: Jossey-Bass, 1995.

Shadish, W. R., T. D. Cook, and L. C. Leviton. *Foundations of Program Evaluation.* Thousand Oaks, Calif.: Sage, 1995.

Shulha, L., and B. Cousins. "Evaluation Use: Theory, Research, and Practice Since 1986." *Evaluation Practice* 18, no. 3 (1997): 195–208.

Sirotnik, K. A., ed. *Evaluation and Social Justice: Issues in Public Education. New Directions for Program Evaluation* 45. San Francisco: Jossey-Bass, 1990.

Smith, M., and B. Leigh. "Virtual Subjects: Using the Internet as an Alternative Source of Subjects and Research Environment. *Behavior Research Methods, Instruments, and Computers* 29 (1997): 496–505.

Smith, M. F. *Evaluability Assessment: A Practical Approach.* Norwell, Mass.: Kluwer, 1989.

Smith, N. L. "Clarifying and Expanding the Application of Program Theory-Driven Evaluations." *Evaluation Practice* 15, no. 1 (1994): 83–87.

Smith, P., and L. M. Kendall. "Retranslation of Expectations: An Approach to the Construction of Unambiguous Anchors for Rating Scales." *Journal of Applied Psychology* 47 (1963): 149–155.

Sonnichsen, R. C. *High Impact Internal Evaluation.* Thousand Oaks, Calif.: Sage, 2000.

Stake, R. E. "The Countenance of Educational Evaluation." *Teachers College Record* 68 (1967): 523–540.

———. "The Case Study Method in Social Inquiry." *Educational Researcher* (1978): 5–8.

———. "Responsive Evaluation." In *International Encyclopedia of Education. Oxford: Pergamon,* 1983.

———. *The Art of Case Study Research.* Thousand Oaks, Calif.: Sage, 1995.

Stewart, D. W., and P. N. Shamdasani. *Focus Groups: Theory and Practice.* Applied Social Research Methods Series, vol. 20. Newbury Park, Calif.: Sage, 1990.

Stewart, T. A. *Intellectual Capital.* New York: Doubleday/Currency, 1997.

Strauss, A. *Qualitative Analysis for Social Scientists.* New York: Cambridge University Press, 1987.

Strauss, A., and J. Corbin. *Basics of Qualitative Research: Grounded Theory Procedures and Techniques.* Newbury Park, Calif.: Sage, 1990.

Stufflebeam, D. L., and A. J. Shinkfield. *Systematic Evaluation.* Boston: Kluwer-Nijhoff, 1985.

Sudman, S., and N. M. Bradburn. *Asking Questions: A Practical Guide to Questionnaire Design.* San Francisco: Jossey-Bass, 1982.

Swanson, R. A., and D. B. Gradous, D. B. *Forecasting Financial Benefits of Human Resource Development.* San Francisco: Jossey-Bass, 1988.

Swanson, R. A., and C. M. Sleezer. "Training Effectiveness Evaluation." *Journal of European Industrial Training* 11, no. 4 (1987): 7–16.

Taylor, F. W. *The Principles of Scientific Management.* New York: Harper and Row, 1911.

Torres, R. T., H. Preskill, and M. Piontek. *Evaluation Strategies for Communicating and Reporting: Enhancing Learning in Organizations.* Thousand Oaks, Calif.: Sage, 1997.

Training. (2000, October). Industry Report 2000: A Comprehensive Analysis of Employer-Sponsored Training in the United States. 37 (10). Minneapolis, MN.

Turner, C. F., L. Ku, S. M. Rogers, L. D. Lindberg, J. H. Pleck, and F. L. Sonenstein. "Adolescent Sexual Behavior, Drug Use, and Violence: Increased Reporting with Computer Survey Technology." *Science* 280 (1998).

Tyler, R. "Evaluation: A Challenge to Progressive Education." *Educational Research Bulletin* 14 (1935): 9–16.

————. *Syllabus for Education 360*. Chicago: University of Chicago Press, 1949.

Tziner, A., R. R. Haccoun, and A. Kadish. "Personal and Situational Characteristics Influencing the Effectiveness of Transfer of Training Improvement Strategies." *Journal of Occupational Psychology* 64 (1991): 167–177.

United Way of America. *Focusing on Program Outcomes: Summary Guide*. Alexandria, Va.: United Way of America, 1996.

Walumbwa, F. O. "Power and Politics in Organizations: Implications for OD Professional Practice." *Human Resource Development International* 2, no. 3 (1999): 205–216.

Wargo, M. J. "The Impact of the President's Reinvention Plan on Evaluation." *Evaluation Practice* 15, no. 1 (1994): 63–72.

Warr, P., and D. Bunce. "Trainee Characteristics and the Outcomes of Open Learning." *Personnel Psychology* 48 (1995): 347–375.

Watkins, K. E., and V. J. Marsick, eds. *Creating the Learning Organization*, vol 1. Alexandria, Va.: American Society for Training and Development, 1996.

Watt, J..H. "Internet Systems for Evaluation Research." In *Information Technologies in Evaluation: Social, Moral, Epistemological, and Practical Implications*, edited by G. Gay and T. L. Bennington. *New Directions for Evaluation* 84. San Francisco: Jossey-Bass, 1999.

Webb, E., D. T. Campbell, R. Schwartz, and L. Sechrest. *Unobtrusive Measures: Nonreactive Research in the Social Sciences*. Chicago: Rand McNally, 1966.

————. *Unobtrusive Measures: Nonreactive Research in the Social Sciences*, rev. ed. Thousand Oaks, Calif.: Sage, 1999.

Webster, J., and D. Compeau. "Computer-Assisted Versus Paper-and-Pencil Administration of Questionnaires." *Behavior Research Methods, Instruments, and Computers* 28 (1996): 567–576.

Weiss, C. H. "Measuring the Use of Evaluation." In *Utilizing Evaluations*, edited by J. Ciaro. Beverly Hills, Calif.: Sage, 1981.

————. "Where Politics and Evaluation Research Meet." In *The Politics of Program Evaluation*, edited by D. J. Palumbo. Newbury Park, Calif.: Sage, 1987.

————. "Theory-Based Evaluation: Past, Present, and Future." *New Directions for Evaluation* 76 (1997): 41–55.

————. *Evaluation*, 2d ed. Upper Saddle River, N.J.: Prentice-Hall, 1998.

Wexley, K. N., and T. T. Baldwin. "Posttraining Strategies for Facilitating Positive Transfer: An Empirical Exploration." *Academy of Management Journal* 29, no. 3 (1986): 503–520.

Wholey, J. S. "Evaluation: When Is It Really Needed?" *Evaluation Magazine* 2, no. 2 (1975).

————. *A Methodology for Planning and Conducting Project Impact Evaluation in UNESCO Fields*. Washington, D.C.: Urban Institute, 1976.

————. *Evaluation: Promise and Performance*. Washington, D.C.: Urban Institute, 1979.

Winston, J. A. "Performance Indicators—Promises Unmet: A Response to Perrin." *American Journal of Evaluation* 20, no. 1 (1999): 95–99.

Witkin, B. R., and J. W. Altschuld. *Planning and Conducting Needs Assessments.* Thousand Oaks, Calif.: Sage, 1995.

Wolf, R. L. "Trial by Jury: A New Evaluation Method." *Phi Delta Kappan* 57 (1975): 185–187.

———. "The Use of Judicial Evaluation Methods in the Formulation of Educational Policy." *Educational Evaluation and Policy Analysis* 1 (1979): 19–28.

Worthen, B. R., J. R. Sanders, and J. L. Fitzpatrick. *Program Evaluation,* 2d ed. New York: Longman, 1997.

Yin, R. K. *Case Study Research: Design and Methods.* Newbury Park, Calif.: Sage, 1989.

———. *Case Study Research: Design and Methods,* 2d ed. Applied Social Research Methods Series, vol. 5. Thousand Oaks, Calif.: Sage, 1994.

Index

About the Authors

Darlene Russ-Eft, Ph.D., is division director of research services at Achieve-Global, Inc., the world's leading resource for obtaining results through performance skills training and consulting. AchieveGlobal works with more than 3,000 organizations worldwide, including most of the *Fortune* 500. She is coauthor of *Everyone a Leader: A Grassroots Model for the New Workplace* (Bergmann, Hurson, and Russ-Eft, 1999, Wiley) and coeditor of *What Works: Assessment, Development, and Measurement* and *What Works: Training and Development Practices* (Bassi and Russ-Eft, 1997, American Society for Training and Development). She is former chair of the Research Committee of the American Society for Training and Development, and former board member of the American Evaluation Association. She received the 1996 Editor of the Year Award from Times Mirror for her research work and the 2000 Outstanding Scholar Award from the Academy of Human Resource Development. She is currently editor of *Human Resource Development Quarterly*. She received her Ph.D. in 1974 from the University of Michigan.

Hallie Preskill, Ph.D., is professor of organizational learning and instructional technologies at the University of New Mexico, Albuquerque. She teaches graduate courses in program evaluation, organizational learning, and training design, development, and delivery. She is coauthor of *Evaluative Inquiry for Learning in Organizations* (Preskill and Torres, 1999, Sage), which won the 1999 Book of the Year Award from the Academy of Human Resource Development, coauthor of *Evaluation Strategies for Communication and Reporting* (Torres, Preskill, and Piontek, 1996, Sage), and coeditor of *Human Resource Development Review* (Russ-Eft, Preskill, and Sleezer, 1997, Sage). Over the past twenty years, she has written articles and book chapters on evaluation theory, methods, and processes, and has designed and conducted numerous evaluations within corporate, nonprofit, health care, human service, and educational organizations. She has served on the board of directors of the American Evaluation Association and the Academy of Human Resource Development, as well as the Research Committee of the American Society for Training and Development. She received her Ph.D. in 1984 from the University of Illinois at Urbana-Champaign.

Rosalie T. Torres, Ph.D., is director of research and evaluation at the Developmental Studies Center (DSC) in Oakland, California, where she implements an organizational learning approach to the evaluation of DSC's educational programs. Torres has coauthored two recent Sage books, *Evaluative Inquiry for Learning in Organizations* (1999) and *Evaluation Strategies for Communicating and Reporting: Enhancing Learning in Organizations* (1996). She has written numerous articles on the theory and practice of a learning approach to evaluation.